Critical Practice in Health and Social Care

Edited by

Ann Brechin, Hilary Brown and Maureen A. Eby
The Open University

SAGE Publications
London • Thousand Oaks • New Delhi in association with

TheOpen
University

First published 2000

 Sage Publications Ltd
6 Bonhill Street
London EC2A 4PU

SAGE Publications Inc
2455 Teller Road
Thousand Oaks, California 91320

SAGE Publications India Pvt Ltd
32, M-Block Market
Greater Kailash – I
New Delhi 110 048

British Library Cataloguing in Publication data

A catalogue record for this book is available
from the British Library

ISBN 0 7619 6492 4 (hbk)
ISBN 0 7619 6493 2 (pbk)

Edited, designed and typeset by The Open University

Printed in the United Kingdom by T. J. International, Padstow, Cornwall

21879B/k302Prelimsi1.1

Contents

Contributors

Ann Brechin is a clinical psychologist with 21 years' experience at The Open University. Her research and writing have focused on disability and learning disability, and she has a particular interest in the relationships between professionals, service-users and families. She is currently training as a systemic psychotherapist. Her chapters introduce themes of interpersonal relationships and inherent power imbalances and draw on principles of anti-discriminatory practice and inclusivity. She co-edited *Care Matters: Concepts, Processes and Research* (Sage, 1999).

Hilary Brown has worked in the health, social services and voluntary sectors with a particular interest in social work. Before becoming Professor of Social Care at the OU in 1996, she was senior lecturer in learning disabilities at the Tizard Centre, University of Kent, where she began a programme of research and policy development around the abuse of vulnerable adults. She maintains academic links with the School but is currently working with social services departments as they implement adult protection policies.

Celia Davies is Professor of Health Care at The Open University. She is a sociologist whose career in research has centred largely on the NHS and the organisation of nursing work. Before joining the OU in 1996, she was Professor of Women's Studies and Director of the Centre for Research on Women at the University of Ulster. Her current research on the history of the UKCC is reflected in Chapter 14. She co-edited the reader associated with this book, *Changing Practice in Health and Social Care* (Sage in association with The Open University, 1999).

Maureen Eby is a senior lecturer in the School of Health and Social Welfare at The Open University. She is a nurse with a foot in both education and clinical nursing as she continues to practise in critical care at a local NHS acute hospital. Her writing was born out of her current research into whistleblowing and nursing negligence.

Linda Finlay is an experienced occupational therapist who now works as a freelance consultant. She has been a long-serving Open University tutor for psychology courses and has a PhD on the life world of the occupational therapist. She co-edited the reader associated with this book, *Changing Practice in Health and Social Care* (Sage in association with The Open University, 1999).

Colin Guest has worked in management and development roles in the public and voluntary sectors. His experience includes developing residential, employment and training services for young offenders and long-term unemployed people. His publications include *Trading Places* (Pavilion Publishing), *Finance Insight* and *Managing Your Resources* (Kent County Council and South East Employers Association).

Bob Hudson is a Principal Research Fellow in the Community Care Division of the Nuffield Institute for Health at the University of Leeds. Before that he was a Visiting Fellow in the Institute for Health Studies at the University of Durham and a Senior Lecturer in Social Policy at New College, Durham. He also has long experience of tutoring for The Open University. Currently he is working on a range of research and consultancy projects related to the reform of the NHS and social care.

Linda Jones is Dean of the School of Health and Social Welfare at The Open University. She writes and researches in the area of health policy and public health with a special interest in children, transport and risk. She co-edited *The Challenge of Promoting Health* (Macmillan in association with The Open University, 1997).

Philip Scarff is a Chartered Secretary and former Director of a large NHS Family Health Services Authority and has held senior management posts in social services. For the past seven years he has been an independent consultant specialising in the public and voluntary sectors and has done several service reviews for quality and value for money. His publications include training courses in financial management and tendering and contracting for public bodies.

Stan Tucker lectures in the School of Health and Social Welfare at The Open University. His main interests are social policy, education, health and social care. He has researched and written extensively in the area of young carers and he is currently involved in a project examining the impact of ME on the lives of children and young people. He is co-editor of *Youth in Society* (Sage, 1997) and *Changing Experiences of Youth* (Sage, 1997).

Acknowledgements

Grateful acknowledgement is made to the following sources for permission to reproduce material in this book.

Figures

Chapter 2

Figure 1: Adapted from Barnett, R. (1997) *Higher Education: A Critical Business*, The Society for Research into Higher Education/Open University Press; *Figure 2:* Braye, S. and Preston-Shoot, M. (1995) *Empowering Practice in Health and Social Care*, Open University Press; *Figure 3:* Dutt, R. and Ferns, P. (1998) *Letting through the Light: A Training Pack on Black People and Mental Health*, Race Equality Unit/Department of Health.

Chapter 3

Figure 1: Adapted from Dodwell, M. and Lathlean, J. (1989) *Management and Professional Development for Nurses*, HarperCollins, Inc.; *Figure 3:* Kolb, D. A. (1984) *Experiential Learning*, Prentice-Hall Ltd.

Chapter 6

Figure 1: Seedhouse, D. and Lovett, L. (1992) *Practical Medical Ethics*, John Wiley and Sons Ltd. Reprinted by permission of John Wiley and Sons Ltd.

Chapter 7

Figure 1: Braye, S. and Preston-Shoot, M. (1995) *Empowering Practice in Social Care*, Open University Press.

Chapter 10

Figure 2: Colebatch, H. K. (1998) *Policy*, Open University Press; *Figure 3:* Winstanley, D., Sorabji, D. and Dawson, S. (1995) 'When the pieces don't fit a stakeholder power matrix to analyse public sector restructuring', *Public Money and Management*, Vol. 15, No. 2, Blackwell Publishers.

Tables

Chapter 5

Table 1: Brown, H., Orlowska, D. and Mansell, J. (1996) 'From campaigning to complaining', in Mansell, J. and Ericsson, K. (eds) *Deinstitutionalization and Community Living: Intellectual Disability Services in Britain, Scandanavia and the USA*, Chapman and Hall; *p. 110:* Barnes, M. and Walker, A. (1996) 'Consumerism vs empowerment: a principled approach to the involvement of older service users', *Policy and Politics*, Vol. 24, No. 4, The Policy Press.

Introduction

This book comes into being with the dawning of the new century. In many fields of human endeavour there is a heightened sense of history, a reflectiveness about what has gone before, and an anticipation of, and an eagerness for, new ways of thinking to take us forward. For health and social care practitioners, however, so many changes, challenges and complexities had beset them by the final decades of the twentieth century that, for some, a sense of resigned helplessness began to set in. This book draws on the strengths of what has been learned from the painful times and builds from the new policies and structures that are beginning to emerge. It looks forward to the role of the practitioner within a new, more negotiated order, as the relationships between professionals and service-users, public and government, shift and adjust to accommodate new understandings of democracy and accountability.

None of this suggests an easier life ahead. Conflicts and power struggles are now more out in the open and there is a growing commitment to recognise and engage with different interests and perspectives. The focus of this book is on what this means for practice. It is concerned with the experiences of those directly involved in one way or another with the delivery or receipt of health and social care. As roles and relationships change, so must ways of working, understandings of the nature of collaboration and underlying assumptions about whose voices should be heard in the decision-making and priority-setting processes. New skills and awarenesses are expected of practitioners. Familiar now with concepts of reflective practice, they must also become both more flexible and more strategic. They must be not only skilled and knowledgeable but also politically aware, accountable, ethically sensitive and responsible, and all within a framework that calls for a collaborative, negotiated and power-sharing approach to their work.

How this book evolved

This book has been written as part of an Open University course that is designed to support all those engaging with such developments. This includes practitioners and front-line managers, whether qualified professionals or not, but particularly those seeking further professional development opportunities, including nurses, social workers, and the professions allied to medicine. Students engaged in post-qualifying or higher award courses, or following social sciences or health studies routes to personal or professional development, will find it particularly pertinent. Educators supporting students or developing related courses, particularly at third level or above in higher education terms, should find it directly relevant to their needs. This book is much more closely integrated than is usual in multi-authored texts. At the same time, each chapter is free-standing and can be read individually. The use of numbered boxes to capture particular perspectives, case studies or issues is an additional feature to support flexible use and ensure direct links with different versions of 'reality'.

Written and compiled by a multidisciplinary Open University team, this book brings a range of experiences from nursing, social work, occupational therapy, psychology, sociology, social policy, adult education and history. In some ways, the experiences of the team in working on this text have mirrored those of practitioners in the field in terms of the challenges of communicating across boundaries of language and experience and differing backgrounds. Arriving at common understandings can be a long and painstaking process.

We were challenged, for example, by how to convey and work with the different meanings attached to even such a core word as 'professional'. In nursing, professionalism is a highly prized attribute, whereas social workers are more likely to want to down-play the professional status of the practitioner. 'Professional', we increasingly realised, is a term that does not translate very well across the health and social care divide. While *professionals* have developed a distinct identity within the health service, and while social work has developed its identity as a distinct profession working within statutory frameworks such as the Children Act and the Mental Health Act, their counterparts in social care, and specifically in residential care, have not traditionally been cast in this role. In social care it is quite clear that people are seen as *staff* or *workers* rather than professionals, however skilled or qualified they may be. These terms have different origins and nuances. Within the 'mixed economy' of care, workers are no longer defining themselves only in relation to large state agencies but also to an assortment of for-profit and not-for-profit agencies, charitable bodies and private companies. Some have chosen to become self-employed. Fragmentation is the defining feature of this shift.

Some might argue that certain groups of workers have been *denied* recognition as 'professionals' and the pay and conditions that go with it. Their job may have been defined as uncomplicated and unskilled (home care workers, for example). From here they may go on to suggest that this evaluation down-plays contributions – because these posts have been traditionally filled by women or black people. Some workers, however, deliberately choose to represent themselves as different from and outside professional cultures, opting instead to ally themselves with users as advocates or campaigners, and perhaps even to place themselves alongside users in opposition to other 'professionals'. Moreover, where users are in control through direct payments, they have chosen to reframe the help they need as 'personal assistance' not 'professional care'.

Within sectors, work is further compartmentalised horizontally between the 'qualified' and the 'unqualified'. How does this line between the professional and non-professional aspects of a task or an intervention get drawn? Who enforces this boundary and what happens when the formal knowledge is held by one person but the service-user prefers to talk to the other, perhaps because they share life experience? As editors and authors we grappled with such issues. Because we were concerned about practice across the whole spectrum of health and social care, we opted in the end to use the term *practitioner*, although this may sound strained in relation to some aspects of care work, or to people whose jobs involve primarily 'management', or perhaps 'advocacy', rather than direct treatment, care or therapy.

Our growing awareness of this varied range of perceptions to be accommodated was further stimulated by feedback from critical readers and developmental testers who routinely read and comment on new Open University courses. Add to this a mixture of personal styles and past experiences, pressures of work and tight deadlines, and the equivalent of many of the tensions and miscommunications of any multidisciplinary team had been fomented. At the same time, there was the potential for the creative thinking that can emerge from uncertainty, conflict and risk, particularly where alternative voices and perspectives are heard and privileged. This book, then, is the product of a challenging process of acknowledging diversity that may ultimately strengthen its relevance to the lived experience of professional practice in health and social care today.

Towards a concept of critical practice

The concept of critical practice lies at the heart of this book. It is designed to create a synthesis that will pull together and integrate many of the above demands. The term 'critical' is used to conceptualise practice as an open-minded, reflexive process, built on a sound skills and knowledge base, but taking account of different perspectives, experiences, assumptions and power relations. Critical practice draws on an awareness of wider ethical dilemmas, strategic issues, policy frameworks and socio-political contexts. It acknowledges that there may be no straightforward 'right' answers and that powerful, established voices will often hold sway over newer, alternative ways of seeing things. The new professional, this book argues, must be a strategic as well as a reflexive thinker, able to understand and work with conflicts and with changing structures. Skills of democratic dialogue are needed to underpin practice. Increasing requirements for openness and accountability can only be met effectively through well-founded and deliberately negotiated processes, and practice which is defensible rather than defensive.

This book is designed to support professional development and addresses this as a topic in its own right. However, it is not a text that simply covers the appropriate base of knowledge and understanding; it is written with a view to engaging the reader in the issues from the perspectives of practice. Different contexts of practice, therefore, are explored, whether residential care, acute sector nursing or community support and whether statutory, private or voluntary sector. All are subject to multiple influences from policy initiatives and to the demand for more flexible, participative and collaborative styles of working. This book considers how practitioners can engage with such developments pro-actively, being influenced by but also influencing and often leading such developments locally from the front.

Structure of the book

Part 1 Professional Development: Contexts and Processes

In Part 1, the contexts and processes of the radical shifts in professional development are framed for the reader, acknowledging past and current change and variation in policy and locating the individual practitioner experience within that. A concept of critical practice is developed to encompass the wider, more strategic vantage point needed by prac-titioners today and based on an assumption of a continuous process of review and development. In Chapter 1, *Exploring continuity and change*, Linda Jones and Stan Tucker consider the changes resulting from the fragmentation of the established order and the emergence and develop-ment of the new diversified contract culture. They look at the impact of changes on the roles, experiences and assumptions of practitioners. In Chapter 2, *Introducing critical practice*, Ann Brechin builds from this starting point, reflecting on the working challenges and dilemmas of practitioners, to frame a three-way concept of critical practice that is central to this book. Critical practitioners, she suggests, are integrating analysis, reflexivity and action as they work and develop on a daily basis, and are striving to establish and hold to principles of openness and equality. Such developmental processes then underpin Chapter 3, *Understanding profes-sional development*. Here, Maureen Eby considers the various schools of thought that have driven forward the notion of continuing professional development. Some emphasise support and empowerment for prac-titioners. Others are more managerial and controlling in their origins and implications. There are important differences, too, between social work and nursing. These strands of influence can be seen to converge, Maureen Eby argues, in a framework that can be used constructively, and the parallels between engaging in a process of continuing professional development and the experience of being a critical practitioner become apparent. These introductory chapters will be of central interest to everyone concerned with the concept of professional development, what it is or might be and what it can or cannot achieve in today's changing world.

Part 2 Challenging Practice

Part 2 moves on to consider different aspects of critical practice. As the double meaning of the title implies, practice is challenging both in and of itself; but equally, many people are engaged in a process of challenging practice. Such challenges come in part from practitioners themselves, but also very powerfully from other interest groups. The two-way nature of such challenges is indeed integral to the nature of critical practice itself. Professionals can no longer be a law unto themselves and, in Chapter 4, Linda Finlay looks explicitly at this issue. *The challenge of professionalism* traces some of the theoretical frameworks that have been developed to clarify the nature of professionalism, and moves on to explore some more recent thinking about complexity and uncertainty which seems to link well with the experiences and expertise demanded of professionals today. Chapter 5, *Challenges from service-users*, takes up one of the most pervasive and central challenges to professionals. Hilary Brown contextualises some of the key underlying developments, such as the disability movement, exploring the emergence of concepts like self-advocacy, independent living and empowerment, and their gradual incorporation into legislation and their impact on practice. In Chapter 6, *The challenge of values and ethics in practice*, Maureen Eby draws on the discipline of ethics to provide a framework for practitioners facing ethical dilemmas and conflicts in practice. The centrality of the value base in health and social care practice requires an increasingly sophisticated capacity to handle such issues and this chapter is a valuable review of current insights and approaches.

Relationships are at the core of the work of care professionals and Chapter 7 addresses one aspect of this by looking at *The challenge of caring relationships*. Getting it right, Ann Brechin suggests, involves awareness not just of the other person's needs and rights to a balance between support and self-determination, but also an awareness of one's own emotional needs and responses, particularly where there may be the risk of emotional or physical abuse. The theme of relationships is continued in the following chapter, *The challenge of working in teams*. There is much rhetoric and exhortation devoted to teamwork and Linda Finlay makes a refreshing change in taking an altogether cooler, calmer look at just what is entailed in working closely and collaboratively with other people. Drawing on recent research, she details some of the difficulties as well as the potential benefits of team approaches. This part of the book ends with Chapter 9, *The challenges of being accountable*. Maureen Eby clarifies the concepts of personal, professional and legal accountability, examining the underpinning concepts of responsibility, liability and autonomy. She takes a critical look at such phenomena as whistleblowing and risk management and charts the background to some of the moral dilemmas which emerge. The question of who is responsible and accountable, to whom and for what, is far from having a clear-cut answer and the

challenges of accountability neatly frame and encapsulate some of the
key themes covered in this part of the book.

Part 3 Working with Changing Structures

In the third part of this book, the focus is on working with changing
structures, addressing the power and significance of the structural
environment within which professionals operate. Such structures mirror
the socio-political climate of thinking and are operationalised through
evolving policy frameworks. Although such frameworks impact on and
significantly control how professionals work, the message of this book is
that the critical practitioner is far from being a passive recipient at the end
of a line of decision making and implementation. Rather there is an
ongoing proactive relationship between practice and policy in which
critical practice has the potential to play a crucial role. Celia Davies sets
the scene for this analysis with Chapter 10, *Understanding the policy process*,
by developing the concept of the 'provenance' of a policy. Understanding
policy more in terms of the interactive processes by which thinking
evolves, and the range of sources and influences on such thinking, makes
clearer the process by which influence can be brought to bear, albeit in the
context of the inevitable privileging of the more powerful voices. Drawing
on the notion of stakeholders, Chapter 10 offers insights designed to
support more active participation by *all* those with a stake in service
development. In Chapter 11, Philip Guest and Colin Scarff take the reader
into an area that cannot be ignored – money. *Counting the costs* is an
account of how budgets work and the surprisingly creative thinking that
can sometimes be involved in solving budgetary problems. Although this
is set in the context of pressures towards the management of scarce
resource, it is not about 'creative accounting', but more about the
imaginative edge needed to think openly about new ways of solving
problems. In Chapter 12 we revisit the issue of collaboration, but from a
new standpoint. Moving on from the earlier teamwork focus, Bob Hudson
looks here at the wider context of collaborative work, exploring some of
the difficulties that have beset the policy-makers and those wanting to
find ways of working together across agency boundaries. Legislation has
often brought in its wake perverse incentives which have made progress
harder, but Chapter 12 sets out to frame and support the opportunities
that exist.

In the final two chapters Celia Davies takes up the story again, leading
the reader into one of two overarching frames of reference for reviewing
policy and structure. *Improving the quality of services*, the title of Chapter 13,
is after all what it is all about ultimately, and this chapter guides the reader
through the maze of standard setting, audits and quality assurance
mechanisms. For the practitioner, quality initiatives can feel like a further
burden. The intention here is to shed light on the essential overlap
between the concerns and objectives of critical practice and the desire to

improve the quality of services. In the final chapter of this book, *Frameworks for regulation and accountability*, Celia Davies completes the picture with a forward-looking review of the sea changes taking place in the external regulation of services and professional work. Inspection systems, reviews, accreditation systems and so on evolve along with other new thinking about the nature of professional work today. The expectation that the professional will know what is best has been replaced by a newer vision of shared and negotiated responsibility for health and social care; one which involves practitioners, service-users and the public as key players in determining and delivering future developments. Regulation and accountability are also in a process of reconceptualisation and rebirth. Patterns in future must reflect awareness of the multiplicity of stakeholders within a more negotiated and openly responsive set of structures.

Defensible practice

The message for the practitioner from this book, however, is not one of a reduced, more passive and defensive role in the context of these wider voices and challenges. Rather the concept of critical practice offers a prospect of harnessing skills and purposes to a shared yoke. Creating dialogue, influencing through negotiation and bringing informed, well-founded argument to bear suggest a more proactive, strategic role in keeping with the calls for greater accountability. Not defensive but defensible practice is the order of the day and this book offers up a mirror to practitioners to suggest the myriad ways in which they are already engaging with such challenges in striving to create enabling health and social care services that can command widespread support in a diverse society.

Part 1
Professional Development: Contexts and Processes

Chapter 1
Exploring continuity and change

Linda Jones and Stanley Tucker

The sovereign consumer making individual
consumer choices from the supermarket
of services.

Introduction

Over the last 20 years there has been tremendous upheaval in the way in
which health and social care services are organised and delivered.
Practitioners, wherever they work, have found themselves trying to
deliver an effective service while at the same time coping with
unprecedented change. It is now impossible to assume that someone
who qualified only a few years ago is up to date with all the changes in
structure and delivery across the health and social care field. Jobs have
'disappeared' or been restructured, roles and responsibilities have changed
and some workers have experienced a complete shift in the status of their
organisation – if it became a trust, was merged with others or transferred to
the private or voluntary sector. Sometimes these experiences have left
people feeling bruised and battered. At other points they may have
welcomed change, at a personal or professional level, as having the
potential to improve services and career prospects.

This chapter puts such personal and professional experience into
context by examining key structural and political influences on health
and social care work over recent years. Chief among such influences have

been the creation of, and more recent retreat from, 'markets' in health and social care, the shift from institutional to community-based and domiciliary care for some service users and providers and the growth of a contract culture. Most of these changes have involved greater regulation of organisations and professionals and a shift of control towards managers and, to an extent, towards 'consumers' or 'service-users'. Accompanying such changes there has been a heightened awareness of risk and a greater emphasis on the knowledge underpinning care. In addition, restructuring in health and social care inevitably raises questions about welfare in general and the influence of broader socio-economic and cultural transformations will also be noted. Whilst the chapter focuses on change, it also acknowledges that there are underlying continuities in service provision and relationships which should not be ignored.

Everyone within the sector has some experience of policy change, but the impact has not been uniform. Consequently, the views of health and social care professionals are very varied. Among some groups, there has been a degree of scepticism about whether professionals can ever influence change. It is seen as imposed from outside, to be grudgingly accepted and then grumbled about. Nurses have sometimes been put in this category of the 'invisible group' in policy making, in spite of their strength of numbers (Strong and Robinson, 1988). However, policy change can represent an opportunity as well as a threat, if professionals are flexible enough in their thinking and able to be responsive to new challenges (Ewles, 1996). Beginning to understand these changes – situating yourself in relation to them and grappling with their significance – represents an important first stage of growth in the journey towards becoming a more reflective professional and engaging in critical practice.

1   Restructuring in health and social care

During the 1980s and the 1990s, the health and social care sector in the UK underwent the most profound changes in structure and orientation that it had experienced since the 1940s, when the welfare state was first established. The characteristic of post-war social policy had been the removal of most welfare agencies from private or voluntary hands into public control. This was most evident in health, where a National Health Service (NHS) was created. In social care, more and more services were provided by the state, through local authority welfare departments or the NHS, although existing private or voluntary organisations, such as Barnardos and the National Children's Society, also continued to provide care. In other sectors, such as education and housing, public ownership was extended and national goals and standards were set down. By no means all services were free or universally available, but the logic of providing services collectively to meet the needs of citizens was generally accepted.

By the 1980s, however, the role of the state in welfare was under serious attack (Mishra, 1984; Deakin, 1988). The efficiency, effectiveness and overall cost of state services for health and social care had been questioned and challenged. The dominance and inflexibility of professionals had been highlighted (Illich, 1976; Johnson, 1972). Some service provision, such as long-stay residential care, was increasingly criticised as inefficient (Audit Commission, 1986) and community-based care was endorsed. Scaling down the state-provided services, such as public housing, moved to the forefront of the Conservative government's agenda. By the late 1980s, the stage was set for significant restructuring in health and social care (see Box 1).

Box 1: The emergence of markets in health and social care

In 1989 the Conservative government set out its plans in two White Papers:

In health care, the government introduced *Working for Patients* (DoH, 1989a), a White Paper which set out plans to create an internal market. Central to this was the designation of some groups as purchasers of health services – the health authorities and fund-holding general practitioners (GPs) – and other groups as providers of services – hospital trusts, most general practices, community services and other public, voluntary and private health care agencies. Purchasers would set out, through contracts, the types of services they required and agree with a provider on the level and cost of such services. The logic of this, it was claimed, was that purchasers would commission the most efficient and economic providers, thus decreasing costs, improving efficiency, treating more patients and gaining better value for public money spent on health care. In a foreword to *Working for Patients* in 1989 Margaret Thatcher, then Prime Minister, wrote:

> We aim to extend patient choice, to delegate responsibility to where the services are provided and to secure the best value for money .... We believe that a National Health Service that is run better, will be a National Health Service that can care better.

In social care, provision had always been a mix of local authority services, voluntary sector and private provision. The reforms of the Conservative government represented another stirring of the pot in which voluntary and private provision were spiced up and made more prominent in the stew. *Caring for People* (DoH, 1989b), emphasised patient choice, the need for better management of services and a more restricted role for local authorities as purchasers of care from other agencies rather than major providers themselves. The government endorsed the view that 'the role of the public sector is essentially to ensure that care is provided. How it is provided is an important, but secondary consideration' (DoH, 1988, p. vii). Local authority social service departments became commissioners, responsible for creating and monitoring care packages for clients. Contracts and service level agreements drove this social care market, creating a 'mixed economy' of care (Wistow *et al.*, 1994).

The NHS and Community Care Act of 1990 had created a health and social services model in which the underlying assumption was that separating purchasers and providers would bring better value for money and increase accountability and efficiency. Nearly a decade later, the new Labour government published a new White Paper on the future of the National Health Service in England, *The New NHS* (DoH, 1997). This claimed that the market model had not delivered on its promises, that billions had been wasted on 'red tape' and that the health service required modernisation 'for the next fifty years' by replacing 'the internal market with integrated care'. The market was associated with 'what has failed: fragmentation, unfairness, distortion, inefficiency, bureaucracy, instability and secrecy' (DoH, 1997, p. 2). This view was echoed in White Papers on the health service in Scotland and Wales and in White Papers on social care. *Modernising Social Services* (DoH, 1998) attacked the policies of privatisation that 'put dogma before users' interests'. In the government's view the market model had perpetuated many of the very problems of waste, poor standards and rising costs that its supporters claimed it was created to solve.

However, *Modernising Social Services* also criticised what had been 'near monopoly local authority provision of social care', with its assumption that 'one size fits all' (DoH, 1998, para. 1.7), and the White Paper *Modern Local Government* (DETR, 1998) criticised inward-looking, unresponsive councils which protected vested interests.

Significant restructuring was proposed, along with increased public accountability and local partnerships with the business and voluntary sectors to obtain 'best value in the delivery of local services'. In health care, reforms of the internal market were proposed in which health authorities gradually ceased to commission services but instead developed a role as co-ordinators and joint planners (with GPs and trusts) of Health Improvement Programmes for the local population. They allocated funds to Primary Care Groups, new groups made up of all general practices, who became the new commissioners of services from NHS trusts – the providers – through long-term service agreements. Public health, rather than the narrower focus on treating presented sickness, emerged as a stronger priority (DoH, 1998). 'Best value' in local government and 'clinical governance' in health care emerged as concepts which encapsulated concerns about public accountability and probity and led to requirements for more stringent methods of self and external policing in public services.

Conflicting values, conflicting priorities

The changes in health and social care structures outlined above represent a significant reconceptualisation of the role of the state in relation to this area of welfare. In the 1940s' welfare state, emerging from a period of 'total war', the central co-ordinating and policy role of government was important and generally accepted. The state was seen as an active player in guiding economic and social change. In the economic sphere, the view of Maynard Keynes that governments could intervene to regulate the economy and control employment was generally accepted. It was claimed that 'full employment in a free society' was a realisable goal (Beveridge, 1942). State planning of welfare was presented as an obvious next stage in creating an efficient modern democracy (Beveridge, 1942; Bevan, 1952). This reflected a general political concern, emphasised by the post-war Labour government but also endorsed to some extent by all political parties, to create a more equal and stable society in place of the gross divisions between wealth and poverty and the social unrest of the pre-war years.

> When wealth is dispersed and distributed in scores of millions of homes the result is not so conspicuous [as] ... the daily display of functionless wealth ... The social scene presents fewer dramatic contrasts. But there is no doubt about which type of society produces more quiet contentment and political stability.
>
> (Bevan, 1952, p. 168)

A strong endorsement of the values of collective organisation and social solidarity underpinned the 1940s' welfare state, ideologically, if not always in fact. This was the logic of seeing essential services as available for all citizens when they were in need. National insurance and assistance schemes created an income 'safety net'; local authority social services helped those who were most vulnerable. Medical care became free at the point of use, funded largely by taxation and determined by professionals (Allsop, 1994).

By the end of the 1980s, all these values had been called into question. Market competition, self-help, and consumer rights and freedoms became more dominant concerns, fuelled by the rise of the neo-liberal 'New Right' in politics – with its aims to reduce public expenditure on welfare and dependency on the 'nanny state' (Deakin, 1988) – and by the powerful critique from the political left of the failures of professionals and state welfare to eradicate poverty and inequality (see Box 2 overleaf). 'It is important to remember that some of the ammunition for [the] attack on state welfare came from critics campaigning for the restructuring and democratisation of welfare services' (Jones, 1994, p. 509).

The challenges to state welfare were also bound up with changes in society in the decades since the 1940s. In the next section some of these key changes are noted: economic and technological transformations, shifts in social structures and relationships, and new cultural affiliations.

2   The challenge of social change

Massive political upheavals in Central and Eastern Europe in the late 1980s added fuel to the flames of the neo-liberal attack on state welfare. The demise of state socialism and the discrediting of central state economic planning offered further evidence of the inability of the state

Box 2: Growing debates about welfare

The political left voiced concerns that Labour governments had fallen short of their promises to create greater equity and that poverty and homelessness were still prevalent (Coates and Silburn, 1971; Townsend, 1962 and 1979). Inequalities in health were still marked despite the welfare state (DoH, 1980). There was also criticism of welfare professions as monopolistic and elitist (Illich, 1976). As state bureaucracies continued to expand in the 1960s and 1970s and professionals pressed for more extensive and expensive services, some reformers questioned whether more provider-dominated services would actually benefit welfare consumers (Donnison, 1975). There were calls for social work to become more locally organised and accountable (Hadley and Hatch, 1981). Most sought to protect and extend welfare entitlements, but also to democratise them.

Neo-liberals, the 'New Right', challenged the whole basis of state welfare, arguing that provision of collective services by the state was both inefficient and inherently wrong-headed:

> The present welfare state, with its costly universal benefits and heavy taxation, is rapidly producing ... economic and spiritual malaise among our people. Planned, introduced and encouraged by good men who believed that state intervention would bring economic and spiritual returns, the end-product is completely different.
>
> (Boyson, 1971, p. 37)

In this view, collective provision of welfare had undermined people's ability to stand on their own feet. The proper role of the state was not to become a service-provider itself but to safeguard the freedom of its citizens and create conditions in which a free market could deliver everything – from toothpaste to palliative care (Jones, 1994). The view of the state as a regulator rather than a provider of services, a minor rather than a major player, underpinned the ideology of market-led solutions in welfare. Linked to it were claims that market competition and business management methods would bring greater efficiency and that services could be transformed by consumers challenging traditional welfare relationships and making supermarket-type choices about health treatments and social care packages (Willetts, 1987; DoH, 1988).

to be efficient and effective, and underpinned claims about the superiority of the free market approach (Jacques, 1988; Squires, 1990). In Western Europe, but also in other countries, such as Australia, New Zealand and Canada, the welfare state came under attack from neo-liberals who argued that the state was overmighty and that welfare budgets were overblown (Ham, 1997).

Interacting with these shifting political ideologies have been more fundamental economic and social shifts in the UK and beyond, which have resulted in the demands for reconceptualisations of health and social care practice. Many of these will be familiar. For example, technological innovation has transformed the mass, unionised workforce and social class hierarchy of industrial society into a more diversified service economy. Life expectancy has risen and with it public demand for health and social support services.

New technologies and medical advances have expanded the range and cost of available treatments (DoH, 1989a). Education and mass media have greatly extended public interest in and knowledge about health and care. New social movements such as women's liberation, anti-racism and green alliances have challenged assumptions and altered people's expectations about what is 'normal' and 'natural'. Social relationships – between the sexes, within households, in the workplace, between cared-for and carers – have been, and are still being, challenged and transformed (Finch and Groves, 1983; Dalley, 1988). Each of these changes has had some impact on the type and range of welfare services provided.

These changes, observers have argued, both reflected and created fundamental economic and socio-cultural transformations, and debates about the nature and extent of them are still continuing (see Box 3).

Box 3: Thinking about change – the 1970s to the millennium

Post-industrial society? As early as the 1970s the pace of economic change had convinced some observers that a new economic order was emerging in which industry and manufacturing were being replaced by a focus on services, knowledge and information (Toffler, 1970). Modern industrial society, with its industrial base, trade union organised mass workforce and social class organisation, was giving way to 'post-industrial' society, characterised by greater diversity in patterns of production, use of technology, lifestyle and social relationships.

In this global economy, mass media communications and transnational corporations operated both to create and to satisfy people's needs and desires. The global market 'commodified' people's lives, offering ever-multiplying goods and services, each of which promised to enhance people's lives and entice them into more and more consumption. It also seemed to offer infinite choice and the potential for people to create and continually change their individual 'lifestyles', piecing together media images and information in new ways and for new purposes. However, some commentators emphasised its negative and exploitative effects, claiming that the 'bottom line' criterion was not to satisfy people's needs for welfare but to maximise the growth of capital (Leonard, 1997). In this view, the market created the mirage of choice and reinforced poverty and inequality.

Post-modern culture? To some social scientists the shift was about not only moving beyond industrial society but also creating a new, 'post-modern' culture (Featherstone, 1991). The old social order with its emphasis on conformity to established cultural and social traditions, values and explanatory systems was being swept away and replaced by a culture which offered more opportunities for ordinary people to be creative and release their potential. The cultural icons – classic literature, music and art – that people had been taught to revere became merely one set of options among many from which they could choose a style of living to suit themselves. Willis (1991) described the process of cultural change in an optimistic way, suggesting that people could create and remodel their identity, their reality and their very 'self'. We needed 'new maps' of contemporary culture because:

> Far from degrading everyday life with a thousand cracked mirrors of human potential, commodity and media cultural abundance has massively widened the daily scope for symbolic creativity. It has done this by increasing the supply of relevant materials for its work, providing usable forms and channels which maintain rather than close the potential of the fragments being formed in new ways to reflect and develop human potential.

> (Willis, 1991, p. 6)

Post-modern culture, in this view, offered people more opportunity to be creative, autonomous and distinctive than did a culture based on dominant values.

Late modernity? Other writers have been more sceptical about the existence of post-industrial society and post-modern culture (Giddens, 1990). The impact of economic change on social life has been overstated and the transforming effects of new technologies such as microprocessing and electronic communications remain unclear. Shifting towards a service-based economy has not meant wholesale restructuring of work or of the socio-economic order. Giddens (1991) has used the phrase 'reflexive' or 'late' modernity to acknowledge that there is indeed less certainty, more fragmentation, more reflexivity and preoccupation with the mental and emotional self and its shifting nature. This said, he has challenged post-modernist claims that we must discount all established accounts and accept that all explanations and value systems are equally worthy of regard. Faced with fragmentation and uncertainty we need more than ever convincing explanations of social structures and relationships and shared principles that we can agree to adopt.

Implications for health and social care

Applying 'post-modernist' claims in relation to health and social care, we could argue that dominant scientific values and the practices which harness scientific methods – such as medicine – have lost their privileged position as explanatory systems. They have become just one more set of claims about what is true and they have to battle it out with other truth claims – for example, those of alternative therapies such as homeopathy or acupuncture. Alongside this culture shift, the economic changes associated with 'post-industrial' society have created greater diversity in service provision and remodelling of services so that they resemble commodities from which consumers can pick and choose. The increasing diversity of public and independent sector care provision and the vast growth of over-the-counter products and services in recent decades provide some evidence of this change. Such outcomes offer consumer choice compared with the monolithic state welfare system of the 1940s.

On the other hand, arguments about 'late modernity' suggest that we need to be sceptical about claims that cultural and economic life has been transformed. For example, many health and social welfare professionals continue to endorse the use of scientific methods because they yield more convincing evidence and remain more open to challenge and objective evaluation. This argument applies not only to the science underpinning health work but also to accounts of social structures and relationships that have been developed by social scientists. On the basis of these shared accounts, welfare can be claimed to be a key element in fostering social connectedness. In spite of significant change in welfare structures and provision there is still a widely-held acceptance of its role in removing some of the risk from contemporary life (Crewe, 1991). Williams (1992), reviewing the shortcomings of 'one size fits all'-type service provision, argued that the real challenge for social welfare in the 1990s was to develop a strategy which combined universality in provision with a sensitive regard for diversity in needs and interests. For example, a maternity service which 'treats everyone as the same' can result in unacknowledged and institutional racism towards black and minority ethnic women whose needs may be different.

Changes in health and social care offer us some, but perhaps not sufficient, evidence of deeper socio-cultural transformations. Individuals and groups are increasingly making consumer choices about their welfare: paying for private care; opting for private treatment; using alternative medicine and non-Western remedies; shopping around for better services (Jones, 1998). Welfare relationships between users and professionals have been significantly changed by contracts, and markets and the service ethic have been undermined by consumerism and economic incentives.

Every opinion poll in the UK throughout the 1980s, however, demonstrated continued support for collective provision of social welfare – even when the emphasis on market values and solutions was at its height (Crewe, 1991). Public and professional attachment to the value of collective services have remained high and the Labour Party's election success in 1997 offered some endorsement of this. In the late 1990s, the Labour government began to put a much greater emphasis on partnership, collaboration and rebuilding trust between professionals and the public. The so-called 'third way', in which the strengths of both a market and a public sector approach were combined, was reflected in White Papers such as *The New NHS* (DoH, 1997), with its emphasis on partnership and consultation.

3   The impact of restructuring at the grass roots

Most important of all, what have these shifts meant to staff working within health and social care? What have been the ramifications of the changing structures and roles? There has been considerable investment in persuading staff that change is 'for the better', which reflects a political awareness that doctors and nurses, and to a lesser extent social workers, attract considerable public support and sympathy. For example, during the launch of 'Working for Patients' in 1989, health authorities were instructed that all staff everywhere in the NHS should see the video and be given a summary of the report within the same week. Managers were gathered together for special briefings before the launch and every attempt was made to persuade them that the reforms would lead to decided improvements. However, there was considerable hostility to the NHS changes from professionals within the sector.

Within social care, the Association of Directors of Social Services, while they were unable to resist the restructuring, expressed continuing concerns about the impact on both professionals and clients and on the relationships between them. They welcomed the decision to give local authorities the lead role in social service commissioning and to protect, at least initially, the community care budget. But there were powerful incentives to find market solutions to care problems; indeed, government funding required that 85% of community care budgets be spent in the non-statutory sector.

There were also limits on the type of care packages available, since the independent sector was predominantly a provider of residential care and only slowly moved into domiciliary provision. The 'snapshots' that follow offer comments on key aspects of the changes from the perspective of different groups within health and social care, reminding us that much of the response to change depends on situational opportunities and constraints. There is no attempt here to be comprehensive but rather to begin to identify some significant features of change.

Contract culture: a view from social services

A key change experienced by those managing and administering public social services in the 1990s was the development of a contract culture (Mather, 1989; Stewart and Walsh, 1992). Providers were charged by purchasers of services with the efficient and effective delivery of services at an agreed price. Contracts specified conditions to be met. Costs, in particular, were a driving force for change, as one local authority social services chair noted:

Let's be quite honest. The reason for considering a not-for-profit trust is because of the government's funding policy, and make no bones about that. The whole point is that if an elderly person is resident in our homes we have to pick up the tab, whereas if they go into the private sector, they can get income support and DSS money. So that's a big influence on one's policy.

(Conservative Chair of Social Services, quoted in Wistow *et al.*, 1994, p. 95)

Contract culture, as we noted earlier, created a very different set of socio-political and economic relationships. It was grounded in principles of market flexibility and assumptions about the efficiency of private enterprise (Green, 1987) and the ability of capitalism to transform itself (Ham, 1996). The outcome was to some extent to mask the political choices in health and social care provision by moving more of it into the market-place. For example, although health authorities and local authorities as major public sector employers had played a significant role in setting standards in the sensitive area of equal opportunities, such standards could not always be written into contracts.

The introduction of contract culture also helped to transform service structures and managerial priorities. Increasingly, local authorities were required to adopt an 'arm's length' strategy of inspecting and regulating these new contract arrangements through local inspection units (Statham, 1996). Subsequently, *Modernising Social Services* (DoH, 1998) proposed regional inspection units rather than local ones.

Doubts have been voiced concerning matters of accountability and how far contracts have actually opened up work processes and institutional arrangements to external scrutiny. Accusations of 'cherry picking' – bidding only for the profitable parts of services – have been made. Service-users have complained of their inability to influence service priorities. Contracts are fixed term and can create tension and uncertainty. Commissioners have highlighted the difficulty of writing contracts: 'If you don't have enough specification then people will find a way through it, and if you write a specification which is overtight, they can't adhere to it and it becomes impossible to monitor' (Wistow *et al.*, 1994, p. 87). Providers have noted the potentially deadening impact of tight regulation on creativity and innovation (Schwabenland, 1997).

But reactions have been mixed (Butcher, 1995). Supporters of contract-ing, including some service-users, have highlighted its flexibility in meeting diverse needs through various forms of provision and the creativity that has been fostered in resource use. 'There was some hard bargaining on the contract but we were none the less able to design the service ourselves' (Schwabenland, 1997). Contract culture has begun to dismantle the 'juggernaut syndrome' of public service care provision, through evaluation of effectiveness and by extending personal and occupational accountability. However, most observers and participants agree that there is much still to do (Hoyes and Means, 1997).

The 'new managerialism'? A view from NHS trusts

The 'new managerialism' as an ideology and a policy initiative entered the health sector in the mid-1980s (Pollitt, 1993), although attempts to make the NHS more business-like have had a much longer history. Initial reactions by health care professionals to the idea of private-sector-style management put forward by Sir Roy Griffiths in his Management Enquiry into the NHS (DoH, 1984) were fairly hostile. This was not surprising since Griffiths, the Chief Executive of Sainsbury's the food retail chain, had been handpicked by the Conservative government to bring the gospel of business efficiency to the health service. 'If Florence Nightingale were carrying her lamp through an NHS hospital today', announced Griffiths, 'she would be asking who was in charge' and this set the tone for his report. He called for the introduction of the general management function into hospitals, by which he meant creating a cadre of decision-makers who would carry operational responsibility and budgetary control. By implication, consensus-style management involving professionals had been found wanting, avoiding the tough decisions.

The general managers who entered the health service over the next decade, however, were by and large not the ruthless private-sector business-types envisaged by Griffiths. Over 60% of them were NHS administrators, whereas only 20% of district general managers and 8% of unit general managers were from outside the NHS (Jones, 1994). However, very few managers at district level had a nursing or medical background and even at unit level only 10% of managers were nurses and 15% had a medical qualification. The initial view from NHS hospitals, therefore, was considerable suspicion of general management and scepticism about its intentions. From a health professional viewpoint, clinicians saw themselves and not general managers as the ones who should be driving decisions about patient care. This was reflected in popular culture, where the doctor and nurse as heroes and the unit manager as villain became a common theme in television soaps.

In spite of the new managerialism, control did not pass from hospital clinicians to managers and Cox (1991) suggested that in the early 1990s managers were very much still junior partners in decision making. Indeed, by unveiling plans for an NHS internal market, *Working for Patients* (DoH, 1989a) shifted direction and focused on turning clinicians into managers. By the late 1990s, more clinicians had moved into management in trusts, although their ability to control clinical colleagues remained limited. Mark (1997, p. 110) suggested that, in spite of NHS management training programmes, doctors may recoil 'where what is experienced is the conflict which will arise for doctors/managers when they fully appreciate that the choices of one role can represent the demands and constraints of another'. The rather ambivalent medical attitude towards NHS management is expressed in the following aphorism:

> Management is the syphilis of the NHS. Doctors usually acquire it in
> unguarded moments. It is much more pleasurable than work, but
> produces delusions of grandeur.
>
> (Hicklin, quoted in Mark, 1997, p. 105)

As managers, doctors were more likely to focus on strategic decision
making, leaving the operational side to a business manager. This
involvement in strategy offered them an opportunity to exercise power
both covertly, through influencing others and managing perceptions, and
overtly, through managing conflict. In this way, doctors sought to 'move
back into the driving seat' and recover the ground lost to the new
managerialism (Mark, 1997, p. 111).

Any assessment of the impact of new managerialism, therefore, needs
to take into account how it has shifted over recent decades. In particular,
in the internal market of hospital and community trusts and GP fund-
holders, it was professionals who were 'managerialised' (Walby and
Greenwell, 1994). For nurses, entering management provided extended
career pathways and progression without having to leave the clinical area.
Social workers, whilst many have negative feelings about their changing
role, also increasingly became managerialised. In place of 'hands on' social
work, they created and managed the care packages for their clients. In the
latest twist of policy, some attempts were made in the late 1990s to de-
managerialise, for example by creating primary health care groups in place
of single GP practices and enabling trusts and health authorities to merge.

The 'mixed economy': a view from outside the public sector

In the UK, as in much of Western Europe, a 'mixed economy' of welfare
developed between the state, profit-making and voluntary sectors (Ely and
Sama, 1996). These new partnership arrangements have had major
implications for organisations traditionally operating outside the boundaries of the public sector.

In health and social care, the 'for-profit' sector grew significantly in the
1980s, assisted by Conservative government policies. North American
health care corporations such as AMI penetrated the UK, encompassing
hospital chains, nursing homes and medical suppliers. Some independent
sector residential homes also amalgamated into chains so that large
corporate players emerged in both health and social care. Changes in
planning guidance allowed private hospitals to be sited next to NHS
hospitals and older people obtained tax relief on private health insurance
(Jones, 1998).

In the voluntary sector, the changes have also been significant. The
history of service development rests on a principle of 'trust' (Kendall *et al.*,
1997) – a 'trust' built on the assumption that the voluntary sector would
'do its best' to champion and advance the various causes and demands of
service-users. Relationships between voluntary and statutory sector

agencies were often loosely defined and constrained by little more than the demand to present an annual report of work done. Where financial support was offered, it was often given in the form of open-ended grant aid and the voluntary sector developed responsive and creative forms of management and service delivery, unhindered by the bureaucratic constraints that controlled and regulated state activities (Popple, 1995).

Market relationships forced many voluntary sector agencies to change and embrace a set of ideas and principles that sat uneasily alongside this cultural inheritance. Demands placed on voluntary organisations to compete for service contracts disadvantaged some smaller, less well-resourced organisations. Volunteer recruitment has suffered, especially where 'traditional volunteers are unsympathetic to the new contract culture' (Kendall et al., 1997). In some cases, where voluntary organisations were tied to particular funding agencies, exposing need and agitating for change has been curtailed (Kendall and Knapp, 1996). Indeed, a voluntary agency has become little more than the conduit for apportioning scarce resources through markets that were never really able to respond to demand.

Of course, the same changes can be read in a very different way: to argue the case that these new arrangements have changed the status of the voluntary sector; that many voluntary agencies became key players in delivering packages of health and social care in the community; that voluntary sector action became more influenced by minority needs of black and Asian groups, women and people with disabilities. The diversity of the independent sector also needs highlighting; some large agencies may have more in common with the public sector than with small voluntary agencies. What can be said with a degree of certainty, however, is that the role of the voluntary sector will continue to change in direct response to the demands placed on it by local and central government.

Sovereign consumer or service-user? Professionals and users talking

Almost all reforms in health and social care have had as one of their stated aims the improvement of services to clients or patients. From assuming that professionals knew what was best for the people they served, we have moved slowly towards relationships of greater equality – or at least where there is more negotiation. Armstrong (1993) has noted how patients moved from being viewed as passive and dependent to being expected to tell their own history and be active in their own case. Political constructions of service-users have evolved in a similarly complex, but different, way.

Three approaches to user involvement illustrate some of the significant changes that have taken place in the 1990s. The model that accompanied the health and social care reforms was that of the sovereign consumer, making individual consumer choices from the supermarket of services

(Winkler, 1987). Winkler has been highly critical of this model in health care, arguing that the actual choices available to users were narrow or non-existent. Evidence of demand from users, when gathered, is often limited to tick-the-box patient satisfaction questionnaires which reveal very little about how to modify or develop services.

In social care, the model of care management and the care package agreed in a contract could only work if real choices were available and resources were able to meet demands (Walker, 1988). In most cases, such choices were unavailable and it was often the carer or relative rather than the client who was making the choice. In many social services departments, care managers have a limited budget, tight restrictions on how they can use it, and a limited choice of providers.

A second model of involvement was public participation in decision making. Decentralisation in some local authority social services has sought to increase 'citizen empowerment' (Hambleton and Hoggett, 1993). The long tradition of community work, revived in the late 1990s, has been about enabling local people to campaign for improvements in local services. In health care, user panels and citizens' juries have been developed. Selected members of the public are given an opportunity to weigh up evidence about policy proposals and participating health trusts are required to allocate resources to enable expenditure on the option the jury chooses, thus ensuring that real decisions can be made by the public rather than superficial consultation. Usman Khan, Chair of Camden and Islington Health Services Trust, sees clarity of aims, timing, audience and method as critical:

> Badly done consultation will cause problems for policy makers, alienate participants and fuel public cynicism ... Ensuring that a consultation exercise is meaningful to all those involved should be the primary concern. In many cases, this involves a health authority or trust delegating some real control over a particular issue.
>
> (Khan, 1998, p. 32)

A third model which presents an alternative vision of consumption is that of the active 'service-user', participating to different degrees in the planning, implementation and evaluation of care. In some areas and services, in particular in mental health and disability, this model is quite widespread and able to begin a process of cultural change. Clare Evans of the Wiltshire Users' Network comments on its aim and purpose as follows.

> It is important that our involvement is based on our terms and within a background of rights: the rights we have as citizens like any others – the democratic right to participate in society and the right to have choice and control over our lives – which must mean that we have as much choice and control as we can over the services we receive ... By enabling local authorities to learn from users' expertise directly, there is the opportunity for those who do choose to participate to change services for all service users ... So it is very much the emphasis of wanting to change the culture from the dependency that we experience as people

who use social services and health services and other agencies to meet
our care needs.

(Evans, 1998, p. 318)

Making the shift from a consumer sovereignty model of limited
consultation to public participation and the full involvement of users in
shaping policy and changing service provision is fraught with difficulty,
not least for professionals who have to share power. Different local
contexts and types of needs require different responses; at the same time,
services should reflect wider social principles of equity and fairness
(Hugman, 1998).

4   Continuity and change – what's new?

The discussion so far has been about restructuring within health and social
care. But continuity amidst change is also visible. In what might appear as
a rush to embrace change, many of the 'old' challenges facing health and
social care continue to influence policy and practice. In some instances,
the tone and language of debate may have shifted, different interests may
have come to the fore and the political landscape may appear to have
altered significantly. Yet practitioners, policy-makers, administrators,
academics and service-users continue to debate the underlying philosophical, ethical and practice issues that should underpin service
development and delivery. Nowhere is this more evident than in the area
of accountability.

Accountability – new concern or old business?

Debates about the need to increase levels of accountability have directly
influenced practice in health and social care settings, as service relationships have been restructured. The concern has been to construct lines of
'financial, organisational and public accountability' (Hughes and Pengelly,
1997, p. 12), in order to formalise the responsibilities attached to
particular kinds of work-place relationships and roles. For example, there
have been attempts to create more clarity about the work that nurses do
through explicit acknowledgement that they may have an 'extended role'
which overlaps with that of doctors. Similarly, the new purchaser and
provider relationship in social care has extended the accountability of
social workers to secure 'value for money' in negotiating care packages
with voluntary and private agencies.

Demands for increased levels of accountability have been stimulated by
various public inquiries into presumed professional incompetence (see for
example, Levy and Kahan, 1991) and have been a factor in political moves
to determine the outline, competencies and outcomes of professional
training through National Vocational Qualifications (Jessup, 1990; Field,

1993). At the same time, internal structures for accountability have blossomed in the form of new line management, appraisal and review arrangements – often requiring workers to provide justificatory evidence for their actions and activities (Thompson, 1995).

The development of quality assurance in 'people work' has also gained significant momentum. Quality assurance, as it has been introduced to the public, voluntary and private sectors, is concerned with ensuring that the 'services provided meet the standards set and the needs of the consumer, both now and in the future' (Taylor and Vigars, 1993, p. 73). Essentially, the work of both managers and practitioners is focused on the construction of standards, and on judgements about how well both individuals and organisations are performing in relation to meeting such standards. In many instances, external and internal auditing systems have been created to review and assess progress. Underpinning this process, and portrayed at times as part of a strategy of Total Quality Management (TQM), is the idea that standards, and the aims associated with them, should be redefined and reassessed at regular intervals.

At first glance this construction of accountability seems quite new, reflecting 'new managerialism', attacking professional accountability, and denying 'the uncertainties, confusions and anxieties that are [part of] human contact' work (Hughes and Pengelly, 1997, pp. 13–14). However, some of the presumed 'new' debate can in fact be seen as a reworking of the ideas and themes of the past. For example, in the 1970s Lipsky, in his discussion of the work of 'street-level bureaucrats' such as social workers, noted how accountability was defined in terms of 'agency preferences' and 'clients' claims' rather than professional responsibility (Lipsky, 1978, p. 19). At the heart of this debate lies a long-running and fundamental tension: is it the professional worker who is ultimately responsible for meeting the needs of the client and/or is it the employing institution? During the 1970s and 1980s, the issue of accountability surfaced through attacks on the efficiency and effectiveness of welfare state professionals and 'the old functionalist and idealising view of the professions fell rather rapidly into disfavour' (Collins, 1990, pp. 14–15). It was replaced by an analysis of the impact of power given, or acquired, by those employed in health, social welfare, education or care work (see Chapter 4).

Debate about the need to create increased levels of public account-ability has also been prominent over time. Accountability proved an effective political weapon for central government as it sought to control local authority spending intentions and policy actions in the 1980s (Rhodes, 1997; Gyford, 1985). In particular, the National Audit Act (1983) was used as an instrument to increase the ability of central government to scrutinise local government expenditure. Sir Gordon Downey, speaking one year after the creation of the National Audit Office, argued that what was needed was an:

> ... examination of value for money – or in the terms of the 1983 Act –
> economy, efficiency and effectiveness in the use of resources.
>
> (Public Finance Foundation, 1985, p. 6)

These particular concerns and expectations have continued to dominate thinking and action. Many of the 'old' debates about the efficient and effective use of scarce resources strongly influence health and social care policy and management agendas. *Modernising Social Services* (DoH, 1998), in this sense, can be seen as one more in a long line of attempts to make local government more accountable; indeed, accountability has been a key part of the Labour government's agenda across all public services in the late 1990s. The principal aim still appears to be one of needing to regularise, scrutinise and pin-point individual and collective responsibility. Accountability, although frequently portrayed as 'new concern', is, in fact, very much 'old business'.

Conclusion

This chapter briefly explored aspects of continuity and change, highlighting not only how restructuring created an internal market system with new priorities, but also how the modification of the health market in the late 1990s emphasised some aspects of co-operation, partnership and accountability. Commonalities in health and social care work mean that, in spite of change, certain issues remain important, such as teamworking and debates about resource allocation and the rationing of care. In tracing some of the key change processes, the influence of ideology in shaping political decision making is also graphically illustrated. Change is frequently underpinned by alternative 'visions' of how health and social care provision should be organised and run. Those changes that are the product of macro-level policy making will, of necessity, have a direct impact on the ground.

Although it is likely that only some of the discussion about policy and practice change will relate specifically to your area of practice, beginning to make links between your own experience and that of other types of practitioner can help you to understand where opportunities for growth and change can occur. Indeed, it becomes possible to view practice from a much wider perspective; a perspective that encourages the linking of theory, practice and experience. This wider picture can provide you with a means of setting your own practice in a framework, seeing how it has developed over time and how it may develop in the future. You will begin to understand not only the processes of change, but also where your efforts and activities fit into the greater scheme of things. Many of the themes you have encountered here will be picked up in later chapters of this book.

References

Allsop, J. (1994) *Health Policy and the NHS towards 2000*, Harlow, Longman.

Armstrong, D. (1993) 'From clinical gaze to regime of total health', in Beattie, A., Gott, M., Jones, L. and Sidell, M. (eds) *Health and Wellbeing: A Reader*, pp. 55–67, London, Macmillan (K258 Reader).

Audit Commission (1986) *Making a Reality of Community Care*, London, HMSO.

Bevan, A. (1952) *In Place of Fear*, London, Heinemann.

Beveridge, W. H. (1942) *Social Insurance and Allied Services*, Cmd 6404, London, HMSO.

Boyson, R. (ed.) (1971) *Down with the Poor*, London, Churchill Press.

Butcher, T. (1995) *Delivering Welfare: The Governance of the Social Services in the 1990s*, Buckingham, Open University Press.

Carter, N. (1994) 'Performance Indicators: 'backseat driving' or 'hands off' control?', in McKevitt, D. and Lawton, A. (eds) *Public Sector Management Theory, Critique and Practice*, London, Sage.

Coates, N. and Silburn, A. (1971) *The Forgotten Englishman*, London, Allen and Unwin.

Collins, R. (1990) 'Changing conceptions in the sociology of the professions', in Burrage, M. and Torstendahl, R. (eds) *The Formation of the Professions, State Knowledge and Strategy*, London, Sage.

Cox, D. (1991) 'Health service management – a sociological view: Griffiths and the non-negotiated order of the hospital', in Gabe, J., Calnan, M. and Bury, M. (eds) *The Sociology of the Health Service*, London, Routledge.

Crewe, I. (1991) 'Values: the crusade that failed', in Kavanagh, D. and Seldon, A. (eds) *The Thatcher Effect: a Decade of Change*, Oxford, Oxford University Press.

Dalley, G. (1988) *Ideologies of Caring: Rethinking Community and Collectivism*, London, Macmillan.

Deakin, N. (1988) *The Politics of Welfare*, London, Methuen.

Department of the Environment, Transport and the Regions (DETR) (1998) *Modern Local Government – in Touch with the People*, London, The Stationery Office.

Department of Health (DoH) (1984) *Griffiths Management Enquiry*, London, HMSO.

Department of Health (DoH) (1988) *Community Care: Agenda for Action*, London, HMSO.

Department of Health (DoH) (1989a) *Working for Patients*, Cmd 555, London, HMSO.

Department of Health (DoH) (1989b) *Caring for People*, Cmd 849, London, HMSO.

Department of Health (DoH) (1997) *The New NHS – Modern, Dependable*, London, The Stationery Office.

Department of Health (DoH) (1998) *Modernising Social Services, Promoting Independence, Improving Protection, Raising Standards*, Cmd 4169, London, The Stationery Office.

Department of Health and Social Security (DHSS) (1977) *The Way Forward*, London, HMSO.

Department of Health and Social Security (DHSS) (1980) *The Black Report*, London, HMSO.

Donnison, D. (1975) *The Politics of Poverty*, London, Allen and Unwin.

Ely, P. and Sama, A. (1996) 'The mixed economy of welfare', in Munday, B. and Ely, P. (eds) *Social Care in Europe*, London, Prentice Hall, Harvester Wheatsheaf.

Evans, C. (1998) 'Disability, discrimination and local authority social services', in Bornat, J. *et al.* (eds) *Community Care, A Reader*, pp. 317–326, Basingstoke, Macmillan.

Ewles, L. (1996) 'The impact of the NHS reforms on specialist health promotion in the NHS', in Scriven, A. and Orme, J. (eds) *Health Promotion: Professional Perspectives*, pp. 66–74, London, Macmillan.

Featherstone, M. (1991) *Consumer Culture and Postmodernism*, London, Sage.

Field, J. (1993) 'Competency and the pedagogy of labour', in Thorpe, M. (ed.) *Culture and Processes of Adult Learning*, London, Routledge.

Finch, J. and Groves, D. (1983) *A Labour of Love: Women, Work and Caring*, London, RKP.

Giddens, A. (1990) *Consequences of Modernity*, Stanford, CA, Stanford University Press.

Giddens, A. (1991) *Modernity and Self Identity*, Cambridge, Polity Press.

Green, D. G. (1987) *The New Right: The Counter Revolution in Political, Economic and Social Thought*, Brighton, Wheatsheaf.

Gyford, J. (1985) *The Politics of Local Socialism*, London, Allen and Unwin.

Hadley, R. and Hatch, S. (1981) *Social Welfare and the Failure of the State*, London, Allen & Unwin.

Ham, C. (1996) *Public, Private or Community: What Next for the NHS?*, London, Demos.

Ham, C. (1997) *Health Care Reform: Learning from Experience*, Buckingham, Open University Press.

Hambleton, R. and Hoggett, P. (1993) 'Rethinking consumerism in public services', *Consumer Policy Review*, Vol. 3, No. 2, pp. 103–11.

Hoyes, L. and Means, R. (1997) 'The impact of quasi-markets on community care', in Bornat, J., Johnson, J., Pereira, C., Pilgrim, D. and Williams, F. (eds) (1998) *Community Care, A Reader*, pp. 293–303, Basingstoke, Macmillan.

Hughes, L. and Pengelly, P. (1997) *Staff Supervision in a Turbulent Environment: Managing Processes and Tasks in Front-Line Service*, London, Jessica Kingsley.

Hugman, R. (1998) *Social Welfare and Social Value*, Basingstoke, Macmillan.

Illich, I. (1974) *Tools for Conviviality*, London, Marion Boyars.

Illich, I. (1976) *Limits to Medicine: The Expropriation of Health*, London, Marion Boyars.

Jacques, M. (1988) 'New times', *Marxism Today*, October, p. 3.

Jessup, G. (1990) 'National Vocational Qualifications: implications for further education', in Bees, M. and Sword, M. (eds) *National Vocational Qualifications and Further Education*, London, Kegan Paul, published in association with National Council for Vocational Qualifications.

Johnson, T. (1972) *Professions and Power*, Basingstoke, Macmillan.

Jones, L. J. (1994) *The Social Context of Health and Health Work*, Basingstoke, Macmillan.

Jones, L. J. (1998) 'Changing health care', in Brechin, A., Walmsley, J., Katz, J. and Peace, S. (eds) *Care Matters*, London, Sage.

Kendall, J. and Knapp, M. (1996) *The Voluntary Sector in the UK*, Manchester, Manchester University Press.

Kendall, I., Blackmore, M., Bradshaw, Y., Jenkinson, S. and Johnson, N. (1997) 'Quality services in quasi-markets', in May, M., Brunsdon, E. and Craig, G. (eds) *Social Policy Review 9*, London, Social Policy Association.

Khan, U. (1998) 'Up and ATAM', *The Health Service Journal*, April, p. 32.

Leonard, P. (1997) *Postmodern Welfare, Reconstructing an Emancipatory Project*, London, Sage.

Levy, A. and Kahan, B. (1991) *The Pindown Experience and the Protection of Children*, Staffordshire County Council.

Lipsky, M. (1978) 'The assault on human services: street-level bureaucrats, accountability, and the fiscal crisis', in Greer, S., Hedlund, R. D. and Gibson, J. L. (eds) *Accountability in Urban Society: Public Agencies Under Fire*, London, Sage.

Mark, A. (1997) 'Doctors in management', in Anand, P. and McGuire, A. (eds) *Change in Health Care*, p. 105, Basingstoke, Macmillan.

Marshall, T. H. (1977) *Social Policy in the Twentieth Century*, London, Hutchinson.

Mather, G. (1989) 'Thatcherism and local government: an evaluation', in Stewart, J. D. and Stoker, G. (eds) *The Future of Local Government*, London, Macmillan.

Mishra, R. (1984) *The Welfare State in Crisis*, Brighton, Harvester Wheatsheaf.

Pollitt, C. (1993) *Managerialism and the Public Services: the Anglo-American Experience* (2nd edn), Oxford, Blackwell.

Popple, K. (1995) *Analysing Community Work, Its Theory and Practice*, Buckingham, Open University Press.

Public Finance Foundation (1985) *Public Accountability: The National Audit Act 1983 and the Work of the Public Accounts Committee*, London, Public Finance Foundation.

Rhodes, R. A. W. (1997) *Understanding Governance, Policy Networks, Reflexivity and Accountability*, Buckingham, Open University Press.

Schumpeter, J. A. (1976) *Capitalism, Socialism and Democracy*, London, George Allen & Unwin.

Schwabenland, C. (1997) 'Elfrida Rathbone Islington: an experience of contracting', in Bornat, J., Johnson, J., Pereira, C., Pilgrim, D. and Williams, F. (eds) *Community Care: A Reader*, pp. 304–316, Basingstoke, Macmillan/ The Open University (K259 Reader).

Squires, P. (1990) *Anti-Social Policy. Welfare, Ideology and the Disciplinary State*, Chichester, Harvester Wheatsheaf.

Statham, D. (1996) *The Future of Social and Personal Care: The Role of Social Service Organisations in the Public, Private and Voluntary Sectors*, London, National Institute for Social Work.

Stewart, J. and Walsh, K. (1992) 'Change in the management of public services', *Public Administration*, Vol. 70, No. 4, pp. 499–518.

Strong, P. M. and Robinson, J. (1988) *New Model Management: Griffiths and the NHS*, Warwick, Nursing Policy Studies Centre.

Taylor, M. and Vigars, C. (1993) *Management and Delivery of Social Care*, Harlow, Longman.

Thompson, N. (1995) *Theory and Practice in Health and Social Welfare*, Buckingham, Open University Press.

Toffler, A. (1970) *Future Shock*, Harmondsworth, Penguin.

Townsend, P. (1962) *The Last Refuge*, London, Routledge and Kegan Paul.

Townsend, P. (1979) *Poverty in the United Kingdom*, Harmondsworth, Penguin.

Walby, S. and Greenwell, J. (1994) 'Managing the National Health Service', in Clarke, J., Cochrane, A. and McLaughlin, E. (eds) *Managing Social Policy*, pp. 57–72, London, Sage.

Walker, A. (1988) *Social Planning: A Strategy for Socialist Welfare*, Oxford, Blackwell.

Walsh, K. (1995) *Public Services and Market Mechanisms, Competition, Contracting and the New Public Management*, London, Macmillan.

Willetts, D. (1987) 'The price of welfare', *New Society*, 14 August, pp. 9–11.

Williams, F. (1992) 'Somewhere over the rainbow: universality and diversity in social policy', in Manning, N. and Page, R. (eds) *Social Policy Review 4*, London, Social Policy Association.

Willis, P. (1991) 'Towards a new cultural map', *National Arts and Media Strategy Discussion Paper 18*, London Arts Council.

Winkler, F. (1987) 'Consumerism in health care: beyond the supermarket model', *Policy and Politics*, Vol. 15, No. 1, pp. 1–8.

Wistow, G., Knapp, M., Hardy, B. and Allen, C. (1994) *Social Care in a Mixed Economy*, Buckingham, Open University Press.

Chapter 2
Introducing critical practice

Ann Brechin

The day to day experience of health and social care work is often one of firefighting...

Introduction

The day-to-day experience of health and social care work is often one of firefighting; managing time constraints; dealing with conflicting demands; setting difficult priorities; managing tricky relationships; finding short cuts; dealing with stress and frustration (both internal and external); and struggling to hang on to simply doing the job. It is about operating within organisational and social constraints as an individual, feeling accountable and responsible, yet often powerless and lacking in any real autonomy (Fish and Coles, 1998).

The challenge is to find an approach which: acknowledges the inadequacies as well as the difficulties of much current practice; recognises the major policy changes that have been taking place; welcomes the increasingly proactive role of service-users; but still values the positive motivation to provide support for others, which takes many practitioners into health and social care work in the first place. This chapter will develop a concept of 'critical practice' as a way of trying to engage with such challenges, particularly at a level appropriate to the experienced practitioner.

1   What is 'critical practice'?

The critical practitioner

The term 'critical' is used here to refer to open-minded, reflective appraisal that takes account of different perspectives, experiences and assumptions. It is not about being critical in the common parlance of being negative and destructive. Taking a constructive critical stance is not, of course, the prerogative of professionals; other chapters address the balance between professional and lay roles more explicitly. Here, however, it is discussed in the professional context with the implication that it encapsulates what professionals and experienced practitioners try, and indeed are called upon, to offer.

What is required increasingly is a capacity to handle uncertainty and change, rather than simply operating in prescribed ways in accordance with professional skills and knowledge. Practitioners must, in a sense, face both ways, to be seen as appropriately knowledgeable and competent but at the same time be continually aware of the relative and contextual basis of their practice. Most practitioners will recognise this continual sense of dilemma. Barnett (1997) puts it like this:

> Professionals have the duty to profess. But professing in a postmodern age calls for the capacity to be open to multiple discourses and to engage, albeit critically, with them.
>
> (Barnett, 1997, pp. 143–4)

A critical approach, of itself, assumes no moral direction. If, however, we assume that there is a fundamental assumption of social justice under-pinning the provision of care for others, it follows that successful caring processes must be both empowering and anti-oppressive. And prac-titioners' purpose will be to achieve solutions that are at some level felt to be just by all parties. Kitwood (1990), in his book *Concern for Others*, talks of 'the converging threads of integrity and integration' as desirable for one's own moral development and, therefore, necessarily for others.

> ... since there is a crucial sense in which all human beings are made of the same stuff, suffer the same kind of anguish, experience similar joys. It is to wish and hope for that same integrity for all persons, within their own particular cultural frame. In short, to seek an inner truth and integration for oneself is of necessity to desire integrity on the part not only of a few close others, but of a much larger circle of friends, colleagues and acquaintances. But if these, then why not all?
>
> (Kitwood, 1990, p. 211)

Kitwood is constructing his argument here within a discussion about psychotherapy, but in the context of a much wider analysis of caring within society. How such issues are thought and talked about within professional discourse will, of course, both reflect and construct what flows in practice. Oppressive patterns, embedded in thought and actions, have to be brought into awareness in order for change to occur. Yet confidence building rather than confrontational challenge seems to be the most fertile ground for development and learning to occur. Self-confidence and self-esteem, built on a sense of personal integrity and integration will, Kitwood argues, create a basis for open and empowering attitudes towards others.

Three case studies are described over the next few pages. Each reflects the complexity of critical practice. They are not so much accounts of the expertise involved in knowing what to do; rather they tell the story of the expertise involved in being able to tolerate the 'not knowing'. They reflect Kitwood's 'converging threads of integrity and integration'. Being able to acknowledge uncertainty and recognise conflicting lines of argument and different perspectives, while staying true to one's own understandings, lies at the heart of much professional work.

Jaqui – a physiotherapist

A young mother of three children has circulatory problems caused by diabetes, leading to progressive breakdown of tissue in one foot and leg. Amputation is inevitable and the surgeon sees his role as minimising the damage by removing as little as is clinically essential at each stage. An initial operation to remove the toes is followed six months later by a removal of half the foot and then the whole of the foot. Jaqui, the physiotherapist, sees from her vantage point the devastation this approach wreaks on the family and the mother's health generally. Each time the disease process reasserts itself to the point of tissue breakdown, with associated stress to other body systems. The procedure involves time in hospital, there is the stress of the operation itself, time off work for the young woman's husband, further separation for the children followed by the period of recovery before any functional rehabilitation can begin.

Jaqui knows that the eventual picture will resolve itself as a below-the-knee amputation, at which point things are likely to stabilise. To move to that point at the outset would mean one traumatic event instead of multiple interacting traumas; it would lead to better health for the mother, rather than for her to be trapped in a cycle of illness and partial recuperation for years, and a satisfactory rehabilitation process with functional prosthesis.

With care and tact, Jaqui attempts to discuss it with the doctor, but to no avail. She considers ways in which she might raise it during a ward round with the doctor in front of the family, or even behind his back, but concludes that the potential damage from such an intervention might be worse for the family than the current position. She recognises that the likelihood of her arguments being accepted would be minimal. Without the doctor's backing, the family are unlikely to accept the idea of a major amputation.

Jaqui's decision not to intervene further flew in the face of what she felt to be the best outcome for the family and was probably harder for her than to argue her case further. Her personal and professional analysis of the situation had to include awareness of the family's likely reactions and feelings as well as the context of the more powerful role of the doctor and the importance of the family's trust in him. The difficulties partly arose, she knew, from the unequal status and consequently limited communications between doctors and therapists. The action she did subsequently pursue was the creation of a multidisciplinary 'journal club' which gave her an occasional platform to begin to present some alternative evidence and perspectives to the doctors, and others, thus opening up some discussion and altering the power imbalance a little.

Adjoa – a community nurse

An experienced nurse working as part of a team attached to a large primary care practice, Adjoa finds the increasing use of agency nurses on temporary contracts very worrying. She has no management or supervisory role and yet is aware of her greater expertise in relation to their often unknown (at least to her) level of experience. As a black, female nurse, she is also conscious of the sensitivity of such tensions about roles and responsibilities when a white, male nurse is appointed on contract.

For a period the male nurse takes over some of Adjoa's excess workload. On revisiting one of her elderly patients (an 80-year-old Asian man), subsequently, she finds that a lesion that had been healing well has begun to break down again because the wrong kind of cream has been used. She finds herself very angry and yet unable to remedy the situation. She confronts the contract nurse who is offhand about the matter, making her acutely conscious of her lack of any formal seniority. She feels her gender and racial and ethnic identity, and those of the client, make matters worse, but does not feel sure whether this is her problem or her colleague's. (Is he being racist and sexist or does she just anticipate that he will be?) Even angrier now, she takes up the matter with her senior, but is effectively made to feel that she is overreacting.

Unlike Jaqui, Adjoa acted on her initial feelings about the situation but ended up feeling that she had 'blown it' by getting so angry. A friend helped her to talk it through some weeks later and suggested that maybe she had every right to feel angry. What seemed to have happened, though, was that her anger had made it very difficult for her to really analyse the situation or reflect on her own reactions. When she could do this, the picture began to change. She could see the problems for the contract nurse, thrown in at the deep end without obvious lines of peer support being established; she could see the financial limitations forcing short-termism in appointments; she could see her own uncertainties, despite her experience, limiting her capacity to offer non-judgemental support to colleagues. At this point she began to formulate a new strategy and approached her line manager to discuss how the team might support itself more effectively in the longer term.

Martin – a residential care home manager

As manager of a care home for young people, Martin found himself faced with a difficult dilemma. Sophie, a 15-year-old, was persistently self-harming and heavily involved in substance abuse. For some time it had been clear that the home could not provide a safe environment for her and after a process of negotiation and consultation a specialist foster placement was found for her, which, combined with intensive support work, offered a good chance for her to make some progress towards recovery. But Sophie refused to go. She understood all the reasons and the arguments, but simply dug her heels in and refused to agree.

All Martin's training and indeed the Children Act 1989 stressed the importance of the young person's right to choose. Yet here he was confronted with a situation where he knew the young person's welfare was seriously at risk. His decision, not taken alone or lightly, was to insist that she must go. He knew he was taking away a part of her autonomy, in the hope that she would gain more subsequently. He also felt strongly that insistence must be presented with explanation and acknowledgement of the conflict, conveying in essence 'I know this is not what you want, but these are the reasons why I believe it is what must happen.'

Martin's difficulty was that whatever action he took or did not take would be wrong in one sense or another. The best he could do was to be clear about the context of his decision and the value base he was drawing upon and on that basis to make the best decision he could. His concern to maintain respect for Sophie's different view was an important part of the story for him. He did not pretend that her view did not matter or that his view was right and hers was wrong. He did not feel comfortable about it, but decided his primary concern must be to protect her welfare in this situation.

Practitioners, as these examples illustrate, cannot occupy some detached space from which vantage point they make 'correct' decisions about their clients. They are in there too, struggling to make sense of things, to communicate, and buffeted in the same way by winds of change, by personal and cultural influences, as are service-users and others. Practitioners face conflicting principles and a context that is complex and requires reflection, rather than the straightforward application of knowledge and skill. These examples argue, then, for a professionalism involving not just the critical appraisal of knowledge and action – not just a critical handling of theory and practice – but also the importance of acknowledging personal involvement.

These three examples illustrate the importance of what Barnett (1997) describes as 'the three domains of critical practice'. Adapting his terminology slightly, we frame these here as the domains of critical analysis, critical action and critical reflexivity. The domain of *critical analysis* can be seen as the critical evaluation of knowledge, theories, policies and practice, with an in-built recognition of multiple perspectives and an orientation of ongoing enquiry. *Critical action* requires a sound skill base, but also calls for a recognition of power inequalities and structured disadvantage and seeks to work across difference towards empowerment. The third domain of *critical reflexivity* presumes an aware, reflective and engaged self; the term 'reflexivity' implies that practitioners recognise their engagement with service-users and others in a process of negotiating understandings and interventions and are aware of the assumptions and values they bring to this process.

This chapter will argue that professional education and development needs to draw out a capacity not only for critical analysis and critical action but also for critical reflexivity, combining to create an awareness of the circular and interactive processes by which the 'self' develops as a critical practitioner. An adapted version of Barnett's three domains of critical practice is shown in Figure 1.

In each of the case study examples, the practitioner was operating across these three domains. Each was drawing upon their professional knowledge and understanding to analyse the situation; each had been

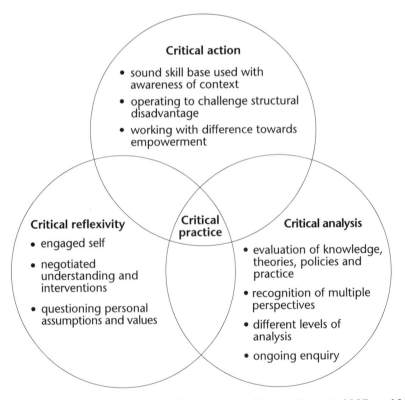

Figure 1   **Three domains of critical practice** (Source: Barnett, 1997, p. 105)

using a repertoire of skilful actions (including inaction); and each held a reflexive view about their own position and feelings. It is artificial, of course, to describe these as separate processes; the reality will be rather more integrated – 'joined up practice', perhaps.

There seem to be some crucial aspects of the process those practitioners were engaged in which span or underpin the three domains. It may help to identify these in terms of two *guiding principles*: the principle of 'respecting others as equals' and the principle of an open and 'not-knowing' approach.

The principle of 'respecting others as equals'

There are many good reasons for enshrining this as a guiding principle. International human rights movements and declarations have raised awareness of the ease and frequency with which people's basic rights can be ignored and the importance of setting up agreed principles and policies to endeavour to protect them. Equal rights movements and anti-discriminatory campaigns have drawn attention, in the Western world in particular, to the endemic oppression of less powerful groups in society: women, black people, disabled people, older people, people with mental health problems, people with learning difficulties, people who are ill, children, people living in poverty and others.

Given the relatively powerful position of professionals in society, and the fact that health and social care practitioners are working explicitly with people in vulnerable positions, it is not surprising that built-in oppression is increasingly recognised. A substantial body of work in the form of research, papers, books, policy documents and practice experience addresses explicitly the problems of the imbalance of power and how attempts may be made to redress it. Not only that, but the concept of establishing a value base, which affords equal rights and respect to all, is at the core of all the vocational qualifications and occupational standards relevant to work in this field. Much of this body of work will be drawn upon in the course of this and subsequent chapters.

One example, for now, can be drawn out from the experience of Martin and the young person in his care. In the field of child care, the legislative and policy frameworks have shifted significantly towards the protection of children's rights to be heard (HMSO, 1989). Against this backdrop, Martin understood the power he had and the state had to intervene in a life. Already a 'looked-after' young person, Sophie was now to be moved again against her wishes, and yet as far as could be foreseen 'in her best interests'. What he could do to acknowledge this imbalance of power was to respect her views and feelings, not by accepting them, but by talking about them and allowing them to be different from his own. Respecting Sophie's rights did not mean that Martin should abdicate his own rights and responsibilities.

Respecting others as equals applies not only to working with service-users but also to working with, including supporting and being supported by, colleagues. Power differentials between professions, hierarchies within professions, and different conceptual, theoretical and practice frameworks all contribute to major difficulties in communication between one practitioner and another. The cases of both Jaqui, in her relationship with the more powerful doctor, and Adjoa, in her ambiguous relationship with her colleague as well as the problems with her line manager, illustrate these difficulties. Interestingly, both of them looked for solutions that involved moving towards greater opportunities for learning and support through establishing more respectful and equal relationships.

This principle is well developed and has a good pedigree. It is not, however, easy to translate into practice. It does not mean denying or disparaging professional knowledge and expertise. Rather, it is about seeking to *share* skills and understandings and *offer* potential interventions or explanation. Such offers will not always be accepted, however, and critical practice will be about struggling to build and sustain respectful and equal relationships within which meanings and ways forward can be negotiated.

The principle of an open and 'not-knowing' approach

The second guiding principle for critical practice is openness. Accepting a degree of uncertainty about any intervention has to be part of the job. There will be conflicting needs and widely varying views about priorities and the desirability of different outcomes. Who is to say, for example, whether a half leg amputation and remaining healthier and more active is more desirable than struggling on with less devastating surgery for a longer period? Who is to say whether insisting on a move to a foster placement will be for the best – and whose best? Using the wrong cream on a wound is almost certainly worse than using the right one! But where does the blame lie and how might best practice be conceptualised, developed and shared with others in that situation?

To take up a position of openness is to accept that professional practice is an evolving process within a social and political context. This is not to deny the importance of established thinking and evidence – far from it. Professional practice is rooted in theories and keeping up with the latest research will continue to be important. It is more like the adage, 'the more you know, the more you know what you don't know'. Openness and 'not-knowing' require engagement with the process of evolving knowledge.

Practice then can be seen as part and parcel of a continual process of theorising. Theories develop as attempts to make sense of how things seem (Howe, 1987; Thompson, 1995). They are not a fixed entity apart – in books. They do not tell some absolute truth, but theorising is part of a human process of trying to make our experiences more intelligible (Argyris and Schön, 1974). Practitioners are, *par excellence*, theorisers, as Schön in particular has argued (Schön, 1983). Thompson suggests it is a mistake for practitioners to see themselves as concerned only with practice, while others attend to the theory. He argues that:

> ... we need to recognise the fallacy of theoryless practice so that we are not guilty of failing to review our ideas and lacking the flexibility to adapt or abandon them in the light of changing circumstances.
>
> (Thompson, 1995, p. 29)

Theories are always 'only theories', but in the positive sense that they are provisional and there to be tried and tested for fit in order to evolve. To accept 'not-knowing' is in the best tradition of philosophers and scientists down the ages. What is strange is how far professionals have been pushed (or have pushed themselves) into a defensive position of seeming to be the opposite – all-seeing and all-knowing. What is suggested here is that critical practice should be seen as part of an ongoing process of theorising within an acceptance of 'not-knowing' and that this should be the second guiding principle.

A theoretical context

Critical practice occurs in a theoretical context, although the influences may not always be very apparent to practitioners. The ideas behind the accounts and analyses of critical practice offered here can be seen as stemming from several interrelated theoretical traditions.

For some, particularly those who have studied sociology at some point, the most obvious link will be to *critical theory* – historically to the work of the Frankfurt School and more recently perhaps to variants of the work of a writer such as Habermas (1972). For others, critical practice will gel with an understanding they have developed of *social constructionism* in psychology or sociology, with its insistence that the social context in which we live is not extraneous reality, but is constructed by us as part of a process of creating that context. The language that we use is seen as part of a process of creating shared meanings and experiences. What this argues essentially is that humans are 'meaning-generating systems'. Such thinking has a long history, but has more recently been extensively debated – for example, by Gergen (1991), Shotter (1993), McNamee and Gergen (1992), Shotter and Gergen (1989), Harré (1986), and Bateson (1972).

Still others might draw a link with *feminist theory* or with *history from below* or with the implications of the *social model of disability*, particularly in the sense that these challenge established ways of formulating and researching issues and insist that, from the standpoint of oppressed groups, there are new questions to be addressed and new ways of collecting data.

While it may be helpful and enrich an understanding of critical practice to be able to make links such as these (see, for example, Porter, 1998;

Layder, 1997), it is by no means necessary to do so. A critical practitioner needs to recognise that the social world operates according to rules that are not the same as those of the material world and to accept in broad terms that:

- social and organisational structures are not given and immutable
- individuals have agency in that they imbue situations with meaning and that these meanings have consequences
- interpersonal relationships and structures reflect and create power imbalances which can be uncovered and challenged
- alternative circumstances, strategies and outcomes can be envisioned and sometimes brought about.

This is not to deny the reality, for example, of disease and the advances that laboratory science has brought working with biological theories of human behaviour. But it is to acknowledge that practitioners in health and social care need to work with a broader theoretical framework in their daily practice – with what one set of authors recently called an integrated 'biopsychosocial model' (Cooper *et al.*, 1996). Acknowledging different discourses cannot fail to bring the questioning stance which is at the heart of critical practice.

Critical practice in action

So how does any of this relate back to the three case studies? It was argued earlier that practitioners are engaged in theorising, but does it make any sense to suggest that they might think in such abstract terms as these? The exercise involves thinking about their arguments and dilemmas in relation to a theoretical framework which takes on board not just a sense of an individual in society but also a sense of how meanings and understandings may be socially constructed.

Jaqui was very clearly aware of the wider context in which both the family and the professional service operated. The issue was not just about physical rehabilitation after an amputation. It was about a young woman in the context of a family life and the particular roles and expectations she would expect and be expected to meet. Jaqui's own role as physiotherapist set her in a particular and subordinate relationship to the doctor in the context of wider professional and regulatory systems. What took her beyond this into the realms of critical practice was her recognition that different meanings could co-exist and have validity; that more powerful voices might hold sway, but that this did not mean they were right, nor necessarily wrong, and that ways might be found for opening up some further dialogue around these meanings.

Adjoa was similarly aware of the constraints of the system on how she and others worked. She also saw the potential of the more powerful white majority to discredit her voice as a black professional and identified her lack of formal status as making it difficult to support or know how to criticise her colleague. As she grappled with the issues, she began to take on a different perspective, realising that her view of things was not the only one or necessarily the most helpful and constructive one. She was able to blend together a view of her own agency, and of the power of existing structures to constrain or facilitate, in a way that provided her with a course of action for the future.

Martin knew the systems in which he and the young person were located; they could not be more clearly spelled out in policy documents in the child-care field. He also understood the importance of the meaning that might be attached to his decision. Inevitably for the young person, it meant her wishes were overruled, at least on the face of it. He hoped that his explanations and respect for her views would create a more positive meaning for her; one that said she had been heard and understood, but that a decision genuinely thought to be more in her best interests had to be taken.

Where does this take us in terms of defining 'critical practice'? Drawing together all these elements, which address process, guiding principles and theoretical perspective, results in the following list.

Critical practice entails

- operating across the three domains of analysis, action and reflexivity

- working within a value base that respects others as equals

- adopting an open and 'not-knowing' approach to practice

- understanding individuals (including oneself) in relation to a socio-political and ideological context within which meanings are socially constructed.

Having framed a concept of critical practice in this way, the rest of this chapter looks at what this means in terms of fundamental, everyday processes – what will be referred to as the three pillars of critical practice: forging relationships, seeking to empower others and making a difference.

2 Becoming a critical practitioner

Forging relationships

What most practitioners are concerned with on a day-to-day basis is being a good enough practitioner, seeking to help and striving at least to do no harm, within increasingly tight budgetary constraints. The case studies offered some examples of what might be described as critical practice in action, where outcomes are not perfect, nor even satisfactory much of the time, but nevertheless good enough decisions must be made on the best information and judgements available. In a sense, the professional has ownership of his or her working role and space and, within that, both experiences and creates professional practice (Kolb, 1995; Tsang, 1998). This second section will unpack those ideas just a little further, exploring what it means to 'respect someone as equal', for example, or to maintain an 'open mind'.

At the heart of health and social care practice, then, there is the first pillar of critical practice: forging relationships with people, whether as clients or colleagues. This requires sophisticated interpersonal skills. Being a good communicator and able to forge good relationships is a starting point, but it has to extend to include, for example, the capacity to establish a dialogue in difficult circumstances: to negotiate, mediate, set boundaries, challenge and influence. Constructive relationships may have to be developed with diverse and challenging clients, relatives, colleagues, managers, juniors, other professions, planners, politicians and often the media and the public. This requires, as we have argued, not only a good understanding of how others may operate but also a sensitive and well-tuned awareness of oneself.

This aspect of direct care work has been described in terms of emotional labour (Smith, 1992) and is beginning to be more widely recognised within training and support. As a professional develops, further emotionally demanding tasks arise. There is the process of balancing priorities in meeting the competing needs of many clients (including potential clients who are not accessing the service); the balancing of time and resource constraints; and the balancing of time for clinical work against time for administration, liaising, supervisory or personal development responsibilities, and a growing sense of responsibility for, or at least awareness of, the direction of the organisation and the professional roles within it on a wider scale. This wider political professional perspective may still remain connected with individual client work. As depth and breadth of understanding and skill grow, so the awareness and critical perspective on work and relationships with individuals has to evolve (Mann, 1998; Allen, 1997).

Within this broader critical framework, interpersonal skills remain central (Thompson, 1996). The professional will be handling communications with a wide range of people. This will involve multiple roles and among these we might identify the following relationships:

- professional–client relationships
- professional–team relationships
- interorganisational relationships
- purchaser–provider relationships
- supervisor–learner relationships
- manager–staff relationships
- relationships with policy-makers or politicians
- relationships with the media or the public.

Not all will be in agreement with each other and the capacity to create and maintain open dialogue while holding on to core principles and negotiating priorities demands sophisticated skills. Forging relationships is not just about being friendly, it is about creating connections and channels through which real communications can occur, bringing opportunities to learn about other views and perspectives, and discovering ways of talking constructively about differences of opinion.

Fundamentally this is about establishing equity and mutual respect. The Rogerian emphasis on warmth, positive regard, genuineness, empathy and equality holds sway here and is hard to better as a foundation (Rogers, 1951). Recognising and respecting the other person's viewpoint and feeling positive and accepting towards them does not mean losing touch with your own beliefs and feelings. Dialogue and partnership essentially involve bringing yourself and your own ideas, principles and knowledge base to the relationship and communication. To do that without disempowering the other, to remain genuinely open to learning from them, to offer ideas without defensiveness or pressure, and to hear and receive in return – those are the sophisticated skills of constructive engagement with others.

Given the multiple differing roles, perspectives and power relations, this will seldom be straightforward. A capacity for mediation and negotiation is required when relationships threaten to break down or cannot easily be established in the first place.

> Negotiation is the only way to achieve the best outcome for individuals or organisations who need things from each other ... You need to get people talking, keep people talking and work towards a better understanding of different parties' needs and wishes.
>
> (Fletcher, 1998, p. 21)

The concept of working together in partnerships and across role boundaries towards goals which may have to be negotiated provokes a very different image from that of the individual autonomous professional fixing something that has gone wrong. The expectation that professionals should be able to work in such a way has increased significantly (Loxley, 1997; Hornby, 1993) and the relational aspect, or forging of relationships, within such work can be seen as central.

Seeking to empower others

The concept of empowerment is the second pillar of critical practice. Concepts such as oppression, discrimination, empowerment and equal opportunities have become part of the language in health and social care work (Dominelli, 1988; Braye and Preston-Shoot, 1995; Thompson, 1998). They have reflected a recognition that less powerful or minority groups tend to become oppressed and disadvantaged and that health and social care services and professionals are so much a part of the status quo that they inevitably and unconsciously play a part in this structured oppression. In recognising this, critical practitioners begin to understand oppressive forces and work to reconstruct power imbalances. What has been learned from disabled, feminist and black perspectives has valuable messages for all critical practice (Pinkney, 1999).

Such messages are also complex, with a growing lexicon of terms which can prove something of a minefield for the unenlightened practitioner. Braye and Preston-Shoot (1995), in looking at empowering practice, use the diagram in Figure 2 to illustrate the difference between anti-discriminatory and anti-oppressive practice. Both, they suggest, attempt to address the problem, the first through 'reform' and the second through more radical, political activity, which they term 'revolution'.

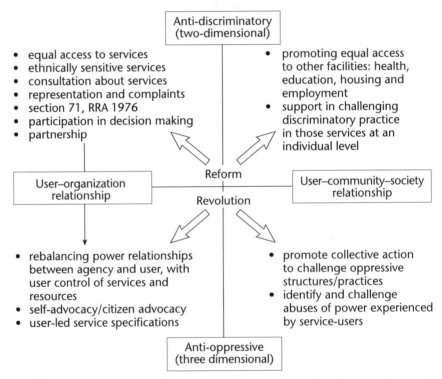

Figure 2 **Anti-discriminatory and anti-oppressive practice** (Source: Braye and Preston-Shoot, 1995, p. 108)

There may be parallels between the shift from anti-discriminatory to anti-oppressive practice and from reflective to critical practice. This is not so much a political question of how 'revolutionary' practitioners ought to be, but more a matter of a shift in perception and understanding to a broader and more politically framed arena. Such debates have become central to professional codes of practice and to professional training (Dominelli, 1988 and 1997; Culley, 1996 and 1999; Doyle, 1997; Pinkney, 1999). This seems to reflect a growing awareness amongst professionals that recognising and tackling oppression in relation to ethnic or other minority group experience is an inherent aspect of critical practice (Dominelli, 1997).

Some of this thinking has begun already. For example, the firm line on anti-oppressive social work practice is being reformulated in terms of inclusivity and citizenship (Thompson, 1999; Clarke and Cochrane, 1998; Saraga, 1998; Pinkney, 1999). The polarising of characteristics by gender, particularly in relation to asserting women's capacity for caring, has been reframed, for example, by Davies (1995 and 1998), who argues that rather than gender attributes, these stereotypes represent 'cultural codes of gender'. The dependency relationships imposed on disabled people by concepts of 'care' rather than 'direct payments' are challenged (Morris, 1991; Swain and French, 1998) by thinking emerging from the social model of disability (for example, Oliver, 1990).

Analyses have tended to polarise people according to particular attributes, whether gender, ethnicity or role. This is described as a form of 'essentialism' (see, for example, Clarke and Cochrane, 1998) in which social behaviour is ascribed to some particular 'essence' of the individual, such as 'blackness' or 'femaleness' or 'disability'. This results in a denial of diversity and difference, assuming that all people who are socially constructed as 'black', 'old', 'disabled' or 'homosexual', for example, share similar experiences and aspirations (SSI, 1998; Pinkney, 1998). Thus power relations and oppressive practice can seem irredeemably embedded in social structures. A more positive formulation may emerge as boundaries and identities become more fluid and are recognised as such.

All this impinges very directly on practice. For example, Pinkney suggests, in discussing 'same race' adoption policies, that current reformulations see the child 'as an individual', with an identity which is multi-layered and complex, rather than one-dimensional. 'Race' is an important feature in this assessment, but so are other factors such as class, gender, health, friends, school, neighbourhood, the child's and their family's wishes, and so on (Pinkney, 1998).

These issues find an echo in health as well as social care, where Culley (1999) argues for such a shift in terms of the limitations of the 'multi-culturalist' perspective which has held sway in nursing:

- It is inadequate and misleading to suppose that education for greater sensitivity amongst health professionals alone can redress the prejudice and discrimination faced by ethnic minority groups in a majority white society.

- Professionals cannot learn all about and have an adequate under-standing of all cultural differences, religious conventions, diet, health beliefs, etc. More appropriate will be an approach to a negotiated understanding which includes awareness of cultural and ethnic diversity.

- There are dangers of 'essentialism' in the multicultural approach, which lead to stereotypical assumptions about the experience of minority groups: for example, passive Asian women, arrogant Afro-Caribbean youth, tightly knit family support networks.

(Culley, 1999, in press)

Culley argues for a shift in emphasis in nursing to a more contextualised understanding of the experiences and impact of racism and calls for research to focus on 'the complex ways in which "race", culture, gender, age and socio-economic dimensions may interact in influencing both patterns of health status and utilisation of health services' (Culley, 1996, p. 569).

Lewis (1996), in research with social workers, describes how race and gender relations emerge from 'situated voices' – in other words, from the way people talk about other people and each other, thus creating complex and shifting, personal meanings about gendered and racial identities, but meanings which arise also from particular historical and social situations. We are all, in Lewis' sense, 'situated voices' playing a part in creating our own and others' understandings and experiences – using our own voices, but voices which carry a heritage, are embedded in a current context and anticipate a future. Such voices will have racial and ethnic elements, gender, sexual orientation, socio-cultural experiences, religious or ideological beliefs, family positions and experiences and social role through work or other contexts.

For white Anglo-Saxons, ironically, owning and valuing ethnic and cultural identity and its influences can be problematic, in the first place because it is rendered almost invisible by being the norm in the UK context. The ethno-centric assumption is that it is others who are different, who have racial and ethnic identities, which are then seen as requiring special pleading. Owning a white cultural identity brings the discomfort of an implicit label of oppressor. Can anyone take pride in that heritage today and not be seen as prejudiced against others who are not white, not Anglo-Saxon? Anglo-Saxon pride seems associated with the National Front and extremes of racism, of the Irish Troubles, of a racist police force. Yet valuing and understanding one's own identity is fundamental to offering empowering help to others (Dutt and Ferns, 1998). One cannot help others from a position of personal shame.

But is awareness enough for critical practice? Can an understanding of identities, oppression and principles of empowerment influence practice and outcomes? Gomm's analysis suggests somewhat bleakly that there is a fundamental paradox about empowerment:

> To empower someone else implies something which is granted by someone more powerful to someone who is less powerful: a gift of power made from a position of power. ... Those people who say they are in the business of empowering rarely seem to be giving up their own power: they are usually giving up someone else's and they may actually be increasing their own.
>
> (Gomm, 1993, p. 137)

Gomm rightly challenges naïve and circular justifications of professional power in practice, in which, for example, 'legitimate power equals expertise' and 'the illegitimate use of power equals professional mal-practice'. He allows, nevertheless, rather grudgingly, that the term 'empowerment' designates many excellent practices and it is hard to see, indeed, how striving towards clearer understandings of and better practice towards empowerment can be a bad thing.

Gomm's concept of empowerment in which 'giving power' to one equals taking it away from another rests on a particular notion of combative power with winners and losers in terms of influence. Ferns, on the other hand, describes empowerment as:

> ... fundamental to equality ... Enabling access to legitimate forms of power and removing discriminatory barriers ...
>
> (Ferns, 1998, personal communication)

Seeking to empower individuals and to challenge oppression and discrimination may involve more than just recognising and challenging on the basis of rather simplistic models of identity and social relations. Increasingly, it becomes part of a wider project of critical practice aiming to facilitate more permeable boundaries, acknowledge more flexible roles and identities and develop more dialogic ways of working with others. It is about supporting the inclusion of people as equal citizens within such processes and negotiations.

Making a difference

The third suggested pillar of critical practice is 'making a difference'. Practitioners assess, judge and intervene with the aim of making something better than before, whether by helping a wound to heal (physically or emotionally) or helping to improve somebody's circumstances or situation in some way. In order to make, and continue to make, 'good enough' interventions, practitioners have to keep up to date with the latest practice and research evidence, weigh up that evidence in relation to their own working practice and situation, and act and evaluate outcomes accordingly.

Scientific method offers an approach to evolving knowledge and practice in this way by testing out beliefs to prove or, more precisely, to attempt to disprove them. The notion of evidence-based practice stems from this tradition (Muir Gray, 1997) and is increasingly forming a basis for policy planning and implementation, for professional practice and audit and for professional training and professional development. Book 2 *Using Evidence in Health and Social Care* examines these ideas in more detail in terms of the relationship between research and practice. Here we can simply indicate some of the issues.

The call for evidence-based practice reflects a rational and, what some would describe as, a Western frame of reference. That does not make it right – or wrong – but it does give it a particular cultural 'style'. Fernando (1991), in discussing mental health services, suggests that 'style' will affect the underlying assumptions and the nature of interventions:

> The goal of all Eastern religions and psychology is enlightenment, subjective experience and meditation. In general, the quest for under-

standing in Western thought is for facts, in the East, for feelings. The
Westerner seeks knowledge, the Easterner seeks to know.
                              (Fernando, 1991, p. 93, quoted in Dutt and Ferns, 1998)

Without necessarily accepting this rather essentialist position on East and
West, the notion of cultural styles may still be helpful. Dutt and Ferns
(1998), in their training pack on 'black people and mental health', draw
upon Fernando's analysis to develop three dimensions of cultural style (see
Figure 3). The first dimension is about achieving understanding: in
'rational' terms, through analysis of formal information; in 'emotional'
terms, through achieving greater self-awareness. The second dimension of
cultural style concerns the response: whether by seeking to control or
eradicate the symptoms, or by acceptance combined with a restoration of
balance. The third dimension addresses assumptions about outcome:
whether a concern with re-establishing the autonomy and interests of the
individual or with the harmony of the social group to which the
individual belongs.

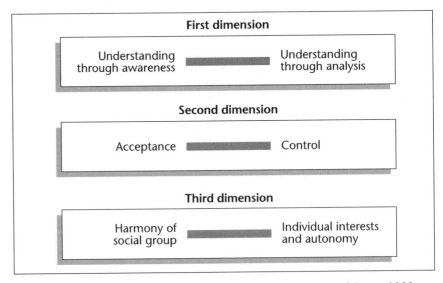

Figure 3   **Three dimensions of cultural style** (Source: Dutt and Ferns, 1998,
p. 29)

In seeking to build partnerships and to empower, it is the professional,
ultimately, who will be expected to 'know' and to be responsible for any
decisions and interventions. Yet professionals have their own ethnic and
cultural origins and styles and, like those people they are working with,
these will vary widely. To some extent such 'differences' will be overruled
by a professional training, which privileges intellectually based arguments
and views, and by the power of the professional to impose those views.
And yet, increasingly, the central importance of recognising and working
across difference, creating dialogue and partnership and respect, calls this
into question.

As well as such concerns about whether practitioners *should* rely solely on rational analytic approaches, there are also reasons to doubt that professionals *do, or even can*, operate in a purely rational way. Theoreticians exploring how people make decisions have struggled to find models which account for how they do so. Typically, these have been cognitive and statistical models, describing the kinds of factors that may be taken into account in thinking rationally about the best decision to reach (Ranyard *et al.*, 1997; Kahneman *et al.*, 1982). Such a formulation would fit comfortably with the implementation of evidence-based practice.

Subsequent work in psychology, however, has suggested that in practice people do not actually operate in this rational way. We tend rather to 'base our choices on rules and strategies derived from past experience with similar problems' (Eiser and van der Pligt, 1988). We are also influenced by our attitudes and values and by the feedback loops from earlier decisions. It is essentially, therefore, they argue, a social process, rather than a rational, individual one. In other words, belief systems and cultural style may have a powerful impact on practice.

From large-scale policy issues to specific practice decisions and the moment-to-moment decisions that are part of an ongoing process – how to respond to a request, how to initiate or conclude a conversation, the tone of voice, the interpretations placed on what is said or done – all will be influenced not just by formal evidence and analysis but by a host of other less formal understandings and feelings (Schön, 1992 and 1994; Lester, 1995; Schell and Ceverso, 1993). Rational, evidence-based practice can be powerfully effective, but it will always depend on what evidence is seen as relevant and what outcomes are seen as meaningful. It is inevitably limited in its range of vision and the critical practitioner seeking to make a difference and also to value difference must draw on it as a tool and source of information, but not as the whole or only story.

Experience and expertise should not be devalued, nor, as Claxton (1998) argues, the power of human intuition. Neither should we ignore the importance of the value base operating alongside our own unconscious motivations and defences. In professions and organisations which are mediating human need and social justice, there is surprisingly little emphasis on the fundamental human processes involved. Kitwood (1990 and 1998) argues for the importance of moral space and draws upon 'depth psychology' to examine caring work. Smith (1992, 1999) talks of 'emotional labour'. Hornby (1993) discusses the essentials of 'self-responsibility and social integration'. Barnett (1997) suggests we cannot have genuine critical thinking and critical action without self-engagement. (These points are discussed further in Chapters 3, 7 and 8.)

We need to recognise these broader frames of reference in thinking about evidence-based practice and professional development. If the professionalisation of work in health and social care is ultimately of value, it must be because it enhances rather than dehumanises our capacity to value and understand ourselves and others as moral and sentient beings – and our capacity to treat others, especially vulnerable others, accordingly, in working to provide health and social care.

Conclusion

The concept of critical practice developed here locates the practitioner within the frame; as an active participant in a process of creating meanings and understandings and forging relationships and dialogue across difference. Rather than presuming a detached, objective and wholly rational role based on assumptions of passive compliance from others, the critical practitioner is seen as reflexive and engaged. Thus in seeking to work in an empowering way, awareness of personal and socio-cultural origins and belief systems is seen as an essential basis for creating respectful and equal relationships and for challenging discriminatory barriers.

Critical practitioners must be skilled and knowledgeable and yet remain open to alternative ideas, frameworks and belief systems, recognising and valuing alternative perspectives. 'Not-knowing' and uncertainty need to be valued as an orientation towards openness and a continuing process of learning, even if, at times, it can be essential to act swiftly and confidently. This sense of critical practice with its dilemmas and conflicts, but also its sense of creative and developmental process, underpins and infuses the chapters that follow.

References

Allen, D. (1997) 'The nursing-medical boundary: a negotiated order?', *Sociology of Health and Illness*, Vol. 19, No. 4, pp. 498–520.

Argyris, C. and Schön, D. (1974) *Theory and Practice*, San Francisco, CA, Jossey-Bass.

Barnett, R. (1997) *Higher Education: A Critical Business*, Buckingham, SRHE and Open University Press.

Bateson, G. (1972) *Steps to an Ecology of Mind*, London, Intertext Books.

Braye, S. and Preston-Shoot, M. (1995) *Empowering Practice in Health and Social Care*, Buckingham, Open University Press.

Clarke, J. and Cochrane, A. (1998) 'The social construction of social problems', in Saraga, E. (ed.) *Embodying the Social: Constructions of Difference*, London, Routledge.

Claxton, G. (1998) 'Investigating human intuition: knowing without knowing why', *The Psychologist*, May, 88, pp. 217–220.

Cooper, N., Stevenson, C. and Hale, G. (1996) 'The biopsychosocial model', in Cooper, N. *et al.* (eds) *Integrating Perspectives on Health*, Buckingham, Open University Press.

Culley, L. (1996) 'A critique of multiculturalism in health care: the challenge for nurse education', *Journal of Advanced Nursing*, Vol. 23, pp. 564–570.

Culley, L. (1999) 'Working with diversity: towards negotiated understandings of health care needs', in Davies, C., Finlay, L. and Bullman, A. (eds) *Changing Practice in Health and Social Care*, London, Sage (K302 Reader 1).

Davies, C. (1995) *Gender and the Professional Predicament in Nursing*, Buckingham, Open University Press.

Davies, C. (1998) 'Caregiving, carework and professional care', in Brechin, A., Walmsley, J., Katz, J. and Peace, S. (eds) *Care Matters: Concepts, Practice and Research in Health and Social Care*, London, Sage.

Dominelli, L. (1988) *Anti-racist Social Work*, London, BASW/Macmillan.

Dominelli, L. (1997) *Sociology for Social Work*, Basingstoke, Macmillan.

Doyle, C. (1997) 'Protection studies: challenging oppression and discrimination', *Social Work Education*, Vol. 16, No. 2, pp. 8–19.

Dutt, R. and Ferns, P. (1998) *Letting through the Light: A Training Pack on Black People and Mental Health*, London, Race Equality Unit and Department of Health.

Eiser, J. R. and van der Pligt, J. (1988) *Attitudes and Decisions*, London, Routledge.

Fernando, S. (1991) *Race and Culture in Psychiatry*, London, Tavistock/Routledge.

Fish, D. and Coles, C. (1998) *Developing Professional Judgement in Health Care*, Oxford, Butterworth Heinemann.

Fletcher, K. (1998) *Negotiation for Health and Social Services Professionals*, London, Jessica Kingsley.

Gergen, K. (1991) *The Saturated Self*, New York, Basic Books.

Gomm, R. (1993) 'Issues of power in health and welfare', in Walmsley, J. *et al.* (eds) *Health, Welfare and Practice: Reflecting on Roles and Relationships*, London, Sage/The Open University (K663 Reader).

Habermas, J. (1972) *Knowledge and Human Interest*, London, Heinemann.

Harré, R. (1986) *The Social Construction of Emotion*, New York, Basil Blackwell.

HMSO (1989) *The Children Act*, London, HMSO.

Hornby, S. (1993) *Collaborative Care: Interprofessional, Interagency and Inter-personal*, Oxford, Blackwell.

Howe, D. (1987) *An Introduction to Social Work Theory*, Aldershot, Wildwood House.

Kahneman, D. *et al.* (eds) (1982) *Judgement under Uncertainty: Heuristics and Biases*, Cambridge University Press.

Kitwood, T. (1990) *Concern for Others: A New Psychology of Conscience and Morality*, London, Routledge.

Kitwood, T. (1998) *Dementia Reconsidered*, Buckingham, Open University Press.

Kolb, D. A. (1995) 'The process of experiential learning', in Thorpe, M., Edwards, R. and Hanson, A. (eds) *Culture and Processes of Adult Learning*, London, Routledge and The Open University.

Layder, D. (1997) *Modern Social Theory: Key Debates and New Directions*, London, UCL Press.

Lester, S. (1995) 'Beyond knowledge and competence: towards a framework for professional education', *Capability*, Vol. 1, No. 3, pp. 44–52.

Lewis, G. (1996) 'Welfare and the social construction of race', in Saraga, E. (ed.) *Embodying the Social: Constructions of Difference*, London, Routledge.

Loxley, A. (1997) *Collaboration in Health and Welfare: Working with Difference*, London, Jessica Kingsley.

Mann, H. (1998) 'Reflections on a border crossing: from ward sister to clinical nurse specialist', in Smith, P. (ed.) *Nursing Research: Setting New Agendas*, London, Arnold.

McNamee, S. and Gergen, K. (1992) *Therapy as Social Construction*, London, Sage.

Morris, J. (1991) *Pride against Prejudice*, London, The Women's Press.

Muir Gray, J. A. (1997) *Evidence-based Healthcare: How to Make Health Policy and Management Decisions*, Edinburgh, Churchill Livingstone.

Oliver, M. (1990) *The Politics of Disablement*, London, Macmillan.

Pinkney, S. (1998) 'The reshaping of social work and social care', in Hughes, G. and Lewis, G. (eds) *Unsettling Welfare: The Reconstruction of Social Policy*, London, Routledge.

Pinkney, S. (1999) 'Anti-oppressive theory and practice in social work', in Davies, C. *et al.* (eds) *Changing Practice in Health and Social Care*, London, Sage.

Porter, S. (1998) *Social Theory and Nursing Practice*, Basingstoke, Macmillan.

Ranyard, R. *et al.* (eds) (1997) *Decision Making: Cognitive Models and Explanations*, London, Routledge.

Rogers, C. (1951) *Client-centred Therapy: Its Current Practice, Implication and Theory*, Boston, Houghton Mifflin.

Saraga, E. (ed.) (1998) *Embodying the Social: Constructions of Difference*, London, Routledge.

Schell, B. A. and Ceverso, R. M. (1993) 'Clinical reasoning in occupational therapy: an integrative review', *The American Journal of Occupational Therapy*, Vol. 47, No. 7, pp. 605–610.

Schön, D. A. (1983) *The Reflective Practitioner*, London, Temple Smith.

Schön, D. A. (1992) 'The crisis of professional knowledge and the pursuit of an epistemology of practice', *Journal of Interprofessional Care,* Vol. 6, No. 1, pp. 49–63 (originally published 1984).

Schön, D. A. (1994) 'Teaching artistry through reflection in action', in Tsoukas, H. (ed.) *New Thinking in Organisational Behaviour,* Oxford, Butterworth Heinemann.

Shotter, J. (1993) *Cultural Politics of Everyday Life,* Buckingham, Open University Press.

Shotter, J. and Gergen, K. (1989) *Texts of Identity,* London, Sage.

Smith, P. (1992) *The Emotional Labour of Nursing,* Basingstoke, Macmillan.

Smith, P. (1999) 'Logging emotions: a logbook of personal reflections', *Soundings,* Vol. 11, pp. 128–37.

Social Services Inspectorate (SSI) (1998) *They Look after Their Own, Don't They: Inspection of Community Care Services for Black and Ethnic Minority Older People,* London, Department of Health.

Swain, J. and French, S. (1998) 'Normality and disabling care', in Brechin, A., Walmsley, J., Katz, J. and Peace, S. (eds) *Care Matters: Concepts, Practice and Research in Health and Social Care,* London, Sage.

Thompson, N. (1995) *Theory and Practice in Health and Social Welfare,* Open University Press, Buckingham.

Thompson, N. (1996) *People Skills: A Guide to Effective Practice in the Human Services,* Basingstoke, Macmillan.

Thompson, N. (1998) *Promoting Equality: Challenging Discrimination and Oppression in the Human Services,* Basingstoke, Macmillan.

Thompson, N. (1999) 'Theory and practice in health and social care', in Davies, C., Finlay, L. and Bullman, A. (eds) *Changing Practice in Health and Social Care,* London, Sage (K302 Reader 1).

Tsang, N. M. (1998) 'Re-examining reflection – a common issue of professional concern in social work, teacher and nursing education', *Journal of Interprofessional Care,* Vol. 12, No. 1, pp. 21–31.

Chapter 3
Understanding professional development

Maureen Eby

... a danger of becoming just another
piece of flotsam on the tide of change...

Introduction

The clock chimes the end of the working day, but in the mind of the
practitioner that working day is by no means over. Questions keep
emerging such as 'What was that I just experienced?'; 'Do I know what
that was about, or is it something I need to find out?'; 'Am I missing
something?' and 'Where can I go to find out more?'; or 'Who should I
ask?' Success in seeking out information that makes sense out of
experience can feel very positive. Addressing these questions as they
emerge not only will make the next time a similar situation is experienced
much easier to recognise but also handling that situation will feel more
comfortable.

This is one part of the story about professional development. It reflects a
personal commitment on the part of individuals to seek out answers to
questions that continually arise in the context of their practice. It often
involves a sense of wonderment, excitement, puzzlement, and at times
frustration when barriers get in the way of seeking out answers. What
helps people to develop this questioning attitude to learning – this
motivation to develop understanding and skill? But, equally, what ensures
that personal commitment leads to appropriate professional development? And who defines what is appropriate professional development?

There is an emerging movement to ensure that individuals maintain and develop their skills, at the very least in order to keep pace with change, but this has come hand-in-hand with a political agenda that is about ensuring the accountability and quality of professional practice across the board. The notion that professionals must be lifelong learners, that their learning is not 'complete' at the point of acquiring a first qualification, stems as much from the accountability, quality assurance and effectiveness lobbies as it does from the developments within educational theory – the advent of the self-directed learner, for example. Lifelong learning is seen as 'a desirable politico-economic activity, necessary to maintain a skilled workforce in a constantly changing world' (Hinchliff, 1998, p. 35). What might once have been regarded as a natural and very individual phenomenon, a natural desire to learn and develop work skills, has over the last 20 years developed into a highly structured, deeply political and, for some, a very successful and thriving business venture in the form of professional development.

Professional development can be defined as:

> ... the maintenance and enhancement of the knowledge, expertise and competence of professionals throughout their careers according to a plan formulated with regard to the needs of the professional, the employer, the profession and society.
>
> (Madden and Mitchell, 1993, quoted in Hinchliff, 1998, p. 38)

When professional development is defined in this way, multiple ownerships of the concept come to the fore and developing practice is no longer a matter of the choices made by individuals. The employer, the profession and even the politician have an influence on patterns of professional development in health and social care. This chapter begins to uncover some of the dynamics of professional development in relation to some of the different groups who have a stake in it. Understanding their perspectives highlights the way in which multiple messages about professional development inform individual decisions and influence the development of professional skills, judgement and communications.

1   Professional development at the individual level

Before focusing on the ways in which people may engage with professional development, it is useful to consider the wider context with its multiple influences on how professional development is conceived and created. One way of thinking about this is to view the individual as an active learner within an environment of demands, pressures and constraints. When thinking of this what comes to mind is an amoeba, a one-cell aquatic organism, functioning within a complex environment, as shown in Figure 1 (overleaf).

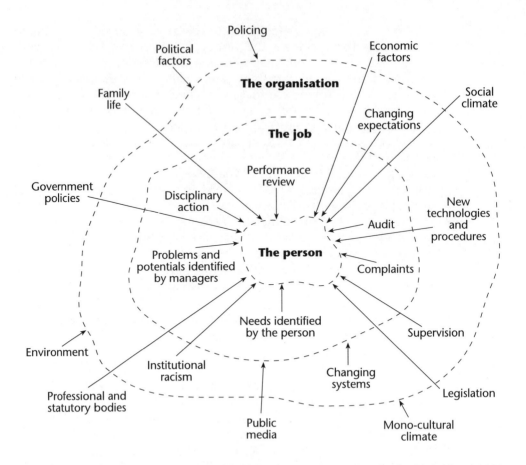

Figure 1 **The amoebic world of practice** (Source: adapted from Dodwell and Lathlean, 1989, p. 11)

Figure 1 highlights a considerable number of ways in which a person may be moulded and shaped by aspects of a job and, just like an amoeba, as one aspect becomes more prominent at a particular time – audit perhaps, or individual performance review – the shape changes to accommodate these pressures. Both the individual and the job are also affected by factors such as new technologies, changing systems of work and changing expectations. Societal, political and economic factors have a major influence, as suggested by the factors in the outer circle of the diagram, among them, family life, the media and what is called here the 'mono-cultural climate'.

How can individuals begin to make more sense of the world they work and live in when all of these factors are pushing and pulling and reshaping the context of their work? The amoeba analogy assumes that people have the ability, and significantly the opportunity, to adapt and change. This is not the whole story, however, as the example in Box 1 (opposite) suggests.

Box 1: Mary – a home care service administrator

Mary, a black administrator for a national home care service, observed that there were no standardised procedures for home carers in several areas of their work. Drawing on her higher education qualifications in law and financial management, Mary began to draft a guidance document, which she thought would be useful for her local team, and presented it to her manager. The manager, however, did not let her finish the document, stating that it was not her job to draft guidance because she was 'only an administrator'. The manager then brought in an agency worker to complete the final version and published the document within the organisation for other teams to use. Mary received no acknowledgement for her work.

What was Mary to make of this? A very different scenario could be imagined where, having presented her draft, Mary was then invited to join a working group (facilitated possibly by an outside agency) that developed the policy further. As things were, however, the events triggered a whole series of questions in Mary's mind. Would there have been a different outcome if she had presented her ideas differently? Should she perhaps have offered to do the job rather than just getting on and doing it and presenting it without warning? Was she being blocked because she was black – and, if she was, was it personal prejudice on the part of her manager or was there deep-seated institutional racism in the organisation?

Drawing on just one account of what happened, as described in Box 1, does not allow for the different ways in which such events may be experienced or understood nor how such accounts may be contested. In analysing the multiple layers of this event, Mary was actively engaging with her situation and exploring different interpretations and possible responses. Without such engagement, there is a danger of practitioners becoming just another piece of flotsam on the tide of change, with no ability to control the direction in which they are headed. The rest of this section explores those processes that enable a practitioner to transcend such uncertainties and conflicts and to develop, in effect, a capacity for critical practice. Subsequent sections go on to situate these important individual processes in organisational and wider contested arenas.

Reflective practice – a developmental process

'We should ... investigate how it is that some people learn the kinds of reflection-in-action essential to professional artistry', suggests Donald Schön in his classic paper (Schön, 1984, republished 1992, p. 62). Any notion of professional development must be predicated on an assumption that people can and do continue to learn. Schön's approach was a direct challenge to the more established school of thought (Schön, 1983). The assumption had been that professional education depended on learning the underlying scientific knowledge base, learning how to apply the knowledge and developing the skills and attitudes necessary to do that effectively (Schein, 1974; Glazer, 1974). This technical rationality model saw uncertainty and indeterminacy as evidence of weakness in the professional base.

What Schön uncovered through his consultation with a wide range of experienced professionals from varying fields was the disturbing realisation that 'the competences they were beginning to see as central to professional practice had no place in their underlying model of professional knowledge' (Schön, 1992, p. 51). The result was a new look at these competencies of professional practice – an account which values the sense of continual learning in action and the capacity to work with, reflect on and learn from the continuous uncertainties in the 'swampy lowlands' of practice. Schön's work on the 'reflective practitioner' underlined professional practice as a developmental process.

The notion of such 'reflection' now forms the bedrock of today's professional development movement. It is repeatedly discussed in text-books, heard on training days, seen in journal articles, and invoked in discussions with colleagues and managers (Richardson and Maltby, 1995; Thompson, 1996; Tsang, 1998; Pietroni, 1992). Reflection is the ability to think and consider 'experiences, percept[ion]s, ideas [values and beliefs], etc. with a view to the discovery of new relations or the drawing of conclusions for the guidance of future action' (Quinn, 1998, p. 122). In other words, reflection enables individuals to make sense of their lived experiences through examining such experiences in context.

Reflection, although a cornerstone of reflective practice, is not the only skill needed. Reflective practice is more than just thoughtful practice. It is the process of turning thoughtful practice into a potential learning situation 'which may help to modify and change approaches to practice' (Schober, 1993, p. 324). Reflective practice entails the synthesis of self-awareness, reflection and critical thinking, as shown in Figure 2 (opposite).

All three of these skills stem from rich philosophical roots. These have helped to shape our understanding of the lived experience. *Lived experience* involves the totality of an experience – the actions, circumstances, nuances, feelings, memories and desires that surround the happenings within that event. As described by the philosopher Wilhelm Dilthey (1833–1911) 'lived experience is awareness of life without thinking about it' (Taylor, 1998, p. 141).

Reflective practice also has roots in critical thinking, which more recently has been influenced by the writings of Jurgen Habermas (b. 1929). He believes that a critical consciousness is developed through reflection. Critical consciousness is the ability to recognise and resist oppression in everyday life in order to foster emancipation. Seen in this way, reflection can become a tool that enhances the learning process in professional development – that 'Ah ha!' experience when insight suddenly translates

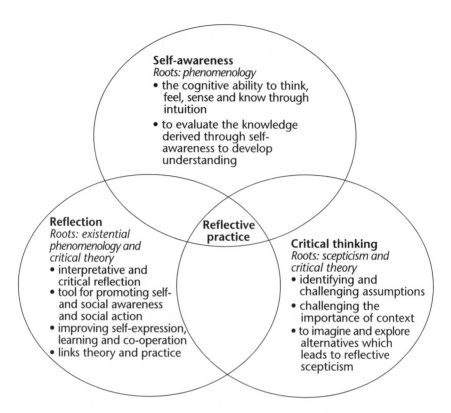

Figure 2   **Skills underpinning the concept of reflective practice**

into understanding. Reflection in this sense underpins the beliefs and values of professional development through:

- promoting self and social awareness and social action
- supporting the principles of lifelong learning
- stimulating self and peer expressions or dialogue
- improving self expression, learning and co-operation, and
- fundamentally by linking theory and practice.

(Hammond and Collins, 1991)

So how does it happen? What are the processes by which professionals can learn and develop as reflective practitioners by reflecting in and on action? One model, which is widely used and quoted, is Kolb's experiential learning model (Figure 3 overleaf).

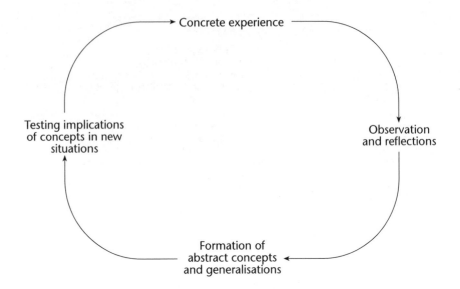

Figure 3   **Kolb's experiential learning model** (Source: Kolb, 1984, cited in Quinn, 1998, p. 126)

Kolb's theory of experiential learning clearly suggests that theory and practice flourish and enrich each other in a never-ending circle. His experiential learning model is a cycle of moving from a 'concrete experience' into a reflecting process which creates, in essence, a kind of theory about the experience. On the basis of this, new ideas about how to act in future may be generated, followed by a phase of testing out such ideas. Other models exist (see, for example, a review by Quinn, 1998), but these tend to focus on reflection located within the individual, occurring in a somewhat closed loop and triggered by a supposedly 'concrete' experience. The implications of this process of learning from experience are examined further in the next section.

   The use of reflection within professional development is not without its critics (Quinn, 1998). The constant use of reflection to promote self-development can lead to a sense of self-doubt and self-disapproval, since endlessly striving to improve leaves little room for a sense of personal well-being. Reflection places the emphasis for the maintenance and improvement of standards of care on the shoulders of the individual, removing from the organisation the responsibility of providing 'adequate staffing levels, effective staff development and adequate resources' (Quinn, 1998, p. 142). And on a practical note, Quinn maintains that nurses are already facing 'navel gazing' overload with all the statutory, professional and organisational demands to keep up to date. One nurse echoes this feeling:

> When I go home to my husband, five children and housework after my nine-hour shift, the last thing on my mind is to sit and write about my day, like a child doing its homework.
>
> (Felix, 1998, p. 23)

Critical practice – a proactive process

The suggestion that models of reflective learning may have a somewhat individualist focus has implications for the theme of critical practice. Other writers (Sheppard, 1995, 1998; White, 1997; Slaughter, 1988 in Davies and Lynch, 1995) have argued that a shift is necessary from what is described as an interpretative position to one identified in Chapter 2 as a critical position. *Interpretative reflection* encourages individuals to understand their experiences by recognising and valuing the significance of their own interpretation. It moves away from a positivist stance, valuing subjectivity as the basis for developing understanding and as a basis for new actions (Taylor, 1998; Sheppard, 1998). The supposedly 'concrete' experience, however, remains the trigger for reflection, and new strategies for problem solving are the desirable outcome.

Being critical, on the other hand, denotes an open-minded, reflective appraisal that takes account of different perspectives, experiences and assumptions in a world of uncertainty and change. As described in Chapter 2, critical practice requires an appropriately knowledgeable and competent practitioner, who continually recognises the relative and contextual basis of his or her own practice, who respects others as equals, who forges relationships through dialogue using mediation and negotiation skills, who seeks to empower, and fundamentally who makes a difference in the lives of others.

A number of significant aspects of critical practice tend to get lost in these individualistic models of reflective learning. This was first identified through Schön's recognition that professional practice is often not so much about problem solving as about the wider social challenge of problem setting. This is illustrated when he says:

> 'Our interest', as one participant put it, 'is not only how to pour concrete for the highway, but what highway to build ...'
>
> (Schön, 1992, p. 50)

Schön might have added whether another highway was needed at all. Where in individualistic reflective models is there room for negotiation and dialogue other than self-dialogue? It would appear that individualistic models of reflective learning have ignored the learning that occurs through dialogue and interaction with others, especially clients and patients, those who have been empowered through such interactions. And whereas individualistic models of reflective learning do imply a reframing of the initial experience, the sense of critical action which is crucial to critical practice is lacking.

To encompass these points it is important to take a step back: to emphasise the importance of recognising competing perspectives and the impact of political and power relations; to stress the practitioner's presence and influence on the situation; and to account for the means by which evidence or opinion may be evaluated as a basis for further practice. That is to say, the models must describe a process of critical practice in which practitioners can not only observe and evaluate the situation and context from a greater height, as it were, but also see themselves as an interactive and influential part of the system they are observing.

A concept of *critical reflection* may offer just that – a critique which takes account of the constraining forces and influences within a given situation, and which enables distorted, hidden and perhaps manipulative communications and actions to come to light. Underpinning critical reflection is scepticism – questioning the source, truthfulness and reliability of knowledge – and critical theory, which 'entails looking beneath the surface of knowledge and reason ... in order to see how that knowledge and reason is distorted in an unequal and exploitative society ... and, in doing so, to point the way to less distorted forms of knowledge and reason' (Porter, 1998, p. 131).

In Box 2, Kate, an experienced staff nurse, describes an ordinary day working on a self-harm unit attached to an Accident and Emergency (A&E) Department in the Midlands.

Box 2: Just an ordinary day

Nick, an angry 20-year-old, was admitted in the night having overdosed on paracetamol and codeine hoping to stop his heroin withdrawal. The night staff had let Nick sleep off the narcotics and so did I. I didn't see the need to wake him. Finally, the psychiatrist, having seen the other patients, went in to see Nick, waking him up. I knew he was awake because from the treatment room came a series of yells and curses. The treatment room door banged open and out rushed Nick, doubled up in pain from the cramps. Sweating profusely, but hugging his parka jacket close to his body, he yelled for help. No one responded. This man's too angry, I thought. If I approach him, he'll lash out. I could certainly hear his anger but what could I do? Looking up, I saw the psychiatrist leaving the treatment room as Nick rushed out of the Unit into the hallway. Hearing the yelling, the medical doctor from next door rushed in only to see Nick leaving the Unit. 'Well', the psychiatrist said, 'I told him there was a three-week waiting list for admission to the Detox Unit. He's only detoxing, it won't kill him.'

By now events started to blur. Nick rushes in and hearing the psychiatrist pulls out a knife, grabbing me and pushing the cold blade into my neck. I'm frozen. That blade is ice and I see fear, though not my own but Nick's. What I see is large, ugly and very frightening. No one moves but, just as quickly as Nick grabs me, he doubles up again in pain from the abdominal cramps. His grip on me loosens and next I see Nick spread-eagled on the floor with two security guards sitting on him. He is yelling in agony. He can't curl up in pain anymore, I thought. 'Well', the medical doctor said to the psychiatrist, 'if you don't section him now, I damn well will!'

(Source: Maureen Eby, July 1998, personal communication)

Clearly, this was a desperately shocking incident for Kate; she needed time afterwards to reflect and to try to understand what had happened. Rather than staying with some 'concrete' notion of the experience, and considering how she might have handled it differently, her thoughts took a much broader sweep.

> I felt unreal as if the world was no longer part of me. I will never forget that feeling, it was as if the air had turned ugly and frightening yet I wasn't afraid of Nick. On reflection, what I felt I can now identify as institutional violence. That is why it was so large and ugly. It is also what Nick was reacting to, for in grabbing me he was attacking the institution. I was merely an instrument of that institution. That's what frightened me so much for it wasn't me as a nurse Nick was attacking but the Unit and its policies that were contributing to his severe pain and distress. In that, I had no control and it was the depersonalisation of me as an individual nurse that has stayed with me from this incident. For one brief moment I was not seen as human, and it is that feeling that has changed me forever.
>
> (Maureen Eby, July 1998, personal communication)

Kate was not reflecting in a vacuum. A myriad of influences, perspectives and pressures, including all her training and experience, affected her thought processes. Kemmis (1985) emphasises that this:

> ... is a social process because the ideas and understandings that we have generated from our reflection are socially constructed, and the actions that flow from these understandings are similarly shaped and con-strained by society.
>
> (Kemmis, 1985, cited in Street, 1990, p. 17)

Sheppard (1998), thinking in terms of social work knowledge, makes a similar point. He draws on the concept of 'reflexivity', arguing that this is essential to a model of knowledge as a process. In reflexivity, individuals not only influence the world around them but equally they themselves are influenced by that world.

> The notion of reflexivity emphasizes the social worker (i) as an active thinker, one able to assess, respond and initiate action, and (ii) as a social actor, one who actually participates in the situation with which they are concerned in the conduct of their practice.
>
> (Sheppard, 1998, p. 767)

Another way of presenting the processes at work here is through a diagram. Figure 4 (overleaf) illustrates how a practitioner interfaces not only with self but also with others within the system. The internal processes of reflection are represented within the circle with elements feeding into a process of continual learning with deconstructions and reconstructions of meaning emerging in the centre. The external interface, represented by outward arrows, indicates the processes of communication about events and experiences through relationship, dialogue, negotiation, review of evidence through written or other information media, and the checking out of these against other legitimating criteria. In turn, this will

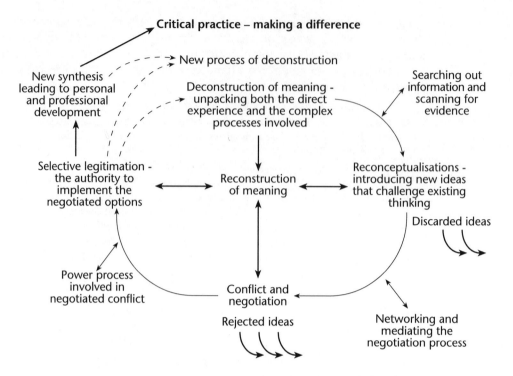

Figure 4   **Process of critical practice** (Source: adapted from Slaughter, 1988, in Davies and Lynch, 1995, p. 387)

lead either to new ways of thinking and action, which lead to further personal and professional development, or to the interface where continual new events and experiences occur, which will feed in turn into the process of critical reflection.

What becomes apparent in perusing this diagram is that, as well as being an illustration of the processes of critical reflection, it could equally be an illustration of critical practice – this seeming to further underline Schön's original concept of practice as 'knowledge-in-action' and Sheppard's sense of 'knowledge as process'. Figure 1 in Chapter 2, showing overlapping circles of critical analysis, critical reflexivity and critical action, could be comfortably superimposed on this figure, not in the sense that it maps over it in the same way, but in the sense that both figures illustrate key aspects of the same overall conceptualisation of practice.

But what else is needed for critical practice? Burnard (1989), drawing upon the work of Brookfield (1987), believes that critical thinkers can identify and challenge assumptions, can challenge the importance of context, and can imagine and explore alternatives, which involves the use of reflective scepticism. Critical thinking involves the use of cognitive skills as described in Box 3 (opposite).

Box 3: The six cognitive skills of critical thinking

- **Interpretation**: comprehending, expressing meaning and significance

- **Analysis**: identifying inferential relationships between concepts, examining ideas, and detecting and analysing arguments

- **Evaluation**: assessing claims and arguments for credibility

- **Inference**: identifying and securing information needed to draw conclusions, querying evidence, imagining alternatives and drawing conclusions

- **Explanation**: stating and justifying the results of one's reasoning, including contextual considerations

- **Self-regulation**: monitoring and reflecting on one's reasoning and correcting one's reasoning when necessary

(Source: adapted from Fonteyn, 1998, p. 15)

For Mary and Kate, these were the skills that helped them make sense of what happened in a way that enabled them to work out where to go from there. As Allen (1985) states:

> ... the advantage of a critical [approach] ... is that it offers an opportunity to shatter the ideological mirror that traps us and our clients in despair and hopelessness. Taken seriously, it forces us to question that status quo at every turn, sifting and winnowing our personal and working lives to enable us to formulate a truly alternative plan.
>
> (Allen, 1985, cited in Emden, 1991, p. 349)

Finally, one aspect that is still not sufficiently emphasised in Figure 4 is the importance of standing back to see the larger picture. Thinking of the amoeba diagram in Figure 1, the individual is continually slipping through those dotted lines that separate the person from the job, the organisation and society. So the following section turns to the organisational and socio-political determinants of professional development.

2   Professional development – everyone's baby

Professional training and career progression – an uneasy alliance

To some extent, it is the employing organisation that sets the professional development agenda. Its written and unwritten policies specify which courses it will fund, who will have access to them and how many days of paid leave a practitioner can take for professional development. This section considers three key sets of related tensions: between career development and professional training; between occupational standards and professional standards; and between management and support agendas in the provision of supervision. It is worth noting how, in the midst of such tensions, it is very easy for the needs and agendas of the service-users in all of this to get lost.

Ideally, career development and professional training progress hand-in-hand. Appropriate and accessible career ladders within an organisation will enable the individual to build on experience and qualifications by moving to more senior positions, offering satisfying challenges together with enhanced status and financial rewards. The reality is somewhat different. The single track into managerial posts and the lack of easy and obvious opportunities for career progression for field social workers, nurses and other clinicians have been long-standing complaints in local government and the NHS. The small size of some voluntary organisations can limit career opportunities and, in all settings, the barriers that unqualified but often highly experienced staff face in making the jump into attaining professional qualifications has long been a source of frustration and complaint. One nurse, Mark Radcliffe, writes:

> Career development is largely a myth, not because nurses cannot plan clinical progression and the development of required skills but because that progression is not accompanied by salary and status development. If you work hard, nurse well, study in your spare time, pay study fees yourself and on occasion undertake patronising and pointless ENB courses then you will get on. But where? There are fewer G grades, fewer H grades, hardly any I grades and it's difficult now to even get an E grade. ... We have invented a way of thinking about nursing that masks the realities of the job.
>
> (Radcliffe, 1998, p. 29)

In a much-cited text from over 20 years ago, nurses were rather disparagingly dubbed 'migrant certificate gatherers' for behaviour that seemed to be just randomly accumulating courses (Dingwall and McIntosh, 1978). Yet in the absence of clearly recognised and supported pathways for clinical rather than educational or managerial development, an opportunistic pattern is not necessarily surprising. For social workers, too, until the post-qualifying framework was introduced in 1990, training opportunities and pathways were also somewhat haphazard.

Even where there are career development opportunities that allow for professional growth and development, there may be barriers to access to them. Findings repeatedly showed disproportionate numbers of women and minority ethnic professionals in the lowest grades of professional practice. A complex array of factors can often be at work here, to do with time, money, access to opportunity to demonstrate potential, as well as discriminatory attitudes and practices (Witz, 1994; Beishon et al., 1995; Miers, 1999; Hanmer and Statham, 1988; DoH/SSI, 1991).

Nevertheless, career and training do tend to interrelate, as illustrated in the following two case studies, which consider the educational opportunities and career progression of the individuals involved. Samuel, a modern languages graduate, followed a path through social work that led him into involvement with the training of social workers, whilst retaining and developing a practice base (Box 4 overleaf). Pat made the transition from hospital cleaner to working as an advanced nurse practitioner in the comparatively short period of 10 years (Box 5 on page 63). Their experiences of professional development reflect considerable determination to seize the opportunities that were available; they also reflect a changing pattern of professional education policy at national level as well as changes in thinking about the organisation of work in both these fields.

When Samuel entered social work in 1969, graduates were rare, and most staff did not hold social work qualifications. Such qualifications, indeed, were seen largely as a means to promotion rather than as a basic requirement for the work.

The Central Council for Education and Training in Social Work (CCETSW), established in 1971, brought several existing qualifications together in the Certificate of Qualification in Social Work (CQSW). This Certificate could be taken at postgraduate level (as Samuel did), at undergraduate level and at non-graduate level, and the length of the training varied. It existed alongside yet another option – the Certificate in Social Services (CSS), designed primarily to allow secondment for training from residential and day care. Seen always, although not officially, as a second-class qualification, the CSS was nevertheless expensive to deliver and few employees could gain the coveted sponsored places. Pressures to rationalise combined with the government's emphasis on vocational and competency-based training resulted in the birth of the present two-year Diploma in Social Work (DipSW) (Weinstein, 1998). This replaced both the CQSW and the CSS, thereby providing one professional qualification for social work and social care (although many social care staff remain unqualified). Academically, the DipSW is set at DipHE level, although it can be taken at Bachelor degree or Master's level.

The emergence of a career grade for social work practitioners in the late 1970s/early 1980s and the subsequent appointment of 'Senior Practitioners' represented an important step in the process of professional development for social workers. The reintroduction of social work specialisms, sometimes by client group, sometimes by organisation (intake teams, emergency duty/out-of-hours teams), also assisted this process. The introduction of the Approved Social Worker under the 1983 Mental Health Act, with mandatory requirements for post-qualifying training, was particularly significant.

Public concern about high-profile child abuse cases leading to inquiries raised further demands for post-qualifying training in child care, especially in child protection. It was not until the early 1990s that CCETSW introduced a comprehensive post-qualifying training framework for the profession, allowing regional consortia of academic institutions and agencies to consider and validate courses, which led to the Post-Qualifying (PQ) or Advanced Award (AA) in Social Work (CCETSW, 1990, 1997).

Box 4: Samuel – a social worker

Samuel came into social work in 1969, shortly after graduating in Modern Languages. He applied to what was then the local authority health and welfare department for a job as a Mental Welfare Officer and was appointed, despite his lack of relevant qualifications. Samuel quickly recognised the need for professional social work training but found the range of courses bewildering. Eventually he chose and was accepted on the one-year postgraduate Certificate of Qualification in Social Work and qualified in 1973.

He returned to the Social Services Department and worked on a team which was concerned almost entirely with children in the care of the local authority and their families. Later he also became responsible for supporting a number of ancillary staff, a student, unqualified staff and trainees. At the time, there was only a small amount of in-service training on offer in his department. Eventually a practice teachers' course was provided by the local university's extra-mural studies department. Taking up this opportunity, he felt better prepared to support the social work students attached to his department, although the issue of improving the development opportunities for unqualified staff still remained. He was frustrated that there were so few opportunities for experienced but unqualified staff to achieve social work qualifications.

Some four years later, Samuel decided to apply for and obtained a first-level management post as leader of a team of social workers and ancillary staff in another part of the same Social Services Department. Again, the work focused on children and their families with the added awareness of 'non-accidental injury' that was such a major part of the 1970s. In the 1980s, Samuel returned to practice as a Senior Practitioner in Child Care, qualified as an Approved Social Worker under the Mental Health Act and resumed his interest in supervising students. He followed a CCETSW-approved Practice Teachers' Award Programme and became an accredited Practice Teacher within his agency.

He now carries half a caseload and supervises students on qualifying courses as well as those on Approved Social Work courses. He has taken additional training with the Practice Teachers' Programme and acts as Mentor/Assessor to Practice Teachers in training. Samuel used his training opportunities to obtain the Advanced Award and a Master's Degree in Advanced Social Work Practice.

After a review of CCETSW and the publication of the government's White Paper *Modernising Social Services* (Department of Health, 1998), which outlined new policy initiatives within social services, further changes were put in place. The intention was that a General Social Care Council would set and enforce standards of conduct and a National Training Organisation would develop and promote training at all levels. Controversies around these changes remain (see Chapter 14), in particular questioning whether

---

Box 5: Pat – an advanced nurse practitioner

Pat, a 44-year-old nurse, has travelled the path from hospital cleaner to advanced nurse practitioner in only 10 years. While raising her family, Pat started as a cleaner part-time on a maternity ward, the same hospital in which her own children were born. The job was hard and demanding, but it gave Pat an insight into the working of the hospital. A nursing auxiliary post became vacant on the ward Pat was cleaning, and she applied for and was offered the job. In her own words, 'I assisted the midwives with deliveries, cleaning the equipment and bathing babies. It was a lovely job and inspired an interest. I decided I wanted to be a midwife.' So Pat applied to her local school of nursing who tried to push her towards enrolled nurse training. Pat comments, 'I think they tried to discourage me because I had young children.' Nevertheless, at 32, Pat did the three-year training course along with 30 other students. 'I did find it a struggle. I had not been in a classroom for 16 years.'

It was in Pat's student placement on A&E that her love of emergency nursing grew. 'There is a buzz in A&E because you never know what will come through the door next.' After registration, Pat took a staff nurse job in a local A&E Department, but felt she wanted more, 'clinically, academically and professionally.' She took the opportunity that had now arisen to convert her registered nurse qualification to a Diploma. This involved a two-year part-time programme while still working in A&E. She was then in a position to 'top up' to a nursing degree at a local university where her research project looked at nursing practice within A&E. Two years on, Pat completed a Master's degree and now has a part-time lecturer practitioner's post in A&E, which combines practice and theory. This was a long journey and, in Pat's words, 'people seem fascinated by my career development through the decade. I suppose I just took the opportunities as they arose.'

(Source: adapted from Carlowe, 1998, p. 32)

---

the DipSW as the basic qualification should have been linked so closely with employer demands and whether a three-year academic course is not fundamental groundwork for the critical stance that a social work professional needs (Dominelli, 1996). Practitioners like Samuel need to make their choices in this complex and changing climate of professional development.

Pat's career developed on the cusp of change. Before the late 1980s, most people entering nursing, like Pat, took a traditional vocational training course of three years, usually based in a hospital and an adjacent school of nursing. Among the factors pointing towards change were widespread dissatisfaction with an education system that used students as 'pairs of hands' in the workforce, increasing difficulties in providing the requisite level of support in settings where workload had intensified, a mismatch between hospital-based training and a growing need for practice in the community. In 1986, the UKCC, as the statutory body with responsibility to improve educational standards, recommended student status and a broad common foundation programme (UKCC, 1986). Project 2000 training, as it came to be known, then moved into universities and nurse registration became linked with a higher education qualification. Pat's story might have been very different had she started five years later.

Progression after registration offers a confusing array of possibilities. Some nurses add further registrations, as Pat would have done if she had continued to become a midwife or if she had been attracted into community nursing or health visiting. Most nurses go on to take a wide array of short clinical courses, and move between areas of practice, rather than follow a conventional career structure. Those who took a Diploma, as Pat did, often did so because they were looking for a broader educational base than their registration programme had given them.

Bringing clarity and order into the Topsy-like growth of post-registration professional development has proved a challenge. Even the statutory requirement of a minimum of five days or its equivalent of study activity every three years for continued registration (UKCC, 1997) did little to provide a cohesive framework for professional development. In 1999, the whole provision of pre and post-registration education was under review by both the government and the UKCC's Commission on Education.

Professional or vocational qualifications – are occupational standards the answer?

In the health and social care professions, there is an increasing tension between what employers want and what those in the profession feel is important for advancing practice within their field. Who should determine an individual's competency within the workplace is also adding to the tension. The role of the professional bodies is no longer sacrosanct. The 1980s saw growing governmental pressure to bring a stronger employer voice to shaping outcome definitions of competence and the emergence of National and Scottish Vocational Qualifications (N/SVQs).

The strong emphasis in the initial N/SVQs on observed task competence, however, did not endear the professions to change. Professionals dismissed what looked like 'knowing how' rather than 'knowing why' and argued that it was inappropriate that their education should be so strongly employer-led. For a time, views were distinctly polarised. Jenny Weinstein, someone who was later to be involved in a competence-based approach to social work training, records how in the late 1980s 'academic, professional and vocational education frameworks were seen as entirely discrete, geared for different purposes and designed for different groups of students' (Weinstein, 1998, p. 170).

The 1990s, however, have seen an important degree of *rapprochement*, with professional and indeed academic education paying more attention to outcomes and competencies, and vocational qualifications broadening out from their task focus to encompass underpinning knowledge and understanding. A government document in 1996 acknowledged that N/SVQs at higher levels could only be a foundation for professional practice, that increasingly sophisticated knowledge is required by professionals and that problem solving, reflection and working with uncertainty are crucial ingredients (DfEE, 1996).

In parallel, occupational standards emerged with, for example, the publication of National Occupational Standards for Professional Activity in Health Promotion and Care in 1998. Occupational standards are agreed benchmarks which specify staff competence and performance outcomes. National occupational standards have been described as:

> ... a powerful strategic and operational tool for organisations and individuals in the health and social care sector, enabling organisations to describe and map what it is they hope to achieve and helping individuals put their decisions about achievements into action in a coherent and informed way.
>
> (Mitchell *et al.*, 1998, p. 158)

As these authors go on to state, national occupational standards are about describing performance. They detail what is expected of the individual within organisations. National occupational standards rely on the ability of the individual practitioner to be both reflective and proactive to maintain these standards. Interestingly, occupational standards, statutory body statements in nursing, post-qualifying and advanced practice requirements in social work seem to be converging. Current thinking in these areas, furthermore, seems to be focusing on an array of skills that link closely with the idea of critical practice as set out in this chapter and Chapter 2. The emphasis is on practitioners who can be open-minded and innovative in their practice, who are flexible in the face of changing demands, who work and communicate well with others, sharing good practice and knowledge, who can work as change agents, and who are challenging and creative in their practice. These are now widespread themes and are likely to continue to underpin the drive for continuous professional development within health and social care.

In years to come perhaps there will not be so great a divide between the aspirations of individual practitioners for professional development and the interests of employers, government and users. Mark Radcliffe might then want to modify his angry comment quoted earlier about career development as a myth. And yet the distinction between 'fitness for purpose' (of an employer) and 'fitness for practice' (of a professional) is perhaps a healthy tension and a useful distinction to retain.

Is supervision a key to professional development?

The term 'supervisor' often brings to mind a picture of rows of assembly-line workers with little interest in or commitment to their jobs, being closely watched on the assumption that without constant monitoring the pace will slacken or standards will drop. In the mental health field, in counselling and in social work, however, the term has long been in use to describe the support that a more experienced practitioner gives to a less experienced one, and to acknowledge the professional development that can come through reflection on and exploration of practice with others.

Thus in social work a practitioner will expect to have the opportunity to discuss aspects of their workload with either their line manager or with a senior practitioner, whose work includes providing supervision without managerial responsibilities. Terms like 'practice supervision', 'group supervision' and 'peer supervision' emphasise the reflection/consultation element of this activity. In the 1990s, 'student supervision' has been replaced by the concept of 'practice teaching', again indicating the emphasis on learning and professional development.

The concept has come to the fore rather more recently in nursing and in the therapy professions. The UKCC (1996) in a position statement endorses the value of clinical supervision as a way of assisting practitioners 'to develop a deeper understanding of what it is to be an accountable practitioner and to link this to the reality of practice' (p. 2). The UKCC argues that the potential benefits are not limited to patients, clients or practitioners, since a 'more skilled, aware and articulate professional should contribute effectively to organisational objectives' (UKCC, 1996, p. 2).

From this point of view, it would seem that supervision can provide an ideal mechanism for encouraging reflection and critical practice. Tensions, however, remain. In the first place, with supervision costs and flatter hierarchical structures and intensified workloads, it may not be feasible to provide it, on any scale. In the second place, there is a fear in nursing, for example, that clinical supervision is or could become a tool for management instead of bringing practitioners together to reflect on practice, discover new solutions to problems and increase understanding of professional issues. The issue of power differentials between the parties, lack of support of the individuals involved, as well as the lack of acknowledgement and support for the risks and emotional labour involved in caring, can also make the participants feel that the process is artificial and unrealistic.

It may be healthy to make these tensions more explicit. Practitioners are employees, paid and accountable for the work they do. As such, they require clear direction and boundaries and there must be quality checks in place to protect everyone's interests – service-users and colleagues alike. At the same time, practitioners are people, struggling to develop their skills and understanding to cope with demanding and often stressful circumstances over which they may have little control. The more effectively they are supported, the more their work may be enhanced. Supervision alone cannot deliver on all these fronts, but it can provide a very effective mechanism for holding and mediating some of these tensions.

Conclusion

This chapter argued that professional development requires individuals to engage as lifelong learners in a continuing process of critical reflection. Professional development is central to practice in both health and social care. There is much that an individual practitioner can do not only in terms of formal courses or the systematic use of a portfolio or reflective diary, but also through the process of acting as a critical practitioner. But professional development, as the definition in the introduction emphasised, is the enhancement of knowledge and competences in the context of a range of powerful agencies and influences outside the individual. Analysing and understanding these agencies and the forces shaping them is very much part of professional development too. Not all health and social care practitioners, after all, are on an equal footing when it comes to the pressures imposed on them in their work settings or the power, or lack of it, of their professions and occupations.

The chapter has tried to set the scene both for critical reflection as an individual activity and for reflecting on the circumstances in which critical reflection – and ultimately the kind of critical practice outlined in Chapter 2 – can occur. The chapters which follow, in their different ways, all seek to take the business of critical practice further.

References

Allen, D. (1985) 'Nursing research and social control: alternative models of science that emphasise understanding and emancipation', *Image: Journal of Nursing Scholarship*, Vol. 17, No. 2, pp. 58–64.

Beishon, S., Virdee, S. and Hagell, A. (1995) *Nursing in a Multi-Ethnic NHS*, London, Policy Studies Institute.

Brookfield, S. D. (1987) *Developing Critical Thinkers: Challenging Adults to Explore Alternative Ways of Thinking and Acting*, Milton Keynes, Open University Press.

Burnard, P. (1989) 'Developing critical ability in nurse education', *Nurse Education Today*, Vol. 9, pp. 271–275.

Carlowe, J. (1998) 'Floors to ceiling', *Nursing Times*, Vol. 94, No. 9, 4 March, p. 32.

Central Council for Education and Training in Social Work (CCETSW) (1990) *The Requirements for Post Qualifying Education and Training in the Personal Social Services*, Paper 31, London, CCETSW.

Central Council for Education and Training in Social Work (CCETSW) (1997) *Assuring Quality for Post Qualifying Education and Training*, London, CCETSW.

Davies, E. and Lynch, S. (1995) 'Nursing: a rhythm of human awakening', in Gray, G. and Pratt, R. (eds) *Scholarship in the Discipline of Nursing*, Melbourne, Churchill Livingstone.

Department for Education and Employment (DfEE) (1996) *Employers' Use of NVQs/SVQs in Human Resource Management*, London, The Stationery Office.

Department of Health (1998) *Modernising Social Services*, London, The Stationery Office.

Department of Health (DoH)/SSI (1991) *Women in Social Services: A Neglected Resource*, London, DoH.

Dingwall, R. and McIntosh, J. (1978) (eds) *Readings in the Sociology of Nursing*, Edinburgh, Churchill Livingstone.

Dodwell, M. and Lathlean, J. (1989) *Management and Professional Development for Nurses*, London, Harper and Row.

Dominelli, L. (1996) 'Deprofessionalizing social work: anti-oppressive practice, competencies and postmodernism', *British Journal of Social Work*, Vol. 26, No. 2, pp. 153–175.

Emden, C. (1991) 'Becoming a reflective practitioner', in Gray, G. and Pratt, R. (eds) *Towards a Discipline of Nursing*, pp. 335–354, Melbourne, Churchill Livingstone.

Felix, C. (1998) '... it just feels as if has been', *Nursing Times*, Vol. 94, No. 12, 25 March, p. 23.

Fonteyn, M. E. (1998) *Thinking Strategies for Nursing Practice*, Philadelphia, Lippincott.

Glazer, N. (1974) 'The school of the minor professions', *Minerva*, Vol. 12, p. 3.

Hammond, M. and Collins, R. (1991) *Self Directed Learning: Critical Practice*, London, Kogan Page.

Hanmer, C. and Statham, D. (1988) *Women and Social Work: Towards a Women Centred Practice*, Basingstoke, Macmillan.

Hinchliff, S. (1998) 'Lifelong learning in context', in Quinn, F. M. (ed.) *Continuing Professional Development in Nursing*, pp. 34–58, Cheltenham, Stanley Thornes.

Madden, C. and Mitchell, V. (1993) *Professions, Standards and Competence: A Survey of Continuing Education for the Professions*, Bristol, University of Bristol, Department for Continuing Education.

Miers, M. (1999) 'Nurses in the labour market: exploring and explaining nurses' work', in Wilkinson, G. and Miers, M. (eds) *Power and Nursing Practice*, pp. 83–96, Basingstoke, Macmillan.

Mitchell, L., Harvey, T. and Rolls, L. (1998) 'Interprofessional standards for the care sector – history and challenges', *Journal of Interprofessional Care*, Vol. 12, No. 2, pp. 157–168.

Pietroni, P. (1992) 'Towards reflective practice – the languages of health and social care', *Journal of Interprofessional Practice*, Vol. 6, No. 1, pp. 7–16.

Porter, S. (1998) *Social Theory and Nursing Practice*, Basingstoke, Macmillan.

Quinn, F. M. (1998) 'Reflection and reflective practice', in Quinn, F. M. (ed.) *Continuing Professional Development in Nursing*, pp. 121–145, Cheltenham, Stanley Thornes.

Radcliffe, M. (1998) 'Who wants to be a millionaire? You don't', *Nursing Times*, Vol. 94, No. 24, 17 June, p. 29.

Richardson, G. and Maltby, H. (1995) 'Reflection-on-practice: enhancing student learning', *Journal of Advanced Nursing*, Vol. 22, No. 2, pp. 235–242.

Schein, E. (1974) *Professional Education*, New York, McGraw Hill.

Schober, J. (1993) 'Frameworks for nursing practice', in Hinchliff, S. M., Norman, S. E. and. Schober, J. E. (eds) *Nursing Practice and Health Care* (2nd edn), pp. 300–327, London, Edward Arnold.

Schön, D. (1983) *The Reflective Practitioner: How Professionals Think in Action*, New York, Basic Books.

Schön, D. (1988) 'From technical rationality to reflection-in-action' (first published 1983), in Dowie, J. and Elstein, A. (eds) *Professional Judgment: A Reader in Clinical Decision-Making*, pp. 60–77, Cambridge, Cambridge University Press.

Schön, D. A. (1992) 'The crisis of professional knowledge and the pursuit of an epistomology of practice' (first published 1984), *Journal of Interprofessional Care*, Vol. 6, No. 1, pp. 49–63.

Sheppard, M. (1995) 'Social work, social science and practice wisdom', *British Journal of Social Work*, Vol. 25, pp. 265–293.

Sheppard, M. (1998) 'Practice validity, reflexivity and knowledge for social work', *British Journal of Social Work*, Vol. 28, pp. 763–781.

Slaughter, R. (1988) *Recovering the Future*, Melbourne, Monash University Press.

Street, A. (1990) *Nursing Practice: High, Hard Ground, Messy Swamps and the Pathways in Between*, Geelong, Victoria, Deakin University Press.

Taylor, B. (1998) 'Locating a phenomenological perspective of reflective nursing and midwifery practice by contrasting interpretative and critical reflection', in Johns, C. and Freshwater, D. (eds) *Transforming Nursing Through Reflective Practice*, pp. 134–150, Oxford, Blackwell Science.

Thompson, N. (1996) *People Skills: A Guide to Effective Practice in the Human Services*, Basingstoke, Macmillan.

Tsang, N. M. (1998) 'Re-examining reflection – a common issue of professional concern in social work, teacher education and nursing education', *Journal of Interprofessional Care*, Vol. 12, No. 1, pp. 21–32.

United Kingdom Central Council for Nursing, Midwifery and Health Visiting (UKCC) (1986) *Project 2000: A New Preparation for Practice*, London, UKCC.

United Kingdom Central Council for Nursing, Midwifery and Health Visiting (UKCC) (1996) *Position Statement on Clinical Supervision for Nursing and Health Visiting*, London, UKCC.

United Kingdom Central Council for Nursing, Midwifery and Health Visiting (UKCC) (1997) *PREP and You*, London, UKCC.

Weinstein, J. (1998) 'The use of National Occupational Standards in professional education', *Journal of Interprofessional Care*, Vol. 12, No. 2, pp. 169–179.

White, S. (1997) 'Beyond retroduction? Hermeneutics, reflexivity and social work practice', *British Journal of Social Work*, Vol. 27, pp. 739–754.

Witz, A. (1994) 'The challenge of nursing', in Gabe, J., Kelleher, D. and Williams, G. (eds) *Challenging Medicine*, pp. 23–45, London, Routledge.

Part 2
Challenging Practice

Chapter 4
The challenge of professionalism

Linda Finlay

I was just born several centuries too early.
Just think, in the future the likes of me
become respected surgeons!

Introduction

Identifying the 'professionals' at first glance seems straightforward. People would name several professional groups such as doctors, dentists, lawyers and the clergy. Some would include nurses, remedial therapists, social workers or teachers. But then the boundaries become blurred. Is a residential care worker a 'professional'? Does a nursing assistant qualify? What of practitioners of alternative and complementary medicine? And if people were asked to explain their understanding of 'professional', how would they do so? Would they refer to specialist knowledge, pay, training or qualifications? What about commitment and the role of moral values? Does the definition rely on the fact that professionals belong to professional bodies that accredit and regulate their members?

These boundaries are further complicated because they change over time and are constantly being renegotiated. Many of the professions allied to medicine (PAMs), such as physiotherapy, occupational therapy, dietetics and orthoptics, have a short history, having been recognised formally as professions only within the last 50 to 75 years. New groups strive to professionalise as part of a dynamic process of advancing claims to expertise, political power and/or formal status.

The fact that the lines between professionals and less 'qualified' practitioners are in constant flux indicates that the concept of professional is far from straightforward. Professionalism is contested. What does it mean to be a professional? Do professionals offer an effective service? In the 1990s, the place of the professions in modern society has become a much-explored area of discussion and research. Some scholars and commentators have been critical of professionals' power and of how they maintain their advantage in society. Others suggest professionals are losing their hold in the face of marketisation, new regulations and consumer power.

This chapter takes a critical look at professionalism by exploring both the challenge of being a professional and how professionalism itself is being challenged. Section 1 looks at what constitutes a profession. Section 2 explores four theoretical approaches, which examine how different groups emerge in a social, political and historical context and how this is fundamentally tied up with the exercise of power. The third section has a more practice-based focus and examines ways in which professional power is currently being challenged with professionals being exhorted to both 'deprofessionalise' and 'reprofessionalise'.

1   Defining the 'professional': characteristics approaches

The stories of the two practitioners in Box 1 raise many questions about what it means to be a qualified professional and about where and how the lines are drawn. Can you be 'professional' in the sense of maintaining high standards if you are not a member of a 'profession'? Are professional groups really better equipped than other workers and, if so, in what ways and for what tasks? Do professionals have more in common with each other than with unqualified workers in their own field? Are some areas of expertise, such as dealing with difficult patients or passing on local knowledge, downgraded and artificially excluded from the professional agenda? Do status differences rest on race, class and gender as much as skill and training?

Behind these questions there are some important concepts about what a 'profession' is and how some occupational groups (and not others) come to be accorded this status or can gain access to qualifications. As part of investigating these questions, several different theories have been put forward which identify particular 'characteristics' of professions. The traditional trait approach and functionalist accounts will be explored here.

Box 1: Two practitioners divided by profession

Elizabeth Smith is an occupational therapist who has recently become a care manager working alongside social workers, a community nurse and care assistants in a local social services learning disabilities team. Although members of the team have different professional backgrounds they do a very similar job. Elizabeth's work involves assessing clients and both designing and costing packages of care, including aids and adaptations to enable greater independence in personal care. Elizabeth delegates the actual work of implementing the care packages to care assistants. She also explores work/leisure roles and refers clients on to day services when social contact is an issue. In carrying out her assessments she draws heavily on her initial training but the managerial aspects of her job involve a range of other skills which she has picked up 'along the way'. She is challenged by her managerial role as she feels her professional training has not equipped her to cope with the tensions between meeting needs and containing costs. Sometimes she feels bothered that she makes recommendations which are incomplete or which fall short of the professional ideals that she had hoped to practise.

Marcia Grant is a care assistant who works with Elizabeth. In her job of teaching people how to use aids and manage their personal care, she often works to care plans that are imprecise or unworkable. If anything unexpected about a case comes up, she uses her ingenuity and tries to get on with it as best she can. She often offers extra advice based on her own local knowledge and on her contacts within the Afro-Caribbean community. She is paid one-third less than Elizabeth and is sometimes resentful that she cannot progress to become a care manager in her own right. In her work she is sometimes subjected to sexual and racial harassment and she is often hassled by people who have had to wait a long time for the equipment or aids they need. If the equipment is not what they wanted, she bears the brunt of the client's frustration. Marcia thinks of herself as a professional and was very annoyed recently when a younger, less experienced member of staff was allocated a new client with complex needs on the grounds that this case needed a qualified person. Although it is never stated in these terms, Marcia wonders if there is a racist streak to this undervaluing of her skills and experience. She has completed NVQs to Level 2/3 but this does not lead to a professional qualification and her only option would be to do a part-time course over four years, which would put a strain on her family finances. In previous years her local authority had sponsored people to go on this course but they have stopped doing this now in the face of recent cuts.

Traditional trait approach

The literature on professionalism which developed in the first half of the 20th century tended to focus on establishing lists of traits professionals were assumed or expected to hold. Some scholars (for example, Millerson, 1964) suggested that 'professions' could be distinguished from 'occupations' by the ethical, altruistic way in which their expertise was applied, in contrast to the self-interested motivations ascribed to other workers. For others, factors such as levels of expert knowledge (see Box 2), autonomy and membership of associations were what singled out the 'professional'. Table 1 sets out the major elements in this traditional 'menu' or lists-of-traits approach.

Table 1 **Defining 'professional' characteristics**

Characteristic	*Definition*
Altruism	Members of a profession act in the best interests of their clients
Trustworthiness	Professions are trusted to give impartial, expert and confidential advice
Skills	Members of a profession have specialist skills
Knowledge	Professions draw on a body of theoretical/scientific knowledge which they apply in their practice
Competence	Members of professions have extended training through which they develop an agreed, and usually assessed, standard of competence
Code of conduct	Professions issue written codes of conduct and ethics which members are expected to adhere to
Organisation	Professions organise themselves within associations (including Royal Colleges, Chartered Societies and trade unions) through which they regulate themselves and monitor standards
Autonomy	Professionals can make independent judgements and decisions about their practice
Power	Professions are consulted with, and thus influence, social policy
Professional culture and etiquette	Professionals are loosely bound to a way of behaving, guided by their codes of conduct, which maintains their status/standing and may exclude outsiders

---

Box 2: Professionalism as 'expert knowledge'

Williams (1993) argues that the key criterion for acceptance as a profession is public acknowledgement of professionals' knowledge base. Agreement about specialist knowledge is what gives an occupation its credibility:

> The claim to specialist knowledge is central, for on it rests the professionals' claim to be qualified to advise, the claim to 'know better' than their clients – and hence the claim for autonomy, for being trusted by the public, for reward and prestige.

(Williams, 1993, p. 9)

On this basis, she says, professions such as medicine have been able to develop 'whole philosophies and systems', and acquire the right to shape public provision. When advice giving is monopolised in this way it is hard for service-users to initiate change or innovation.

Some kinds of knowledge are seen as more valid than others. In general, scientific knowledge carries more weight and respect than practical, experiential knowledge. In an effort to gain recognition of their professional status, many 'newer' professions in recent years have driven to establish a more expert knowledge base and increase their academic and scientific credibility. In the last 20 years, 'semi-professionals' have campaigned to extend existing diploma training to degree level and replace on-the-job training with university-based study. Turning away from common-sense knowledge, they have struggled to develop their professional research base to show the worth and value of their work.

In these early studies of professionalism, occupations vying to be considered as professions often measured themselves against supposedly impartial, value-free lists of traits such as that in Table 1. Using this model, occupations such as nursing, social work and the remedial professions were classified as '*semi*-professions' as they were seen to have developed some of the characteristics of the full professions but not others. The shortfalls which assigned these occupations to this 'not quite' status were that they lacked a clear scientific knowledge base; they had not yet achieved autonomous self-regulation and that their work rested on 'skills' rather than 'knowledge' (see Hugman, 1991, for a broader discussion).

Such views gave the semi-professions impetus to 'professionalise'. They were exhorted to develop their academic base, develop more theoretical models, do more research. Noting that occupational therapy was regarded as a lesser profession, West (1989), for example, avowed that 'few among us would contest the need for greatly increased efforts to transform solid conviction and partial demonstration into the scientific documentation that is required to merit professionalism' (cited in Irvine and Graham, 1994, p. 11).

Functionalist accounts

Listing supposed traits of professionalism has been criticised as being too simplistic an approach. Other scholars, in seeking to define what constitutes a profession, have focused on the issue of function: what professionals do; the roles they play. Functionalists argue that society wants professionals, for example, to cure illness and deal with social problems, and that these professionals need to be well trained and well rewarded. To enable them to do their job, professionals are given status and the legal authority. In return, society expects professionals to commit themselves to an ethic of service.

Southon and Braithwaite (1998) offer one such functionalist account which focuses on key tasks done by professionals. They argue that these tasks are characterised by high levels of *uncertainty* and *complexity*. Medicine is offered as an example of a successfully and necessarily professionalised occupation because practitioners have to cope with high levels of both uncertainty and complexity. Because they treat a wide range of illnesses, doctors' practice is highly unpredictable and context-dependent (Cox, 1995). Within the profession, of course, the nature of medical practice varies. A general practitioner deals with high levels of uncertainty but reduces complexity by referring difficult cases to specialists. On the other hand, specialists deal with complex cases and highly specialist techniques, but the fact that their referrals are more predictable reduces uncertainty.

Southon and Braithwaite develop their argument by suggesting that when uncertainty is minimal, even if the task is complex, then the task can be standardised and is therefore to be seen as a technical rather than professional concern. An example here is a therapy assistant who is 'unqualified' (in terms of therapy) but is trained to carry out a standardised 'dressing practice' protocol. Likewise, a reduction in complexity, even in a situation of high uncertainty, is seen to require intelligence and motivation, but little specialist training or knowledge. The home carer who uses her own personal skills rather than having a specific professional training would be an example of this.

Other researchers (for example, Jamous and Peloille, 1970) emphasise the role of *indeterminacy*, arguing that the wider the scope for interpretation or dispute, the greater the professional's autonomy. For example, the work of lawyers is seen to involve much interpretation of the law where there is a need to make judgements on precedents. The lawyer's professional knowledge and decision-making practice cannot be communicated as a set of rules. The more professionals are seen to have expertise which cannot be easily routinised into a set of codes, the greater the dependence of clients on professional advice. In this way, professionals maintain and reinforce their special position (Turner, 1985).

Evaluation of characteristics approaches

Characteristics approaches to defining professionals have had a great deal of impact in practice. The assumptions and principles of these theories are embedded in the discourse of much of the professional literature. Images and representations (that is, ideologies) of what professionals are, or should be, have guided practitioners to develop down certain paths. They have also coloured the mind of the general public who have then laid certain expectations on professionals. These ideas are used by many semi-professionals as a conceptual map, charting the direction they must take in the future in order to attain full professional standing (Irvine and Graham, 1994).

Whilst characteristics approaches seem unproblematic at first glance, they have also been criticised heavily by academics and professionals who argue that 'shopping lists' obscure the social and historical context within which certain groups define themselves, or are defined by others, as a profession. Simply describing what constitutes 'the professional' cannot take us very far. The differences in power and status between professions – differences which are sometimes as great as that between professional and non-professional work – also need to be explored. There is, too, the process of negotiation involved in becoming a professional and the degree to

---

Box 3: Transforming professions

Professions emerge in a social, political and historical context: the 1980s and 1990s have witnessed the birth and death of several professions. For example, dramatherapy has emerged as a new profession and is now formally (that is, legally) recognised as a profession supplementary to medicine. Previously, many dramatherapists tended to be teachers or occupational therapists, but gradually the training for dramatherapy was extended until it justified a separate and distinct qualification.

In the field of social care, generic social work first included specialists such as child care workers, probation officers and hospital almoners. More recently, these boundaries have been redrawn and new designations have emerged, such as 'care manager'. An example of a profession that has disappeared is remedial gymnasts. They opted to merge themselves under the banner of 'physiotherapy', a step which involved losing their name, their unique identity and some of their specialist knowledge.

which different occupational groups 'professionalise' over time (see Box 3 on page 79). Critics also contend that such lists are insufficiently critical. Are professionals really as competent, knowledgeable and altruistic in their day-to-day practice as traditional views would have it?

To move beyond definitions, we need to enter the world of theory – the subject matter of the next section.

2   Explaining professional power

Four different theoretical approaches to professionalism which locate professionalisation in a socio-historical context are explored in this section: neo-Weberian, neo-Marxist, feminist and critical discourses approaches. Whilst each focuses on a different dimension, they all aim to explain how professionals exercise power and how this power reflects or magnifies the relatively privileged positions professionals hold in class, race and gender hierarchies. Until recently, for example, medicine was dominated by middle class, white males; and working class, black women remain disproportionately represented in low-status occupations (Hugman, 1991).

The four approaches discussed in this section apply a more critical eye to the role of professionals in society than do characteristics approaches. Specifically, they emphasise the self-interested involvement of groups and how professional behaviour, in practice, may not always work to the advantage of the public. These approaches, in short, offer a *critique* of professionalism.

Evolving professional status: neo-Weberian approaches

Neo-Weberian approaches to professionalism focus on how groups and organisations gain status and maintain their advantage in a competitive employment market. In the 1920s, Weber (1968) analysed what he saw as certain groups regulating market conditions in their favour. Faced with competition over scarce resources, these groups closed ranks against outsiders. This idea was developed into the notion of *social closure* – the process whereby groups seek to maximise their rewards and status by restricting opportunities or controlling access to resources on behalf of their 'insider' circle. Professions, by this view, are no more than privileged groups who manage to monopolise social and economic opportunities.

In the Weberian tradition, Parkin (1979) explored how closure operates. He argues that groups exclude others from sharing their advantages by defining them as 'ineligible' or somehow 'inferior'. Professions do this on the basis of *credentialism*; individual competitors in the job market are stopped from entering an area of work because an existing profession has placed restrictions around certain tasks. Access is therefore restricted to 'credentialled' individuals, typically those with the 'right' qualifications (see Box 1 on page 75). Closure also operates at group level. Established professions make sure that other professions are not allowed to expand into their areas of work (this is termed *exclusion* in Weberian discourse). For example, very few professional groups are allowed to prescribe medication: those which can retain an exclusive power and locus of control as arbiters of who gets what treatment and how. It is interesting to see how specialist nurses have recently attempted to wrest some of this authority away from doctors (an activity termed *usurpation* in Weberian theory), as they have fought to be able to prescribe as independent practitioners: a power which has in limited circumstances been conceded by doctors.

Numerous examples of social closure and credentialism can be identified in the field of health and social care (see, for example, Saks, 1998 or Donnison, 1977). Many professional groups operate a system of legal registration that confirms which individuals have undergone a particular training. We have already encountered the case of 'qualified occupational therapists' and 'unqualified care assistants' – a distinction which leads to inequalities in both pay and status. Not surprisingly, such divisions can be a source of tension between groups – as, for instance, when assistants feel they are doing the job of the formally qualified person without adequate recognition of their experience. Professionals, likewise, feel aggrieved when employers hire less qualified staff to take over some of their roles: this both dilutes their skills and burdens them with more work as supervisors.

Neo-Weberian scholars focus on the degree to which different occupations can organise themselves and gain the power to control the type of work done and under what conditions. The idea that highly specialised training and expert knowledge are pivotal features of a profession's status is thus challenged. For instance, Freidson (1970) compared pharmacy and optometry in the USA. He notes that, although both require similar levels of training and knowledge, optometrists may legally diagnose and prescribe whilst pharmacists remain subordinate to the medical profession. In an account of competition between pharmacists and doctors, Turner (1985) explains this in terms of the doctors' 'collegiate control', that is their success at controlling their own work through successful political organisation.

In a later analysis, Freidson (1994) identified occupational *monopoly* and *authority* as the key criteria for differentiating labour groups. He sees the medical profession exercising power not only in relation to its own members but also in relation to other professions. The medical profession, he believes, determined how and when physicians were trained and licensed, thereby controlling the labour market. It also exercised supervisory power over a range of technical workers who could not work without medical authorisation (for example, laboratory technicians).

These neo-Weberian theories offer interesting insights into the emergence of different professions over time and into the ways occupational groups have jostled and competed with each other for advantage. Using this type of analysis, we might look at the 'semi-professions' not in terms of shortfalls against a list of features but in terms of their having been defined *in relation to*, and to some extent *by*, a more powerful professional interest group. This question of how power is exercised by a privileged few is pursued with more vigour by the other theoretical approaches.

Professions divided by class: neo-Marxist approaches

Marxists understand the rise of modern professions in a modern context of industrial capitalism and class exploitation. Occupational specialisation is seen to have a role in a class-divided, highly unequal society governed by the pursuit of profit. Several different strands of analysis are put forward.

Some Marxists focus on the way the work of professionals has become so routinised they are effectively labourers and part of the exploited working class. The logic of capitalist expansion (that is, the ceaseless search for profit) means that all workers – including professionals – will eventually be reduced to proletarian status and stripped of their control over the terms and conditions of work (a process known as *proletarianisation*). Applying these ideas to doctors, for example, it has been argued that as physicians have been incorporated into large-scale bureaucracies (rather than small independent practices) their work has been routinised by protocols and technology, rationalised and divided into specialist tasks. Such developments allow certain types of work, previously handled by doctors, to be done by less qualified, cheaper workers, such as nurses.

Other Marxists (see Navarro, 1978) argue against applying the proletarianisation theory to doctors and other senior professionals. They counter that true labourers do not have the kind of expertise that is credentialled by the state, do not supervise others and do not control the way production is organised (Annandale, 1998). These scholars highlight the *élitist* character of 'establishment' professions, such as medicine and the law, documenting the extent to which they remain bastions of wealth and privilege.

Bringing these different arguments together, some neo-Marxists view professionals in terms of 'contradictory class location' (Wright, 1985) and suggest a trend towards an increasing *polarisation* of the classes. A few professionals, they argue, are well placed to accumulate capital, whilst most of the others (particularly in the public sector) are increasingly deskilled and exploited in terms of low pay and status. For these researchers, the growth of trade unionism among white collar professionals is symptomatic of distress caused by pressures to downgrade skills and deprofessionalise (see Box 4 opposite).

A different argument, which focuses more on the professional–client relationship, has been put forward by other Marxists. They argue that

---

Box 4: Trade union versus professional body

The 'proletarianisation of professional labour' thesis emphasises how professionals have become increasingly deskilled (Braverman, 1974) and under the control of management. Some theorists argue that practitioners in health and social care should recognise that they are employed labour (that is, skilled working class) and should therefore join trade unions such as UNISON rather than Royal Colleges or other professional bodies. Trade unions are seen to define the interests of practitioners as employees – people who are essentially under the control of the employer. Trade unions recognise that the interests of worker and employer may conflict. Professional bodies, in contrast, emphasise the corporate nature of occupational groups and underplay the significance of the wage contract. Professional bodies are viewed as seeking to maximise professional advantages.

When trade unions and professional bodies are separated, the practitioner has a problem. With which organisation do they more strongly identify? Which organisation is likely to act in the practitioner's best interest? Does the answer depend on whether the practitioner sees himself or herself as a 'lower status worker' or a 'higher status professional'? Does the answer depend on whether the practitioner identifies a common interest with service-users or with service-providers?

---

professionals such as teachers and social workers are 'agents of the State' whose role is essentially to preserve, uphold and perpetuate the existing distribution of power (Althusser, 1984). In this context, the caring professions are seen to exercise control over their clients, who are often poor and disadvantaged.

These professionals are also seen to act on behalf of the capitalist state by individualising social problems and suggesting that individuals are essentially responsible for the plight in which they find themselves. This attitude and practice of 'blaming the victim', say Marxist scholars, shifts attention away from the structural inequalities.

These ideas have had an impact on the work of professionals in different ways and at different points in time. The radical social work movement of the 1970s, with its mission to combat inequality, was influenced by such arguments. Community workers sought to cement common interests with service-users and to empower them to improve their situation through collective action by tenants' associations, trade unions and so on (see Loney, 1983, on the rise of Community Development Projects). As Abbott and Meerabeau (1998) note, however, the response of successive governments to such analyses and action was negative, and eventually funding for various community action projects was withdrawn.

Professions as gendered: feminist approaches

Turning away from class divisions in society, feminist theories focus more specifically on the significance of gender for professionalism, and the relationships between the professions. Traditional analyses have explored the position of women in terms of discrimination and exclusion (for example, Crompton, 1990). Here, analyses of occupational segregation by gender is evidenced both *vertically* (within professions women are usually clustered at the bottom of the hierarchy) and *horizontally* (with women, or men, clustered in particular occupations).

A different feminist argument is put forward by Davies (1995, 1998) in reference to the health care field. She notes how current notions of 'professionalism' are tied to a long tradition of masculine ideals which stress mastery of knowledge, control, detachment, competition and autonomy. Both bureaucracy and the professions, she argues, draw upon the putative masculine attributes of heroic individualism, and independent, rational and boundaried (stand-alone, one-off) interventions. She argues that the important issue is not that individual women have been excluded from these male-oriented professions but that women's professions have been defined in relation to them, and in order to complement them. Comparing the 'professional work' of men with the 'supportive activities' of women, she notes that the high status, 'fleeting encounters' type of professional consultation can be contrasted with the ongoing, low status support work on which it relies. In this analysis, women are not seen as being *excluded* from professions but *included* as an essential bedrock without which the work of the traditional men's professions, and of the newer emerging women's professions, would not be possible. This helps us to understand professions and social closure from a different perspective: although not part of these traditionally powerful professional élites, woman were there all along, allowing men to function in their 'arm's length' way, preparing for and then clearing up after the fleeting encounters and the heroic interventions.

This understanding of professions and power provides a crucial backdrop to change. Witz (1992, 1994) locates changing professional practices in nursing in the context of wider power relations. She discusses recent efforts made to reconstruct the nursing role to allow greater autonomy and independence from medical dominance. However, whilst doctors may not be adverse to offloading some routine work on to nurses, they are less keen to accept practices which threaten their power base, namely the move into 'cure' rather than 'care'. Witz explains this as:

> ... the enhanced 'carative' route of upskilling nurses [which] ... instates the nurse–patient partnership as an alternative to the doctor–patient relationship, and puts into practice a radical new philosophy of patient-centred work which undermines traditional, medically created distinctions between care and cure ...
>
> (Witz, 1994, p. 37, cited in Murphy, 1996, p. 98)

Witz remains sceptical about whether nurses will be able to 'pull off' their challenge to medicine.

In this context it is important to consider the ubiquitous split between the 'qualified' and 'unqualified' and to reflect upon the extent to which the work of qualified practitioners is predicated on the input of assistants (who are often poorly paid women). We also need to examine how far the professions define and police the boundary between professional tasks and support tasks they consider 'beneath' them. Lee Treweeke (1994) pointed to this dynamic in residential care for older people when she wrote of the 'bedroom' tasks of care assistants whose job it was to cope with bodily functions and intimate care, preparing and transforming people's bodies so they could enter the public space of the living room where qualified staff would deal with cleaner tasks, such as planning, leisure and managing visitors.

At a macro level, this division can also be seen to operate in health and social care. Here, the 'fleeting encounters' that are part and parcel of the acute health care services work on the assumptions that there are care services to pick up the pieces when a patient returns home.

Power through language: critical discourse approaches

Critical discourse approaches perceive professionals as socially constructed and recognise that power derives from the way in which ideological messages are transmitted through cultural representations (see Box 5).

Box 5: Power and professional knowledge

Foucault's (1978 and 1983) post-structuralist critique argues that in modern societies, populations are controlled and disciplined by the knowledges and practices of medicine, psychology, criminology and so on. His analysis stresses how fields of science and medicine make knowledge claims and create situations where professional definitions of social problems come to be seen as natural and unchallengeable. He illustrates the way knowledge is constructed with the example of 'homicidal monomania' – a category now consigned to the history books. 'Nineteenth century psychiatry invented an entirely fictitious entity, a crime which is insanity, a crime which is nothing but insanity, an insanity which is nothing but a crime' (1978, pp. 5–6). Foucault urges us to resist scientific expertise (scientists' knowledge being the agent of power in the modern state) where people are coerced by ideas and professionals' standards.

Critical discourse theory highlights the importance of language in shaping and confining our thinking. It examines how different discourses within society shape the way the world is perceived and experienced (Potter and Wetherell, 1987). Applying these ideas to the professionalism debate, three points are emphasised:

1 **Professional discourse can be stigmatising.** The use of 'jargon' or the practice of stereotypically labelling patients can preserve professional authority (Kelly and May, 1982; Johnson and Webb, 1995). Health care research reveals a ubiquitous use of moral evaluations, with professionals being forced to judge the social 'worth' of people in order to balance competing claims on time and resources. Crucially, these evaluations carry with them critical consequences where people are stigmatised and treated differently according to their illness, class, behaviour or appearance (Finlay, 1997). There is a classic illustration of this in Jeffrey's often-quoted 1979 study of how medics in Accident and Emergency departments routinely classified some patients as 'normal rubbish' (for example, the 'normal drunk' or the 'normal overdose') and how that label carried significant consequences, for example, delaying resuscitation.

2 **Professional discourses can be disempowering.** For example, Woollett and Marshall's (1997) analysis of discourses around pregnancy (building on the work of Oakley, 1979, and others) revealed that traditional medical ways of describing pregnancy relegated the mother to a passive role and reduced women's varied physiological changes to simplistic categories of 'normal' or 'abnormal'. In contrast, the women's own accounts were much more complex and emphasised how bodily changes took place in a social context, for instance how tiredness interfered with care of the family.

3 **Professionals have the power to impose their own definitions of clients' needs.** Ultimately, expert knowledge can give professionals the power to enforce their definitions through legal sanctions. A case in point is the legal authority social workers have to take children away from their families and into care. In probation work and social work with young offenders, the use of trained professionals enables social control to work through the guise of social care (Hugman, 1991). A probation officer can ask a court to review a probation order and can use this 'threat' explicitly or implicitly in relationships with clients (Day, 1981; Rodger, 1988). Similarly, social workers and health care professionals can play a major role in compelling patients to receive treatment (Olsen, 1984; Hugman, 1991).

Professionals, then, have both formal power to impose punitive sanctions on their clients and informal power to control their relationships with clients by more subtle means, such as use of language, organisation of time and reinforcement of gender and racial stereotypes (Miell and Croghan, 1996).

Evaluation of the four approaches to professionalism

All four theoretical approaches discussed in this section recognise the changing nature of the different professions, placing the process of professionalisation in a social–historical context. Whilst the approaches present different accounts of professional power (focusing variously on status, class, gender and language), they each offer a critique of how power can be both used and abused.

Each approach reveals strengths and weaknesses in its attempt to explain the nature of professional power. In terms of strengths, the neo-Weberian approach offers a clear account of the dynamics of coalition and subdivision amongst professional groups as they jostle for status in a competitive job market. The neo-Marxist and feminist approaches offer particularly strong analyses of power which explain how social (class and gender respectively) divisions impact on professionals themselves and on the relationships between professionals and service-users. The critical discourse approach spotlights how language can be used in a disempowering way and how ideological discourses are embedded in our social structure. The latter three approaches offer a radical dimension (compared with neo-Weberian approaches), in that they seek to uncover inequalities that are accepted 'givens' in our social institutions; they aim to bring about social change.

Each approach also has weaknesses which emerge when the competing approaches engage in a critical dialogue. Neo-Weberian approaches can be seen to focus unduly on group dynamics, glossing over the inequalities within the broader social structure and the way professionals exploit their power. Neo-Marxist arguments are challenged for their preoccupation with the impact of capitalism on class which underplays the significance of other social divisions, whilst feminist approaches are criticised for prioritising patriarchy. Critical discourse theory is accused of attending too much to language and relative meanings at the expense of 'real' material inequalities.

All the approaches may be challenged for being too critical, for over-generalising, for exaggerating the extent of professional power and for adopting a rather 'anti-professional' stance. Further, they sometimes seem to overlook the fact that professionals do valuable, caring, conscientious work and that aspects of professionalism can be a relatively benign, even positive, force.

3   Challenging professional power

Managing the myths: heroes and demons

Professions carry considerable status in our society. They are associated with relatively high levels of income, authority and power. But they are also dogged by myths about their power to help and to heal. Such heroic images are commonplace within popular culture, for instance, in hospital docu-dramas and soap operas – the Lone Ranger of the 1950s having given way to the lone doctor or vet of the 1990s. Whilst individual professionals are often criticised, the public continue to invest an enormous level of trust and faith in the professions in general. Ordinary people can be unquestioning about professional expertise and passive in the face of professional authority (Murphy, 1996).

At the same time, professionals also have to cope with negative representations of their services. Glastonbury *et al.* (1982) make this point in relation to media images of social workers in the recent past, arguing:

> ... periodic eruptions in the national press have suggested that social services have encouraged scroungers, sapped personal initiative, allowed children to be battered to death, overlooked hypothermia in the elderly, negotiated immoral 'contracts' with teenagers, broken up families, dragged children away from loving parents into care, and illegally cajoled people into psychiatric hospital against their will. Worst of all, in the view of the media, some social workers have gone on strike to get better wages.
>
> (Cited in Hugman, 1991, p. 109)

These kinds of representations, both positive and negative, are challenging at many levels. Service-users may try to block professionals' attempts to resist the hero myths. Then, when professionals cannot meet excessively idealised expectations, service-users are left feeling angry about the professionals' failure to deliver (Cornwell, 1984). Professionals, too, feel disappointed and frustrated as they internalise such messages of failure (Finlay, 1998).

The negative representations are equally problematic. They reflect the negative self-image of many professionals who struggle to carve out a more positive identity. Such images can also be used by antagonists as weapons in debates about funding, autonomy and training (Hugman, 1991).

Challenging traditional boundaries

Over the past two decades, professionals have been under growing pressure to justify their existence or else relinquish some authority. Such challenges have occurred in the context of far-reaching changes in health and social care.

In particular, the rise of the new right and its 'free market' ideology heralded major reorganisations of care delivery (see Chapter 1). First, the move towards a purchaser–provider split and the rise of the private, voluntary and community sectors transformed care services. Second, as the state became a regulator rather than a provider, 'élitist' professionals came under attack and it was claimed that a business management approach would be more efficient. At the same time, free market ideas about 'profit', productive efficiency, cost-effectiveness and value for money replaced traditional notions of service and placed constant pressure on professionals to demonstrate their worth. Third, as the boundaries between professionals and managers have blurred, intra-professional solidarity has been further undermined. Finally, with developments such as the Patient's Charter and the expansion of user groups, consumers have been encouraged to stop being passive recipients of services and voice their demands.

Creek and Ormston (1996, p. 9) express these trends in terms of a new professional vulnerability:

> Another consequence of changes within the culture and political structures of current ... care provision is the stigmatising of the term 'professional'. It has become unfashionable to champion the right for a profession to be self-organised and regulate itself, or for professionals to owe allegiance to their peers and their profession. 'Providing' has become the saleable commodity in a new business-like health service ... We see the emergence of new breeds of 'quasi-professionals' who are generic, defined by tasks and techniques, and recognised through specific competencies; for example, care managers, 'rehabilitation therapists' and generic support workers. This focus on task and practice, which exists remote from philosophy or theory, further undermines the vulnerable position of a profession ...

Professionals are thus being challenged in at least three ways.

1   **Changing care contexts challenging traditional role boundaries.** The shifts towards private, voluntary and community services have fundamentally redefined professional power. New generic roles have evolved where professionals have been forced to learn new skills and become more flexible, expanding their areas of concern. At the same time, they have lost their profession-specific support and supervision structures. With the breakdown of traditional role boundaries,

professionals have had to negotiate new roles within the wider care teams. In particular, professionals have been forced to become managers – managing care, managing teams, managing budgets. In all these ways, professionals can be seen to be engaged in a process of *re*-professionalising (Finlay, 1998).

2 **New social policy challenging professional accountability.** The erosion of power has been reflected in, and spearheaded by, a range of government policies. Southon and Braithwaite (1998) argue that new reforms, such as those requiring the use of protocols and performance measures, have heralded attempts to diminish professional skills and increase management control. Davies (1999) argues that proposed changes to statutory regulation for the health professionals (for instance, the current proposals for the Professions Supplementary to Medicine Act) represent a withdrawal of trust in the professions. The self-regulation of professions seems set to be replaced by a different model of statutory professional regulation (see also Chapter 13).

3 **A newly empowered public challenging professional decision making.** Service-users are increasingly finding their voice both as individuals and as members of collectives. Whilst users mostly express satisfaction about their care, they are also increasingly criticising professionals for being too distant or arrogant. As Thompson (1984, p. 87) notes:

> ... dissatisfaction with medical communications remains the most prominent of patient complaints and a major factor in the move to alternative medicine, with its focus on good and reassuring communications and the patient as an informed participant.

User groups are turning away from professional or medical definitions and favouring their own experiences, which are located in more social definitions (see Chapter 5). An increasingly knowledgeable general public, informed by a watchful media, has taken to challenging professional mistakes and abuses of power (for example, Ward, 1998; Karpf, 1988).

Pressures to deprofessionalise

Under mounting pressure to redefine themselves and reprofessionalise, professionals have also been challenged to relinquish some of their professional trappings: in short, to *de*professionalise.

Here, we see professionals engaged in projects designed to empower and equalise their relationships with service-users. Embracing the mantle of 'advocate', professionals have rejected traditional definitions – a move much supported by practitioners favouring the radical social work critiques of the 1970s (for example, see Cohen and Wagner, 1982).

Pressures to deprofessionalise have also occurred in the context of organisational structures and work in changing care contexts. In particular, as social care has increasingly moved out of institutions and also become more sensitive to the need to destigmatise people who receive services, social care workers have found their professional status undermined. The language used to describe the work they do, as well as changing organisational structures and employment conditions, has weakened their position.

Although the move to community-based services has led to new patterns of work, job titles, skills and responsibilities, the majority of workers in new community services (as opposed to the highly unionised nursing staff in long-stay hospitals) are 'unskilled' and 'unqualified'. The day-to-day job of 'looking after' people in the community was increasingly separated out and characterised as 'ordinary' and unexceptional (see Box 6). A commitment to enhancing the status of users and overcoming public prejudices hassled both managers and workers to downplay the difficulty of the work, inadvertently undercutting claims that the work was skilled, required knowledge and/or deserved professional rates of pay. Employers and funders have been able to use such arguments to resist claims for higher status and better employment conditions.

Modelling new services on small family homes reinforced the relationship between gender and the giving of care. Care assistants and house companions do work that so resembles housework it is easily categorised as unskilled – the 'natural' domain for women. As Brown and Smith (1993, p. 189) remark, this has produced a vicious circle:

> ... the fact that women do the work makes it appear unskilled and undemanding, the fact that they are skilled enough to care without straining the appearance of an 'ordinary' relationship further undercuts their need for proper recompense.

Box 6: Discourse of 'ordinariness'

The deceptively simple language of 'ordinariness' coined in the UK publication *An Ordinary Life* (King's Fund Centre, 1980) has been central in debates about new service models. Ordinariness, defined as the opposite of professionalism, has involved a rejection of professional knowledge in favour of 'common sense'. Ordinariness could be portrayed as the key qualification of staff in new community services only if the specific needs of people with complex difficulties or multiple impairments were downplayed. The analogue of 'ordinary living' was used to suggest that service-users needed only low-level inputs.

An additional barrier to claiming professional status was the confusion surrounding the theoretical underpinning of the new service models. The onslaught on institutional service models was so successful it undermined claims that new community workers were drawing on any relevant and/or ethical models of physical, mental or intellectual disability. The theoretical basis for the work has been a point of debate ever since: in so far as the bio-medical model was rejected out of hand, the yet-to-be-developed social model consisted of more moral imperatives than useful techniques (see Chapter 5).

A new professionalism?

Professionals, then, are under pressure, facing challenges to their power and authority from both within and outside their professions. They are being exhorted to organise themselves, to improve their knowledge, to offer a better service. They are also being urged to give up some of their power, to redraw traditional role boundaries and embrace new, more flexible ways of working.

Against this backdrop, there are growing calls for a 'new professionalism'. Hugman (1991) argues for greater partnership and participation in a democratic professionalism that empowers both users and professionals. Davies (1995, 1998) claims the new professional should be one committed to reflective practice which empowers clients, and is one who engages in mutually supportive, collective team relationships. Davies' vision favours the caring practitioner who is:

- neither distant nor involved but *engaged*
- neither autonomous nor passive/dependent but *interdependent*
- neither self-oriented nor self-effacing but accepting of an *embodied use of self as part of the therapeutic encounter*
- neither instrumental nor passive but a *creator of an active community in which a solution can be negotiated*
- neither the master/possessor of knowledge nor the user of experience but a *reflective user of experience and expertise.*

(Davies, 1995, pp. 149–150)

Such empowering relationships depend on the willingness of professionals to relinquish their traditional status as 'experts' and ally themselves with service-users. At a UNISON/IMPACT conference in Belfast in 1997, Inez McCormack, then Regional Secretary of UNISON, argued the case thus:

Many people forget just who the expert is when it comes to the provision of care. The professional is the person with power over resources. However, the expert is the person with the need. What balances this relationship is mutual respect between the two; i.e. the powerful with the resources and the powerless with the expertise. It is only in the context of rights that such a relationship of mutual respect can be achieved.

(McCormack, 1998, p. 31)

Professionals are thus being asked to value the contributions of both service-users and other professionals. They are being challenged to relinquish the idea that their knowledge base gives them special rights to define problems and solutions for others. They are being pushed to acknowledge their power is problematic and can be abused. What is unclear is how professionals can meet these challenges at the same time as holding useful expertise and offering a positive contribution.

Conclusion

This chapter explored what it means to be a professional. The contested nature of this concept was emphasised by contrasting different theoretical approaches to, and critiques of, professionalism. This chapter also examined how professions are socially constructed, how they evolve in social, political and historical contexts. Over time, professions have faced pressures to (re)professionalise and deprofessionalise. Currently, they face multiple challenges arising from ideology, changing care contexts, new social policy and increasing public demands. Calls for a new democratic professionalism are propelling professionals to empower users and engage in mutually supportive professional relationships.

The gauntlet has been thrown down. Professionals face a dual challenge: to both examine their power and seek to empower others. Is it time for professionals to embrace such change? Can this be realistically achieved in the present climate?

References

Abbott, P. and Meerabeau, L. (1998) 'Professionals, professionalization and the caring professions', in Abbott, P. and Meerabeau, L. (eds) *The Sociology of the Caring Professions* (2nd edn), London, UCL Press.

Althusser, L. (1984) *Essays on Ideology*, London, Verso.

Annandale, E. (1998) *The Sociology of Health and Medicine: A Critical Introduction*, Cambridge, Polity Press.

Braverman, H. (1974) *Labor and Monopoly Capital*, New York, Monthly Review Press.

Brown, H. and Smith, H. (1993) 'Women caring for people: the mismatch between rhetoric and women's reality', *Policy and Politics*, Vol. 21, No. 3, pp. 185–193.

Cohen, M. B. and Wagner, D. (1982) 'Social work professionalism: reality and illusion', in Derber, C. (ed.) *Professionals as Workers: Mental Labor in Advanced Capitalism*, Boston, G. K. Hall.

Cornwell, J. (1984) *Hard-earned Lives: Accounts of Health and Illness from East London*, London, Tavistock.

Cox, K. (1995) 'Clinical practice is not applied scientific method', *Australian/ New Zealand Journal of Surgery*, Vol. 65, p. 553.

Creek, J. and Ormston, C. (1996) 'The essential elements of professional motivation', *British Journal of Occupational Therapy*, Vol. 59, No. 1, pp. 7–10.

Crompton, R. (1990) 'Professions in the current context', *Work, Employment and Society* (special issue), pp. 147–166.

Davies, C. (1995) *Gender and the Professional Predicament in Nursing*, Buckingham, Open University Press.

Davies, C. (1998) 'Care and the transformation of professionalism', in Knijn, T. and Sevenhuijsen, S. (eds) *Care, Citizenship and Social Cohesion: Towards a*

Gender Perspective, Utrecht, Netherlands School for Social and Economic Policy Research.

Davies, C. (1999) 'Rethinking regulation in the health professions in the UK: institutions, ideals and identities', in Hellberg, I., Saks, M. and Benoit, C. (eds) *Professional Identities in Transition: Cross-cultural Dimensions*, Gothenburg, University of Gothenburg/Swedish Humanities and Social Sciences Research Council.

Day, P. R. (1981) *Social Work and Social Control*, London, Tavistock.

Donnison, J. (1977) *Midwives and Medical Men*, London, Heinemann.

Finlay, L. (1997) 'Good patients and bad patients: how occupational therapists view their patients/clients', *British Journal of Occupational Therapy*, Vol. 60, No. 10, pp. 440–446.

Finlay, L. (1998) *The lifeworld of the occupational therapist: meaning and motive in an uncertain world*, unpublished PhD thesis, The Open University.

Foucault, M. (1978) 'About the concept of the "Dangerous Individual" in 19th century legal psychiatry', *International Journal of Law and Psychiatry*, Vol. I, pp. 1–18.

Foucault, M. (1983) 'Afterword', in Dreyfus, H. L. and Rabinow, P. (eds) *Michel Foucault: Beyond Structuralism and Hermeneutics* (2nd edn), Chicago, University of Chicago Press.

Freidson, E. (1970) *The Profession of Medicine*, New York, Dodd, Mead and Co.

Freidson, E. (1994) *Professionalism Reborn: Theory, Prophesy and Policy*, Oxford, Polity Press.

Glastonbury, B., Cooper, D. and Hawkins, P. (1982) *Social Work in Conflict – The Practitioner and the Bureaucrat*, Birmingham, BASW.

Hugman, R. (1991) *Power in Caring Professions*, London, Macmillan.

Irvine, R. and Graham, J. (1994) 'Deconstructing the concept of profession: a prerequisite to carving a niche in a changing world', *Australian Occupational Therapy Journal*, Vol. 41, pp. 9–18.

Jamous, H. and Peloille, B. (1970) 'Professions or self-perpetuating systems: changes in the French university-hospital system', in Jackson, J. A. (ed.) *Professions and Professionalisation*, Cambridge, Cambridge University Press.

Jeffrey, R. (1979) 'Normal rubbish: deviant patients in casualty departments', *Sociology of Health and Illness*, Vol. 1, pp. 98–107.

Johnson, M. and Webb, C. (1995) 'Rediscovering unpopular patients: the concept of social judgement', *Journal of Nursing*, Vol. 21, pp. 466–475.

Karpf, A. (1988) *Doctoring the Media: The Reporting of Health and Medicine*, London, Routledge.

Kelly, M. P. and May, D. (1982) 'Good and bad patients: a review of the literature and a theoretical critique', *Journal of Advanced Nursing*, Vol. 7, pp. 147–156.

King's Fund Centre (1980) *An Ordinary Life: Comprehensive Locally Based Residential Services for Mentally Handicapped People*, London, King's Fund Centre.

Lee Treweeke, G. (1994) 'Bedroom abuse: the hidden work in a nursing home', *Generations Review*, Vol. 4, No. 1, March, pp. 2–4.

Loney, M. (1983) *Community against Government*, London, Heinemann.

McCormack, I. (1998) 'Developing mutual understanding and partnership: towards a common purpose', *Conference Proceedings – The Quality of Social Care in Ireland, North and South: New Perspectives*, UNISON/IMPACT Conference 1997, Belfast.

Miell, D. and Croghan, R. (1996) 'Examining the wider context of social relationships', in Miell, D. and Dallos, R. (eds) *Social Interaction and Personal Relationships*, pp. 267–318, London, Sage Publications.

Millerson, G. (1964) *The Qualifying Associations*, London, Routledge.

Murphy, J. (1996) D317 Trigger Unit: *Using health and illness to understand social psychological problems and perspectives*, Milton Keynes, The Open University.

Navarro, V. (1978) *Class Struggle, the State and Medicine: An Historical and Contemporary Analysis of the Medical Sector in Great Britain*, London, Robertson.

Oakley, A. (1979) *Becoming a Mother*, Oxford, Martin Robertson.

Olsen, M. R. (ed.) (1984) *Social Work and Mental Health*, London, Tavistock.

Parkin, F. (1979) *Marxism and Class Theory: A Bourgeois Critique*, London, Tavistock.

Potter, J. and Wetherell, M. (1987) *Discourse and Social Psychology: Beyond Attitudes and Behaviour*, London, Sage.

Rodger, J. J. (1988) 'Social work as social control re-examined: beyond the dispersal of discipline thesis', *Sociology*, Vol. 22, No. 4, pp. 563–581.

Saks, M. (1998) 'Professionalism and health care', in Field, D. and Taylor, S. (eds) *Sociological Perspectives on Health, Illness and Health Care*, London, Blackwell.

Southon, G. and Braithwaite, J. (1998) 'The end of professionalism?' *Social Science and Medicine*, Vol. 46, No. 1, January, pp. 23–28.

Thompson, J. (1984) 'Communicating with patients', in Fitzpatrick, R. *et al.* (eds) *The Experience of Illness*, London, Tavistock.

Turner, B. (1985) 'Knowledge, skill and occupational strategy: the professionalisation of paramedical groups', *Community Health Studies*, Vol. IX, No. 1, pp. 38–47.

Ward, D. J. (1998) *Homicide, mental illness and public inquiry: an evaluation of the recommendations and responses*, unpublished MA thesis, University of Hull.

Weber, M. (1968) *Economy and Society*, New York, Bedminster Press. (Originally published in German in 1922.)

Williams, J. (1993) 'What is a profession? Experience versus expertise', in Walmsley, J. *et al.* (eds) *Health, Welfare and Practice: Reflecting on Roles and Relationships*, pp. 8–15, London, Sage Publications.

Witz, A. (1992) *Professions and Patriarchy*, London, Routledge.

Woollett, A. and Marshall, H. (1997) 'Discourses of pregnancy and childbirth', in Yardley, L. (ed.) *Material Discourses of Health and Illness*, London and New York, Routledge.

Wright, E. O. (1985) *Classes*, London, Verso.

Chapter 5
Challenges from service-users

Hilary Brown

Users may not be in a position to complain
like shoppers can.

Introduction

In this chapter we shall look in more detail at the dynamic between users
and professions, not only as individuals but also collectively. We shall
explore what happens when user and carer movements develop enough
momentum to engage with, and challenge, the knowledge on which
professional interventions are based. We shall explore what happens when
they challenge the status and rewards which accrue to professional groups
in contrast with their own, often precarious and marginalised, economic
status. We will see that, increasingly, service-users assert their own skills
and resources for dealing with problems and create their own networks.
These developments impact on the way in which individual professionals
interact with users, but they also affect recruitment, policy and resource
allocation at a more strategic level.

Not all people who use health and social services identify themselves
strongly as 'service-users'. Many people have occasional contact with
primary or acute health services on a more or less transitory basis – they

may visit their GP three times a year, be booked for day surgery, or receive treatment over a short contained period of time. These contacts with services are often fairly routine and go unremarked. None of these encounters will lead to significant changes in the person's social roles or economic status. For these 'users' involvement is going to matter most at a personal level, in terms of shared decision making about their particular case and the specifics of treatment and intervention. They may worry about when they can receive treatment so that it least disturbs their work or family responsibilities and be concerned that they are accommodated in comfortable surroundings with reasonable privacy, nice food and so on. These concerns are often wrapped up in the rubric of 'consumerism', as these people 'consume' a discrete service for a limited period in their otherwise busy and valued lives.

But for some groups, whose use of services is more protracted and pervasive, and/or who belong to communities at risk of being marginalised, the relationship with 'services' is very much more problematical. Within these groups, assertive individuals may have an impact in their day-to-day dealings with health and social care professionals but it is as collectives – as user groups and movements (the disability movement, mental health survivors, people with AIDS and HIV, carers' groups and the black pressure groups, women's and gay and lesbian networks within them) – that they have had the most impact. We shall see that user-led organisations have begun to offer services as well as use them and have taken on a more formal identity as they interact with statutory agencies within a contract, as opposed to a campaigning, culture.

Even for these groups the term 'user' is not ideal in itself. Øvretveit (1997, pp. 83–4) remarks:

> Many of the commonly-used terms fail to describe or connote the kind of relationship which some practitioners seek to create. 'Patient' is too passive for many roles, especially in rehabilitation. It is too medical for people with mental health problems and learning or physical disabilities. 'Consumer' and 'customer' are at the other end of the extreme, implying confidence, self-possession and certainty rather than a willingness to form a partnership to work together. Whilst 'user' may be appropriate in some settings where the aim is to discourage any dependency, it gives the impression of someone exploiting the practitioner and does not advance the idea of partnership ...

Øvretveit coins the term 'co-service' for the style of work he believes practitioners and service-users are aspiring towards in these long-term services.

This chapter assesses these challenges from individual service-users and the user movement as a whole and identifies conflicts of interest that can be experienced by workers who find themselves straddling uncomfortable boundaries. For example, they may take on roles advocating for users on issues that bring them into conflict with their own or a related professional group. Practitioners may be sharing the care of service-users with relatives and unpaid carers whose commitment and skill rival their own. Workers may find themselves being both a user or carer *and* a professional (Lindow and Rooke-Matthers, 1998). To what extent have professional cultures and training adapted to these more equal, two-way working partnerships? Can individual professionals help and actively facilitate users or is their role inevitably to stand back? When service-users define their own goals and strategies, where and how do professionals fit in and work within the agenda they have defined?

The dilemmas set out in Box 1 are echoed in a range of user-led initiatives and service settings. To explore these, Chapter 5 is divided into three sections:

- Understanding the challenges from people who use services, in terms of the theory generated by user groups and its practical applications.

- Listening to feedback, through a range of channels, mechanisms and 'sound barriers'.

- Redesigning services so that user involvement is enshrined in the decision-making structures of social care organisations.

Box 1: The deaf community – working towards equality and participation

The deaf community is one example of a disadvantaged minority group often ill-served by mainstream services. Deaf people need health services not only on account of their deafness but also when they are ill, getting older or experiencing mental health problems. The research study 'Looking on: deaf people and the organisation of services' (Young *et al.*, 1998) illustrates some of the barriers that stand in the way of more equal involvement of deaf people in service provision. This study explores the position of deaf workers in two mental health settings and in a school for deaf children. The authors describe a number of tensions that arose in these workplaces despite the fact that they had taken the first steps towards partnership by recognising the importance of employing deaf staff.

Challenges were seen to operate at three levels – theoretical, interpersonal and structural. Inequalities at one level were mirrored at another so that narrow interpretations of the problems faced by individual service-users led to: inappropriate models of service; inaccessible environments (both physical and linguistic); feelings of exclusion; and unfair employment practices surfacing as personal resentments. Because these layers 'bleed' into each other, change is not easy. Commitment to an ideal, such as user involvement, or in this case equality between hearing and deaf workers, falters without tireless attention to detail. Change entails restructuring roles and responsibilities, attending to the training needs of both new and established workers, and creating more flexible routes for participation and career progression. This study will serve as a reference point throughout Chapter 5.

1   Understanding the challenges from people who use services

Broadening the knowledge base

Service-users have not only focused on the way they want services delivered but also challenged the relevance and appropriateness of the knowledge base upon which professionals traditionally draw. User movements have increasingly been involved in generating theory about their position in the world – theory which rests on the analysis and lived experience of people who use health and social care services.

'Theory' in this context is both explanatory and anticipatory: it is a body of knowledge that helps to locate causes and predict what might happen. Bio-medical theories have a very precise focus on individual impairment or illness, and on the causes and treatments of conditions at the level of the individual and the disease, but they do not 'explain' the impact of social and economic factors on people's lives. Nor does a medical perspective address the reactions of other people to disability or illness or the persistence of barriers in the social and physical world. For disabled people the bio-medical model is not enough because it leaves them in the role of 'tragic individuals' with no model of how to achieve change.

Social models, such as those developed by disabled academics and activists, extend the scope of what is under examination, looking for broader, often interlocking explanations. A social model of disability looks beyond the causes of an individual's impairment to the causes of their exclusion from, and disadvantages in, social and civic life, housing, employment and culture (see, for example, Oliver, 1990). Within the social model, disabled people discriminate between their impairment and the extent to which it is allowed, by society, to disadvantage them (that is, their disability). This 'social model' is mirrored in the movements of people using mental health services and people with learning disabilities who have developed their own understandings (Goodley, 1997) about the mechanisms of exclusion and strategies for change.

In the services for deaf people, the first challenge to orthodox practice rests on a redefinition of 'the problem'. Deafness is understood no longer in terms of a medical model (in which deafness is seen as an individual impairment) but from a linguistic or cultural perspective. Deafness has traditionally been thought about in terms of what is missing but this alternative view:

> ... emphasises what is *present* – a living language and a unique community. Deafness is defined in terms of a way of life, not in terms of a medical condition. Deaf people are valued for their own cultural identity ... They are not seen as impaired versions of hearing people ...
> (Young *et al.*, 1998, p. 1)

This shifts the focus of problem solving on to external barriers and leads to different kinds of remedies, such as access to environments in which signing and visual cues are maximised and campaigns for freedom from discrimination in the job and housing markets are pursued.

This position has often been stated *in opposition* to bio-medical models and to the power dynamics generated by a model whose only focus is on what was 'wrong' with the individual. Partly this was a reaction to the fact that the medical establishment had set up hegemony over other kinds of theorising and over spheres of intervention that their 'model' failed to address. Most people would argue that medical intervention at the time of an illness or injury should give way to social action and personal assistance (not care) when people come to (re)build their lives (Øvretveit, 1996). But professionals working within a medical model claim the right to adjudicate beyond their initial rehabilitative remit into these broader arenas. Often they end up directly or indirectly (through rationing practical assistance) exerting control over all aspects of the lives of individual disabled people. Thus, for example, doctors and other professional groups have seen themselves as being the arbiters of ethical issues such as whether disabled people should be 'allowed' to have sexual relationships or bring up children. Disabled people may well need specific assistance around sexual health and fertility issues, but doctors and related professionals had grown used to stepping outside their 'provider' remit and acting as the judges not only of *whether* this treatment should be offered but also of the *rightness* of it. Their explicit role as gatekeepers and rationers of publicly funded services maintained them in this powerful role.

The social model leads to very different conceptions of helpful interventions. In relation to deafness, for example, the social model would question the prioritising of 'normalising' strategies, such as publicly funding cochlear implant programmes, over sign language and community education programmes (Hogan, 1997). The social model also places more emphasis on ongoing practical assistance than time-limited professional assessments and input. One disabled woman reported that:

> 'If I had had more help with my children I would not have felt so isolated. For instance, if I had been provided with a driver I would not have felt more disabled but more empowered as a disabled mother. They sent me an awful health visitor with very narrow views about disabled mothers.'
>
> (Cited in Gillespie-Sells *et al.*, 1998, p. 114)

The solution proposed by the woman herself fundamentally challenged the role of professionals and the appropriateness of 'health-based' interventions. The mother perceived the health visitor's role as starting from an assumption that she would not be able to cope rather than from a commitment to tailor practical help in such a way that it underpinned her ability to manage. The social model shifts the focus from personal inadequacy to the availability and adequacy of services.

One way of understanding this challenge to the knowledge base of professionals is to see it as a demand that the knowledge that comes from lived experience be revalued, not necessarily in opposition but alongside more specific professional discourses and bodies of knowledge. For example, disabled people claim direct knowledge of how to cope in a culture which 'segregates and penalises differences' (Gillespie-Sells *et al.*, 1998, p. 83). Integrating this new perspective requires action at interpersonal and structural levels when devising new models of service and forms of organisation.

Working with (unpaid) carers

Carers also lay claim to a body of expertise that challenges professional dominance but their distinct and sometimes competing interests can place them at odds with those they care for and the professionals with whom they interact. These potential conflicts of interest complicate their position in relation to service agencies despite legislation that assures them of a separate assessment of their own needs.

The role of carers is often defined by default to include those things services will not provide. Models of service that may be more 'flexible' or 'efficient' for their relatives may impose increased responsibilities on them, as for example when five-days-a-week day placements for adults with learning disabilities give way to shorter, more targeted involvement or day activities, or when hospitals move in the direction of providing only acute care or day surgery.

Sometimes shifts are initiated because of a wish to improve the service for the primary service-user but fiscal limits also play a part in moving the share of care provided from professionals to the family – from a public to a private and personal responsibility. Glazer (1990) describes how, in the USA, limits on acute hospital budgets, forced by insurance companies' insistence on paying a standard price, made carers at home take on increasingly technical tasks in caring for relatives discharged from hospital. When tasks change hands in this way there is often a shift in language or ideology that demotes complex areas of care and reframes them as less difficult. Glazer (1990) talks about this process as 'work transfer' and equates some changes in health care to self-service policy in cafeterias and do-it-yourself or self-assembly strategies in other industries. Here change in one area (of paid work) is seen to prompt change in another (of unpaid work). Tasks are reassigned to the family solely because they are no longer paid for out of the public purse. Home then becomes not only a site of professional health care work but also a substitute for it – a 'provider unit' in its own right.

These changes may not always be welcome as carers can feel overburdened both physically and emotionally (Bibbings, 1994).

When seriously ill patients are discharged early from hospital it is often assumed that family members will be there to care for them and that these family members will be both willing and able to provide care. Little planning is done around either the caring work or the other responsibilities of family members who are to take on this role. Visiting professionals may assume that carers have no other commitments and avoid discussing the implications for them of the caring tasks they already do. Moreover, turnover and 'flexibility' amongst the workforce works against consistent partnership and often leaves carers carrying the responsibility for continuity of care.

Relocation of caring work challenges the legitimacy of professional input, skills and knowledge. Teaching, albeit in an unobtrusive way, becomes a new skill for practitioners and a difficult one to perform within a relationship in which they may have more knowledge but so much less ongoing responsibility.

In hospital settings, carers and relatives are also being drawn in and their input needs to be contained and managed. One nurse, cited in a study of lay participation on a hospital ward in which caring alongside relatives was being encouraged and evaluated, said:

> 'I think it's a really good idea ... and at the same time I think it is really difficult ... I find it difficult to know what sort of tasks to give them to do and sometimes I find myself hanging on to it all because that's my role and you know it's easy to hide behind the nurse's role. I can ... get on and do it, and it is more difficult and perhaps takes longer to involve them in care ...'

(Cited in Meyer, 1993, p. 60)

The benefits of user involvement

Given that it is not always easy to facilitate user and carer involvement, it is helpful to dwell on the positive outcomes that arise out of it. In the study of services for deaf people (Young *et al.*, 1998) several very tangible benefits were identified when deaf people were recruited as staff to work with deaf users. The deaf workers fulfilled four important roles. In addition to their obvious signing skills and firsthand knowledge of deaf culture, deaf workers were thought to be able to: empathise with the particular forms of exclusion experienced by deaf people; provide role models for deaf people; and educate their hearing colleagues about deaf issues, thereby dispelling stereotypes. The value of role models and the visible presence of deaf adults in services for deaf children was particularly valued because the children's confidence rose through '[recognising themselves] in some of the adults around them' (p. 6).

These advantages of user involvement in service delivery can be extrapolated to other settings. People using mental health services based on user involvement may be more sensitive to and tolerant of other users who are experiencing distressing symptoms. The Clubhouse service model for mental health services is built on this principle. Self-help groups for survivors of abuse, people with alcohol problems and so on also work on this basis. There may be particular issues to be faced in facilitating user involvement in services for older people, however, which have yet to be articulated.

The presence of people who use, or have used, services in caring and leadership roles is not enough to guarantee a good service but their absence undermines the commitment to empowerment that is often set out in mission statements and public declarations. It also robs people who use services of valuable insights; it leaves them without role models and it prevents disabled adults from passing on their stories.

2   Listening to feedback

Approaches to consultation

At an individual level, users are more or less disempowered in their relationships with professionals unless shared decision making is actively embraced. Øvretveit (1996) produced a typology with particular reference to shared responsibility and decision making. He identifies four levels of user involvement in personal decision making:

- giving the person information about what has been decided
- consulting them (in the sense of seeking, but not being bound by their advice)
- jointly deciding (where either has a veto)
- giving responsibility for the service-users to decide or act themselves.

Often well-meaning attempts falter because it is unclear which level is actually in operation. Campbell and Lindow (1996, p. 22) stress the need to be 'honest about decision-making. Who will make the decision? Is anyone else being consulted?'

Lukes (1977) offers an analytical tool to explore different degrees or levels of power (see Box 2 overleaf).

This lack of clarity is also reflected at an organisational level when user influence is channelled through a range of ill-defined consultation exercises. These are structured in different ways and have more or fewer 'teeth' when it comes to biting hands that may sometimes also feed them. Residents' committees, user panels, customer surveys and suggestions boxes are all found in a range of services, backed up by statutory complaints procedures that are supposed to be well publicised and easily accessed. Consultation may take place at the planning and service-shaping stage or retrospectively in the form of customer feedback.

Box 2: Three levels of power applied to decision making

Using Lukes' ideas, power can be conceptualised in terms of:

(i) who is influencing the *decisions*

(ii) who is setting the *agenda*

(iii) what the underlying *biases* are within the social structure.

These ideas can be applied to examine how much power service-users wield over decisions about their own care. In Lukes' terms, service-users might be seen as having some power (at the first level), in terms of giving feedback or expressing preferences. Service-users have less power to decide on the type of care being offered (second level). At the third level, many service-users may not even see they have a role and right to comment in the first place and so they leave the decision making to the professionals involved.

A number of mechanisms have been devised to obtain this feedback, ranging from service-led initiatives for seeking the views of users to campaigns by user groups determined to offer their views whether or not they have been asked for (Peck and Barker, 1997). The London Boroughs Grants Committee (1997) identified a number of methods of actively seeking feedback from users, including the following.

1 Involving users on a management committee.
2 Inviting users to sit on forums or working parties that are looking to improve or develop particular parts of a service.
3 Establishing focus groups of users.
4 Encouraging a regular users' forum.
5 Initiating a users' conference.

Many service-providers opt for high profile public meetings in preference to ongoing involvement and consultation but, while commissioners often favour the concept of the public meeting as 'they are a good means of demonstrating publicly a commissioner's commitment to consultation' (Alcohol Concern, 1996, p. 7), there may be scepticism in that 'many appear to be called only when commissioners have something to "tell and sell"' (p. 7). A further limitation can be public meetings' inability to attract a representative audience:

> They can attract a very narrow section of service users, and experience suggests that they are the favourite of the vociferous, the articulate, and the axe-grinding 'dissidents', most of whom because of their confidence or zeal to bash the system also find other ways of making sure their views are known. Even so, public meetings can have their cathartic uses. Users can let off steam, and can feel all the more satisfied if commissioners are present to hear their opinions.
>
> (Alcohol Concern, 1996, p. 7)

To offset this, Campbell and Lindow (1996, p. 21) argue that it is necessary to 'place special emphasis on involving users/survivors from groups who experience discrimination within society' and they recommend giving priority to black and other minority ethnic service-users.

This commitment needs to rest on a critical approach to the issue of representativeness and its reverse face, 'tokenism'. At its simplest, tokenism can be seen in situations where individuals are asked to represent others without being supported to access user networks to feed into their participation. Where they do speak for other service-users their legitimacy may be challenged: when they speak for themselves their views may be discounted. Situations may be set up in such a way as to minimise their chances of being powerful. For example, users are often isolated on committees or boards, leading Campbell and Lindow (1996, p. 22) to advise:

> Never place one or two service users in a position of being greatly outnumbered by professional people. This can be an overwhelming situation.

But there is also genuine confusion about what role individuals can play and Beresford and Campbell (1994, p. 323) identify a conflict between:

> ... competing models and cultures of democracy. While movements of disabled people and other service users have placed an emphasis on a participatory model of democracy the service world is firmly located in a representative system of democracy and bases its efforts to involve service users on a representative model of democracy.

Users who represent the movement may not be 'representative' in the sense of being 'typical' – they may indeed be more forceful than other users. This may be used to challenge the legitimacy of their position in speaking for others where, for example, a forceful hospital consultant would not be so challenged. Beresford and Campbell (1994, p. 317) declare that users who do the representing rapidly turn into activists who challenge assumptions, commenting that:

> ... getting involved may not only lead to change, but also change *us*. We become different. We become 'unrepresentative' in ways some service providers do not want. We become confident, experienced, informed and effective.

User consultation is not a cheap option and funds need to be identified from the outset to support its implementation (Campbell and Lindow, 1996). Easily quantifiable costs include the training of participants, their expenses, room hire and refreshments, but it is also important to make an allowance for the administrative costs which might seem minimal to the agency but prove prohibitive for users. Beeforth (1993, p. 94) points out that:

> ... users are poor; they are usually on benefits; and they do not have access to typewriters, photocopiers, telephones, secretaries etc. The importance of the absence of these facilities is rarely appreciated by those who have grown accustomed to using them. It is amazing how

much users can achieve with a fraction of the resources available to
professionals.

Nor is user involvement a panacea. There are often tensions within these
movements as well as at the interface with services. For example, in the
disability movement gender and/or sexual orientation may be as salient as
(dis)ability in relation to some issues, and fractures may appear.
Shakespeare *et al.* (1996, p. 182) remark on this potential for contradictory
attitudes to inclusiveness:

> Within identity group politics, it has always to be remembered that there
> are minorities within minorities, that there are multiple oppressions,
> and that being progressive about one issue does not automatically mean
> being progressive about other issues.

Carers also have a right to be consulted but the potential for conflicts of
interest with those they are caring for puts them in an ambivalent position
and weakens their claims to advocate on behalf of their relatives. Brown
et al. (1996, p. 227) argue that:

> New service models framed in terms of choice for individuals who use
> the service neglect parents' [of disabled children and adults] secondary
> reliance on services to enable them to work or attend to other family
> relationships or activities. Because the service is never explicitly
> acknowledged as being for the parent as well as for their son or
> daughter, their voices are easily silenced: they can be characterized as
> neither unbiased advocates for their relatives nor legitimate complai-
> nants on their own behalf.

Despite this ambiguous position, relatives and carers' groups may embark
on a range of campaigning activities in their own right as well as
ostensibly on behalf of their relatives: activities span 'preventing,
improving, maintaining, extending, augmenting or replacing current
service provision' (Brown *et al.*, 1996, p. 235) (see Table 1).

Clearly, there is a distinction between running an organisation and
being asked to give your views on the services offered to you – the
difference between being a member of the board and a regular customer.
Winkler (1987, p. 1) remarks that consumer models tend to redefine
'structural problems as problems of communication' and that this:

> ... vision of customer relations extends to reducing the waits at the check-
> out counter and exchanging faulty goods with the minimum of questions
> asked. It does not extend, even at Marks and Spencers, to inviting
> customers on to the board, nor to consulting them about investment or
> even about what should be on the shelves, let alone in their products. The
> supermarket model certainly does not mean that retailers help customers
> sue manufacturers of products that have caused harm.

Barnes and Walker (1996) also point out the problems of relying on
individuals to act as 'consumers' when they may be 'mentally disabled,
frail or vulnerable' and when they are not in a 'position to shop around or

Table 1 Continuum of parent action

Aim in relation to existing service	Prevent	Improve	Maintain	Extend	Augment	Replace
Definition	Here the aim is to close a bad service or remove an individual member of staff. Examples include ward closure, exposing abuse, mismanagement or severe limitations in quality	In this case the aim is to change one aspect of the service without jeopardising other aspects. This will usually take the form of a complaint or campaign *against* a particular aspect of practice	Here the goal is to protect the service from threatened cut-backs or contraction – the concern is to maintain present availability and not allow standards to slip	Expanding the service and gaining access for additional service users adds up to a 'more of the same' approach wherein quantity and access to the service will be a more important issue than quality	Here the emphasis is to add on a new component to an existing service or programme meeting additional or specialised needs without removing the current core activities. In this case there will be a campaign *for* something new to be added to the service	In this mode parents will create an innovative service and be willing to let go of an existing service in order to create a new model over which they can exercise some control in the planning phase, possibly throughout imlementation and almost certainly in ongoing quality control
Example at an individual level	Challenging physical or sexual abuse of an individual through the courts	Complaining about lack of leisure activities in a group home for an individual with multiple [disabilities]	Refusing to allow an individual's day placement to be reduced from five days a week to three	Asking for respite care every fortnight rather than once a month	Campaigning for access to a generic mental health service for someone with a learning disability and an additional mental health problem	Using the care management process to plan an alternative day service for an individual with special needs to replace segregated provision with supported, community-based activities
Example at local group level	Closure of a ward, hostel or deregistration of a private home after ongoing abuse has been discovered	Campaigning for improved staffing ratios at the weekend so that residents of a group home are able to go out and participate in household activities	Lobbying councillors to prevent charges for day services currently provided free of charge and to prevent reduction in the service county-wide	Campaigning for more group homes so that people currently living with their families do not have a worse service than people moving out of hospital	Campaigning for speech therapy services in an area to meet the needs of children assessed under the Education Act 1981	Designing and setting up a parent-led supported employment service which enables people with learning disabilities to come off benefits
Example at national or policy level	Campaigning to stop institutional provision	Redirection of resources to improve quality of residential environments	Public campaign to oppose cuts in services	Campaign to increase national availability of day places	Use of legislation and legal precedents to establish rights to speech therapy for all children under the Education Act 1981	National policy framework to establish innovative services for people with challenging behaviours

(Source: Brown *et al.*, 1996, pp. 236–7)

have any realistic prospect of exit' (p. 379). Carpenter (1994, pp. 90–1) takes a pessimistic view, arguing that:

> The new public management also has no strategy for tackling the social causes of disadvantage because it largely takes for granted the wider social context of inequality in which public services operate ... it has no realistic strategy for dealing with the fact that inequalities of class, gender, 'race', disability and age constrain the ability of people to act as informed and assertive 'consumers'.

Instead, Winkler (1987, p. 2) argues that 'the key to any serious concept of consumerism is the principle of outside scrutiny' and she proposes four models: Community Health Councils (and their equivalents in Scotland and Northern Ireland); strengthening of democratic accountability; user power (as opposed to consultation); and partnership between providers and users. She argues that the latter could only be achieved if structural change underpinned emerging partnerships by making the relationships between users and practitioners more equal.

Learning from complaints

Another avenue for user feedback is through informal and formal complaints but, as we have seen, users may not be in a position to complain like shoppers can. Brown *et al.* (1996) argue that it is critical to take into account people's dependence on services and unwillingness to 'rock the boat' if, by openly challenging services, they risked losing needed assistance. They argue that people often tolerate the mediocre where the penalty might be to lose a service altogether and they will often only seek radical alternatives if the current service drops way below an acceptable level.

Inequalities form a pervasive backdrop to the operation of both informal and formal (statutory) complaints systems. A naïve view of complaints procedures might assume that a lack of complaints means all is well. This needs to be challenged by urging service agencies to create a context within which it is possible to complain. A service with no complaints is not necessarily a good service – merely one in which users feel unable to voice their concerns. Conversely, a service where people do complain is not necessarily a bad one. It may simply indicate that people feel free to assert themselves. See Box 3.

People may not complain about a service if their views have been consistently suppressed within it. Services that fail to make space for users to comment on what is on offer and to shape the design of future services are more likely to make users complain than to generate complaints.

Box 3: Making complaints and levels of power

Wood (1995) used Lukes' analysis of different levels of power as a framework to describe different patterns of complaint making and resolution in mental health services. She distinguished between services in which there were:

- many complaints but few were upheld (in Lukes' model this is one-dimensional power), in that 'one side has more resources – in this case credibility – and this enables them to prevail at times of conflict

- few complaints (in Lukes' model, two-dimensional power) where power is used to create barriers to complaining, which prevent complaints being made rather than dismissing them once they have surfaced

- no complaints (in Lukes' model, three-dimensional power) which prevents people 'from having grievances by shaping their perceptions, cognitions and preferences in such a way as they accept their role in the existing order of things'.

(Source: Lukes, 1982, quoted in Wood, 1995, p. 11)

So how does a service set out to help service-users complain? A number of Health Trusts provide patient advocates who operate across and outside traditional line management structures to facilitate complaints and to help resolve them at an early stage (NAHAT, 1996). This can be a difficult 'go-between' role to manage, as it involves maintaining a distance from one's professional colleagues. Often the role involves remedying mis-understandings and re-establishing communication (especially where insufficient allowance has been made for the distressed state of patients and relatives) but it can also involve troubleshooting between professions and bolstering the status of knowledge held by people 'lower down' in the organisation. Sometimes the role extends to enabling patients to make formal complaints or seek legal redress but often complaints can be resolved at an earlier stage through counselling and mediation. Some might argue that this neutralises legitimate anger and softens any challenges brought to the traditional structures and practices of profes-sional power. Others would accept that the presence of an advocate may facilitate the acceptance of feedback, since informal complaints are less likely to be dealt with in defensive mode.

Resolving complaints is a role that highlights the conflicts of interest that can arise for practitioners working outside their usual roles or in a different relationship from their usual hierarchies. Williamson (1992) argues that professionals who move into advocacy roles may find themselves in the same position as "male feminists" in that they advocate for the rights of patients against the interests of their own professional colleagues. Others, working for user-led organisations or as employees of individual service-users, may also feel divided loyalties or feel that the user-led agenda is being used against less powerful sections of the workforce. Carpenter (1994, p. 87) argues that some of these structures:

> ... attempt to drive a wedge between workers and managers of services and place the latter in a pact with consumers.

Direct care workers often bear the brunt of criticism of public services despite their relative powerlessness within them. This pincer movement is central to the issues with which this chapter is concerned. While users experience direct care workers as powerful in relation to them, workers often experience themselves as powerless in relation to their work, their managers and their working conditions. Carpenter (1994, p. 89) calls this 'a "zero sum" notion of power':

> ... in which power is exercised by providers at the expense of users, unless the reverse is made to happen. The possibility that both providers and users might be jointly empowered is not entertained ...

except in this chapter!

3   Redesigning services to take users into account

Inclusive organisational cultures

Empowering services require more flexible organisational cultures, roles and structures. Barnes and Walker (1996, p. 379) contrast bureaucratic with empowering organisational cultures, which they see as two ends of a continuum:

Bureaucratic	Empowering
Service-provider orientated	User orientated
Inflexible	Responsive
Provider-led	Needs-led
Power concentrated	Power sharing
Defensive	Open to review
Conservative	Open to change
Input orientated	Outcome orientated

In the study of services for deaf people referred to earlier, the researchers homed in on the mismatch between the low occupational status of deaf workers and the high intrinsic value they brought to service delivery. They characterised this as trying to 'fit a square peg into a round hole, where the round hole would not change shape' (Young *et al.*, 1998, p. 9). Hearing staff voiced concern about exploiting their deaf colleagues whose job descriptions usually failed to describe their jobs accurately. Should they ask them to do more than they were being paid for? Should they invite them to management meetings when others at their grade would not be expected to attend? How could they be promoted when they had come in to the work through an untraditional route with skills that were not recognised or accredited?

Few deaf people hold related professional qualifications often because of educational barriers so, in these settings, they had been 'slotted in to' ready-made posts which hearing people used to occupy, for example posts as nursing auxiliaries or teaching assistants. Roles such as these are usually low status, unqualified and unskilled roles which do not recognise unique contributions such as those brought by deaf workers. Then, because in these services the deaf workers were mostly slotted in to these low status posts, there were few opportunities for them to access training or contribute to decision making. Young *et al.* (1998, pp. 6–7) argue that this low status/high value tension 'disrupts' the normal expectation that qualifications, skills and experience would be brought together in individual practitioners. The presence of unqualified deaf people:

> ... provoked uncomfortable questions for both deaf and hearing people. People questioned the value of professional qualifications if those without them nonetheless had fundamental skills that enabled them to do the job ... if deaf staff's contribution was really so important ... why were the majority of them the ones who did the most menial jobs?

The researchers located both the problems and the potential solutions at a structural, rather than an interpersonal, level. They advocated breaking down traditional roles and placing emphasis more on competence than qualification. They suggested allowing deaf workers the opportunity to acquire more formal skills such as counselling and requiring professionally qualified staff to acquire more deaf-orientated skills (for example, by becoming proficient in signing). They conclude that:

> A situation is created in which individual professionals, be they deaf or hearing, are unlikely to possess all the pieces of the jigsaw that would allow them to do their job: professional qualifications, deaf centred skills and experience. Rather, these three elements are distributed *between* deaf and hearing staff – each making a vital contribution.
>
> (Young et al., 1998, p. 30)

There are parallels here with the disadvantaging of black staff within services, which in turn militates against black service-users receiving appropriate and valuing services. Where black staff *are* employed it is also often in low-level jobs where they cannot input their lived experience of racism or their own specific cultural identity to important decisions being made about individual service-users or about the appropriateness of service provision.

Women, similarly, are also often clustered at the bottom of hierarchies and trapped in menial roles within service settings. Their lack of influence may lead to the oversight of practical difficulties, such as the problems of travelling with young children at certain times of the day, or to the downplaying of whole areas of health or social care, like treatment for infertility or varicose veins. The failure to value lived experience works against the full employment of staff whose lives echo the difficulties that have brought users into contact with services. This, in turn, sends an ambivalent signal to service-users about just how valued they are.

Developing organisational structures that facilitate user involvement

When it comes to running services, users can be found on a continuum from complete control and governance of their own autonomous organisations through to more marginal forms of consultation and influence. Services working within the social model aim to place users firmly in control of their own service but also to embed user involvement in the structure of service agencies and their governance.

The structure of these organisations says far more than the rhetoric when it comes to user involvement. Service-providers have to attend to several functions and networks. They need to ensure clear lines of accountability and governance, whether through traditional line management structures or through management/trustee committees. For example, the Spinal Injuries Association have embedded user control within their constitution to ensure that spinally injured people have the major voice in running their affairs – as much as 75% of its management committee has to be spinally injured and elected by the membership. Users in other organisations might find themselves marginalised within more traditional hierarchies or clumsy federal arrangements. Disabled people are not well represented on the governing bodies of agencies serving them and the proportion of disabled people is usually outweighed by non-disabled 'experts' (Brown *et al.*, 1999).

The underlying thinking behind structures such as the Clubhouse services described in Box 4 is to ensure that all the day-to-day tasks, such as providing lunch and administering the transitional employment programme, become opportunities for co-working.

Other organisations *of* (as opposed to *for*) disabled people function as independent agencies – they may provide services and information to their members (as descendants of the 'self-help' movement, which pioneered user-led agendas and service provision) and/or contract with the statutory sector to provide services to clients of health and social care services. This is an important distinction and some commentators have suggested that, by becoming service-providers, the voluntary sector has lost some of its independence when it comes to campaigning or challenging statutory services. The community care reforms in the early 1990s promoted the idea that statutory services should spend a larger proportion of their total social care budget in the independent sector. This led to a fundamental shift within voluntary organisations which had to equip themselves to provide specific services to local authorities rather than be funded in such a way that they could remain as independent campaigners on behalf of service-users.

Box 4: Clubhouse services – a model for mental health user involvement

Clubhouse services provide a model for mental health services, which has been explicitly designed to support user involvement. Clubhouse services are for people with enduring mental health problems and work without a hierarchy between users (referred to as 'members') and staff. This approach is designed into the service at each layer of the organisation. Internally, members sit on staff interview panels and are involved in staff supervision; *all* meetings are open to members and staff; and all the space is equally accessible under an 'open doors' policy. Clubhouse services belong to a federation which sets out standards designed to guarantee this high level of user involvement by stipulating how such a service can work. Articles displayed by a Clubhouse service in Maidstone, for example, say:

Clubhouse staff are sufficient to engage the membership yet small enough in number to make carrying out their responsibilities impossible without member involvement.

And:

Members have the opportunity to participate in all the work of the Clubhouse, including the administration, research, intake and orientation, reach out, hiring, training and evaluation of staff, public relations, advocacy and evaluation of Clubhouse effectiveness.

Black voluntary organisations have been particularly affected by this shift, as they were often smaller and more local than the large charities that have moved wholesale into a service-provider role. SIA (a different organisation from the Spinal Injuries Association) is a National Development Agency for the black voluntary sector that aims to build an infrastructure to support black-managed groups and agencies in this context. SIA has called for a separate 'compact' between the government and the black voluntary sector acknowledging 'racial discrimination and oppression and the way it systematically excludes and curtails the participation of Black communities from everyday life' (SIA, 1998).

We have seen that disabled people's organisations and other service-user movements have challenged professionals to operate within limits and to make their expertise available within more equal relationships. They are not asking professionals to give up their knowledge but to give up the control that went with it and to operate alongside people whose lived experience feeds into a broader analysis. Barnes and Walker (1996, p. 380) argue that:

... professionals should cease to exercise dominant power over users. Instead, authority deriving from professional knowledge [should be] balanced by authority deriving from the experiential knowledge of the user who is able to exercise greater self-determination in decisions concerning their care.

'Direct payments' enable disabled people to manage their own care and dismantle many of the 'givens' in the user–worker relationship. New types of direct health care work or personal assistance place individual workers in a very different hierarchical relationship from their 'user–employer'. The relationship has been redefined as 'working *for*' and this provides another very fundamental challenge to professional identities and ways of working. Service-users in these schemes employ their assistants directly, manage the worker directly, and cut across existing career paths and employment patterns. There are some problems in that bulk provision is cheaper and more reliable, workers may miss out on opportunities for support or training, some service-users are at risk of exploitation, and some groups may miss out on their entitlements but, nevertheless, many users prefer cash to services:

> ... the arguments in favour of cash are that people are placed in control and the money is symbolic of this control.
>
> (Doyle, 1995, p. 43)

Black service-users in one study were shown to be more in favour of direct payments than their white counterparts (Doyle, 1995), perhaps reflecting their greater disempowerment in relation to traditional service-providers.

Conclusion

In this chapter we have seen how user and carer movements have challenged professional practice at several levels. Disabled people and other user groups have theorised their position in broader social terms and have challenged both the rationales for the service models on offer and the way these are delivered. They have argued for different kinds of input to and from service agencies – involvement which allows them to control practical assistance in their own lives while contributing to wider societal changes. Within services, they have moved into management roles in their own organisations and have taken on the role of arranging their own care as individuals and collectives. In larger, more traditional service organisations, users are routinely consulted and complaints are encouraged and actively facilitated. This has necessitated new skills for professionals as well as new organisational structures.

This is not to say that disabled people and other user groups have stopped wanting and needing 'professional' health and social care but rather that they want to access it, shape it, monitor it and evaluate it for themselves and on their own terms. User-focused services rely on open channels for feedback, complaints and accountability. This is a fundamental challenge to professional structures, which in turn has produced a significant shift in the division of labour. It has grown out of, and now rests on, a broader knowledge base – one that integrates specific 'professional' expertise with the resources and resilience that grow out of lived experience.

Acknowledgement

We are grateful to Clare Croft-White, independent consultant to the voluntary sector, for contributing references and ideas to this chapter.

References

Alcohol Concern (1996) *Consulting People Who Use Alcohol Services*, London, Alcohol Concern.

Barnes, M. and Walker, A. (1996) 'Consumerism vs. empowerment: a principled approach to the involvement of older service users', *Policy and Politics*, Vol. 24, No. 4, pp. 375–93.

Beeforth, M. (1993) 'What does it mean to have user participation in planning?', in Leiper, R. and Field, V. (eds) *Counting for Something in Mental Health Services: Effective User Feedback*, pp. 89–95, Aldershot, Avebury.

Beresford, P. and Campbell, J. (1994) 'Disabled people, service users, user involvement and representation', *Disability and Society*, Vol. 9, No. 3, pp. 315–25.

Bibbings, A. (1994) 'Carers and professionals – the carer's viewpoint', in Leathard, A. (ed.) *Going Interprofessional: Working Together for Health and Social Welfare*, pp. 158–71, London, Routledge.

Brown, H., Orlowska, D. and Mansell, J. (1996) 'From campaigning to complaining', in Mansell, J. and Ericsson, K. (1996) *Deinstitutionalization and Community Living: Intellectual Disability Services in Britain, Scandinavia and the USA*, pp. 225–78, London, Chapman & Hall.

Brown, H., Croft-White, C., Stein, J. and Wilson, C. (1999) *Taking the Initiative: Supporting the Sexual Rights of Disabled People: A Service Agenda*, Brighton, Rowntree/Pavilion Publishing (in press).

Campbell, P. and Lindow, V. (1996) *Changing Practice: Mental Health Nursing and User Empowerment*, London, RCN with Broadmoor Patients Council.

Carpenter, M. (1994) *Normality is Hard Work: Trade Unions and the Politics of Community Care*, London, Lawrence & Wishart/Unison.

Doyle, Y. (1995) 'Disability: use of an independent living fund in south east London and users' views about the system of cash versus care provision', *Journal of Epidemiology and Community Health*, Vol. 49, pp. 43–7.

Gillepsie-Sells, K., Hill, M. and Robbins, B. (1998) *She Dances to Different Drums: Research into Disabled Women's Sexuality*, London, King's Fund.

Glazer, N. (1990) 'The home as workshop: women as amateur nurses and medical care providers', *Gender and Society*, Vol. 4, pp. 479–500.

Goodley, D. (1997) 'Locating self-advocacy in models of disability: understanding disability in the support of self-advocates with learning difficulties', *Disability and Society*, Vol. 12, No. 3, June.

Hogan, A. (1997) 'Issues impacting on the governance of deafened adults', *Disability and Society*, Vol. 12, No. 5, pp. 789–803.

Lindow, V. and Rooke-Matthers, S. (1998) 'The experiences of mental health service users as mental health professionals', *Findings Series*, April, Rowntree.

London Boroughs Grants Committee (1997) *A Guide to User Feedback Methods*, London, LBGC.

Lukes, S. (1977) *Power: A Radical View*, London, Macmillan.

Meyer, J. (1993) 'Lay participation in care: a challenge for multidisciplinary teamwork', *Journal of Interprofessional Care*, Vol. 7, No. 1, pp. 57–66.

NAHAT (National Association of Health Authorities and Trusts) (1996) *Complaints: Listening, Acting, Improving. Guidance on Implementation of NHS Complaints Procedures*, Leeds, Department of Health.

Oliver, M. (1990) *The Politics of Disablement*, London, Macmillan.

Øvretveit, J. (1996) 'How patient power and client participation affects relations between professions', in Øvretveit, J., Mathias, P. and Thompson, T. (eds) *Interprofessional Working for Health and Social Care*, London, Macmillan.

Peck, E. and Barker, I. (1997) 'Users as partners in mental health – ten years of experience', *Journal of Interprofessional Care*, Vol. 11, No. 3, pp. 269–77.

Shakespeare, T., Gillespie-Sells, K. and Davies, D. (1996) *The Sexual Politics of Disability: Untold Desires*, London, Cassell.

SIA (1998) *Newsletter*, No. 29, July.

Williamson, C. (1992) *Whose Standards? Consumer and Professional Standards in Health Care*, Buckingham, Open University Press.

Winkler, F. (1987) 'Consumerism in health care: beyond the supermarket model', *Policy and Politics*, Vol. 15, pp. 1–8.

Wood, D. (1995) *Complaint Procedures in Mental Health Services*, Tizard Centre, University of Kent, Canterbury, SETRHA.

Young, A., Ackerman, J. and Kyle, J. (1998) *Looking On: Deaf People and the Organisation of Services*, Bristol, The Policy Press.

Chapter 6
The challenge of values and ethics in practice

Maureen Eby

Ethics is a boat adrift at sea being blown in various directions by winds from different philosophical directions but without sight of a secure harbour in which to seek refuge.

Introduction

Living and working in today's complex society raises all sorts of questions about the rights or wrongs of decisions and actions that confront us on a daily basis. Just listening to the news will stir a mixture of feelings ranging from amazement and disbelief to uncertainty and doubt. The individual is left thinking was that the right decision? Or could a better choice have been made? These questions and more are asked not only about the larger issues such as abortion, consent, euthanasia, or resource allocation but also each day by individuals of themselves. Did I do the right thing? Should I have looked the other way? Was I wrong? Was there another way of looking at this? These are the sorts of questions that lead to the process of critical practice.

Often these questions remain unanswered because there is not enough time to think through the consequences of actions or because life is too short to ruminate over past decisions. But these unanswered questions do leave a legacy that lingers within the individual and keeps on surfacing with each new difficult encounter or decision. Living with this tension is hard for anyone who is trying to exercise responsibility creatively and with integrity. The challenge to all individuals within health and social care is to find ways of ensuring that ideas and aspirations are not totally lost whilst being utterly realistic about the constraints that exist in any organisational, and indeed personal, context.

The aim of this chapter is to reflect on how individuals can creatively juggle and balance the constraints and opportunities found within today's health and social care practice for the benefit of those concerned – the individual, the patient/client and the organisation. But herein lies the conflict for what is desirable for the individual may not be for the patient/client, for the organisation or for the other employees. All of them have a perspective which adds to the debate and understanding of everyday decisions but these multiple perspectives can at times feel quite conflicting. Yet working with these multiple perspectives can also lead to exciting and new ways of thinking which is inherent within the process of critical practice.

This chapter, through focusing on some common approaches to the understanding of ethics, will enable practitioners to recognise these alternative perspectives when faced with the unanswered questions or concerns of everyday practice, thus enabling the creation of new and potentially helpful options within the decision-making process.

1   Values and ethics

Through the use of self-awareness and reflection, personal beliefs and ideas arise that can have a direct impact on decision making. It is recognising the anchors of personal belief systems that helps to free an individual from the constraints of dogma and ideology. Identifying personal values through reflection is the first step in understanding why in some situations or decisions the individual can feel uneasy.

Values

Values are in essence a set of beliefs, ideas and assumptions that both individuals and groups hold about themselves and the society they live in. Values are a part of the culture and societal norms that guide people's daily lives, but values can also be formed that do not conform with these societal norms. For example, loyalty (fidelity) to one's family is an important value which maintains the social cohesion of society; however, loyalty to one's family to the point that an individual would lie about a family member to protect that person from imprisonment for murder is not in the best interest of society.

Everyone holds their own personal set of values, just as their families, friends and neighbours do. As values are personal to the individual, sometimes they may never be articulated or shared. People may also belong to different social groupings, such as work, leisure or religious, which generally also share a common set of values that may or may not separate that grouping from others. Values when not made explicit can be deduced from behaviour, but people may also claim to hold a set of values which is not evident by their behaviour, such as a person who believes in the sanctity of confidentiality yet breaks any confidence at the first opportunity.

Competing values

People generally have a set of values, which may have an overarching loose framework holding them together, such as religious or patriotic beliefs. However, one value may conflict or compete with another value thus creating a sense of dissonance within that individual as shown in the scenario in Box 1.

Box 1: John

John, a 54-year-old lorry driver, has recently been admitted to hospital suffering acute pain in his left leg and is awaiting amputation due to insufficient blood supply caused partly by his smoking. Medication only dulls the pain and, in an attempt to feel relaxed, he insists on smoking despite him being on oxygen and the patient in the next bed recovering from an acute asthmatic attack.

John wants to smoke to help him relax from the unrelenting pain in his left leg (the value of self-determination or autonomy), yet he is aware that the person in the next bed is recovering from an acute asthma attack (upholding the value of non-maleficence – to do no harm) and that in the presence of oxygen a fire could start (again the value of non-maleficence). These two values, autonomy and non-maleficence, are competing with each other. Exercising an individual's right to autonomy – John's right to smoke – can in fact harm those near to him. Autonomy and non-maleficence are discussed further in Section 2.

When a person is faced with two or more competing values, such as John who is faced with his own autonomy versus not harming others, a sense or feeling of disharmony or dissonance can occur as the individual decides which value will override the other. But it becomes more complex when other sets of values are imposed within a given situation as described in the scenario in Box 2.

Box 2: Rebecca

Rebecca, a social worker, has recently been approached by her line manager to head-up a new project focusing on the issue of teenage pregnancy. Acceptance of the offer would mean promotion but Rebecca knows she will need to pursue strategies in her work that she would find difficult to accept. As a Catholic, she firmly believes that the use of contraceptives is against God's will, yet she is asked to work with these young women and implement and subsequently evaluate a strategy for this project, which includes an educational programme on contraception that has been agreed by her local authority's Social Services Committee.

Rebecca's personal belief system values the observance of God and the sanctity of life, yet professionally social work values are directed at encouraging the client's personal autonomy and self-determination (upholding the value of freedom) (Banks, 1995). As a social worker, Rebecca accepts a need to be non-judgemental (the value of respecting others) while her employer, the local authority, needs to ensure that local monies are targeted to meet the needs of vulnerable groups within their authority (justice) and that this funded programme's evaluation provides value for money (effectiveness and efficiency).

On a personal level, Rebecca is struggling with her personal beliefs, which stand to be compromised by aspects of this project, and her own self-worth. On a personal/professional level, Rebecca's personal belief in the sanctity of life is in direct conflict with her professional value of respecting others in this particular project for, despite believing that contraception is denying the sanctity of life, her client group, teenage women, are being educated to use this method to reduce the number of teenage pregnancies. On a personal/employer level, the tension between Rebecca's beliefs and those of her employer, who wants to provide an efficient and economical means of reducing teenage pregnancies, is also creating conflict. So for Rebecca there are three levels of conflicting values operating: the values of the individual, the profession and the organisation. How does the individual separate out and prioritise these competing values? Developing an understanding of ethics will help in dealing with these issues.

Ethics: the study of morals

Morals are 'the actual standards of behaviour or conduct held by individuals or groups' (Eby, 1994a, p. 22). Ethics, on the other hand, is that branch of philosophy concerned with the systematic study of human values and the principles and methods for distinguishing right from wrong and good from bad. Ethics is 'thinking and reasoning about morality' (Rowson, 1990, p. 3). But ethics is also about being human and living in today's world, as Verena Tschudin, a nurse ethicist, describes:

> Ethics is not only for philosophers. Ethics is something which is done every day. It is not only about long words and dilemmas, but ethics is first and foremost about people: people with different views, values and experiences. It is not a question of who's right and who's wrong, but of how you can know what you believe is valuable, and stand by that value, and respect other people's values. It is about understanding how your feelings and society's norms relate to each other, and how you decide for yourself and others.
>
> (Tschudin and Marks-Maran, 1993, p. 3)

Ethical problems: distress or dilemmas

How do ethics and values interact? When two or more values or moral principles are present within a situation, and they are not creating any problems or conflicts for the people involved, then an ethical issue has arisen. However, when these values or moral principles are in conflict, which poses a challenge about what to do, then an ethical problem has occurred (Purtilo, 1993). For instance, if John in the example in Box 1 wanted to have a shot of whisky instead of a cigarette, the value of autonomy would not be in conflict with the value of non-maleficence for, unlike a cigarette, one shot of whisky does not pose a health risk to the other patients or staff within the ward. This is an example of an ethical issue. However, if John did light his cigarette while still receiving oxygen then an ethical problem has occurred because these two values, autonomy and non-maleficence, are now creating a conflict for the other patients and staff due to the very high risk of explosion and fire.

Two forms of ethical problems are ethical distress and ethical dilemmas. Ethical distress occurs when barriers prevent a course of action perceived as right by the individual from happening (Purtilo, 1993). In Rebecca's situation, her personal values would favour her arguing for a programme of support for teenage women who became mothers rather than one on contraception; yet this course of action is stymied through her employer's (the local authority) decision to implement a preventative programme of sex education for young women within the project that has been approved. This situation is likely to produce ethical distress for Rebecca if she accepted the promotion to head the funded project.

An ethical dilemma occurs either when there is a choice between two courses of action that are both morally right but only one choice can be made (Purtilo, 1993) or when either course of action, if chosen, would lead to the compromise of values or principles (Beauchamp and Childress, 1994). Rebecca is facing two choices. She can accept the promotion and implement the agreed project that includes an educational programme on contraception; or she can turn down the promotion and seek support for her idea of helping teenage mothers and their new-born babies through alternative sources of funding such as local charities. Both courses of action would affect teenage pregnancies: one would reduce the number of teenage pregnancies; the other would provide support to help young mothers continue to study and develop work skills. The ethical dilemma for Rebecca is which course of action to take. However, both courses also entail a compromise of values. If Rebecca accepts the promotion then her personal belief that contraception is against God's will would be compromised. Yet if she makes the alternative choice, the professional values of promoting client autonomy and self-determination will be compromised.

Ethical dilemmas can occur between competing personal and professional values as well as between personal and organisational values. On a personal level, the value of autonomy or individual freedom can often conflict with the value of non-maleficence (to do no harm). This is usually seen as a conflict over personal lifestyles such as between one's beliefs and behaviours over smoking or drinking alcohol, but dilemmas can also occur between other values such as veracity (truth telling) and non-maleficence. For example, if you are aware your friend is going out with someone you know is married, do you tell her, realising that it might cause her great pain, or do you not tell her and risk losing the friendship if she finds out later that you knew? This conflict between veracity and non-maleficence can also occur at a professional or an occupational level. For example, a homeless man has come to the Accident and Emergency Department because it is cold and wet outside. Both the doctor and the nurse, not wanting to cause further harm by sending him outside again, admit the 'patient' for observation of his blood pressure, ensuring that he will have at least one warm, dry night with a hot meal before he is discharged.

At an organisational level, individuals may have to decide between upholding their professional code or risk losing their job or, in the case of many health professionals, their registration to practise in situations where the organisation has compromised on quality and service due to financial constraints. What about the people who worked with the social worker in Hackney who later died of AIDS who had concerns about his activities with the children in his care (Hunt, 1998); or colleagues of the nurse suspended because of his concerns over poor staffing levels on the ward that was compromising patient care (Pilgrim, 1995)? It is this sense of unease or tension that is experienced with conflicting values that very often drives the person to seek out answers (Eby, 1994b).

The study of ethics entails more than just identifying what is right and/ or wrong about a situation or behaviour. Ethics is also about developing skills – the cognitive skills of reasoning, reflection, analysis and logic. These are not skills that individuals working in health and social care have necessarily had in their basic or initial education or training but they are essential to individual development and add considerable meaning to the critical practice of health and social care.

Health and social care practitioners intervene in other people's lives and this creates power. But how should this power be exercised? In everyday practice, people are enacting values, making decisions and encountering situations with an ethical dimension. Becoming more aware of ethical and value choices will enable the health and social care practitioner to have critical distance – space to embrace or change ways of thinking or acting. Remember:

> Ethics is not only about giving the right *answer*, but also about seeking the right question, and seeking to understand what a person's world and meaning is [about].
>
> (Tschudin and Marks-Maran, 1993, p. 17)

2   Approaches to understanding ethics

People often become perplexed about the sheer complexity and diversity of thought in the field of ethics, as so aptly described in the following metaphor:

> ... ethics is a boat adrift at sea being blown in various directions by winds from different philosophical directions, but without sight of a secure harbour in which to seek refuge. There are just too many disconnected moral vocabularies in modern use.
>
> (Warren, 1993, p. 188)

Ethics can be approached in a variety of ways, from the principle-based approach often found in health care ethics (Edge and Groves, 1994), or the theory-based approach such as deontology or utilitarianism found in most philosophy texts on ethics (Frankena, 1973), to the practical approach such as Seedhouse's ethical grid (Seedhouse and Lovett, 1992) or Niebuhr's response ethics (Niebuhr, 1963 in Tschudin, 1994) found in the many 'how to' books on ethics. Six of the most common of these approaches to the understanding of ethical issues are described in this section. This is by no means meant to be a definitive discussion of these approaches but rather a synopsis that will enable you to engage in the many differing debates that surround the ethical issues in everyday practice. Table 1 (overleaf) summarises these approaches.

Table 1   **Six approaches to understanding ethics**

Approach	*Major assumptions*	*Critique of assumptions*
Principles approach	• Easy to understand as it is based on simple words or statements, e.g. the right to life, or justice, truth telling • Even though it is based on logic, it still incorporates the emotive aspects • Flexible and adaptable approach which applies universally to all groups • Can resolve a variety of conflicts	• Too simplistic for modern life • Difficult to question due to historical precedent • Narrowing life's conflicts into four or five principles is too rigid
Virtues approach	• Attempts to create a good or virtuous person • There can be both a virtuous act and a virtuous person • Stresses moderation in both feelings and actions • Encourages freedom within the virtuous individual to know and do the right thing	• Assumes that virtues are naturally inherent in all human beings • Who decides what constitutes a virtue? Is happiness a virtue? • Does not provide a specific direction in ethical decision making • Relies too heavily on the past and traditional practice
Duties approach	• Goodwill is the most important human attribute, followed by reason • There are absolute moral rules that are established through reason that are obeyed out of a sense of duty in order to be a moral person • Individuals are never used as a means to another's ends • Right act will always be guided by moral duties, responsibilities and rights	• Too rigid for real life and very difficult to just derive morality from reason as pain and pleasure also make up our sense of right and wrong • Fails to take account that the consequences of an action can have disastrous results • Duties can clash – duty to your family, your employer, your profession • A sense of duty tends to lead to a blind acceptance of and obedience to authority • There are no exceptions to the rules
Consequences approach	• Apparently a simple and clear doctrine to understand and use in practice • The concept of happiness is far easier to grasp than that of natural rights or duties	• Difficult to know what all of the consequences of an action will be • How do you measure happiness and how do you compare the happiness of one with that of another?

Approach	Major assumptions	Critique of assumptions
	• Maximising happiness offers a decisive and accurate procedure for decision making • Very attractive as a method of public decision making • Achieving the end does justify the means necessary	• Individuals value other concepts besides happiness, such as justice and equality • Confuses morality with expediency since the good of one person can be sacrificed for the good of many • Does not take into account motive when weighing up the consequences of an individual's actions
Emotive approach	• In making moral judgements the individual is expressing without stating or declaring their feelings and attitudes • Reason is and ought only to be the slave of passions • All moral statements attempt to persuade others to share one's own attitudes about the rightness or wrongness of certain acts • Care must be taken of the emotive meanings of ethical terms used and individuals need to distinguish their evaluative function from their descriptive function	• Stating something is good or bad does not always mean the individual is stating their own opinion or attitude • There is more to life than just right and wrong • Excludes rationality from moral arguments • Fails to distinguish serious moral arguments from irrational or non-rational propaganda
Feminist approach	• Ethics of care offers a new and vital direction of enquiry • Stresses that everyone is vulnerable to oppression and abandonment • Challenges traditional approach's denial of women's moral agency and the devaluation of women's experiences • Refuses to dominate or to be dominated • Ethics ceases to be an instrument of restraint and constraint, instead it empowers women with meaning	• Justice and care are not different approaches but are complementary, equally necessary components of morality • Glorifying care as normative for women only worsens the position of women • Caring can be abusive • Has yet to develop a substantial moral theory • Women are not morally perfect creatures • Seems to assert feminist values as superior to masculine values

Principles approach

Probably the most often described approach to understanding ethics in textbooks is the principles approach. Principles are general guides that have become so fundamental in everyday thinking that they are no longer questioned (Beauchamp and Childress, 1994). For example, the principle of retribution established in the phrase 'an eye for an eye or a tooth for a tooth' originated from the Code of Hammurabi in 2100 BC, which stated 'If a man destroy the eye of another man, they shall destroy his eye' (Infopedia, 1995, p. 1).

A variety of principles can be found in ethics textbooks but fundamental to health care ethics there are four basic principles: respect for autonomy, beneficence or doing good, non-maleficence or avoiding harm, and justice (Beauchamp and Childress, 1994). These four principles, described in further detail in Box 3, form the foundation of ethical practice and conduct which underpins professional workers' decision making. Principles help to determine the right course of action within any situation.

Box 3: Principles of health care ethics

Respect for autonomy – asserts the basic right of individuals to participate in and make decisions about and for themselves. Three basic elements are incorporated within this principle: the ability to decide, the power to act upon choices and decision, and respect for the individual autonomy of others.

Beneficence – asserts the duty of practitioners to seek the good for patients under all circumstances.

Non-maleficence – asserts the duty to avoid or prevent harm to individuals. If the practitioner cannot do good for the patient then at least the practitioner should not harm the patient.

Justice – asserts that it is not enough to do good and avoid bad but that some effort must be made to distribute the good and bad resulting from action which is distributed equally or according to need, effort, contribution, merit, ability or decided by some other means.

(Source: based on Edge and Groves, 1994, pp. 28–29, 36–37, 39–40)

These principles can be seen in the case of John in Section 1. The principles approach is widely used because it is based on such simple truths. However, basing ethical decisions on these four principles can seem simplistic at times for today's complex world. Not every situation can be reduced to just these four principles. For example, in predictive testing when some of the individuals concerned do not know that a relative has been genetically screened as positive for developing bowel cancer, especially if these family members are no longer in contact; or xenografting where the use of animals to provide organs and tissue for transplantation means the death of that animal.

Virtues approach

The virtues approach is based on the idea that if the virtues of people are encouraged then there would be no need for problem-solving methods for moral dilemmas since each and every individual would be acting from the goodness of their heart. Greek philosophers talked about the cardinal virtues of wisdom, courage, temperance and justice. Virtues not only move the individual into right action but also specify what that right action ought to be (Pellegrino and Thomasma, 1993). However, virtue ethics has been criticised for relying too heavily on past and traditional practices rather than on reason which can thwart creative solutions or personal autonomy (Edge and Groves, 1994). Virtue ethics has also been criticised for generally not providing a specific direction in ethical decision making: the fact that the virtuous person will know the right action does not always hold true, especially when competing external factors are at play.

Truth telling or veracity is a virtue that is enshrined in most professional codes. Is it always ethically right to tell the patient or client the truth even though the truth might cause pain or further suffering? Is there ever any justification in withholding the truth from the patient or client? One line of argument is that it is sometimes in the patient's best interest for the truth to be withheld. This is seen as a paternalistic attitude which relies on the ethical concept of beneficence or doing good. But what about the patient or client's own sense of autonomy and respect for people? What if the patient or client does not want to be told the truth? Is telling the patient the truth in these circumstances or even lying to patients or clients respecting them as autonomous individuals?

Duties approach

The central issue of the duties approach is the principle of doing good – beneficence. It is generally felt that doctors, nurses, social workers and others in the caring fields have a duty to do good, to benefit their clients and patients. Nurses and doctors are told they have a duty to care and this duty is embodied within the principles of negligence as stated by Lord Hewitt in the case of *R. v. Bateman* (1925): 'If a person holds himself out as possessing special skill and knowledge, and he is consulted, as possessing such skill and knowledge, by or on behalf of a patient, he owes a duty to that patient ...' (Korgaonkar and Tribe, 1995, p. 2). Local authorities have a duty under Section 47(1) of the National Health Service and Community

Care Act 1990 to not only assess a client's needs but also provide for those services identified as needed from that assessment (Dimond, 1997).

This duty to care is an obligation which spells out what ought to be done in a given situation. But this notion of obligation is based on two assumptions: first, that the person can actually do or perform the action so obliged; and second, that there is a choice of whether to act or not (Fletcher *et al.*, 1995). It has been argued that, in fact, professional codes actually prevent individuals from fulfilling their obligations because they prevent choice. Professional codes are discussed in Section 3.

In essence, the duty-based approach forces a person to be the moral agent. In other words, 'a person is good when their only motive for doing something is that it is their duty to do it' (Palmer, 1999, p. 108). This approach stems from the work of Immanuel Kant (1724–1804) whose philosophy, known as deontology, makes the concept of duty central to morality. Kant firmly believed that the right act would always be guided by moral duties, responsibilities and rights; thus some actions will always be considered immoral, regardless of their positive benefits (Fowler and Levine-Ariff, 1987).

However, opponents feel that it is very difficult to derive morality just from reason alone, for in fact both pain and pleasure, which are not considered by the duties approach, are a central platform for the development of goodness and our sense of right and wrong (Edge and Groves, 1994). Not looking to the consequences of our actions can also lead to disastrous results, as in John's case when without thinking he lit a cigarette while still receiving oxygen through his face mask. It is also possible to be faced with a conflict between two duties, such as the case of a young single mother who, despite being on full benefits, is moonlighting as a bar maid to make ends meet. The social worker's duty is to maintain the client's confidences but the social worker also has a duty to the state to report fraud. So which duty takes precedence?

Consequences approach

In the consequences approach, what really matters ethically speaking is the consequences of an action, which should be beneficial and not harmful to the individual. An action is right or wrong based on the consequences produced as measured against a specific end that is sought, such as pleasure, utility or dispassion (Fowler and Levine-Ariff, 1987). Consequentialism applies even if achieving the end result means that an individual's rights are ignored or rules are broken.

One form of consequentialism is utilitarianism, an ethical theory proposed by Jeremy Bentham (1748–1832) and later refined by John Stuart Mill (1806–1873). Bentham identified the goal of morality as the greatest happiness for the greatest number and, in consequentialist fashion, claimed that an action is right in so far as it tends to promote that goal. As a philosophical proposition, utilitarianism is hampered by the fundamental difficulty of comparing quantitatively the happiness of one person with that of another, even though Bentham devised a method for calculating the quantity of pain or pleasure called the hedonic calculus (Box 4).

Box 4: Hedonic calculus

The amount of pleasure or pain is calculated by an individual based on the cumulative value that individual places on the following seven dimensions:

- its intensity

- its duration

- its certainty or uncertainty

- its propinquity or remoteness

- its fecundity or the chance it has of being followed by sensations of the same kind

- its purity or the chance it has of *not* being followed by sensations of the opposite kind

- its extent, that is the number of persons to whom it extends or who will be affected by it.

(Source: based on Palmer, 1999, pp. 69–70)

Nevertheless, utilitarianism is particularly attractive as a method for public decision making and it is strongly opposed to deontology, the view that the worthiness of an action depends upon its conformity with duty or its respecting the rights of other individuals. Deontologists characteristically complain that consequentialism leads to a confusion of morality with expediency, since consequentialism seems to allow that the good of one person may be sacrificed for the good of many (Johnstone, 1989).

Allocation of resources, which is established on the principle of justice and fairness, is often based on the consequences approach. Does society treat individuals randomly like in a lottery on a first come first served basis, as is the case with waiting lists or triaging those who are in most need of treatment, which occurs currently in Accident and Emergency Departments? What about treating the greatest number of individuals possible with the finite resources available? Would you treat two individuals with liver transplants or give ten people hip replacements? Just who does make these decisions? Health economists have tried to address these questions through the use of cost–benefit ratios and the development of QALYs or quality-adjusted life years (Newdick, 1995).

Emotive approach

The emotive approach claims that moral judgements do not state anything that is capable of being true or false even subjectively but merely express emotions. Emotivism is based on the belief that moral decisions have nothing to do with reason or rationality but that morality is all about feelings.

According to the US philosopher Charles Stevenson (b. 1908):

> The emotive meaning of a word is the power that the word acquires, on account of its history in emotional situations, to evoke or directly express attitudes, as distinct from describing or designating them.
>
> (Stevenson, 1944, p. 33, quoted in Johnstone, 1989, p. 57)

Stevenson argues that all moral statements are essentially an attempt to persuade others to share one's own attitudes about the rights or wrongs of certain acts. 'The reason we can't define "good" in purely descriptive terms is that "good" is emotional' (Gensler, 1998, p. 62).

Emotivism is criticised for its exclusion of rationality from moral arguments and its failure to distinguish serious moral arguments from irrational propaganda. Not all moral judgements are emotions; some are unemotional, such as paying taxes (Gensler, 1998). Emotivism is seen by its critics as having trivialised ethical debate for, in the main, it 'is not much different from simple common sense!' (Harmon, 1977, pp. 39–40, quoted in Johnstone, 1989, p. 58).

The emotive approach has had a strong impact on organ donation. Transplantation is widely seen as the best option for end-stage organ failure as there is no other treatment available. Without a replacement organ, people with end-stage failure of their heart, lungs, liver or kidneys will die. Unfortunately, there is a severe shortage of organs available for transplantation, thus the use of organ donor cards is strongly advocated to keep a pool of readily available organs at all times. However, in the UK even a signed organ donor card does not necessarily mean that organs will be harvested at death because of the current practice of requesting the next of kin's consent (BBC, 1998). Why, when an organ donor card has been signed indicating express consent, does the medical profession still require the family's consent before they proceed? As the King's Fund Report states, 'whilst presumed consent may, in the short run, furnish more organs for transplants, in the long run its systematic effect on the institutions of medical care could be depressing and corrosive of that trust upon which the doctor–patient relationship depend[s]. And, even in the short run, public controversy can adversely affect donation rates' (New *et al.*, 1994, quoted in McHale *et al.*, 1997, p. 919). So, even though the law is clear on the consent given with a signed organ donor's card, it is still the feelings and emotions of the family involved that necessitate the additional consent for donation (BBC, 1998).

Feminist approach

Feminist ethics expands the boundaries of traditional ethics. It has different methods and priorities which render visible the realities and structures previously obscured in patriarchal ethical perspectives. As philosopher Betty Sichel writes:

> 'Feminine' at present refers to the search for women's unique voice and, most often, the advocacy of an ethics of care that includes nurturance, care, compassion, and networks of communication. 'Feminist' refers to those theorists ... who argue against patriarchal domination, for equal rights, a just and fair distribution of scarce resources, etc.
>
> (Sichel, 1991, p. 90, quoted in Tong, 1997, p. 37)

The feminine or care-focused feminist approach identifies the failure of those perspectives based on duty and utility to understand the attitudes and insights of women whereas a feminist or power-focused approach searches out the oppressive elements of society, rendering the invisible visible.

Carol Gilligan and Nel Noddings, both feminist moral theorists, write about the care-focused approach. Gilligan's work (1982) was an empirical study of the ways in which children look at moral issues. She concludes that girls tend to approach moral issues by examining the relationships involved rather than searching out moral rules as did boys. Noddings (1984) attempted to base ethics upon natural caring rooted in receptivity, relatedness and responsiveness. This approach contrasted sharply with an ethics built upon moral rules, rights, duties and principles found in the other approaches. When a caring relationship succeeds, in Noddings' belief, the cared-for person actively receives the caring thoughts and deeds of the carer, who spontaneously shares her or his aspirations, appraisals and accomplishments with the cared-for person.

The power-focused feminist approach to ethics asks questions about male domination and female subordination before it asks questions about whether an instance or an object is morally good or evil or just or unjust. Alison Jaggar (1991), writing on this approach, believes that the subordination of women is morally wrong and that the moral experiences of women are as worthy of respect as men's. In her view, feminist ethics must articulate moral critiques of actions and practices that perpetuate women's subordination, prescribe morally justifiable ways of resisting such actions and practices, and envision morally desirable alternatives that will promote women's emancipation (Tong, 1997).

A feminist approach to ethics expands the voices heard within ethical debate. It can accommodate different voices, stories, methods and perspectives and it recognises that there is not just one language of ethics. Broadly speaking, feminist ethical approaches value and render visible the following elements, which are often ignored in other approaches to understanding ethics:

- the importance and effect of power relationships
- connectedness rather than individualistic autonomy
- lived human experience
- varieties of human communication and interpretation, including those that are not based on literacy and rational expression such as stories, gossip, anecdotes, touch and gesture
- communities and collectivities rather than individualism
- different ways of knowing
- the importance of the everyday and the ordinary.

Critics of the feminist approach question the absolute adherence to values of trust and non-oppression situated against the realities found within the present system of patriarchal power in today's society. However, the ethical approaches discussed in this chapter have embedded values and presuppositions within them and often their protagonists are a good deal less willing to look critically at these, seeing themselves as having access to reality in the form of reason while seeing others as being based on non-rational systems of myths and magic. Also the care-focused feminist approach is criticised for perpetuating its own brand of stereotyping, which 'can lead to an absolute equation that woman = caring and man = instrumental' or action (Porter, 1998, p. 192).

Major issues addressed within the feminist approach to ethics are abortion, artificial insemination and *in vitro* fertilisation, surrogacy, genetic screening and counselling, contraception and sterilisation, eating disorders and court-authorised Caesarean sections. As Susan Sherwin, Professor of Philosophy at Dalhousie University, Nova Scotia, writes:

> [The] principal task of feminist medical ethics is to develop conceptual models for restructuring the power associated with healing by distribut-ing medical knowledge in ways that allow persons maximum control over their own health. It is important to clarify ways in which dependence can be reduced, caring can be offered without paternalism, and health services can be obtained within a context worthy of trust.
>
> (Sherwin, 1992, p. 28)

3 Values and ethics in practice

An understanding of the different approaches to ethics can assist in deconstructing the multiple meanings in problematic situations in health and social care and help to broaden the choices available. However, knowing about different perspectives does not by itself help an individual arrive at a decision. What else is needed? Hussey (1996, p. 251) believes that a professional is 'someone who has: a heightened sensitivity to the presence of a moral issue; an improved ability to reason and decide on moral questions ... of their work; enhanced skills in implementing moral decisions and acting in morally demanding situations; and the motivation to use these attributes and abilities.' To facilitate this process both professional codes and ethical decision-making frameworks are tools that can help with decision making.

Challenging professional codes

Professional codes are primarily seen as a statement of the values and beliefs of a particular professional group which are designed to serve the interests of the profession and to protect the public. Generally, professional codes contain ethical principles which underpin the approach of professional practice such as autonomy, respect for people, promotion of welfare; ethical rules, the do's and don'ts of each code; and practice rules which are specific to each profession, such as not advertising or declaring a bequest from a client's will (Banks, 1998). Professional codes have several functions, which are described in Box 5.

Box 5: Functions of professional codes

1 **Guidance** – serve to remind professionals of their duties and obligations, to guide practice and to facilitate them in their work.

2 **Regulation** – prescribe the standards of behaviour and moral responsibility expected of professionals.

3 **Discipline** – identify areas of transgression, which enables the governing body to justify the use of penalties to sanction its code.

4 **Protection** – protect the public through the setting of standards of behaviour and conduct of its practitioners.

5 **Information** – inform the general public of the standards of that profession, thus encouraging trust and confidence.

6 **Proclamation** – proclaim to the general public that in fact its members are professionals who have moral respectability and autonomy.

7 **Negotiation** – can be used as a tool of negotiation in disputes between colleagues and/or professionals and can serve as the justification for taking a particular course of action.

(Source: based on Hussey, 1996, p. 252)

Given these functions, just how useful are professional codes? They tend to be fairly brief, often stating broad and general principles; for example, '... shall act, at all times, in such a manner as to: safeguard and promote the interests of individual patients and clients' (UKCC, 1992, p. 1). Are individuals meant to know what these acts are? What about giving an injection which can cause pain and suffering but yet is an instrument of healing through the medication inside the syringe? Or sectioning a patient under the Mental Health Act 1983, which denies that person his or her freedom? Is that promoting and safeguarding an individual's interest and well-being?

Codes can often be contradictory; for example, exhorting a practitioner to work with families, clients and patients as well as other professionals. Yet the interests of these differing groups are not the same; in fact they may well be at odds with one another. For example: Rebecca, the social worker, works with teenage women who want contraceptive advice and access to the morning after pill, yet some health care professionals want to restrict access to contraception to the over-16s and/or the morning after pill to the over-18s; or the school that wants to ensure that teenagers stay in school and gain certificates rather than opt out to raise a family – they all have different agendas.

Professional codes place great emphasis on the duties approach to understanding ethical issues. Codes often look like a list of duties that need to be fulfilled, for example: 'attempts to relieve and prevent hardship ...' (BASW, 1996, p. 2); 'work in an open and co-operative manner ...' (UKCC, 1992, p. 1); 'accept referrals which [are deemed] to be appropriate and for which they have the resources' (BAOT, 1997, p. 34); 'to increase personal knowledge and skill ...' (BASW, 1996, p. 2); 'protect all confidential information ...' (UKCC, 1992, p. 2); and 'must not be under the influence of any toxic substance ...' (BAOT, 1997, p. 35).

These lists of duties, reinforced through the discipline function of codes (see Box 5), require individuals to follow the code's prescribed set of rules and obligations with no questioning allowed. Some codes try to ameliorate this through offering interpretative statements as further explanation, such as the *Code of Ethics for Social Work* (BASW, 1996) or the *Code of Ethics and Professional Conduct for Occupational Therapists* (BAOT, 1997), while the nurse's *Code of Professional Conduct* (UKCC, 1992) has over the years needed additional booklets of further guidance on aspects of the code.

Another difficulty with imbuing professional codes with a duties approach is that the world in which large organisations such as the National Health Service or local authorities operate is the world of the utilitarian, which is concerned not with individuals but with communities and societies – the greatest good for the greatness number. The reality is that professionals working towards a code that fosters duty and virtue are in fact working in a world where utility overrides duty and virtue. This disjuncture is responsible for a great deal of ethical distress and dilemma.

Furthermore, individuals are keeping their personal and working lives separate. They feel that what they do in private is private and of no concern to their employer or their profession. A recent example involved a nurse who in her spare time was also a prostitute (Payne, 1999). As reported in the nursing press, she was fired from her Trust, yet the nurse's regulatory body, the UKCC, took the view that 'The evidence wasn't such that she could be removed from the register' (Payne, 1999, p. 10). Thus, in fact, professional codes perhaps have not enhanced the morality of today's society but rather have placed an unreasonable burden of obligations on individuals who have neither the support nor the resources to fulfil those obligations. Professional codes cannot strengthen the power of the individual to secure the moral duties they impose on their members.

How do professional codes serve those who are conscientiously raising questions about standards of practice and allocation of resources? Individuals who have been in these whistle-blowing situations have said professional codes do little or nothing to support conscientious employees. Graham Pink, a nurse who raised the alarm over staffing levels on a ward caring for elderly people, took the view:

> ... it [the UKCC's *Code of Professional Conduct*] should be scrapped. I have upheld the Code religiously, and as a result I face losing my job ... I see it as a very negative force at the moment. If you break it you get struck off, but it certainly doesn't do any good for patients ...
>
> (Cole, 1991, quoted in Tadd, 1994, p. 17)

So what do professional codes have to offer individuals facing ethical issues in their everyday practice? Do they use these professional codes as part of their decision-making process? In a survey of 10,800 registrants by the UKCC in 1997, '93% find the code useful and only 1% do not' (Norman, 1998, p. 21). Codes are often kept in handy places to be referred to when needed, for example so that employees can confirm their professional identity when asked by management to work beyond their scope of practice (Banks, 1998). As one social worker commented:

> ... if you come to my office you'll see the BASW principles up on the wall, which I always have and sort of look at and remind myself about: like being clear about whether you are speaking as a professional person or as an individual.
>
> (Banks, 1998, p. 29)

Professional codes do have a role to play in practice for they help practitioners apply general principles in practice settings. Codes:

- offer practical guidance on behaviour, especially those professional codes containing interpretative or explanatory statements
- delineate and identify professional boundaries and are very useful in setting standards by which agency policy and practices can be judged
- give an overriding responsibility to the public above that of an individual or employee when resources are scarce and standards are slipping
- remind practitioners that they possess particular knowledge and skills that are used to benefit vulnerable individuals and that 'they have a duty to inform governments and agencies of inequities, lack of resources or the need for policy changes' (Banks, 1995, p. 92).

There is always the job of analysing, assessing, taking a critical stance, engaging with varying perspectives, and facing conflict. In this climate, professional codes become a resource to aid decision making.

Ethical decision making

Whereas professional codes can provide a framework for decision making, often decisions have to be made when time is just not available to consult the code or the broad-brush framework of the code is not enough. So what can a health and social care practitioner use to help with making decisions? There are numerous decision-making frameworks available. Some are based on a process-type framework, which asks the individual to gather all the information, identify the problems, seek out solutions, choose a solution and then evaluate the response to that solution (Eby, 1994b). Other frameworks are based on a grid system (Seedhouse and Lovett, 1992) or algorithms (Johnson, 1990).

Seedhouse's Ethical Grid (Figure 1 opposite) was designed to help health care professionals' decision making. It consists of four different coloured boxes, which represent different levels of analysis, and within each box there are different prompts to help the individual decide on a strategy. Starting from the innermost box, the blue box represents the principles behind health care; these are the major assumptions underpinning health care work. Moving outwards, the red box represents the level of duties while the green box represents the level of consequences. Finally, the outer black box represents the level of practicality. Each of the sections within the different boxes is detachable and the person considering an issue using this grid takes from each box those sections which illustrate aspects of the issue.

For example, if a surgeon was considering whether to operate on a well-informed patient where the risks and benefits were evenly matched, that is there was a 50% chance of survival, the surgeon might select the following sections: 'respect autonomy' from the blue box, 'tell the truth' from the red box, 'most beneficial outcome for the patient' from the green box, and 'the risk' from the black box. These four sections help to remind the surgeon what to consider when making the decision along with the patient (Seedhouse and Lovett, 1992).

Another framework to consider here is H. Richard Niebuhr's response ethics (1963) which asks just two questions. The first is what is happening? The answers to this first question prepare the groundwork for finding answers. This is not a simple question with few answers but its breadth consists of seeking out information about the people involved, the acts that occurred within that situation, the consequences of these acts, the intentions or values underpinning this situation, and any rules or codes or moral frameworks that might apply to the situation.

The information obtained in seeking out the answers to the first question will often answer Niebuhr's second question – what is the fitting answer? What is the fitting answer may well not be the correct or right or dutiful answer but it will be the one that best fits that particular situation.

Asking these two questions and seeking out the answers leads to a pattern of response, interpretation, accountability and social solidarity.

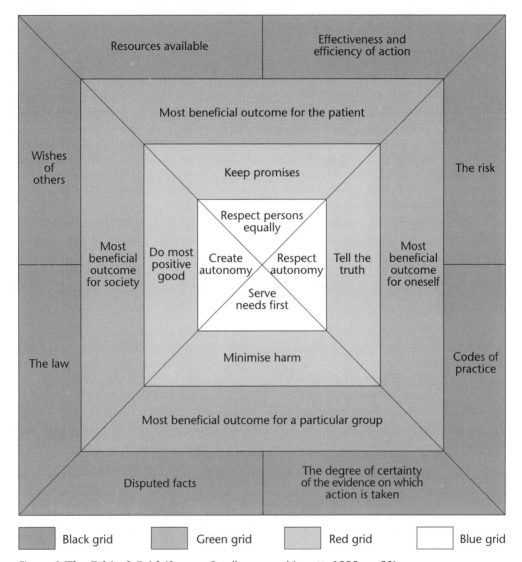

Figure 1 **The Ethical Grid** (Source: Seedhouse and Lovett, 1992, p. 20)

The latter occurs when the fitting answer leads to a gain by the participants – a greater communication, a greater community spirit, because this answer was arrived at by all parties working together. Verena Tschudin writes:

> *Social solidarity* is a wider conclusion than that reached by simply asking what has happened? or by making an evaluation. Not only should all the people immediately involved in this situation feel that their effort in coming to the fitting answer was worthwhile, but they should also feel that their decision will have advanced society in its thinking and acting.
>
> (Tschudin, 1994, pp. 32–33)

Conclusion

One of the fundamental goals of the study of ethics is to help practitioners develop practical reflective skills that can be used on a day-to-day basis to consolidate and reinforce ethical awareness and analysis as a vital, interesting and enriching part of everyday practice. Using an understanding of the various philosophical approaches to ethics and some sort of decision-making framework will enhance individuals' ability to work through their thinking on these issues and contribute to the decision-making process. However, it is equally important to recognise that understanding ethics as an isolated individual process will only lead to sterile decision making, often to no one's gain or understanding. The main thing is to get other people in on the thinking and decision making, as this is the first step towards effective ethics, which essentially is a social activity oriented to how people should live with and regard each other. It therefore makes sense to do ethics with other people and not on one's own, as a means as well as to attain a desired end.

References

BAOT (British Association of Occupational Therapists) (1997) 'Code of ethics and professional conduct for occupational therapists', *British Journal of Occupational Therapy*, Vol. 60, No. 1, January, pp. 33–37.

BASW (1996) *The Code of Ethics for Social Work*, Birmingham, British Association of Social Workers.

Banks, S. (1995) *Ethics and Values in Social Work*, Houndsmill, Macmillan Press.

Banks, S. (1998) 'Codes of ethics and ethical conduct: a view from the caring professions', *Public Money and Management*, January–March, pp. 27–30.

Beauchamp, T. and Childress, J. (1994) *Principles of Biomedical Ethics* (4th edn), Oxford, Oxford University Press.

British Broadcasting Corporation (BBC) (1998) 'Health: doctors reconsider transplant stance', *BBC News*, 28 December, London, BBC. (http://news.bbc.co.uk/hi/english/health/newsid_243000/243500.stm – accessed 12 July 1999)

Cole, A. (1991) 'Upholding the code', *Nursing Times*, Vol. 87, No. 27, pp. 26–29.

Dimond, B. (1997) *Legal Aspects of Care in the Community*, Basingstoke, Macmillan.

Eby, M. A. (1994a) *The Law and Ethics of General Practice*, Beckenham, Kent, Publishing Initiatives.

Eby, M. (1994b) 'Competing values', in Tschudin, V. (ed.) *Ethics: Conflicts of Interest*, pp. 85–109, London, Scutari Press.

Edge, R. and Groves, J. (1994) *The Ethics of Health Care: A Guide for Clinical Practice*, Albany, NY, Delmar Publishers.

Fletcher, N., Holt, J., Brazier, M. and Harris, J. (1995) *Ethics, Law and Nursing*, Manchester, Manchester University Press.

Fowler, M. and Levine-Ariff, J. (1987) *Ethics at the Bedside*, Philadelphia, J. B. Lippincott.

Frankena, W. (1973) *Ethics* (2nd edn), Englewood Cliffs, NJ, Prentice Hall.

Gensler, H. J. (1998) *Ethics: A Contemporary Introduction*, London, Routledge.

Gilligan, C. (1982) *In a Different Voice*, Cambridge, Massachusetts, Harvard University Press.

Harmon, G. (1977) *The Nature of Morality*, New York, Oxford University Press.

Hunt, G. (1998) 'Whistleblowing and the crisis of accountability', in Hunt, G. (ed.) *Whistleblowing in the Social Services*, pp. 1–15, London, Arnold.

Hussey, T. (1996) 'Nursing ethics and codes of professional conduct', *Nursing Ethics*, Vol. 3, No. 3, pp. 250–258.

Infopedia CD-ROM (1995) 'Punishment', in *Merriam Webster's Dictionary of Quotations*, London, SoftKey.

Jaggar, A. M. (1991) 'Feminist ethics: projects, problems, prospects', in Card, C. (ed.) *Feminist Ethics*, p. 366, Lawrence, University of Kansas Press.

Johnson, A. (1990) *Pathways in Medical Ethics*, London, Edward Arnold.

Johnstone, M.-J. (1989) *Bioethics: A Nursing Perspective*, Sydney, Harcourt Brace Jovanovich, Publishers.

Korgaonkar, G. and Tribe, D. (1995) *Law for Nurses*, London, Cavendish Publishing.

McHale, J., Fox, M. and Murphy, J. (1997) *Health Care Law: Text and Materials*, London, Sweet and Maxwell.

New, B. *et al.* (1994) *A Question of Give and Take: Improving the Supply of Donor Organs for Transplantation*, London, King's Fund Institute.

Newdick, C. (1995) *Who Should We Treat? Law, Patients and Resources in the NHS*, Oxford, Clarendon Press.

Niebuhr, H. R. (1963) *The Responsible Self*, New York, Harper and Row.

Noddings, N. (1984) *Caring: A Feminine Approach to Ethics and Moral Education*, Berkeley, University of California Press.

Norman, S. (1998) 'Are we reading the same code?', *Nursing Times*, Vol. 94, No. 48, 2 December, p. 21.

Palmer, M. (1999) *Moral Problems in Medicine*, Cambridge, Lutterworth Press.

Payne, D. (1999) 'Prostitution poser raises prospect of UKCC referendum', *Nursing Times*, Vol. 95, No. 1, 6 January, p. 10.

Pellegrino, E. and Thomasma, D. (1993) *The Virtues in Medical Practice*, Oxford, Oxford University Press.

Pilgrim, D. (1995) 'Explaining abuse and inadequate care', in Hunt, G. (ed.) *Whistleblowing in the Health Service*, pp. 77–85, London, Edward Arnold.

Porter, S. (1998) *Social Theory and Nursing Practice*, Basingstoke, Macmillan.

Purtilo, R. (1993) *Ethical Dimensions in the Health Professions* (2nd edn), Philadelphia, W. B. Saunders Company.

Rowson, R. H. (1990) *An Introduction to Ethics for Nurses*, Harrow, Scutari Press.

Seedhouse, D. and Lovett, L. (1992) *Practical Medical Ethics*, Chichester, John Wiley and Sons.

Sherwin, S. (1992) 'Feminist and medical ethics: two different approaches to contextual ethics', in Holmes, H. B. and Purdy, L. M. (eds) *Feminist Perspectives in Medical Ethics*, pp. 17–31, Bloomington, IN, Indiana University Press.

Sichel, B. (1991) 'Different strains and strands: feminist contributions to ethical theory', *Newsletter on Feminism 90*, No. 2, Winter, p. 90.

Stevenson, C. L. (1944) *Ethics and Language*, New Haven, Yale University Press.

Tadd, V. (1994) 'Professional codes: an exercise in tokenism?', *Nursing Ethics*, Vol. 1, No. 1, pp. 15–23.

Tong, R. (1997) *Feminist Approaches to Bioethics*, Boulder, CO, Westview Press.

Tschudin, V. (1994) *Deciding Ethically*, London, Baillière Tindall.

Tschudin, V. and Marks-Maran, D. (1993) *Ethics: A Primer for Nurses*, London, Baillière Tindall.

UKCC (1992) *Code of Professional Conduct*, June, London, UKCC.

Warren, R. C. (1993) 'Codes of ethics: bricks without straw', *A European Review of Business Ethics*, Vol. 2, No. 4, October, pp. 185–191.

Chapter 7
The challenge of caring relationships

Ann Brechin

Even relatively straightforward encounters
challenge the capacity of the practitioner
to be on the right wavelength.

Introduction

This chapter is concerned with caring relationships and with the contexts
and circumstances that help to sustain, or mitigate against, positive
experiences of care and caring. For the 'caring professions' care is
implicitly central to the work, yet only recently are the challenges
inherent in such relationships beginning to be acknowledged and
addressed in professional training and support. Caring, like mother-love,
risks being seen uncritically as warm, wonderful and quite unproblematic
– and indeed, like mother-love, is assumed to be richly rewarding and
empowering for both parties. The challenge to the carer, however, is to
find out whether this can be made to work in practice.

Caring relationships offer a particular challenge in that they must take
account of the desires, needs and expectations of those on the receiving
end. Providing good care, therefore, cannot be formulaic. For some
people, warmth and support may be welcome and valued; for others, a
more detached form of help and advice may be what is wanted, with 'care'
seen as intrusive and inappropriate. Care, however, is not about
responding to one individual's needs in a vacuum. Another challenge is
to make caring appropriate within the wider cultural and socio-political

context. Care is, for example, a form of social control in relation to child protection or mental health procedures or in terms of assessing need and rationing resources. For the carer personally, whether professional or unpaid, to care at all is, in a sense, to be continually open and vulnerable to challenge. Learning to be respectful and supportive of others, often in very difficult circumstances, may be the biggest challenge of all.

This chapter opens three different windows on the complex and challenging terrain of caring relationships, each offering a view of particular aspects and issues. First, it looks at various struggles to conceptualise what care is all about, exploring who does what and why, how we try to make sense of it, and how we may try to do it better. Then we look through another window to focus on the extreme, although not unusual, challenge of violent, aggressive or abusive behaviour within caring relationships. Finally, the third window looks in on how successful care relationships may be created and models a framework for thinking about contexts and processes which may help this to happen. Rather than focusing on three unrelated accounts of caring, these windows or vantage points can be seen as offering different views over the same territory, with the intention of arriving at a more multidimensional sense of how the land lies.

1   Care tasks and processes

Who does what and why?

Different professions have different frameworks for understanding the care they offer. Social work emphasises the enabling, empowering focus of such work and struggles to move away from perceptions of interfering busybodies who think they know best (Dominelli, 1997; Braye and Preston-Shoot, 1996). Social workers see their work as primarily facilitative, although also on the boundaries of enforcement, given their statutory roles in child protection and mental health sectioning procedures. This controlling face of care can also seem more pervasive, particularly where assumed 'responsibility for' the cared-for person can be seen to threaten independence and autonomy. Care is thus seen as central, but also as deeply problematic.

Nurses, on the other hand, welcome caring as central to their role (for example, Leininger, 1988; Kirby and Slevin, 1992). For them the challenge is to embrace humanistic, holistic care as part of establishing a non-medically dominated professional image. It is often hard to maintain this in the face of time pressures and increasingly high-tech medicine, where nurses may find themselves caught up in the same fleeting encounters as the doctors. Barker *et al.* (1995) also point out that care cannot be seen as somehow exclusive to nursing, nor fixed for all time.

A study of occupational therapists and their relationships with clients suggests awareness of both a caring and a power relationship, which is likely to be familiar to other therapists too:

> They feel degrees of caring, compassion and even love. They also care, by feeling concerned about their patients and wanting to help. ... But alongside this caring, therapists grapple with a power dimension which is embedded within all their relationships.
>
> (Finlay, 1999)

Some service-users are particularly aware of this power dimension. Disabled people, who tend to have extended exposure to the 'caring professions', argue that care is not what they need or want and, moreover, that it is oppressive, restrictive and dependency inducing (Morris, 1993; French and Swain, 1998; Wood, 1992). Mental health service-users, or 'survivors' (of services), also subscribe to this view of 'care' as simply a form of control or repression. In order to retain any power and autonomy in their lives, they must be able to determine what they need – and, the argument goes, what they need is support rather than care.

There seems to be a paradox in talking about such dilemmas in relation to caring. Caring is after all an essentially 'natural' human process. Without care, infants and young children cannot survive and, without mutual caring adult relationships, involving support, sharing provisions, shelter and co-operation in defence and development, there would be little chance of successful reproduction and survival for a species which depends more on its combined wits than on tooth and claw. What is more, the term 'care' is in widespread use, not least embedded in policy documents addressing 'care in the community'. Whilst using the term here, however, we shall bear in mind and continue to question the appropriateness of different approaches to and understandings of care.

The construction of care

Care is generally agreed to include 'caring for' and 'caring about' (Parker, 1981; Graham, 1983) in the sense of covering both the caring tasks involved and the caring feelings. These can be seen as two sides of one coin or as quite different issues. Dalley (1988), for example, argues that the debate has become distorted by the tendency to see these as features of a womanly art of caring. Such assumptions have been an inevitable backdrop for community care policies, which are often seen as pushing female carers to take on extra burdens. Informal care is frequently interpreted negatively in terms of the burden of care on the carers (Finch and Groves, 1980; Glendinning, 1983). Dalley (1988) and others (for example, Twigg and Atkin, 1994) argue that we have to escape from that blinkered view to arrive at a fuller analysis covering informal and formal, paid or professional caring.

Davies (1995) frames a three-way distinction of such caring:

- 'caregiving', primarily informal amongst family and friends
- 'carework', mostly low-paid and female-dominated work, with low status and minimal training, but demanding quite a high level of skill which goes unrecognised
- 'professional care', based on systematic and formal training but, nevertheless, with minimal identification of what precisely is meant by caring skills.

This sets the scene for an exploration of the hidden assumptions bound up in gender stereotypes and gendered language which, Davies argues, restrict progress in our understanding. In particular, they restrict our ability to resolve the apparent dichotomies between task-based caring and emotional/labour-based caring – the caring for or caring about split (Graham, 1983) or 'labour versus love', as Davies (1995) bills it. Her definition of care, striving to integrate these strands, is that it involves 'attending physically, mentally and emotionally to the needs of another and giving a commitment to the nurturance, growth and healing of that other' (pp. 18–19).

Taking another approach to defining care, Hopson (1981) outlines a range of 'strategies for helping' on which the list below is based.

1 Direct action, involving doing something to or on behalf of the other person.
2 Physical therapies, working with the individual towards improved functioning.
3 Giving advice or information, which may provide a basis for the other person to make more informed choices.
4 Providing instruction, to assist the acquisition of skills.
5 Supportive companionship, sharing daily living and leisure activities in an enabling way.
6 Counselling, helping the individual to explore problems and choices.
7 Influencing other people, contexts and systems, including through advocacy or supported self-advocacy.

In the same way that Hopson saw these strategies as forms of helping, they can equally well be seen as forms of caring. Any of them may involve a commitment to nurturance, growth and healing. This may involve comfort and protection from some of life's demands and stresses – an implied lifting of burdens – as in, for example, the provision of relief from pain and stress for dying people or, more contentiously, the 'protection' of vulnerable people from risk or harm. But care may also be seen as directed towards enhancing autonomy (the capacity for self-determination), rights, control and freedom of choice, with a varying emphasis on the degree of responsibility and developmental effort to be taken on by the cared-for individual.

Braye and Preston-Shoot (1996) offer a triangulated version of such conflicting drives (Figure 1). They counterpose protection, empowerment

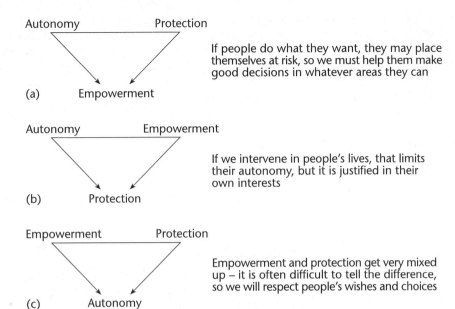

Figure 1 **Triangulation of autonomy, protection and empowerment**
(Source: Braye and Preston-Shoot, 1996, p. 96)

and autonomy, showing how all three are in continual tension with each other, but may be privileged differently by different people in different circumstances.

The challenge might be seen as keeping all three drives in the frame and in balance: for example, the enhancement of autonomy in the context of support and comfort. Care, or support, must always seek to respond, therefore, to the particular needs, circumstances and preferences of the individual. The example in Box 1 illustrates how easily, by ignoring those, care can be counterproductive.

Box 1: Hanif

Hanif, a 14-year-old Asian boy with learning disabilities, was diagnosed as being 'autistic' with 'challenging behaviours' and was placed in a 'special' unit for young people with challenging behaviours. He became increasingly disturbed. He began to throw his food away and would also make attempts to get into the kitchen and throw things about in there as well. All the white staff had assumed he was 'too disabled' to have any concept of his race, culture, religion or diet and no provision for these issues was made in his care at the unit, although his parents were devout Hindus and had always encouraged Hanif to participate in prayers and attend festivals. An Asian visitor immediately attracted the boy's attention and, when he was offered an Indian snack, he accepted it without a fuss.

(Source: case study provided by Peter Ferns)

There was no starting-point there for enhancing autonomy or providing comfort or support, as Hanif's individual needs and identity were not respected. Providing such care successfully through respecting individuality, however, can be achieved, even when needs are complex or hard to understand. The rest of this section explores an approach to the care of people with dementia.

Caring for people with dementia

Dementia is a debilitating process, resulting in death, which robs people progressively of their mental faculties, their memories and often their personality. Working with or caring for someone with dementia has been seen as a process of providing physical and protective care, while the disease process takes its course. Kitwood (1997) began to question what was happening.

His intention and primary focus was on improving the quality of life of people with dementia. This involved working out what life might feel like for someone with very limited remaining capacity. On that basis, then, he could ask what kind of care might be appropriate; and, finally, how might those doing the caring, whether relatives or professional carers, be helped to provide such care?

Three strands to the work can be identified, reflecting these key questions. First, thinking about what quality of life might mean led into a detailed critique of the disease model and a reformulation of it to encompass the notion of continued personhood in the process (Kitwood, 1997). A disease focus, particularly with a dementing process as central, leads easily to dehumanising assumptions. If there is nothing medical that can be done, and if people are assumed not to understand much anyway, then profound pessimism and helplessness set in for any care regime. Care becomes physically focused and basic or worse and the individual is no longer visible. Kitwood describes such care in terms of a series of depersonalising tendencies (Box 2).

If, however, people with dementia are still people with integrity and personhood and, most of all perhaps, with feelings and emotions then different responses come into play. As people they deserve respect for their individual choices and preferences, and respect for their dignity, their privacy and their feelings. The second strand of work, therefore, involves translating these insights and formulations into detailed care guidelines. What exactly does it mean to treat someone with respect – or not to do so? What kind of choices could someone with dementia possibly be capable of, and so on? The answers, evolved over a period of time, are detailed and include checklists. They build from what has been called 'dementia care mapping' and provide an account of 'positive person work' (Box 3 overleaf).

Box 2: Depersonalising tendencies

Treachery: using deception to achieve compliance

Disempowerment: not letting or helping a person to use abilities they have

Infantilisation: treating a person patronisingly, like a young child

Intimidation: inducing fear through threats or physical power

Labelling: using category of dementia as basis for interaction and explanation

Stigmatisation: treating person like an alien or outcast

Outpacing: going too fast for them to follow

Invalidation: failing to acknowledge subjective reality and feelings

Banishment: sending away or excluding – physically or psychologically

Objectification: pushing, pulling, lifting without recognising sentient being

Ignoring: carrying on as if the person were not there

Imposition: forcing, overriding desire or preventing choice

Withholding: refusing attention or to meet need

Accusation: blaming for actions or inactions the person cannot help

Disruption: intruding disturbingly upon someone; breaking their frame of reference

Mockery: making fun of, teasing, making jokes at their expense

Disparagement: giving messages that are damaging to self-esteem

(Source: adapted from Kitwood, 1997, pp. 46–47)

The third strand of Kitwood's work, though, recognises that arriving at guidelines is only one small part of trying to support changes in practice. Carers, whether nurses, care workers or informal carers, tap into deep psychological processes within themselves in caring intimately for others. To respect and respond to someone, respecting their integrity and personhood, means making real contact with them. Making real contact with another person involves a real part of yourself. It will inevitably bring strong feelings with it, perhaps sorrow, grief, anxiety, anger or love and joy, in a complex response to the way the other person's feelings tap into your own past and current emotions. Kitwood's approach to this is to encompass such issues explicitly within any training and support schemes for carers.

Box 3: Positive person work

Recognition: acknowledgement as a person, known by name, affirmed as unique

Negotiation: recognition of preferences, giving degree of control and power

Collaboration: working together; care is not 'done to' a person

Play: encouraging spontaneity and self-expression of value in itself

Timalation: sensuous or sensual interactions (from *timao* in Greek, I honour)

Celebration: sharing joyfulness, not just for special occasions; includes spirituality

Relaxation: low intensity, but may need company and quiet contact to achieve

Validation: acknowledging the reality of a person's emotions and feelings

Holding: holding safe in a psychological sense, from, or through, trauma and fear

Facilitation: enabling half-formed intentions to be realised; supporting agency

(Source: adapted from Kitwood, 1997, pp. 90–91)

---

2   Challenges and conflicts

Working with violent or distressing feelings and actions

Having taken a fairly broad view through the first window on how care is understood and what it may involve, we now adopt a different vantage point, which brings into our frame some of the most challenging aspects of caring.

The focus here is on abuse which may harm, or at least challenge, the carer. This is not to ignore the serious issue of abuse by carers. Sometimes this is systematic and planned; or it may be abuse resulting from a temporary failure to handle frustration and anger; or it may be more insidious – Kitwood's depersonalising tendencies can certainly be seen as forms of abuse which flow naturally from negative stereotypical and dehumanising assumptions.

The Utting Report (Department of Health, 1997), which was concerned with the abuse of children and young people in care, defines abuse as 'action or conduct by another person which causes physical or psychological harm', including 'physical, sexual and emotional abuse'. Abuse scandals have forced attention on to the contexts which not only enable such abuse to occur but also seem almost to facilitate and camouflage them as control and oppression become the norm (Martin, 1984; Levy and Kahan, 1997) – what the Utting Report describes as 'a malignant institutional culture'. Wardaugh and Wilding (1993) go further in seeing aspects of the settings for any care relationships as having a corrupting effect on care.

It will always be necessary to create systems and policies that attempt to safeguard people 'in care' against such abuse. Other chapters (13 and 14, for example) address this more explicitly, looking for instance at quality assurance mechanisms and at regulation and accountability. At the margins of abuse and harm, however, there are interactions which are difficult to handle, where practitioners and informal carers may find themselves drawn into abusive and angry responses. Even if these are controlled at the time, such feelings of frustration or fear or resentment are likely to colour subsequent care relations. Practitioners are, after all, only human. Support to enable them to find more effective ways of responding to challenge or abuse will help to create a more nurturing and less 'malignant' environment all round.

In Box 4 (overleaf) there are brief examples of a range of abusive, dangerous, unacceptable or particularly stressful, worrying, upsetting or difficult situations. They include situations of threat or risk to the professional or carer; to others including other clients; or the threat of self-harm. They also include emotional, physical and sexual stresses, threats or abuse. It is difficult to put together such examples, because each one individually risks negative stereotyping. Yet such experiences do occur and are the harder to handle just because they are so hard to talk about.

Some of these examples are extremely dangerous situations. Others are worrying and stressful. Most are acutely distressing and painful, arousing emotions it is hard for anyone to deal with. Practitioners have to find ways of handling such situations that enable them to continue to provide care. (Would that we could all come up with the wonderful 'Hey, baby' retort just when it is needed.) Experience suggests that focused research and the development of practice and policy guidelines within clear legal frameworks are necessary to inform practice in such cases. Essentially these are about trying to find optimal ways of responding which do not inflict more pain. They can at least supply a measure of support and the security of knowing what one is supposed to do.

The emphasis emerging from new work with men with learning difficulties who have difficult and/or sexually abusive behaviour, for example, is on the importance of greater clarity (Thompson et al., 1997; Thompson and Brown, 1998).

Greater clarity means making it more explicit that carers have to give clear messages about what is acceptable and what is not. Greater clarity gives staff the go ahead and the security to intervene on behalf of others and also not to put up with unacceptable behaviour themselves. This will include keeping careful records of incidents and working out how to react

Box 4: Carers' experiences of conflict

Verbal aggression

He stood very close in front of me and started to shout about waiting times. He then yelled that none of us were fit to be nurses. He followed me down the corridor shouting that I was a f***ing slag, a bitch and so on. All this in front of my unit, full of patients and visitors.

(Coombes, 1998, p. 12)

'Known to be at risk'

Jenny (working in a forensic psychiatric unit): He's a bit predatory in that he will follow you down corridors. We, obviously, we don't walk down the ward on our own, but he will follow you down corridors. He had actually ... crept up behind me, cause he's very quiet, when you think you are sort of off the ward and you are safe, he'll have you cornered really ... because I am known to be at risk, I'm watched a lot, which is really comforting ...'

Interviewer: 'Why are you known to be at risk?'

Jenny: 'Because every time he comes into contact with me he will do something. He will try to touch me, he will make a comment ... this time that he got me cornered in the gym he said, "They can't watch you all of the time, and I'll get you." That was about 18 months ago so I am still waiting for this to happen.'

(Finlay, 1998, interview with occupational therapist)

A health support worker

This elderly patient had been in once before, and during that stay he would often play with his penis and ask me to get into bed with him. When he returned I think he remembered me and while I was washing him he would be touching me all over. I basically had to keep hold of one of his hands and wash him with my free hand.

(Mahony, 1998, p. 27)

'A very strange job'

Mr C is thirty-two and is regarded as one of the most able residents living in a large residential service for people with learning difficulties. A woman who lives in the same service disclosed ... that Mr C was her boyfriend and he was 'doing it to her'. She also said, 'it hurt when he put it in'. The worker was particularly surprised about hearing this because there was no knowledge of any relationship between the two individuals. In fact Mr C tended to ignore this woman in the course of their activity and work sessions and was very public about having a relationship with another woman who also attended the day centre.

(Thompson and Brown, 1998, p. 8)

Yvonne – forensic nurse

Sometimes patients within the forensic system would concentrate their anger on me, calling me a black bitch. During my first week in a forensic setting a patient walked up to me and said, 'Hey baby, I would kill you for free' ... because I was black.

I was very scared, but didn't want him to see he was getting to me. I dropped my voice down low and said, 'Hey baby, people like you I eat for dinner.'

If you take everything to heart, you will end up sick yourself.

(Mahoney, 1998, p. 27)

'Intimate' care

Mr D lives in a group home staffed by both women and men. The women staff were complaining that when they were helping him with intimate care he would start to masturbate. Also he would regularly come down from his bedroom early in the morning naked looking for a reaction from the women staff – this did not happen when any of the male staff were on duty.

(Thompson and Brown, 1998, p. 9)

Working with people with learning difficulties who self-injure

'I was horrified ... especially with P., because he used to crash hell out of his head ... it was just awful, you know ... '

'It just makes me so ... angry sometimes ... when he just has to do it and I get ... hooked into it ... and it makes me so mad. And then I feel bad about that too, I mean that's [caring] what I'm here for, isn't it?'

'I found that very frightening ... and very disturbing ... because I didn't know whether he could be outwardly aggressive.'

'If I knew why he did it ... it would be ... more understandable, and I'd cope better ...'

'It's sort of like ... um ... a feeling inside ... like a volcano inside you ... it's churning you up ... it keeps winding you up ... '

(Anderson, 1997, pp. 121–30)

and what to say; or it may mean devising a behaviour management programme for someone who has minimal verbal comprehension. The messages, however clear, must still be respectful rather than demeaning. Poor self-esteem is already likely to be a contributory factor to such behaviour and shaming someone is the least likely approach to lead to positive change. So the approach recognises the need to protect the interests of everyone involved, including the perpetrator, while making it a priority to protect anyone who has been abused or is at risk.

While awareness of the men's limitations and an understanding of what may contribute to such behaviour are important, this approach does not see any label of 'different' as providing any blanket excusal, nor requiring any stigmatising blame. Focusing on the particular behaviours and the circumstances and the individuals involved ensures an approach which deconstructs rather than stereotypes difference. Such a framework of thinking would seem to have a wider relevance and, indeed, there are echoes in the approach described overleaf.

Using physical interventions

A carefully devised policy framework exists on the use of 'physical interventions' (Harris *et al.*, 1997); also, as it happens, in working with people who have learning difficulties. The authors cite violence towards others, self-injury, or reckless disregard for safety, such as wandering into traffic, as the kinds of behaviours that might lead to physical intervention. They start, however, by listing reasons why physical intervention should always be the last resort:

- using force may lead to further injury
- may provoke high levels of stress for staff and service-users
- the force may be unlawful
- may lead to abuse of service-user by carers
- may not be in service-user's best interests
- non-physical methods may be more effective
- may lead to escalation of challenging behaviours
- may conflict with key service values, such as respect, dignity and choice.

Bearing all that in mind, there will still be circumstances in which physical intervention seems necessary, or at least the best option, and guidance will be necessary to protect the interests of the service-users, primarily, but also the staff. Harris *et al.* suggest there may be three kinds of physical intervention:

- direct physical contact, such as guiding away from danger or holding to prevent an attack on someone
- use of barriers, such as locked doors or door catches out of reach
- materials or equipment to restrict movement, strapping someone into a wheelchair, splints on arms or legs.

The authors exclude absolutely any physical intervention designed to cause pain or to punish, but it is not difficult to see how easily any physical intervention, particularly in the heat of the moment, may carry an overlay of anger or panic and take on a punitive aspect.

The approach and guidance offered is based first of all on a primary commitment to the best interests of service-users. Starting with an analysis of challenging behaviour as part of a broader context of personal and environmental factors, Harris *et al.* emphasise the importance of preventive strategies to reduce the likelihood or provocation of incidents that may require physical intervention. They suggest attention to the 'setting conditions', including the surrounding circumstances and the feelings of the individual concerned, is vital, as illustrated by the case in Box 5.

> ## Box 5: 'Setting conditions' for violence
>
> Jim shares a house with four other people with learning disabilities. One morning recently, he woke up with a heavy cold, feeling tired and irritable. Even on a good day he doesn't like to be hurried, but there were staff shortages and everyone seemed to be rushing around. The staff who usually work with Jim know that if he is asked to do something, he responds best to simple verbal instructions and lots of gestures. On this particular morning a new relief worker asked Jim to get some clean towels from the airing cupboard: 'Jim, pop upstairs and get me three clean towels, not hand towels; they're on the middle shelf. Oh and bring me down a clean shirt for yourself while you're there.' Jim knew that he was expected to do something, but he wasn't sure what. As he stood looking confused, the member of staff said 'Come on, Jim, we're running late you know.' Jim began to feel uneasy and under pressure. The member of staff came up close to him and saying 'Jim, we need some clean towels, NOW!' Jim resolved a confusing situation where he felt under pressure in the only way he knows. He punched the member of staff in the face.
>
> The incident report begins *'For no apparent reason ...'.*
>
> (Doyle *et al.*, 1996, quoted in Harris *et al.*, 1997, p. 19)

The setting conditions for Jim's outburst included: Jim was not feeling very well; he was given instructions he could not follow; he was harassed under pressure – not exactly 'no apparent reason'.

Primary prevention should be in place as a strategy to 'modify the setting conditions to reduce the likelihood of challenging behaviours occurring' (Harris *et al.*, 1997, p. 21). Secondary prevention strategies then come into play to ensure that any 'problematic episodes are properly managed with non-physical interventions before service-users become violent or aggressive' (Harris *et al.*, 1997, p. 22). For example, do not box people into a corner, make options available, allow space and time for soothing and calming, reduce demands, facilitate talking about what concerns the person (that is, not about the anger itself).

Finally, when physical intervention is required, it should still be used with the best interests of the service-user in mind. This means using minimum reasonable force for the minimum necessary period of time. Where the problem is anticipated, a detailed assessment and plan should have been carried out, so that the response has been carefully considered. But in any case, risks should be minimised and every attempt made to ensure that the intervention is designed to maintain and support the physical and psychological well-being of the service-user. Finally, staff need to be properly trained (on knowledge, skills and values, not just restraint procedures) and supported. Their interests count too.

3   Building supportive relationships

Co-ordination and communication

We now move to the third window with quite a different view over the
terrain. From here we shall look at how care relationships develop. The
suggestion is that in order to understand how 'good care' can be achieved,
we need to look at *how* such relationships are developed – *how* they are
made – by the people involved in them. We need to understand not only
what happens between people but also *how* it comes to happen and *how* it
can change.

This does not imply a narrow focus on actions and experiences at an
individual level. People will operate within their socio-cultural and
professional contexts, within their understandings of their roles and the
scope of their practice. By their actions and their developing experiences,
they will further affect and help to create those contexts. It is also possible,
taking this focus on how supportive relationships may be built, to look at
how such relationships themselves can be supported in their turn. The
contexts, management styles, supervisory and support arrangements,
policies, working environments and professional expectations will all
contribute to the 'setting conditions', which may help or hinder the
development of good care relationships.

The 'co-ordination' diagram in Figure 2 offers one way of representing
the context for this process. It is based on ideas developed from systemic
psychotherapy, emphasising a relational approach (for example, Pearce,
1989). It is also reminiscent of the concept of 'situated voices' (Lewis,
1996) referred to in Chapter 2, Section 2.

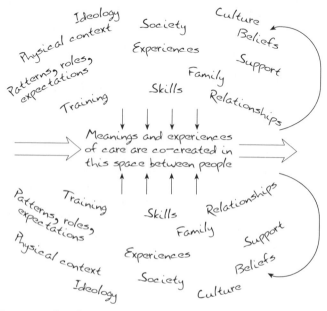

Figure 2   **A context for the co-creation of care**

The arrows at the centre of the diagram represent the encounters between individuals; each individual carries and draws upon a lifetime's set of influences, resources and constraints, which contribute to both the public and the personal context for the care relationship. It is in that metaphorical space between those individuals that the meanings and experiences of care are co-created (that is, created by all those involved). The larger directional arrows indicate the sense in which the negotiation of the relationship is an ongoing process over time, rather than a static entity.

This emphasis on the 'how' of relationships suggests a way of thinking about what is meant by 'care relationships which work', or by 'good care', 'good practice' or 'critical practice', or whatever other term is used to imply some measure of successful outcome. One way of judging could be simply whether they are sustainable. Do they, given the assumptions of individual practitioners and clients as well as those around them, enable a process and relationship to occur that meets expectations? Can they make sense of each other and to each other and share in a mutually satisfactory exchange? Where the process of communication is sufficiently 'co-ordinated', each will feel the satisfaction of being heard, understood and appreciated.

The challenge for the professional can be seen as striving to achieve such 'co-ordination'. Where it fails, the difficulties are often explained away by seeing the 'other' as mad, bad or sick (Pearce, 1989) – or just plain wrong. This has also been argued elsewhere in terms of the importance of seeking to deconstruct devalued difference; in other words, finding a way out of the trap of knee-jerk assumptions and negative stereotyping. The more stressful the experience and the more vulnerable the carer's self-esteem and competence becomes, the more likelihood there is of the other person being pathologised and viewed through the familiar frame of devalued difference (Brechin, 1998).

Trying to see where the other person is coming from (to borrow a rather hackneyed but very useful phrase), and, equally, recognising where they themselves are coming from, are the skills needed to achieve co-ordination, particularly where there are differences of experience and assumptive worlds to be negotiated (remember Hanif, for example). Section 2 gave some extreme examples of failure in co-ordination, but even relatively straightforward encounters challenge the professional to be on the right wavelength – to be able to use that space to co-create effectively. The deconstruction of difference implies a shift in perspective and practice to encompass the complexity of the whole individual, including an understanding of particular difficulties and circumstances and how they impinge on that person.

The example in Box 6 describes an attempt to 'import' palliative care into an acute hospital setting. This is about more than just the co-ordination between individuals in a care relationship. It is also about the challenges of co-ordination between two very different traditions. The hospice tradition and Macmillan nursing have a primary emphasis on care in circumstances where prospects for cure have receded entirely. To

---

Box 6: Importing palliative care into a general hospital

Janet, a Macmillan nurse with many years of experience leading a team in the community and attached to a hospice, was then seconded to the local general hospital with an open brief to try to influence palliative care practice across the board in the hospital. Despite high-level support and a few allies within the hospital, she faced a considerable degree of incomprehension, mistrust and defensiveness. She saw the struggles as being about trying to establish effective communication across the barriers of the very different paradigms underpinning palliative care and acute sector care.

'It's a very complex organisational structure so just finding the points of contact is hard. And getting beyond the sense that it's only relevant for dying patients ... When it's about palliative care which is really relevant for very many more. But it needs such a shift in terms of how people think about the ways they relate to patients – and to relatives.

I have found I have to really work with the practicalities of what happens – whether that's in outpatients or in a ward. At the end of the day, it may not be so much about influencing emotional attitudes to dying – that's what they are expecting from me, all the touchy-feely stuff – but it might be about where the records are or whether the drug administration practices can accommodate the precision and flexibility needed for effective pain management. And then they know that I've understood too.'

(Source: personal communication, name changed)

'import' this into an acute hospital involves complex attention to the processes by which such co-ordination may be achieved.

For Janet even to begin to communicate, let alone influence hospital practice, she needed to find some points of contact. Making those contacts, and beginning to negotiate meanings and assumptions about palliative care, about the constraints and demands of acute sector practice, can all be seen as a process of creating that space within which co-ordination could begin. She had to work with an openness to their assumptive worlds as well as her own. Then the process could begin and could continue.

The feedback arrows on the co-ordination diagram, looping back from the care process into the wider context of influence, show how the experiences and perceptions of today's points of contact and negotiation then become part of tomorrow's resources. Sometimes, of course, practices or patterns are fixed and rigid and we tend to reproduce the resources in the same way they existed and influenced us before. Things can change, though:

More often than we are aware, the practices in which we participate 'construct' a set of resources that differ in significant ways from that which existed before. We call this 'learning', trauma', 'growth', or 'catastrophe', depending on the details.

(Pearce, 1989, p. 46)

Or, we might call it 'professional development'. Some of this professional work or development, however, is, as Pearce suggests, out of our awareness. This aspect of the *how* of care relationships is the subject of the next sub-section.

Unconscious aspects of care work

Different authors focus on various terms, sometimes interchangeably, when talking about the unconscious aspects of care: psychotherapeutic understandings (Smail, 1987); depth psychology (Kitwood, 1990); psycho-analytic frameworks (Menzies, 1960; Hirschhorn, 1990); systemic patterns (Bateson, 1973; Gorell Barnes, 1998). They do have particular and differing meanings, but many more similarities.

Distress, pain, loss, confusion, anger – such emotions can be very intense and hard to handle. The demands of the caring process have been described in terms of the *emotional labour* involved (Smith, 1992, 1999). A professional, of course, may have their own personal emotional stress to contend with – bereavement, separation, depression, anger, or equally, perhaps, feelings of joy and excitement. The emotional labour involves handling one's own feelings *and* supporting clients who are experiencing their own feelings and reactions. Even relatively minor episodes requiring intervention or support from professionals can be extremely stressful; and clients may face extreme stresses, such as having children taken into care, having a terminal illness diagnosed, experiencing pain or fear, being sectioned.

Handling intense feelings tends to tip people back into strategies from early childhood. Whatever school of psycho-dynamic theory is drawn upon, there is a shared set of assumptions that unconscious or 'out of awareness' processes are at work for most people, which in some way reflect habitual early patterns. These can be seen as creative adjustments rather than defence mechanisms and may be quite functional much of the time, but in the face of stressful, unusual or particularly prolonged emotional challenges, they can make successful adaptation hard to achieve.

Box 7 summarises some key explanatory concepts used within counselling and psychotherapy in order to facilitate therapeutic commu-nication and support emotional growth and development. Such frame-works might be of value in understanding other 'caring' relationships. Indeed, the Kitwood frameworks of 'depersonalising' versus 'positive' care interactions are based on precisely such conceptual frameworks as these.

Box 7: Psychological processes that affect coping and caring strategies

Defences (or creative adjustments or habitual patterns): ways of coping with an overwhelming, invasive or isolating environment (Perls *et al.*, 1951; Sills *et al.*, 1995). They are usually patterns laid down in early childhood and can become fixed behaviours, triggered in particular by stressful encounters or circumstances.

Projection: involves getting rid of feelings seen as inappropriate or bad, by detaching from them and projecting them on to someone else (akin to 'splitting'; Klein, 1975). We might see others as in need of comfort by projecting our own unrecognised need on to them. This can sometimes be so powerful that the others take on the feelings and behaviour being projected (projective identification [Klein, 1975] or countertransference).

Retroflection: holding in feelings – for example, of anger or distress – by tightening muscles, holding our breath or turning against ourselves. People who retroflect a lot tend to feel physically tired, stiff and achy. They may also begin to self-harm.

Introjection: introjects are usually involved in the above behaviours. From babyhood we take in (introject) how others behave towards us and this becomes how we see ourselves and the world; for example, I don't deserve comfort; boys don't cry; anger isn't safe.

These forms of defence seem to come into being to protect us from being overwhelmed at times by pain and distress. Paula's brief account in Box 8 is a reminder of how hard it can be to handle that openly.

Box 8: Too close for comfort?

Paula: 'We shared a lot of things, you know, they both shared a lot of things with me about their life, and whatever, and I really did get so involved with those people, that when he died, oh it was just horrendous, it really was!'

Interviewer: 'I can see you're upset even now.'

Paula: 'Yes, oh I am, he was so nice, and yet his death was so ... how she described it ... that's why I got upset, because she described it in such detail to me ... I went to see her afterwards, immediately afterwards, it all just came pouring out. And it was so sad that ... that was very, very hard.'

(Finlay, 1998, interview with occupational therapist)

The difference here, and in Paula's subsequent reaction, was that she was able to make a conscious choice about how to try to handle this then and in the future. The process was within her awareness.

And that made me realise I can't do that, because so many people do die, that you go and see, and you need to be conditioned ... you couldn't do what you do ... you have to go in on a certain level ... I go in with the attitude 'Right, what can I do for these people? How can I make their situation easier?'

Making such a choice, to hold feelings at bay in order to cope, is vital for most practitioners much of the time. This is not the same as pretending the feelings do not exist or being unaware of them through unconscious denial. Being in touch with those feelings may be an essential part of being able to be in contact with the feelings of the person they are seeking to support – or in other words, being able to co-ordinate with them. Their feelings and behaviour too are likely to be filtered through mechanisms designed to protect them, which in their turn may distort and disrupt the process of co-ordination. It can take time to work through to a point where some understanding can occur and, even in fleeting encounters, the best rule of thumb is probably not to jump to conclusions.

In 'dialogue', it is suggested (for example, Buber, 1965; Yontef, 1993), both you and I are emotionally open, free of defences; I am aware of my needs and feelings and you of yours and I am attending to you and you to me. We are separate and connecting. These moments have an impact on both human beings. Holding on to such openness and respect may be necessary, but it is not easy. Each section of this chapter has referred to the importance of support and training in relation to caring roles and this final section is called 'Building supportive relationships'. In the last sub-section we look at this aspect of the caring context.

Support

'A commitment to the nurturance, growth and healing' of the other person is Davies' (1995) phrase to encapsulate caring. Such a phrase might equally well describe the kind of support that carers themselves may need. Whether family carers, residential carers or care professionals, all will fare better if they in turn are cared for. If we leave aside just for a moment conventional notions of training and supervision, we can think rather in the broader terms of what enables us to flourish, what helps us function at our best, develop and grow; then the answers come in terms which have more in common with care relationships than with a curriculum or professional standards.

In itself, attention to nurturance, growth and healing may not be the whole story but, without that, acquiring and developing caring skills and the personal insights which underpin them and evolve alongside will be hampered. To be able to value, respect and co-ordinate with others, including those in severe difficulties with challenging patterns of behaviour, requires that you too be valued, respected and in co-ordination with supportive others. There is a multilayered model at work which, in contrast to the old story of boss shouts at worker, worker goes home and shouts at wife, wife shouts at child, who grows up to repeat the pattern, offers instead a positive feedback loop of co-ordinated and therefore supportive interactions.

Encounters, whether fleeting or longer term or intense, can bring to them an intention to co-ordinate with the other person or to ignore them – to treat them in effect as a cipher rather than as a whole human being. To co-ordinate successfully requires absolutely a commitment to recognise, respect and seek to understand the other's position but, equally, a commitment to respect and seek to understand one's own position.

As we saw earlier, the contexts (settings, organisational and support structures, etc.) in which care occurs can be seen to make good care more, or often less, likely to develop and be sustained. Menzies' work (1960) in an acute sector hospital was seminal in portraying damaging and difficult processes, arising from unconscious mechanisms for dealing with anxiety, which became embedded in the routines and organisational strategies of the institution – to no one's advantage. More recent work (Smith and Agard, 1997; Smith, 1999) describes the emerging structures of new managerialism and the contract culture in terms of their impact on care work – or emotional labour. Smith suggests that these may not provide the ideal environment for good care.

Hard-nosed, resource-led and evidence-based approaches are more likely to be at the cutting edge for service planning and evaluation than a concern about relationships. Nevertheless, the language of negotiation, co-operation and partnership is prevalent in planning and policy documents. Maybe the way forward is to avoid the potential polarisation of organisational constraints and practice and instead to focus on a primary commitment to co-creating both care encounters and care environments through co-operative and co-ordinated relationships.

Conclusion

As we have seen through the three windows on care, providing care is challenging because it involves not just executing care tasks but being in a relationship with another person. Whether this is fleeting or long term, role-bound or relatively flexible, such relationships will be constituted through processes that are both personal and political. How such relationships manifest themselves and how the meanings and experiences of care are created will be negotiated and co-created by the individuals involved, although the practitioner will still tend to have a more powerful voice in the process.

A critical awareness of the personal and political challenges is necessary, to enable a creative approach to such relationships to flow. The good practice and strategies developed to respond constructively to acutely difficult, stressful and potentially damaging encounters can be seen to have relevance for practice and relationships across the board. Where positive care relationships do occur, there will be benefits and rewards to both parties which go far beyond any task-based evaluation.

References

Anderson, M. (1997) 'The necessity of ambivalence: the emotional labour of caring for people with learning difficulties who engage in self-injurious behaviour', unpublished PhD thesis, The Open University.

Barker, P. J., Reynolds, W. and Ward, T. (1995) 'The proper focus of nursing: a critique of the "caring" ideology', *International Journal of Nursing Studies*, Vol. 32, No. 4, pp. 386–97.

Bateson, G. (1973) *Steps to an Ecology of Mind*, London, Paladin.

Braye, S. and Preston-Shoot, M. (1996) *Empowering Practice in Social Care*, Buckingham, Open University Press.

Brechin, A. (1998) 'What makes for good care?', in Brechin, A., Walmsley, J., Katz, J. and Peace, S. (eds) *Care Matters: Concepts, Practice and Research in Health and Social Care*, pp. 170–187, London, Sage.

Buber, M. (1965) *The Knowledge of Man: A Philosophy of the Interhuman* (translated by Friedman, M. and Smith, R. G.), New York, Harper and Row.

Coombes, R. (1998) 'Violence: the facts', *Nursing Times*, Vol. 94, No. 43, pp. 12–13.

Dalley, G. (1988) *Ideologies of Caring: Rethinking Community and Collectivism*, Basingstoke, Macmillan.

Davies, C. (1995) 'Competence versus care? Gender and caring work revisited', *Acta Sociologica*, Vol. 38, pp. 17–31, reprinted in Brechin, A., Walmsley, J., Katz, J. and Peace, S. (eds) *Care Matters: Concepts, Practice and Research in Health and Social Care*, pp. 126–38, London, Sage.

Department of Health (1997) *People Like Us* (The Utting Report), London, HMSO.

Dominelli, L. (1997) *Sociology for Social Work*, Basingstoke, Macmillan.

Finch, J. and Groves, D. (eds) (1980) *A Labour of Love: Women, Work and Caring*, London, Routledge and Kegan Paul.

Finlay, L. (1999) 'The life of the occupational therapist: meaning and motive in an uncertain world', PhD thesis, The Open University.

French, S. and Swain, J. (1998) 'Normality and disabling care', in Brechin, A., Walmsley, J., Katz, J. and Peace, S. (eds) *Care Matters: Concepts, Practice and Research in Health and Social Care*, pp. 81–95, London, Sage.

Glendinning, C. (1983) *Unshared Work? Parents and their Disabled Children*, London, Routledge and Kegan Paul.

Gorell Barnes, G. (1998) 'The intersubjective mind: family pattern, family therapy and individual meaning', in Yelloly, M. and Henkel, M. (eds) *Learning and Teaching in Social Work*, London, Jessica Kingsley.

Graham, H. (1983) 'Caring: a labour of love', in Finch, J. and Groves, D. (eds) *A Labour of Love: Women, Work and Caring*, London, Routledge and Kegan Paul.

Harris, J. *et al.* (1997) *Physical Interventions: A Policy Framework*, Kidderminster, British Institute of Learning Disability.

Hirschhorn, L. (1990) *The Workplace Within: Psychodynamics of Organisational Life*, London, MIT Press.

Hopson, B. (1981) 'Counselling and helping', in Griffiths, D. (ed.) *Psychology and Medicine*, London and Basingstoke, British Psychological Society and Macmillan.

Kirby, C. and Slevin, O. (1992) 'A new curriculum for care', in Slevin, O. and Buckenham, M. (eds) *Project 2000: The Teachers Speak – Innovations in the Nursing Curriculum*, Edinburgh, Campion Press.

Kitwood, T. (1990) *Concern for Others: A New Psychology of Conscience and Morality*, London, Routledge.

Kitwood, T. (1997) *Dementia Reconsidered: The Person Comes First*, Buckingham, Open University Press.

Klein, M. (1975) (ed.) *Envy and Gratitude and Other Works 1946–1963*, New York, Delacorte Press.

Leininger, M. (1988) *Caring: An Essential Human Need*, Wayne State University Press, USA.

Levy, A. and Kahan, B. (1997) *The Pindown Experience and the Protection of Children: The Report of the Staffordshire Child Care Enquiry 1990*, Stafford, Staffordshire County Council.

Lewis, G. (1996) 'Situated voices: "black women's experience" and social work', *Feminist Review*, Vol. 53, pp. 24–56.

Mahoney, C. (1998) 'Patients behaving badly', *Nursing Times*, Vol. 94, No. 39, pp. 26–29.

Martin, J. P. (1984) *Hospitals in Trouble*, Oxford, Blackwell.

Menzies, I. E. P. (1960) 'A case study in the functioning of social systems as a defence against anxiety: a report on the nursing service of a general hospital', *Human Relations*, pp. 95–121.

Morris, J. (1993) *Independent Lives: Community Care and Disabled People*, Basingstoke, Macmillan.

Parker, R. A. (1981) 'Tending and social policy', in Goldberg, E. M. and Hatch, S. (eds) *A New Look at the Personal Social Services*, London, Policy Studies Institute.

Pearce, B. (1989) *Communication and the Human Condition*, Southern Illinois University Press, USA.

Perls, F., Hefferline, R. F. and Goodman, P. (1951) *Gestalt Therapy: Excitement and Growth in Human Personality*, London, Souvenir Press.

Sills, C. *et al.* (1995) *Gestalt Counselling*, Bicester, Winslow Press Ltd.

Smail, D. (1987) *Taking Care: An Alternative to Therapy* (2nd edn 1997), London, Constable and Co.

Smith, P. (1992) *The Emotional Labour of Nursing*, Basingstoke, Macmillan.

Smith, P. (1999) 'Logging emotions: a logbook of personal reflections', *Soundings*, Vol. 11, pp. 128–37.

Smith, P. and Agard, E. (1997) 'Care costs: towards a critical understanding of care', in Brykczynska, G. (ed.) *Caring: The Compassion and Wisdom of Nursing*, pp. 180–204, London, Arnold Hodder Headlines.

Thompson, D. and Brown, H. (1998) *Response-ability: Helping Services to Work with Men with Learning Difficulties Who Have Unacceptable or Abusive Sexual Behaviours*, Brighton, Pavilion Publishing.

Thompson, D., Clare, I. and Brown, H. (1997) 'Not such an ordinary relationship: the role of women support staff in relation to men with learning disabilities who have difficult sexual behaviour', *Disability and Society*, Vol. 12, No. 4, pp. 573–92.

Twigg, J. and Atkin, K. (1994) *Carers Perceived: Policy and Practice in Informal Care*, Buckingham, Open University Press.

Wardaugh, J. and Wilding, P. (1993) 'Towards an explanation of the corruption of care', *Critical Social Policy*, Vol. 37, pp. 5–31.

Wood, R. (1992) 'Care of disabled people', in Dalley, G. (ed.) *Disability and Social Policy*, London, PSI.

Yontef, G. M. (1993) *Awareness, Dialogue and Process: Essays on Gestalt Therapy*, New York, The Gestalt Journal Press.

Chapter 8
The challenge of working in teams

Linda Finlay

··· with doctors labelled as 'pill pushers',
social workers as 'bleeding hearts', and occupational
therapists as 'basket weavers'.

Introduction

> Louise, younger sister of Jasmine Beckford, was first admitted to hospital with severe physical injuries on a Saturday. The admitting junior doctor did not inform the hospital social worker and so Jasmine, still at home, remained unprotected. On the Monday, the hospital social worker informed social services, who made an unsuccessful attempt at a home visit. The next day, Jasmine, too, was taken to hospital with non-accidental injuries.
>
> (Reder *et al.*, 1993, pp. 80–81)

This description of a well-publicised child abuse scandal demonstrates the significance of multidisciplinary teamwork and exposes the damage that can occur when communication breaks down between health and social care agencies. The tragic story of Louise and Jasmine, along with many others (some well publicised and others not), prompted numerous inquiries and investigations. Some of these inquiries (for example, the

1988 Butler Schloss inquiry into child abuse in Cleveland) have resulted in recommendations for co-ordinated multidisciplinary teamwork and for more effective collaboration between agencies. In 1991, the Home Office concluded that: 'Inter-disciplinary and inter-agency work is an essential process in the professional task of attempting to protect children from abuse' (Hornby, 1993, p. 190).

Teamwork is firmly on the agenda as government policy-makers, consumer groups and the range of people working in health and social care all call for greater commitment towards integrated care. Alongside calls for multiprofessional working comes the breaking down of traditional professional boundaries. Increasingly, professionals are being asked to co-ordinate and manage service-users' total care irrespective of traditional role and location boundaries. Thus, individual practitioners face the dual challenge of holding on to their own knowledge or skill base while entering into the work of other professionals, which inevitably means developing new team relationships and ways of working.

All these developments suggest that teamwork is desirable, essential even, for providing effective treatment. Yet is this always the case? What constitutes good teamwork? Can a teamwork approach ever be counter-productive? Is it an effective way of patching up fractures within or between different services? What factors constrain teamwork and how can positive collaboration be fostered? This chapter aims to answer these questions by taking a critical look at teamwork and examining how it works in practice. The focus here will be on how practitioners with different areas of expertise work together in a team, rather than looking at inter-agency collaboration – the subject of Chapter 12.

Section 1 starts by exploring what constitutes co-ordinated multi-disciplinary teamwork. It recognises that different models of teamwork operate in practice. Section 2 challenges the assumptions behind the commonplace view that teamwork is necessarily an effective way of working and analyses the value and limitations of teamwork. Section 3 examines the challenges to teamwork and how the conflicts inherent in multidisciplinary working can constrain attempts to collaborate. Finally, different strategies for fostering positive teamwork are explored in Section 4.

1 Exploring the concept of 'the team'

In this chapter, a team is defined as a group of individuals, with varying backgrounds, perspectives, skills and training, who work together towards the common goal of delivering a health or social care service. Ideally, team members collaborate and value one another's different contributions.

'Co-ordinated profession' or 'collective responsibility' teams?

Within the broad definition given above, teams can be organised in many ways, with different degrees of co-operation and collaboration. Consider Boxes 1 and 2: they describe the way two different teams operate in practice.

Box 1: A multidisciplinary team

Team members

1 consultant, 3 junior doctors, 15 nurses and nursing assistants, 2 physiotherapists, 1 occupational therapist and 1 helper, 1 part-time social worker, associated students.

The way the team is organised/functions

The consultant has overall medical responsibility and (through the junior doctors' efforts) oversees all admissions, discharges and treatment decisions. The nurses implement the patients' treatment, much of which is prescribed by the doctors. Written referrals are made to the remedial therapy staff who have a degree of professional autonomy to decide their particular interventions. Otherwise, decisions about treatment strategies are largely made by the consultant on the daily ward round consisting of the junior doctors and senior nurses on duty. The routine format is that the nurses and doctors give a verbal report to the consultant on a patient's progress. The consultant outlines the next step for treatment after listening to the reports and conferring with the patient. The senior therapists and nurses meet on a weekly basis to discuss the overall management of particular patients' treatment. It is in this forum that the therapists make their reports and recommendations. The senior nurse is supposed to pass these on to the consultant but this does not occur consistently. Some communication between team members also occurs through the writing of daily care notes in the nursing handover book but this carries little overall status and is mainly for nursing consumption. Broader policy decisions regarding changes to ward practice are generally imposed by management.

Closeness of team relationships and degree of interaction

Relationships tend to be formal with interactions generally task-focused, not socially focused. The quick turnover of staff means that several of the team members do not know each others' names. However, uniforms and badges depicting their roles ease interactions as members adopt relevant professional behaviours. Some team members collaborate more closely than others – for instance, warm relationships can be found within the nursing staff as a whole. The three therapists also liaise closely as they negotiate a relevant division of labour.

Box 2: An interdisciplinary team

Team members

1 team leader (qualified nurse), 4 community psychiatric nurses, 1 occupational therapist, 1 psychologist, 1 social worker, 1 part-time consultant psychiatrist, associated students.

The way the team is organised/functions

The team members gather at a weekly referral meeting to allocate newly referred clients to the most suitable staff member who will act as key worker and primary therapist. Thereafter the key worker sees the client for an initial assessment and negotiates treatment goals. The staff team meets regularly to review the progress of the clients in each key worker's caseload. In this meeting the key worker discusses his or her interventions and gains support and advice from the other members. The key worker can also refer the client to other team members for specific interventions as relevant. The team leader chairs the meetings and is the manager with overall responsibility. Policy decisions regarding day-to-day team practice are created jointly by the all team members and regularly reviewed.

Closeness of team relationships and degree of interaction

The team members work closely together and collaborate on several projects (for instance, co-leading therapy groups and having joint supervision). In general their relationships are positive and friendly. Many of the team members also see each other socially. Sometimes conflicts and tensions in the team surface and are usually related to defending role boundaries or not feeling sufficiently valued by others. This can sometimes be felt acutely as the team's work involves a blurring of traditional role boundaries which can leave the members feeling insecure about their contribution. Sometimes members vie to treat 'interesting' clients and the nurses can feel resentful as they see themselves as the ones who always get allocated the more 'routine' clients with long-standing mental health needs. Occasionally, team members clash in terms of their professional beliefs – for instance, about the role of medication. In general, though, team members feel united against outside agencies and units (for example, they all tend to disparage the traditional practices of the local psychiatric hospital unit).

In the example in Box 1 the degree of collaboration and sense of unity of purpose amongst the professionals is limited. The consultant takes responsibility for all the key decisions within the context of a meeting where relevant professionals are absent. Treatments are carried out in parallel rather than being co-ordinated. The exception to this is the weekly management meeting which offers potential for some of the (senior) professionals involved to work together. It is notable that nursing and therapy assistants do not play a part in decision making and that the patients also have a limited voice. The label 'team' would be much more convincing if: (a) the consultant listened to comments from the different professionals and patients involved (see Box 3); (b) the whole team participated in decision making; and (c) the route of communicating through the written care plans was more valued.

Box 3: The patient/client as a team member?

Ideally, patients/clients and their carers should be considered as members of the team in so far as they are centrally involved in carrying through any treatment or care plan. The degree to which this happens in practice is open to question. Patients/clients may be asked to express their 'problem' or give their perspective, but often they do not take part in the actual decision making. The traditional practice of ward rounds is a good illustration of this: patients may be asked how they feel now and whether they are ready to go home, but the clinical decision about when to discharge them is left firmly to the 'expert professionals' involved.

In the example in Box 2 the regular, collaborative team meetings give the key workers a sense of participation and having a team behind them. This prevents practitioners from becoming too isolated and offering parallel services. The fact that there are also conflicts and tensions within this team does not unduly damage the sense of team identity and approach.

Øvretveit (1997a) picks up the contrast between multidisciplinary and interdisciplinary teamwork by distinguishing between a 'co-ordinated profession team' and a 'collective responsibility team'. The former consists of a loose network which acts as a focus for referral and communication but then delivers separately organised and accountable services. The latter involves a close working group which pools its resources, for instance in team meetings and joint case notes, and takes shared responsibility for the use of resources (even where individuals take clinical decisions separately). In a co-ordinated profession team individual members are likely to be bound by the policies and priorities of their own profession or agency, whereas in collective responsibility teams, individual team members are more accountable to the team for the way they deploy their own time and resources.

Three models of teamwork

Another way of characterising the differences between how teams operate is to distinguish between the 'parallel team', the 'hierarchical team and the 'collaborative team'. The hierarchical and collaborative models have already been examined in Boxes 1 and 2. The parallel team describes the situation where several autonomous professionals deal with their own specialist area with little or no collaboration. A primary health care team set within a GP practice is an example of this. Here, GPs, district nurses, health visitors, a physiotherapist, a podiatrist and administration staff all carry their own case or work load. Whilst some liaison occurs between the GPs and each of the other services, these services rarely deal directly with each other. They operate as a loose network and liaise pragmatically where necessary.

In practice, teams often operate a combination of these models as members work both in parallel and in collaboration, whilst simultaneously being a part of a hierarchy. Also the type of teamwork engaged in can change according to the task at hand and to the composition of team members at the time. For instance, whilst the example of a team in Box 1 most closely resembles a hierarchical team, the remedial therapists work in parallel with the medical team, and collaboration takes place within smaller sub-teams. Øvretveit (1997b) reviewed the way a community mental health team functioned and found a range of practices. For instance, day centre staff collaborated as a sub-team but, in terms of links between them and the other services, they operated as parallel teams and contact was largely *ad hoc* or dependent on personalities.

The work of most health and social care teams is too complex to be easily classified. However, it is useful to distinguish between different models to help us understand the structure and processes of a working team more closely. Table 1 (overleaf) contrasts three models of teamwork and draws out different patterns of team behaviour.

Having distinguished between the different models, the question remains: which type of team and teamwork is best? In practice, each has a role depending on the demands of the situation and the function of the team. A collaborative team, or a well co-ordinated parallel team, would probably be the choice to provide a long-term, holistic package of care to a group of clients who have multiple and complex needs (for instance, in a rehabilitation or community-based unit). In such a context, care would need to be taken to ensure team members value each others' different professional interventions and so avoid unnecessary duplication. In situations requiring quick decisions and interventions (for example, an acute surgical ward), a hierarchical structure might be more appropriate. However, in this context care would need to be taken to ensure that professionals do not feel disempowered by the hierarchy and, hence, inhibited about contributing. This again could result in the patients not getting the best service.

The issue for teams, then, is not that some ways of operating are 'good' and others 'bad'. Instead, the working of the team should be appropriate to its purpose and function in terms of the services it is supposed to offer and the decisions it needs to take. The challenge for all teams, and team leaders, is how best to organise themselves to achieve these ends. In practice, teams do not necessarily operate as effectively as they might do.

Table 1   **Three models of teamwork – structure and processes**

Team behaviour	*Parallel team*	*Hierarchical team*	*Collaborative team*
Team decision making	Decisions taken by the individual professionals involved who have a high degree of autonomy	Team leader sets agenda and prescribes action after attending to other team members' reports	Team shares responsibility for goal setting and negotiates team decisions
Referral of clients	To individual team members as relevant, usually in the form of a written referral	Mostly formal referrals where the senior professional delegates tasks	Two-way referrals, often negotiated at both a formal and an informal level
Treatment/care delivery	Carried through by specialist professionals working in parallel	Carried through by practitioners working in parallel under the gaze of the senior professionals involved	Joint working common (e.g. joint domiciliary visiting)
Perception of roles	Some understanding but also some misunderstanding likely (e.g. as seen with stereotyping others' roles)	Some understanding but also some misunderstanding likely	Roles clearly understood and mutual respect given although tensions may occur over role blurring and boundaries
Professional status	Individual professional contribution valued so differences seen as less relevant	Inequalities and differences between professionals can inhibit co-operation	Differences either ignored or not valued; negative use of power or status is challenged
Interaction in the team	Very little and irregular, mostly at a pragmatic, formal level	Regular interaction, mostly formal; closer collaboration can occur between some members	Close regular interaction and collaboration between members

(Source: adapted from Pritchard, 1995, p. 208)

2   The rhetoric and the reality

Challenging assumptions

That teamwork is desirable and an efficient, effective way of delivering health and social care is often taken as self-evident. Practitioners are forever being exhorted to collaborate and work within teams. This rhetoric comes from many quarters: government, professional bodies, management, user groups and the media, among others. In the late 1990s, the Department of Health set out the strategic objectives of the NHS, which included a 'seamless service working across boundaries', and it acknowledged the importance of health and social care professionals having clear understandings of each others' roles (DoH, 1997). With regard to professional education, the national Occupational Standards for professional activity in health promotion and care developed through the 1990s suggested collaboration was essential and called for more interprofessional training opportunities. (The impact of such policies is explored more fully in Chapter 12.)

But to what extent do the assumptions match up to reality? It is important to examine the claims and the counter-claims.

Three basic assumptions underlying the rhetoric can be identified:

• Teamwork offers a way of providing a comprehensive service.
• Teams are cost-effective and efficient.
• Teams offer a source of positive experiences.

Do teams provide a more comprehensive service?

The first advantage claimed for teamwork is that it offers the possibility of delivering a comprehensive range of treatment and care services. The point of having team members from different disciplines is that each person can offer skills and knowledge arising from their particular discipline. The complex health and social needs of a diverse range of service-users can only be met through an equally complex and specialised division of labour (Loxley, 1997). By combining the different areas of expertise and dovetailing contributions to ensure they are both timely and relevant, the service-users can be treated more holistically.

In practice, the quality of care delivered is sometimes less than ideal and different problems emerge. First, from the point of view of the service-user, it can be confusing, even disempowering, to have many different disciplines offering a service. For example, the team can prove destructive if team members offer contradictory 'expert' advice (say about taking medication). Øvretveit's study (1997b) of the work in one community mental health team reveals how some clients were given contradictory advice and how there was a failure to carry out a mutually reinforcing care programme.

Sheldon (1994) argues that, in some cases, treatment by a single profession has been demonstrated to work more effectively and that there are real difficulties in interprofessional working when interventions may be based on mutually conflicting knowledge bases and research evidence. He makes his point thus:

> The different theoretical assumptions about mental ill health held by psychiatrists, nurses, social workers and the staff of voluntary bodies stand as serious and definite obstacles to co-operation. Mention the 'medical model' on a social work course and you will hear the kind of

background hissing once reserved for the characters with moustaches and black hats in silent movies.

(Sheldon, 1994, p. 89)

Secondly, and paradoxically, a negotiated division of labour between members can actually result in less holistic practice as each member concentrates on a small aspect of treatment. From the patient/client's point of view the treatment received can feel fragmented with no one attending to the overall package of care. In order to combat such fragmentation, teams may experiment with different ways of organising their workload (such as adopting a key worker or case manager system). Indeed, many social care agencies have adopted the case manager model to such a degree that they have turned away from team approaches in favour of the 'generic worker'. The degree to which key worker systems are effective depends largely on: (a) the skills of the individual workers concerned; (b) the extent to which the worker is supported by other team members; and (c) the extent to which the worker can draw on other team members' expertise when necessary (see Box 4).

Box 4: The case for and against key working

The National Health Service and Community Care Act 1990 called for the bulk of care for clients in the community to be provided by a designated key worker who would co-ordinate the client's total care. This required professionals to work more autonomously (compared with their previous team-based experience within institutions). It also meant that the key worker could call on wider team resources if clients' needs extended beyond practitioners' expertise (Morgan, 1993). Key working also occasionally required practitioners to be more accountable to colleagues from other disciplines – for instance, where a nominated key worker is accountable to the care manager who has budgetary responsibility for the overall care package. The value of a key working system is that it ensures a co-ordinated approach within a team and allows in-depth relationships between client and worker to be developed. In practice, however, key working may simply replace team working as key workers may not be able to enlist wider team help (given other members have their own heavy workloads). Thus clients may not be able to draw on a team of different experts with specialised skills.

Are teams cost-effective and efficient?

The second commonplace assumption made about teamwork is that it is an efficient, cost-effective way of allocating resources. Offering a co-ordinated package of care based on a division of labour between team members is useful as it can eliminate unnecessary duplication of effort. Also, where a division of labour between members of the team is negotiated the best (or cheapest) person for the job can be selected (for instance, the move to train nurses to do routine medical tasks). This economic rationale for teamwork fits well with the logic of marketisation and the reality of limited resources. For instance, managers may well support the idea of nurse specialists working alongside, and to some extent replacing, (more expensive) doctors.

Against this, it can be argued that teamwork may well prove inefficient and expensive, particularly where team members do not communicate adequately (Mackay *et al.*, 1995). For one thing, using a team approach can lead to unnecessary duplication. Øvretveit's (1997b) evaluation of the work of a community mental health team points out how some clients had many different duplicating review meetings (held by day centre staff, care co-ordinators, hostel staff, and so on).

A further experience of many new hospital patients is being given an 'initial interview' by every member of the team. So the patients repeat the same basic information, explaining their problems several times over. In such situations, it is not uncommon to hear the patient complain, 'Don't you people talk to each other?' (Øvretveit, 1997a, p. 9). Such duplication is not only a potential waste of time and resources, it can also be distressing for the service-users as they feel that the professionals have not listened to previous accounts and that the different team members have not been adequately briefed.

It can also be argued that teamwork is inefficient in that it requires so much extra work in the form of team meetings and strategic negotiations. It is not uncommon to hear staff complain that they do not have time to see their patients! Further, the many accumulated hours spent trying to liaise and collaborate could arguably be more usefully spent in direct patient/client contact.

Do teams offer a good experience?

The third claim made about teamwork is that it can be a positive experience for the team members themselves. The team offers each member a source of meaning and identity as well as learning opportunities, professional stimulation and challenge. The team is also a source of support, positive feedback and satisfying social interactions. In a stressful work situation where professionals struggle with difficult patients/clients and inadequate resources, the team can be experienced as the one positive force that keeps members going. The team in this context empowers. Cohesive teams give individuals strength and confidence as they know that they have the team's backing and that responsibility is shared. In other words, strength is drawn from the group.

However, the obverse can also sometimes apply (see Box 5 overleaf). Team member interactions can be unsupportive, or even negative, and power can be abused. Where there is an over-abundance of conflict and undue competition between members, the team becomes a source of problems as well as solutions and political decision-making can take precedence over clinical decision-making (Morrison, 1994; Finlay, 1999). Ironically, strong teamwork can prove disempowering and problematic for service-users (for an illustration see Griffiths and Luker's study described in Box 5).

Box 5: Some research on teamwork in primary care

1   Jones (1992), reporting on one study in a primary care setting, shows families receiving team care had fewer hospitalisations, operations and physician visits for illness than control families.

2   Wood *et al.* (1994) found primary care teamwork was reported to improve both health delivery and staff motivation.

3   Wiles and Robison (1994) interviewed practice nurses, district nurses, health visitors and midwives in 20 practices. Issues identified as problematic included: team identity, leadership, access to GPs, philosophies of care, misunderstandings or disagreements about each others' roles.

4   Poulton and West (1999) studied 68 primary health care teams and found that effectiveness (in relation to teamwork, efficiency and care given) was related to team processes (such as amount of participation) rather than structure.

5   West and Field (1995), reporting on interviews with 96 team members, refer to failures of leadership, and lack of meeting time to define objectives, clarify roles or tasks, encourage participation and cope with change. Differences in status, power, educational background and personal assertiveness were also seen as problematic.

6   Griffiths and Luker (1994), in a study of district nurses working together in a primary health care team, found that: 'the professional culture of community nursing has led to the development of organisational rules which, in a quest to avoid conflict between team members, potentially militates against patient choice' (p. 1038). These researchers cite several rules, such as the need to keep up a united front and preserve weekends, which are seen to benefit the team but may not be in the best interests of the service-users.

Different teams, different advantages

Teams, when they work well, can be a valuable vehicle for the delivery of effective treatment and care, but there is nothing inevitable about this process. Whether teams are a beneficial or destructive force depends on how they work in practice, given the particular situation, constraints and people involved. Also, different types of team have different values and limitations (see Table 2).

A *parallel* team allows professionals to practise autonomously and draws specifically on their expertise. However, poor team communication can result in fragmented or contradictory treatments and unnecessary duplication. Hierarchical and collaborative teams are likely to have a co-ordinated division of labour which offers the possibility of more holistic, integrated care. A *hierarchical* team, with clear lines of accountability, can ensure an efficient use of resources but team relationships can

Table 2 **Values and limitations of different types of team**

	Parallel team	*Hierarchical team*	*Collaborative team*
Values	Professionals have autonomy Service-users can benefit from individual professional attention and expertise	Co-ordinated division of labour enables holistic, integrated care Efficient use of resources can minimise duplication Lines of accountability and responsibility are clear	Co-ordinated division of labour enables holistic, integrated care Service-users can benefit from interdisciplinary knowledge and respect Team relationships can be empowering and supportive
Limitations	Poor team communication can result in fragmented treatment and unnecessary duplication Team members can be split and played off against each other Service-users can become confused when contradictory approaches are adopted	Team relationships can be experienced as disempowering and unsupportive Tensions and inequalities can inhibit co-operation Conflict may impact negatively on service-users	Team members may become self-absorbed and unduly focused on team relationships, putting these ahead of service-users' needs Collaboration can be time-consuming and so more expensive Responsibility is diffused and lines of accountability are unclear

be experienced as disempowering and unsupportive. Tensions and inequalities can inhibit co-operation and impact negatively on service-users. By contrast, a *collaborative* team has the potential to empower its members and service-users are likely to benefit from greater interdisciplinary respect. On the negative side, it can be time-consuming (and so more expensive) to engage in collaboration and team members may become self-absorbed, putting team concerns ahead of service-users.

Engaging in teamwork is always challenging. Rather than simply accepting the view that teamwork is good, we need to be critical and question: (a) whether teamwork is the best way of delivering services in the first place; (b) which way of organising the teamwork will provide the optimum service; and (c) how the challenges of actually engaging in team collaboration can be faced. As Loxley (1997, pp. 2–3) argues:

> Collaboration is not a universal panacea, nor is it cheap, though it must be efficient if it is to be justified. Understanding its costs tempers enthusiasm with reality ... interprofessional and interagency collaboration must become an activity which can be reliably prescribed when it is

judged necessary for effective service. Collaboration should not be a panacea, nor an article of faith, nor dependent on haphazard circumstances, but a taught and resourced part of each profession's repertoire of skills, organisation, and culture.

The first step to minimising the costs and maximising the benefits of teamwork is to understand more about the dynamics of how the team is functioning – the subject of the next section.

3   Understanding divisions, problems and conflicts

Conflict is interwoven with interprofessional collaboration because there are deep-rooted social differences in the division of labour which has developed over the last 200 years in the health and welfare service.
(Loxley, 1997, p. 1)

Consider the scenario in Box 6 which exposes some of the divisions, problems and conflicts that can occur in a team.

Box 6: Problems in a multidisciplinary team

The doctors and nurses on an acute admission ward want to discharge a patient (in part to release bed space). They argue that the patient is 'well enough' to go home; however, the occupational therapist would like to make a home visit to check on home circumstances before discharging the patient.

On the next ward round, the doctors consult with the nurses and they discuss the possibility of discharging this patient. The consultant asks the occupational therapist whether the patient can function independently in terms of washing and dressing. She replies that on her limited assessment thus far he is independent, but that a fuller assessment of his needs is necessary. The occupational therapist wants to argue against discharging the patient too soon but feels unable to assert herself directly with this senior consultant. The nurse at this point tries to back up the therapist and suggests that a discharge date later on in the week would allow time for a home visit. The consultant asks the patient whether he would like to leave the hospital today and whether a family member can pick him up.

After the ward round, the therapist and nurse let off some steam about how they had felt 'put down' by the consultant's unduly authoritarian approach. A junior doctor walks into the room and all conversation stops.

The patient is discharged later that day. He lives alone and arrangements for activating some support systems in the community have not been made. A week later the patient is readmitted with additional problems, which might have been prevented had someone arranged to check on his progress.

Several different problems confront this team. Conflicts between different professional values and team member priorities occur in a context of unequal status and power. Destructive sub-grouping further compounds failures to communicate. At a 'micro' level of analysis these problems can be seen to arise because of a clash of values between individuals or professional groups (say between the doctor and therapist). Equally, problems may be due to the nature of the group dynamics as a whole (for instance, the way the team engages in decision making may have become established as a norm). At a broader level of analysis, issues such as leader effectiveness, how the team functions as a system and how decision making is organised need to be examined. Finally, underlying 'macro' issues need to be explored as the functioning of a team may have a good deal to do with professional and power issues, in the context of how health or social care is organised.

To understand what is happening in a team, it can be useful to examine three different, and to some extent competing, levels of analysis (see Figure 1):

- the *group* in terms of interpersonal dynamics
- the *organisation* in terms of decision-making structures
- the *society* in terms of power and broader structural issues.

Group

Teams can be analysed in terms of individual and group dynamics and processes. What roles do people play? What norms operate? What level of group cohesion exists?

Organisation

Teams can be understood in terms of how they are set up, organised and managed. What communication networks and decision-making systems are in place?

Society

Teams can be seen to reflect the social relationships and structures of society as a whole. For instance, to what extent does the team reproduce broader social divisions and power relations?

Figure 1   **Three levels of analysis**

Group level of analysis

The roles played by different members can have a major impact on how a team functions. The type of leadership role taken, for instance, can radically shift the way a team responds. An overly authoritarian leader, for example, tends to create either a passive/dependent or an angry/resistant team. As another example, the informal role of 'clown' can both enable and impair teamwork. Sometimes the clown may joke to relieve tensions and, in so doing, absolves others from having to take the social initiative. On the negative side, the clown role can be a source of irritation when it prevents a team getting on with the task at hand (Finlay, 1993).

Group dynamics can also be relevant at a more unconscious level. A team may put up psychological defences, such as stereotyping, denial, blaming and avoidance, to combat the anxieties and stresses of work (Menzies Lyth, 1988). These defensive behaviours enable the practitioners to cope, but they may also be maladaptive and produce additional problems. Box 7 illustrates how defensive behaviour can get in the way of effective work.

As another example, a team can unite against an outside threat (commonly, management or another agency). This may result in a more cohesive, collaborative team, but it can also have a negative impact on professional relationships and the delivery of health and social care.

Box 7: Example of conflict in a social work team

A child protection social work team meets fortnightly with a supervisor to discuss their work. The process of talking about the nature of the work (for example, assessing levels of child abuse) and sharing their different experiences about how they handled situations was stressful to the team members. The social workers often felt 'exposed' and vulnerable. In one such tense group meeting, a team member started to cite some heavily theoretical research. The other members quickly joined in with similar references. The discussion soon became academic and well distanced from the difficult emotions and feelings of inadequacies aroused by their work and the group itself. When the supervisor pointed out the group's use of intellectualisation to deny and avoid their painful emotions, the group's members were forced to confront their own behaviour. This challenge enabled them to refocus on giving each other emotional support.

(Source: adapted from a case illustration cited in Hornby, 1993)

Organisation level of analysis

Problems at organisation level emerge when team members and their managers are not clear about their responsibilities and the team's division of labour. Øvretveit (1997c) argues that team leaders have a responsibility to ensure effective systems are in place and that there is an appropriate division of labour between members. He identifies (p. 50) common problems for team leaders and managers to look out for when they are reviewing a (collective responsibility) team including the following.

- Team meeting problems – frequent absences, avoiding issues, too many issues which do not need team discussion, unclear decision-making processes, inadequate chairing.
- Emergency work driving out longer-term more effective work, or too much long-term work without review.
- No team influence over closure decisions, making it difficult to allocate new cases or work.
- No agreement over priorities, or priorities are not defined in specific terms to monitor whether they are being met.
- No forum for in-depth discussion of selected cases.
- Separate professional information and record systems, or difficulties getting information from others.
- Insufficient administration support and inadequate team base (no good coffee/meeting area).
- Leadership with no authority.

Society level of analysis

At a society level, teams are understood to reflect the relationships and structures of society as a whole. In particular, teams are seen to reproduce broader social divisions (class, race, gender) and power relations. Practitioners in a team are likely to have different status, power, pay, experience and conditions of work – and all of these are a potential source of tension and are disempowering for team members. Cott (1998) suggests team structures commonly reflect social class distinctions as high status professionals assume responsibility and control and lower status workers carry out the tasks, leading to a 'we decide, you do' division of labour. Similarly, hierarchical attitudes to gender may contrast the 'professional work' of men with the 'supportive activities' of women. Dalley (1989) argues that nurses are trapped in a deferential relationship with doctors.

Competition amongst team members, arising in the context of marketisation where practitioners compete with each other for contracts, for funds and even for their jobs, also leads to splits in the team. Competition can impact negatively as it may involve destructive sub-grouping, as sub-groups attempt to usurp power and exclude others (Parkin, 1979), and negative stereotyping of the 'other' (for instance, other professional groups are commonly put down, with doctors labelled as 'pill pushers', social workers as 'bleeding hearts' and occupational therapists as 'basket weavers'). The team is unlikely to function effectively in the face of such processes. Moreover, if practitioners are spending their time protecting their own territory and guarding their backs, they do so at the expense of thinking about patients' and clients' needs.

4   Rising to the challenge of teamwork

> The real benefit from teams comes not just from co-ordinating separate professions' activities but from melding them in new and creative ways and hence producing a sum which is greater than the parts.
>
> (Øvretveit, 1995, pp. 41–2)

Enabling a team to work together more positively involves working at different levels and drawing on a combination of strategies related to: (a) team building; (b) reviewing the team's organisation; and (c) challenging power structures.

Team building

An extensive range of literature details different staff development activities designed to promote a sense of 'team-ness' and to develop teamworking skills. Typically, 'time out' is recommended, where the team put aside their daily responsibilities and carve out a focused space for some shared endeavour. The sharing involves whatever is appropriate to the team, be it a common meal, a day of staff development at a local hotel or bonding together on a mountain survival exercise! The aim of such activities is to develop a sense of team spirit through shared collaboration and participation. Individuals need to feel actively included and be given opportunities to contribute. They may also gain from learning new team skills, such as negotiation and effective leadership.

Another common team-building strategy is the use of 'sensitivity' groups. Here, the team meet on a regular basis to express and explore individuals' feelings and team issues. Sometimes an outside facilitator is brought in to challenge the team to look at its interpersonal dynamics and defensive practices. These types of group can be threatening but also empowering as members 'connect' emotionally and offer mutual support. In Box 8, Hornby (1993) describes how discussion helped some groups of practitioners move from being defensive and isolated in their professional identities towards having a shared identity.

Box 8: A group discussion – sharing

In a discussion about families with problems and the responsibilities of practitioners, criticism was directed at the social workers in the local area office.

AREA SOCIAL WORKER: We don't always get the support we would wish, particularly from GPs.

HEALTH VISITOR: You can't get out of it by blaming someone else.

SOCIAL WORKER (angrily): Well, health visitors can visit and be seen as kind and helpful, and the social workers get turned into the 'baddies' because they have the power to take children away. You hide behind us.

ANOTHER SOCIAL WORKER: Often in this group you have been hinting that we were not doing our job properly. You seem to think you know it all.

HEALTH VISITOR: (after a short pause, and in an unexpectedly distressed voice) I don't know it all. I wish I did. Sometimes I feel I am no help at all to the families I work with.

(silence)

SOCIAL WORKER: I feel just the same.

A wave of fellow-feeling swept the group. The tone changed completely. Suddenly people were free to express doubts about their work. They spoke of cases which had gone from bad to worse or certainly had shown no signs of improvement.

SOMEONE: Sometimes I go home at the end of the day, wondering why I do this job. It all seems so hopeless.

ANOTHER: There are so many problems that are beyond us to put right.

(long silence)

HEALTH VISITOR (who had sparked off the discussion): I feel better having said what I did, because I realise that I'm not the only one, and I do know that sometimes I can make a difference to a family.

SOCIAL WORKER: I know you can, from some of the cases of yours that have come my way.

SOMEONE: Then perhaps we should look at what it is possible for us to do – given that we work in an inner-city area and we're none of us superhuman ...

(laughter)

(Source: Hornby, 1993, pp. 171–2)

Reviewing a team's organisation

Effective teamwork demands that the team engages in regular evaluation of its processes and outcomes. Is the service being delivered appropriate and effective? Are the team members and service-users satisfied? What decision-making and conflict-resolution structures are in place? Evaluation must take into account the type and purpose of the teamwork involved. For instance, close, mutually satisfying team relationships will be less of a goal for a multidisciplinary team than for a transdisciplinary team.

Ideally, the team should regularly review how it functions in terms of the contributions individuals make to the whole. Members' roles and channels of communication need to be reviewed in the context of team goals. For example, the physiotherapists and occupational therapists in a team might decide a division of labour (to avoid duplication of effort) whereby the physiotherapists work on patients' lower limb function and mobility while the occupational therapists focus on upper limb and daily living activities.

It can be argued that the most important individual role to review is the work of the leader or leaders. What type of leadership is required to meet the team goals? Might it be useful to distinguish between different leader roles and allocate responsibilities according to individual members' expertise (see Box 9)? What style of leadership is most appropriate – directive or democratic?

Beyond individual member roles, the team needs to explore opportunities for creating a spirit of joint enterprise. Examples could include collaborating on therapy or research projects, or engaging in interdisciplinary supervision. Joint management and recruitment strategies can also be useful in this context. For example, when a professional is being appointed to work in a multidisciplinary team, other members of the team could be present at the selection interview.

Box 9: Distinguishing between different leadership functions

1 **Team manager** – responsibility for the long-term development of the team and services offered to service-users

2 **Chairperson** – responsibility for chairing particular meetings

3 **Facilitator** – responsibility for enabling participation amongst team members

4 **Key worker or care manager** – responsibility for co-ordinating services for specific client cases

5 **Medical/care director** – responsibility for overall medical treatment or care delivered

---

Challenging power structures

The first step to challenging power structures is for the team to be 'reflexive' and consciously critical about how they go about their daily work. Where team relationships are problematic, the team needs to give itself time to reflect on what is happening and why. Is the conflict best understood at a micro or a macro level? How does the conflict impact on the team's functioning? What should be done about it?

More specifically, team members may need to confront defensive, destructive, discriminatory and disempowering practice. As Opie (1997, p. 273) notes: 'Working reflexively includes acknowledging the inevitability of differential power relations between clients and health professionals and the development, and on-going critique, of modes of interaction which seek explicitly to minimise that difference'. Teams need to react when they see they are putting their own professional or team needs before those of service-users or when unduly hierarchical practice inhibits the potential contribution of different individuals. Members may also have a fight on their hands to challenge the use of negative stereotypes within the team and to promote mutual respect instead.

Collaboration: the key to working with 'difference'?

Where teams are concerned, conflicts are inevitable: by definition, teams involve 'difference'. It is differences that make teamwork such a demanding and difficult task. As Loxley (1997, p. 1) puts it:

> There are differences of knowledge, of ways of working, of priorities. There is competition for resources and for power among professions. Collaboration is not experienced as easy. It is, however, recognised as sometimes necessary in meeting the complex needs of individual patients or clients, or responding to complex social problems.

Here, Loxley is arguing in favour of *collaboration* (not simply co-operation) between team members. She explains how collaboration means working across boundaries and that this:

> ... challenges the safe reductionist view, the adequacy of tunnel vision, the security of the territorial forces, the hard-won power and influence, the taken-for-granted nature of the perception. Collaboration requires communication across open boundaries, the willingness to take risks, the reciprocity of costs and gains.
>
> (Loxley, 1997, pp. 49–50)

Handy (1990) goes even further and recommends team leaders adopt a collaborative style and focus on how problems can be solved in ways which develop others' success.

One answer to the question of how to work with difference is to learn to value or celebrate it. Difference can be a source of tension but the greater the differences the more we stand to gain from the expertise of others. It is only on this basis that we can really work together. Davies has expanded on this using the concept of *reflective solidarity:*

> Each of us may arrive at a position we were not previously in – a position we could not have reached by dint of struggle on our own, or by dint of seeking support from those whose histories and perspectives are similar.
>
> (Davies, 1998, p. 51)

She argues that the jolt of challenge from difference 'gives expression to some of the most powerful and energising moments in social life' (1998, p. 52). Davies goes on to offer a vision of what it is to work collaboratively. Too often, she argues, we work with a notion of each other as bounded and fully knowledgeable individuals. Yet this can sometimes get in the way of real collaboration. She contrasts traditional team styles with more collaborative styles (see Table 3).

Table 3 **Two team styles**

Concept of the individual	Bounded	Connected
Group process/style	Formal	Relaxed
	Adversarial	Co-operative
	'Explaining'	'Exploring'
Outcomes	Resolution is imposed	Agreement is tried
	Assumption of finality	Expectation of change
	Vindication and elation	Enhanced commitment
	or	Stronger bonds
	Defeat and despair	Personal renewal

(Source: Davies, 1998, p. 52)

Anyone with experience of good teamwork will recognise this sense of learning from others. In a collaborative team, members have the opportunity to connect with each other. It is the challenges we pose to each other that enhance us, renewing us personally and stimulating us professionally. In this sense, the collective really can be seen to possess the potential to produce better solutions.

Conclusion

This chapter has critically examined the nature of teamwork. It started by distinguishing different models of teamwork and how these relate to the different purposes and functions of teams. Widely-held assumptions that teams are an effective way of organising the delivery of health and social care were questioned. Teams have values and limitations. In practice, teamwork can be problematic, inefficient and even damaging. The process of engaging in team collaboration is always a challenge given the conflicts which can arise. It is the challenge of working with difference that all team members need to grasp. It requires a willingness to listen and a desire hear what others are saying. It requires the courage to let go of one's own perspective and actively to value the contributions of others. Are we up to this challenge?

References

Cott, C. (1998) 'Structure and meaning in multidisciplinary teamwork', *Sociology of Health and Illness*, Vol. 20, pp. 848–73.

Dalley, G. (1989) 'Professional ideology or organizational tribalism? The health service and social work divide', in Taylor, R. and Ford, J. (eds) *Social Work and Health Care*, London, Jessica Kingsley Publications.

Davies, C. (1998) 'Care and the transformation of professionalism', in Knijn, T. and Sevenhuijsen, S. (eds) *Care, Citizenship and Social Cohesion: Towards a Gender Perspective*, Utrecht, Netherlands School for Social and Economic Policy Research.

Department of Health (1997) *The New NHS: Modern, Dependable*, London, The Stationery Office.

Finlay, L. (1993) *Groupwork in Occupational Therapy*, London, Chapman and Hall.

Finlay, L. (1999) 'Safe haven and battleground: collaboration and conflict within the team', in Davies, C., Finlay, L. and Bullman, A. (eds) *Changing Practice in Health and Social Care*, London, Sage/The Open University (K302 Reader 1).

Griffiths, J. M. and Luker, K. (1994) 'Intra-professional team work in district nursing: in whose interest?', *Journal of Advanced Nursing*, Vol. 20, pp. 1038–45.

Handy, C. (1990) *The Age of Unreason*, London, Arrow.

Hornby, S. (1993) *Collaborative Care: Interprofessional, Interagency and Inter-personal*, Oxford, Blackwell Scientific.

Jones, R. V. H. (1992) 'Teamwork in primary care, 1, Perspectives from practices', *Journal of Interprofessional Care*, Vol. 6, pp. 25–29.

Loxley, A. (1997) *Collaboration in Health and Welfare: Working with Difference*, London, Jessica Kingsley Publishers.

Mackay, L., Soothill, K. and Webb, C. (1995) 'Troubled times: the context for interprofessional collaboration', in Soothill, K., Mackay, L. and Webb, C. (eds) *Interprofessional Relations in Health Care*, London, Edward Arnold.

Menzies Lyth, I. (1988) 'The functioning of social systems as a defence against anxiety', *Containing Anxiety in Institutions, Selected Essays*, Vol. 1, London, Free Association Books.

Morgan, S. (1993) *Community Mental Health: Practical Approaches to Long-term Problems*, London, Chapman and Hall.

Morrison, P. (1994) *Understanding Patients*, London, Baillière-Tindall.

Opie, A. (1997) 'Thinking teams thinking clients: issues of discourse and representation in the work of health care teams', *Sociology of Health and Illness*, Vol. 19, pp. 259–80.

Øvretveit, J. (1995) 'Team decision making', *Journal of Interprofessional Care*, Vol. 9, pp. 41–51.

Øvretveit, J. (1997a) 'How to describe interprofessional working', in Øvretveit, J., Mathias, P. and Thompson, T. (eds) *Interprofessional Working for Health and Social Care*, Basingstoke and London, Macmillan.

Øvretveit, J. (1997b) 'Evaluating interprofessional working – a case example of a community mental health team', in Øvretveit, J., Mathias, P. and Thompson, T. (eds) *Interprofessional Working for Health and Social Care*, Basingstoke and London, Macmillan.

Øvretveit, J. (1997c) 'Planning and managing interprofessional working and teams', in Øvretveit, J., Mathias, P. and Thompson, T. (eds) *Interprofessional Working for Health and Social Care*, Basingstoke and London, Macmillan.

Parkin, F. (1979) *Marxism and Class Theory: A Bourgeois Critique*, London, Tavistock.

Poulton, B. C. and West, M. A. (1999) 'The determinants of effectiveness in primary health care teams', *Journal of Interprofessional Care*, Vol. 13, No. 1, pp. 7–18.

Pritchard, P. (1995) 'Learning how to work effectively in teams', in Owens, P., Carrier, J. and Horder, J. (eds) *Interprofessional Issues in Community and Primary Health Care*, Basingstoke and London, Macmillan.

Reder, P., Duncan, S. and Gray, M. (1993) *Beyond Blame: Child Abuse Tragedies Revisited*, London, Routledge.

Sheldon, B. (1994) 'The social and biological components of mental disorder: implications for services,' *International Journal of Social Psychiatry*', Vol. 40, pp. 87–105.

West, M. A. and Field, R. (1995) 'Teamwork in primary health care, 1, Perspectives from organisational psychology', *Journal of Interprofessional Care*, Vol. 9, pp. 117–22.

Wiles, R. and Robison, J. (1994) 'Teamwork in primary care: the views and experiences of nurses, midwives, and health visitors', *Journal of Advanced Nursing*, Vol. 20, pp. 324–30.

Wood, N., Farrow, D. and Elliot, B. (1994) 'A review of primary health care organizations', *Journal of Clinical Nursing*, Vol. 3, pp. 243–50.

Chapter 9
The challenges of being accountable

Maureen Eby

The whistleblower has only one sting
to use and using it may well kill off
one's career.

Introduction

> You've got to watch your step and cover your back! Document
> everything! Make sure you follow the guidelines and you keep the
> patients safe! That's the bottom line – you've got to be safe.
>
> (L. Finlay, personal communication, 12 March 1999)

These sentiments, expressed to Linda Finlay by a physiotherapist working
in a hospital, highlight the experience of many health and social care staff
who are conscious of the need to ensure their standards, procedures and
protocols have been carefully followed. Practitioners are constantly
reminded to be safety-conscious, to be vigilant when assessing levels of
risk. Above all, they are becoming aware of the need to document
everything. In short, in this increasingly litigious climate, health and
social care workers are becoming more conscious of the imperative to be
accountable.

But it is not easy to be accountable in contexts where practitioners feel
under pressure and face diminishing resources and increasing workloads.
Further, they may well face contradictory challenges to be accountable
coming from service-users, their employees and their professional bodies.

Thus, individual practitioners can get caught between the demands of their own sense of responsibility and the demands of the organisations and society to which they belong.

This chapter aims to explore some of these challenges. It looks at how individual workers are held to account in their dealings with patients and service-users, being both monitored by their employer and in some cases regulated by their profession. The focus in this chapter is on the individual operating through four dimensions of accountability – social, ethical, legal and professional. The accountability found within institutions, such as financial accountability and public accountability, is discussed in Part 3.

1   Social accountability

In everyday interactions, individuals are accountable in a variety of ways. Explaining the reason for being late to work, or asking the garage why the car repair bill exceeds the estimate, or turning down a friend's invitation to dinner because of a headache, or asking the grocer whether the vegetables are fresh – these accounts illustrate the dimensions of social accountability that occur within the social fabric of daily life.

As part of a social grouping, individuals either offer or are asked to give accounts both to explain actions in an effort to mitigate or alter another's opinion or perspective or to recast an action in another light. Suppose someone was seen striking another person with a hammer. When asked to give an account, this individual could say it was an accident as the other person got in the way of the hammer hitting the nail; or it was inadvertent as the individual did not see the person while hitting the nail; or the individual mistook the person for someone else who previously had hit them; or it was self-defence as the individual thought the person was about to attack; or it was through provocation; or the individual was bullied into hitting the person; or quite simply the individual was raving mad and not responsible for their actions (Buttny, 1993).

Each one of these seven accounts recasts the original act in a very different light, illustrating the importance of unseen factors such as motivation, the contextual antecedents and the individual's intended outcome within any account. These different accounts also have different consequences. Whereas the first two may well result in an apology with forgiveness as an outcome, the account of provocation might well result in further retaliative action rather than a resolution. Social accountability eases the stresses and strains in society as it '... lubricate[s] social relations by discursive means' (Buttny, 1993, p. 8).

Social accountability also sets the parameters of acceptable behaviour or etiquette within society, as action is constrained by the boundaries of language and the ability of the individual to explain. This dimension of social accountability cuts across the variety of roles individuals have within society. An employee explaining an absence from work, or a nurse explaining to the UKCC (the nurse's registering body) that the cheque for re-registration was lost in the post, or the care worker's account to the client blaming the car's flat tyre for missing that home visit – these accounts occur in work or professional situations. They rely on the individual offering or being asked to give accounts that both explain actions in an effort to mitigate or alter another person's opinion or perspective and recast that action in another light.

2   Ethical accountability

Being accountable implies values such as honesty, duty and trust. Fowler and Levine-Ariff (1987, p. 48) argue that 'being answerable in this regard is a moral obligation and is derived from the nature of the implicit trust relationship between client and ... [the health and social care worker]'. This ethical dimension of accountability stresses values and principles, which can be viewed in terms of the various ethical frameworks or approaches discussed in Chapter 6. To illustrate, the duty-based approach focuses on the duty of health and social care workers to be accountable, while the consequences-based approach focuses not on the explanation or the individual but rather on the consequences of an account. The virtue-based approach focuses on the integrity of the accountable individual and has faith in that person's knowledge of what is the right explanation to give. The principle-based approach considers that truth telling and honesty are the fundamental principles upon which to base an account. The emotive approach might well focus on the fear surrounding accountability. Ellen Annandale's research in the mid-1990s makes this even clearer. She quotes one nurse: '... you feel you've got to watch your back all the time. ... if you're talking to somebody you've got to be careful. That's the feeling: the openness has gone' (Annandale, 1998, p. 279).

The impact of these different ethical approaches to accountability affects not only the nature of an individual's explanation but also the response to that account, as illustrated in Box 1.

Box 1: Case study – David, a trainee social worker

A young mother was referred to a family centre because of feelings of social isolation. During a counselling session with her key worker (David, a trainee social worker), and while discussing budgeting and the problems caused by spending any time away from her daughter, the young mother revealed that she was claiming income support while still working nights as a cleaner. David's thoughts on hearing this were 'Should I ignore it? Or should I report this to the Benefits Agency? Do I have a duty to uphold the principle of confidentiality in this case?'

(Source: adapted from Banks, 1995, pp. 145–46)

This young mother's account creates a dilemma for David who does not know what to do with the information received. Although specifically the questions raised relate to duty and the principle of confidentiality, David is also raising questions about responsibility and autonomy – two concepts that are very closely linked with accountability.

Responsibility

Responsibility is often used synonymously with accountability. Wagner (1989) and Bergman (1981) see responsibility as the main component of accountability. Responsibility is a duty or a task. It is the acceptance of a course of action as well as the acceptance that an individual should be willing to give an account for the nature and conduct of that task. For example, David, the trainee social worker in Box 1, was fulfilling his responsibility to conduct a counselling session. Responsibilities can be seen as tasks that go with the job and, in that sense, they may be unproblematic in terms of accountability. In accepting responsibility for counselling, other issues came into the arena, rendering questions of responsibility more problematic.

One reaction is to stay silent and not to bring difficult issues into the open. French (1993, quoted in Brykczynska, 1995, p. 157) remarks: 'no wonder that avoidance of responsibility has become almost an art form, one that is learned and practised relatively early in life and honed to the end'. Robyn Holden, an Australian nurse teacher, criticises those nurses for hiding from their responsibilities through their 'compulsive, ritualistic behaviour' (Holden, 1991, p. 398). She continues:

> Procedure manuals stipulate the step by step prescription for the performance of various psychomotor skills; prescriptive ward routines are followed without deviation; there is the practice of checking and counter-checking in an effort to minimise mistakes; and any challenge to the system is generally regarded as heretical. Such compulsive behaviour not only denotes responsibility avoidance, but also implies an absence of the freedom to choose ...
>
> (Holden, 1991, pp. 398–99)

So, for Holden, those individuals who continue to adhere to ritualistic, regimented patterns of work are unable to choose freely one course of action over another. This argument has echoes of Menzies' classic work, first published in 1960, concerning the way routines in a hospital ward served as a defence against anxiety (Menzies, 1960), and repeated in Annandale's study (1998) of defensive behaviour by nurses when confronted with factors today, such as fear of litigation and complaints.

Holden, as the quotation above makes clear, links responsibility with the freedom to choose. In her example, regimentation meant that nurses were denied such freedom. Batey and Lewis (1982) warn:

> We must be careful not to confuse responsibility with the state of being responsible. While responsibility denotes a charge, being responsible or having a sense of responsibility is the acceptance of a charge. It denotes that one knows what the charge is and is willing to fulfill it.
>
> (Batey and Lewis, 1982, p. 14)

This brings us back to the case of David, the trainee social worker, who is faced not with rules and constraints but with autonomy.

Autonomy

Personal responsibility as an attribute or a virtue denotes a sense of free will. Individuals have the freedom to choose their actions and how those actions will be carried out. Autonomy reflects the independence of an individual to make decisions based on his or her own abilities rather than on organisational position. Sometimes it is difficult for people within a given work situation to recognise autonomy, preferring instead to think of themselves as subject to the control of others. But in reality, individuals do have autonomy although some may have less than others. To illustrate this from the case study in Box 1, David is raising questions about the autonomy within that situation. Does a trainee social worker have the autonomy to ignore or act upon what the young mother said? The ability to make that choice is autonomy. Autonomy also includes the notion of self-determination or self-direction – that ability to direct one's own life even in the working environment. Hall (1968) identifies two types of autonomy – structural and attitudinal:

> Structural autonomy exists when professional people are expected to use their judgement to determine the provision of client services in the context of their work. Attitudinal autonomy exists for people who believe themselves to be free to exercise judgement in decision making.
>
> (Hall, 1968, quoted in Duff, 1995, p. 53)

It could be argued that David has both attitudinal and structural autonomy in this case. He may well choose to ignore what the young mother has said about working and not even record it in the notes, which would illustrate his attitudinal autonomy. However, David may well choose not to ignore the information that the young mother had also disclosed she was leaving the child unattended while at work and report this to his superior. In this case, David is using his judgement based not only on the ethical principle of non-maleficence in the case of the child but also on the guidelines for child protection set out within the local authority. In the first case, David has chosen not to be accountable by not documenting the young mother's account in the notes. In the second case, he has chosen to be accountable by reporting the situation to child protection officers.

Whistleblowing – ethical accountability at work

But what if David discovered that many of the clients within the authority are both claiming benefit and working? Having raised conscientious concerns within the social services department, no action seems to have been taken. The subsequent expression of these concerns into the public arena is through *whistleblowing*.

Essentially, whistleblowing is the ancient art of bringing to light wrongdoing in any area of life (Eby, 1994a). It is the act of bringing to public attention abuses or dangers that jeopardise public safety and would not otherwise be publicised (Chadwick and Tadd, 1992). As Gerald Vinten writes:

> [Whistleblowing is] the unauthorised disclosure of information that an employee reasonably believes is evidence of the contravention of any law, rule or regulation, code of practice, or professional statement, or that involves mismanagement, corruption, abuse of authority or danger to public or worker health and safety.
>
> (Vinten, 1994, p. 5)

In Vinten's words (1994, p. 10), the whistleblower 'has only one sting to use, and using it may well kill off one's career'. Within health and social care there have been some very widely publicised whistleblowers. Graham Pink voiced concerns about staffing levels in a care of the elderly ward, which were later picked up by the press (see also Chapter 6, Section 3). He was sacked and later won £11,000 compensation from an industrial tribunal. In Graham Pink's words:

> I know I was right to go public – but I was near retirement, and as a single man I didn't have the welfare of a family to consider. ... I simply wanted to be able to look after my patients properly. I wrote to all my managers. I tried in every possible way to raise my concerns within the NHS and solve the problems internally, but eventually I became so disheartened that going public seemed the only option.
>
> (World in Action, 1994, p. 1)

Susan Machin blew the whistle on abuses of power at Ashworth Hospital. She too was sacked and later received compensation from an industrial tribunal. Mike Cox resigned as a generic social worker after he complained about alleged poor policies and practices in child care, and Alison Taylor complained about abuses in children's homes in North Wales. She also was sacked but later received damages for unfair dismissal from an industrial tribunal (Cervi, 1996).

Whistleblowing is one way out of an ethical dilemma. It can be viewed from three approaches. First, whistleblowers can be seen as rats undermining their company and seeking to leave a sinking ship, one that they helped to sink. A second approach is to view whistleblowers as tragic individuals. Research certainly has indicated that people suffer equally from not blowing the whistle as when they do blow the whistle (Hunt,

1995). A survey of 161 whistleblowers in the USA found that severe retaliation and overwhelming personal and professional hardships were reported by the respondents. Glazer and Glazer state:

> Virtually all of the ethical resisters we studied had long histories of successful employment ... they began as firm believers in their organisations, convinced that if they took a grievance to superiors, there would be an appropriate response. This naivety led them into a series of damaging traps. They found that their earlier service and dedication provided them with little protection against charges of undermining organisational morale and effectiveness.
>
> (Glazer and Glazer, 1986, p. A23, quoted in Winfield, 1994, p. 22)

A small-scale survey of 35 whistleblowers in Australia (Lennane, 1993) found that: 83% experienced victimisation immediately after their first internal complaint; 20% had long-term relationships break up; 43% were on long-term drug treatment; and 49% considered suicide. Income was reduced by 75% in 40% of the cases. Lennane (1993, p. 670) concluded that 'although whistleblowing is important in protecting society, the typical organisational response causes severe and long-lasting health, financial and personal problems for whistleblowers and their families.'

The third approach views whistleblowing as an obligation, especially when there is potential serious harm to the public; or after all other internal channels within the organisation have been exhausted and no response is offered; or when there is documented evidence that would convince a reasonably impartial observer there is a serious risk of harm to the public; or when an individual has good reason to believe that blowing the whistle publicly will bring about necessary change.

In July 1998, the Public Interest Disclosure Act, the first whistleblower's protection legislation, became law and came into force in July 1999. This Act protects employees from being dismissed or victimised when disclosing information in good faith and with reasonable grounds for the belief in what is disclosed. Disclosure by an employee will only be protected if it is made to the employer or to the person responsible for the matter, or to a Minister in the case of civil servants or their equivalent, or to a designated regulatory body identified in Statutory Instrument 1999 No. 1549 (HMSO, 1999), or in the course of obtaining legal advice. Essentially, this Act makes changes to the Employment Rights Act 1996 and enshrines the protection of employees from the consequences of such a disclosure. Victimised employees can now seek redress through industrial tribunals for compensation and, according to a Department of Trade and Industry press release (1999, p. 2), 'there will be no limit on compensatory awards in cases of dismissal, ensuring that employees at all levels of an organisation – from the factory floor to the board room – will be fully compensated if they lose their jobs for blowing the whistle.' Individuals may also seek a re-employment order to return to their former employment. The Public Interest Disclosure Act illustrates the relationship between ethical and legal accountability, which is discussed in the next section.

3   Legal accountability

Being accountable is also enshrined in law through acts of parliament, case law and the various public mechanisms that serve the public, such as tribunals and inquiries. It is an accountability to society at large. Individuals working within health and social care not only face legal accountability as individuals within their own community, such as obeying the rules of the road or paying income tax, but also they face legal accountability through their work in areas such as health and safety and negligence (see Box 2).

Box 2: Case study – manager of a residential home

The manager of a residential home was recently instructed by his employer, a multinational corporation, to cut costs and to implement a chill–cook system of meals to replace freshly prepared meals. Unfortunately, soon after implementing this new system, 10 of the residents developed salmonella poisoning and the environmental health inspector is now asking for the name of the chill–cook meals supplier.

This residential care manager is facing legal accountability as he has been asked to explain the source of the food given to the residents of this residential home. Did the manager follow his company's policies in selecting this supplier? Selecting a supplier was the manager's responsibility. Did he undertake this task in a responsible manner by requesting references or inspecting the premises of the supplier before entering into a contract with them?

Suppose now that the supplier of the chill–cook meals turned out not to be the source of the salmonella. Instead, one of the care assistants brought in some home-made mayonnaise to use in bedtime snacks for the residents. This care assistant was just newly appointed and had not had a chance to do the basic food hygiene course that all employees attend. She had no idea that her home-made mayonnaise was contaminated. Yet it clearly states in the company policy, which this employee had read before starting her care duties, that home-made foods are not to be given to the residents for health and safety reasons. Was this care assistant being responsible? Clearly not. Was she accountable? She would be accountable not only to the manager of the residential home through her employment contract but probably also to the environmental health inspector under health and safety law. If one of the residents died as a result of this incident, further action possibly leading to a criminal action might well ensue.

This case study illustrates that an understanding of both authority and liability is crucial to legal accountability.

Authority

Authority is defined as 'the rightful [legitimate] power to fulfill a charge [responsibility]' (Batey and Lewis, 1982, p. 14) and it is derived from three sources: the situation, expert knowledge and the position (Duff, 1995).

Authority arising from the situation occurs when circumstances demand that action is taken quickly, say to save life or prevent harm. For example, in an emergency and in the absence of a doctor, a nurse can attempt cardiopulmonary resuscitation and even administer cardiac drugs under suitable protocols to ensure a rapid response. A social worker has the authority to remove a child from the home in case of immediate danger under an emergency protection order (Hendrick, 1993; Hoggett, 1993).

Authority derived from expert knowledge is the basis of professional power and is awarded on the basis of prior academic achievement and often statutory registration; while authority stemming from position is derived from the organisational role an individual has or from the occupational grouping to which they belong. For example, the police have authority based not only on the legal system that created a police force but also on the trust given by the public to the police. It is when this trust breaks down that this form of authority is challenged. Health and social care workers often do not recognise within themselves this form of authority, as we saw earlier in the case of ritualistic adherence to procedures (Section 2).

In the case of approved social workers, authority is drawn from all three sources – the situation, expert knowledge and the position. Mental health legislation in Britain provides for compulsory admission to psychiatric hospital in particular circumstances. Social workers approved under the Mental Health Act 1983 in England and Wales, the Mental Health (Northern Ireland) Order 1986 and the Mental Health (Scotland) Act 1984 (known as approved social workers in England, Wales and Northern Ireland and mental health officers in Scotland) are entrusted with the responsibility of assessing whether compulsory admission is necessary. It is clear from the legislation that responsibility for deciding whether to use compulsory powers rests with the approved social worker (ASW) alone. The ASW will take into account matters such as medical opinion, the wishes of the client and his or her relatives, past history and present circumstances, alternatives to hospital admission, and any other factors. However, the final decision rests with the ASW.

Thus, respected commentators on mental health law, such as Richard Jones, state that the ASW acts independently and therefore carries personal responsibility for those decisions. In his words:

> An approved social worker is personally liable for his [sic] actions whilst carrying out functions under this Act. He should therefore exercise his own judgement and not act at the behest of his employers, medical

practitioners or other persons who might be involved with the patient's welfare ...

(Jones, 1994, p. 51, para. 1-098)

This strongly suggests that, in acting independently, an ASW is not subject to managerial control, because he or she cannot be ordered to compulsorily admit someone to psychiatric hospital. This situation is quite unique in a local authority social services department, since in every other situation a social work practitioner is under managerial control. As a last resort, the Director of Social Services (or a manager to whom the Director's authority has been delegated) can order the practitioner either to take a particular action or to face disciplinary proceedings. In Jones' final analysis, the Director of Social Services cannot order such an action. Thus ASWs derive their power from the situation in which an individual is being considered for detention, from their expert knowledge of the Mental Health Act 1983, and from the position they hold in securing the detention order.

Liability

Broadly speaking, liability asks who is responsible for such action or decision? However, in a legal sense, liability is the obligation one individual incurs to another person or organisation as a result of harm or injury caused by the actions of that individual. This is illustrated by the following equation:

act (or omission) + causation + fault + protected interest + damage = liability

(Cooke, 1997, p. 4)

Within health care, liability is often associated with negligence, as described by Lord Atkin in the case *Donoghue* v. *Stevenson* (1932):

You must take reasonable care to avoid acts or omissions which you can reasonably foresee would be likely to injure your neighbour.

(Cooke, 1997, p. 29)

Failure to take this reasonable care can lead to negligence. There are three fundamental conditions to negligence. First, a duty of care must be owed; second, that duty of care must have been broken; and, third, the breach in the duty of care must have caused the damage (Eby, 1994b, p. 11). The standard used in determining whether there has been a breach in the duty of care is known as the *Bolam Test*, after the judgement in the case *Bolam* v. *Friern Hospital Management Committee* (1957). It was alleged in this case that the doctor administered electro-convulsive therapy to Mr Bolam without anaesthetic or muscle relaxants. Mr Bolam suffered a fractured jaw. In his judgement, Mr Justice McNair stated:

The test is the standard of the ordinary skilled man exercising and professing to have that special skill. A man need not possess the highest expert skill ... it is sufficient if he exercises the ordinary skill of an ordinary competent man exercising that particular art. ... a doctor is not guilty of negligence if he has acted in accordance with a practice accepted as proper by a responsible body of medical men skilled in that particular art. ... Putting it the other way round, a doctor is not negligent, if he is acting in accordance with such a practice, merely because there is a body of opinion that takes a contrary view.

(Eby, 1994c, p. 9)

The case of *Wilsher* v. *Essex Health Authority* (1986) involved the monitoring of oxygen in an infant, Martin Wilsher. A junior, inexperienced doctor, unsure whether he had inserted the monitoring catheter in the right place, asked his senior registrar to check. The senior registrar not only failed to notice that the oxygen-monitoring catheter was in a vein rather than an artery but also later reinserted another oxygen-monitoring catheter into the vein as well. As the medical staff thought Martin's oxygen levels were low, he was administered a high dose of oxygen. Although the allegation that the dosage of oxygen caused Martin's blindness failed to be upheld, this case is important because it has modified the *Bolam Test*, especially in situations of expanded role. As Lord Justice Glidewell stated:

In my view, the law requires the trainee or learner to be judged by the same standard as his more experienced colleagues. If it did not, inexperience would frequently be urged as a defence to an action for professional negligence.

(Tingle, 1998a, p. 54)

To illustrate, if a nurse increases his or her abilities and assumes the doctor's responsibilities, for example prescribing medication, then that nurse's prescribing is judged by the standard set by doctors, not that of other nurse prescribers. The importance of these issues and some of the complexities they raise at the medical/nursing interface have been visibly illustrated in recent research (Dowling, 1996).

There are three types of liability: *direct liability* is when an individual is injured not by another person but by defective equipment or product or if the organisational system itself failed resulting in injury; *personal liability* is the liability any individual has if someone is injured as a result of failing to meet the standard of care of the ordinary individual in any given situation; and *vicarious liability* is the liability an employer has as a result of the actions of its employees (Tingle, 1998b). Employees of the NHS, the private sector or local government working within health and social care settings face either direct or vicarious liability as illustrated by the case study of food poisoning in a residential home (Box 2).

Had the cook–chill meal system been the source of the salmonella poisoning, the meal supplier and possibly the residential home would have faced direct liability. However, since the salmonella poisoning was apparently the result of the staff's actions, vicarious liability would apply. It is highly unlikely that the care assistant would be personally sued under personal liability. Since her financial worth would be far smaller than that of the multinational corporation, there would be very little to recover in compensation. So, in this case, the employer would be liable for the acts through the vicarious liability not only of the manager but also of the care assistant, although there may well be an argument that the care assistant was not covered by vicarious liability because of not following company policy. The care assistant, though, could plead mitigating circumstances since she had not done the basic food hygiene course. In this case, both the manager and the care assistant would provide statements or accounts of what exactly happened.

Public mechanisms of legal accountability

Examples of legal accountability also emerge from public inquiries, inquests and tribunals. These are public arenas in which individuals working within health and social care may find themselves needing to explain and defend their practice in general or in relation to a specific incident, event or case.

Inquiries

Public inquiries are usually convened through government ministerial action. It is a method by which individuals and groups are given the right to be heard before a decision is made, for example, in the case of environmental matters. Public inquiries are also used to investigate the reasons why events happened, as in the Blom-Cooper Inquiry into Ashworth Hospital (1992) or, more recently, the Fallon Inquiry (1999) into the alleged abuse of patients and children at the same hospital. Inquiries are about finding out what has happened, and often about allocating blame, and they provide an opportunity for lessons to be learned and recommendations to be followed. However, it has been argued that inquiries, in fact, are nothing more than icing on the cake (Smith, 1999). The Fallon Inquiry was the second major inquiry into Ashworth Hospital and its main recommendation to the government was that the hospital should close (Fallon *et al.*, 1999, p. iv). Inquiry recommendations are not binding on government, as illustrated by Ashworth Hospital not closing. Instead, the government announced that it would look again at the wider issue of special hospitals and the treatment of personality disorders, proposals being announced at the time of writing this chapter granting 'new legal powers for the indeterminate detention of dangerously personality disordered individuals' whether they were before the court on offence or not (Munro, 1999, p. 16).

Inquests

Inquests are judicial inquiries which set out to determine matters of fact. A coroner's inquest is a legal inquiry in England, Wales and Northern

Ireland that has to take place in the event of a sudden, violent or suspicious death, in order to determine the cause (Bird, 1983). Coroners' inquests are sometimes held before a jury but they are not criminal proceedings. If an inquest finds that a particular person caused the death in circumstances amounting to homicide, the inquest proceedings are passed to the Crown Prosecution Service (CPS), who consider whether that person should stand trial. Other verdicts may be death from natural causes, accidental death, or death by suicide. The coroner may make recommendations (for example, about a dangerous product) to prevent similar deaths in future. In Scotland, the procedure for handling these types of case is different. The coroners' work is handled by the Procurator Fiscal of the Sheriff Courts and the police do the investigations on the Fiscal's behalf (Knight, 1992).

Tribunals

A tribunal is appointed to adjudicate on disputed matters, for example between a citizen and a government department, or between individuals. Examples are social security tribunals or industrial tribunals, which hear disputes between employers and employees. The Registered Homes Tribunal hears cases brought against residential home owners under the Registered Homes Act 1984. Tribunals are usually presided over by a legally qualified chairperson, but they are largely composed of lay people, and are less formal than courts of law. Tribunal decisions, while based on rules of law, often concern broad discretionary issues and require members to bring their own experience to bear in reaching their conclusions. Tribunals, rather than adhering to court procedures, observe instead the rules of natural justice and act within the limits of their jurisdiction and prescribed procedure (O'Donnell, 1996).

4   Professional accountability

Professional accountability relies on individuals recognising that they are members of a profession and 'accepting that status, with the rights and responsibilities that go with it' (McGann, 1995, p. 18). This ethos of accountability is clearly stated in the UKCC's *Guidelines for Professional Practice*:

> Accountability is an integral part of professional practice, as in the course of practice you have to make judgements in a wide variety of circumstances. Professional accountability is fundamentally concerned with weighing up the interests of patients and clients in complex situations, using professional knowledge, judgement and skills to make a decision and enabling you to account for the decision made.
>
> (UKCC, 1996a, p. 8)

Professional accountability relies on the two interrelated concepts of ability and competence, which are further described below.

Ability

Ability is seen as 'the relevant knowledge, skills and values [required] to make decisions and to act' (Bergman, 1981, p. 54, quoted in Rodgers, 1995, p. 70). Without knowledge and/or skills, individuals would not be able to act in a purposeful way. It would be difficult to become a social worker or a nurse without the knowledge and skills needed. Values are also important for they convey the essence of the profession and ensure that individual members work towards enhancing its values. But knowledge and skill are not static; they need updating to reflect current thinking. This responsibility of individuals to incorporate new knowledge and skills has been enshrined in social workers', nurses', midwives' and therapy professionals' codes of practice. Individuals are now held to account for maintaining that ability.

Competence

Competence is the ability to perform a responsibility with appropriate knowledge and skill. However, there is more to competence than just the ability to perform a responsibility. Competence denotes both the scope and the quality of performing that responsibility. As Eraut (1994, p. 167) states:

> The *scope* dimension [of competence] concerns what a person is competent in, the range of roles, tasks and situations for which their competence is established or may be reliably inferred. The *quality* dimension concerns judgements about the quality of that work on a continuum from being a novice, who is not yet competent in that particular task, to being an expert acknowledged by colleagues as having progressed well beyond the level of competence.

As individuals progress through their careers, the scope of their competence expands as they gain in experience or, perhaps, through additional skills training or moving into newly developing areas of work or through changing their job or organisation. But also over time, the quality of an individual's competence develops as they continue to strive, to sharpen their knowledge and skills, leading to proficiency and expertise as acknowledged by their colleagues. There is also a distinction between performance that is 'directly observable' and competence which, as Gonzi *et al.* (1993, p. 6, quoted in Eraut, 1994, p. 179) state, is 'not directly observable, but it is inferred from performance'. Thus in day-to-day activities an individual's performance may not always reflect their level of competence.

Public mechanisms of professional accountability

However, it is the role of professional law that greatly affects professionals, for, as well as being accountable as an individual and an employee, many professionals have an entirely new layer of legal accountability to contend with in the shape of statutory bodies that regulate professions. A professional is accountable and responsible to their statutory body and usually this accountability occurs through the work of a professional conduct committee. These committees can expect accountability from their registered members and decisions about a member's continued registration depend heavily on the quality of that accountability and the responsibilities involved. Professional conduct committees cannot impose financial liability on professionals, though, for they do not have the statutory power to impose a financial obligation – only the court currently has that power. What they can do in the most serious cases is to remove a name from a register and effectively deny an individual the right to practise.

Professional conduct committees

Working along the lines of a tribunal, there are professional conduct committees such as the General Medical Council (GMC), which examines cases of 'serious professional misconduct', and the UKCC, which looks at 'professional misconduct'. If cases are proven, these organisations may remove names from the register. While UKCC cases are heard in public, GMC cases are not. However, an exception was made in the Bristol heart surgeons case, conducted by the GMC from 1997 to 1998, where the transcript of the hearing was released to the public. The GMC found that two consultant heart surgeons and the former chief executive of Bristol Royal Infirmary, also a doctor, had failed to pay sufficient regard to the safety and best interests of their patients. One of the consultants and the chief executive were struck off the medical register while the second consultant was barred from operating on children for three years. He later was dismissed from employment at the Bristol Royal Infirmary. A public inquiry is currently under way into this case (Pook and Copley, 1998).

Box 3 (overleaf) details the mechanics of professional conduct for nurses, midwives and health visitors. In 1997/8 the UKCC considered complaints in 997 cases, a 6% increase over the previous year, which resulted in 84 practitioners being removed from the register and 18 being cautioned. One-third of the complaints resulting in removal or caution involved physical and verbal abuse of patients and clients. Other reasons for removal or caution were failure to attend to basic needs (13%), unsafe clinical practice (8%), and failure to keep accurate records or report incidents (5%); and 18% of complaints stemmed from mental health nursing while 25% involved practitioners working in nursing homes (UKCC, 1998).

Box 3: UKCC – United Kingdom Central Council for Nurses, Midwives and Health Visitors

The Preliminary Proceedings Committee (PPC) considers all cases that arise from convictions in criminal courts, reports received from employers and complaints made by private individuals or professional colleagues. The PPC investigates the case and either dismisses the complaint or refers it to either the Health Committee or the Professional Conduct Committee (PCC). At the PCC the evidence is again examined by a panel of council and lay members in a public hearing with a legal assessor to advise on admissibility of evidence and points of law and a council officer to advise on the Council's procedures and relevant background to the case. The standard of proof used is 'beyond a reasonable doubt' – the criminal standard of proof – not the lesser standard of the civil courts – 'on the balance of probabilities'. The UKCC can either caution the individual or remove them from the register. The UKCC also has the power to impose an interim suspension of registration in certain circumstances where there is a real risk of danger to the public pending an outcome of a PCC hearing. Outcomes of the PCC are subject to judicial review if application is made within three months of the decision.

(Source: based on Eby, 1994c, pp. 14–15 and UKCC, 1996b, pp. 2–3)

In social work, as in nursing, there are codes of conduct, giving guidance to professionals on their accountability. These are issued by a professional body, the British Association of Social Workers (see Chapter 6). Social work has never had a registration system and disciplinary procedures of the same form, although developments are currently in progress (see Chapter 14).

Ombudsmen

Ombudsmen are '... the independent upholder of the highest standards of efficient and fair administration' (Whyatt, 1961, p. 77, quoted in Allsop and Mulcahy, 1996, p. 56). There are several ombudsmen who oversee particular areas. Some of them, such as the Health Service Commissioner and the Commissioners for Local Administration, have a basis in statutory law but others, such as the Banking Ombudsman and the Corporate Estate Agents Ombudsman, are private schemes set up and funded by the relevant industry (Allsop and Mulcahy, 1996).

The Health Service Commissioner (HSC) received 2660 complaints in 1997–98, a 20% increase on the previous year, and 120 of these went on to a full investigation. The majority of complaints involved the operation of the NHS complaint procedure itself and the independent review. However, despite the HSC taking on two new additional areas of investigation (family health service practitioners and the exercise of clinical judgement), out of all the complaints received only 36 were about NHS practitioners, of which 27 were general practitioners, and 26 complaints involved clinical issues. Two major areas of complaint highlighted by the Commissioner in his report were care and treatment (36 complaints, of which 18 were upheld) and communication (29 out of the 37 complaints were upheld). These two areas were the most common for complaints about the actions of nurses and midwives (House of Commons, 1998).

The Local Government Ombudsmen investigate complaints of injustice arising from the maladministration by local authorities and certain other public bodies, for example, education appeal committees, national parks authorities, fire authorities. In 1997, the first digest of cases was published covering the year 1996 and including 10 cases involving social services (Local Government Ombudsman, 1997).

5   Risk management: accountability in action

A discussion of accountability would not be complete today without reference to risk and risk management. The term 'risk' has a long history stemming from the seventeenth century and the development of probability theory (Hacking, 1975, quoted in Heyman, 1998). Risk has its roots in both epidemiology and economics through such methodologies as cost–benefit analysis. But despite the proliferation of risk assessment technology, Giddens (1991) argues that there is still 'the inability to predict what is going to happen next in society' (quoted in Higgs, 1998, p. 177). This underlines the fact that the step from assessing a risk to managing a risk is a big one.

Only in the 1990s has the concept of risk crept into the fields of health and social care, mainly through the growing litigious culture of health. Skolbekken (1995, quoted in Higgs, 1998, p. 181) 'points out that since 1987 more than 80,000 articles on risk have been published in medical journals'. He draws attention to the fact that most of these studies lack any coherent understanding of what constitutes risk and, in fact, 'there are many different notions of the concept to which various ideological meanings have been attached' (Skolbekken, 1995, p. 297, quoted in Higgs, 1998, p. 182). Nevertheless, the ever-increasing costs of medical negligence, accidents to both staff and patients/clients, occupational sickness, the growing emphasis on cost effective and efficient care, as well as the loss of Crown immunity, have meant that risk has been high on the agenda of NHS Trusts and other public bodies. The role of risk management in clinical governance within the NHS (see Chapter 13) also reinforces the idea of:

> ... anticipating and preventing potential problems, learning from critical incidents and patient complaints and providing systems to help clinical staff reflect upon and develop their practice.
>
> (RCN, 1998, p. 3)

Despite the concerns of Giddens (1991, 1994) and others (Beck, 1992; Bauman, 1995, 1996) that the assessment of risk is now so overwhelming that it actually enhances risk, risk management itself can be particularly helpful in maintaining a questioning attitude to established practice and reviewing options and alternatives. Giddens (1994) refers to the 'autotelic self', an individual:

> ... with an inner confidence which comes from self respect, and one where a sense of ontological security originating in basic trust allows for the positive appreciation of social difference. It refers to a person able to translate potential threats into rewarding challenges ... [and] ... does not seek to neutralise risk or to suppose that 'someone else will take care of the problem'; risk is confronted as the active challenge which generates self actualisation.
>
> (Giddens, 1994, p. 192, quoted in Higgs, 1998, p. 178)

Box 4 lists 13 key questions vital to the conduct of a risk assessment. A critical practitioner will want to take these questions and others on board as part of providing accountable and defensible practice.

Box 4: Risk-taking assessment strategy

1   Is the proposed action a gamble, a risk or a dilemma?

2   List all the possible benefits for the patient/client of the risk.

3   List all the possible benefits and knock-on effects for staff and other people.

4   Analyse the likelihood of each of these benefits occurring.

5   Manipulate the risk by taking steps to make the benefits more likely to occur.

6   List all the possible kinds of harm to the patient/client of the risk.

7   List all the possible kinds of harm and knock-on effects to staff and other people.

8   How likely are these to occur?

9   Manipulate the risk by taking steps to reduce the likelihood of harm occurring.

10 List any important duties in this risk assessment.

11 Obtain the patient's informed consent.

12 Obtain the informed agreement of colleagues.

13 Decide whether the risk should be taken at this time.

(Source: based on Carson, 1990, pp. 83–84)

Conclusion

This chapter focused on four dimensions of accountability – social, ethical, legal and professional – and how, as an individual, an employee and/or as a professional, accountability has impacted on the daily practice found within health and social care. In the words of Diane Marks-Maran, a nurse educator:

> An accountable person does not undertake an action merely because someone in authority says to do so. Instead, the accountable person examines a situation, explores the various options available, demonstrates a knowledgeable understanding of the possible consequences of options and makes a decision for action which can be justified from a knowledge base.
>
> (Marks-Maran, 1993, p. 123)

This is accountable practice that acknowledges the element of risk. Having this awareness will help in understanding the complexities of practice and this, in turn, will help practitioners to generate more informed decisions and to give an account of these decisions in the diverse contexts in which such an account is required.

References

Allsop, J. and Mulcahy, L. (1996) *Regulating Medical Work*, Buckingham, Open University Press.

Annandale, E. (1998) 'Working on the front line: risk culture and nursing in the new NHS', in Allott, M. and Robb, M. (eds) *Understanding Health and Social Care: An Introductory Reader*, pp. 279–86, London, Sage Publications.

Banks, S. (1995) *Ethics and Values in Social Work*, Basingstoke, Macmillan and BASW.

Batey, M. and Lewis, F. (1982) 'Clarifying autonomy and accountability in nursing service: Part 1', *Journal of Nursing Administration*, Vol. 12, No. 9, September, pp. 13–18.

Bauman, Z. (1995) *Life in Fragments*, Cambridge, Polity Press.

Bauman, Z. (1996) 'On communitarians and human freedom: or how to square the circle', *Theory, Culture and Society*, Vol. 13, No. 2, pp. 79–90.

Beck, U. (1992) *Risk Society: Towards a New Modernity*, London, Sage.

Bergman, R. (1981) 'Accountability – definition and dimensions', *International Nursing Review*, Vol. 28, No. 2, pp. 53–59.

Bird, R. (1983) *Osborn's Concise Law Dictionary* (7th edn), London, Sweet and Maxwell.

Brykczynska, G. (1995) 'Working with children: accountability and paediatric nursing', in Watson, R. (ed.) *Accountability in Nursing Practice*, pp. 147–60, London, Chapman and Hall.

Buttny, R. (1993) *Social Accountability in Communication*, London, Sage Publications.

Carson, D. (1990) 'Taking risks with patients – your assessment strategy', in Professional Nurse, *The Staff Nurse's Survival Guide*, pp. 83–87, London, Austen Cornish.

Cervi, B. (1996) 'Blasts from the past', *Community Care*, No. 1131, 1–7 August, pp. 16–17.

Chadwick, R. and Tadd, W. (1992) *Ethics and Nursing Practice*, Basingstoke, Macmillan.

Cooke, J. (1997) *Law of Tort* (3rd edn), London, Pitman Publishing.

Department of Trade and Industry (1999) 'New protection for whistleblowers starts in July', Press Release P/99/480, 8 June.
(http://www.nds.coi.gov.uk/coi/coipress.n...f19ec4c5bf38025678a0052-c550?OpenDocument – accessed 4 July 1999)

Dowling, S. *et al.* (1996) 'Nurses taking on junior doctors' work: a confusion of accountability', *British Medical Journal*, Vol. 312, 11 May, pp. 1211–14.

Duff, L. (1995) 'Standards of care, quality assurance and accountability', in Watson, R. (ed.) *Accountability in Nursing Practice*, pp. 49–69, London, Chapman and Hall.

Eby, M. (1994a) 'Whistleblowing', in Tschudin, V. (ed.) *Ethics: Conflicts of Interest*, pp. 56–84, London, Scutari Press.

Eby, M. (1994b) *The Law and Ethics of General Practice*, Beckenham, Kent, Publishing Initiatives.

Eby, M. (1994c) *Legal Issues in Nursing Practice*, Beckenham, Kent, Publishing Initiatives.

Eraut, M. (1994) *Developing Professional Knowledge and Competence*, London, The Falmer Press.

Fallon, P. *et al.* (1999) *Report on the Committee of Inquiry into the Personality Disorder Unit, Ashworth Special Hospital*, Volume I, Cm 4194-II, London, The Stationery Office.

Fowler, M. and Levine-Ariff, J. (1987) *Ethics at the Bedside*, Philadelphia, J. B. Lippincott.

French, P. (1993) *Responsibility Matters*, Lawrence, Kansas University Press.

Giddens, A. (1991) *The Consequences of Modernity*, Cambridge, Polity Press.

Giddens, A. (1994) *Beyond Left and Right*, Cambridge, Polity Press.

Glazer, M. and Glazer, P. (1986) 'The whistleblower's plight', *New York Times*, 13 August, p. A23.

Gonzi, A., Hager, P. and Athanasou, J. (1993) *The Development of Competency-Based Assessment Strategies for the Professions*, National Office of Overseas Skills Recognition Research, Paper No. 8, Canberra, Australian Government Publishing Service.

Hacking, I. (1975) *The Emergence of Probability: A Philosophical Study of Early Ideas about Probability, Induction and Statistical Inference*, Cambridge, Cambridge University Press.

Hall, R. H. (1968) 'Professionalisation and bureaucratisation', *American Sociological Review*, Vol. 33, pp. 92–104.

Hendrick, J. (1993) *Child Care Law for Health Professionals*, Oxford, Radcliffe Medical Press.

Her Majesty's Stationery Office (1999) *Statutory Instrument 1999 No. 1549*, London, The Stationery Office.

Heyman, B. (1998) *Risk, Health and Health Care: A Qualitative Approach*, London, Arnold.

Higgs, P. (1998) 'Risk, governmentality and the reconceptualization of citizenship', in Scambler, G. and Higgs, P. (eds) *Modernity, Medicine and Health: Medical Sociology Towards 2000*, pp. 176–97, London, Routledge.

Hoggett, B. (1993) *Parents and Children* (4th edn), London, Sweet and Maxwell.

Holden, R. (1991) 'Responsibility and autonomous nursing practice', *Journal of Advanced Nursing*, Vol. 16, pp. 398–403.

House of Commons (1998) *Health Service Commissioner Fifth Report for Session 1997–98*, London. (http://www.health.ombudsman.org.uk/hsc/document/h-811.htm – accessed 13 July 1999)

Hunt, G. (1995) *Whistleblowing in the Health Service: Accountability, Law and Professional Practice*, London, Edward Arnold.

Jones, R. (1994) *Mental Health Act Manual* (4th edn), London, Sweet and Maxwell.

Knight, B. (1992) *Legal Aspects of Medical Practice* (5th edn), Edinburgh, Churchill Livingstone.

Lennane, K. (1993) 'Whistleblowing: a health issue', *British Medical Journal*, Vol. 307, 11 September, pp. 667–70.

Local Government Ombudsman (1997) *Digest of Cases*, London, The Stationery Office.

Marks-Maran, D. (1993) 'Accountability', in Tschudin, V. (ed.) *Ethics: Nurses and Patients*, pp. 121–34, London, Scutari Press.

McGann, S. (1995) 'The development of nursing as an accountable profession', in Watson, R. (ed.) *Accountability in Nursing Practice*, pp. 18–29, London, Chapman and Hall.

Menzies, I. (1960) 'A case study in the functioning of social systems as a defence against anxiety: a report on a study of the nursing service of a general hospital', *Human Relations*, Vol. 13, No. 2, pp. 95–121.

Munro, R. (1999) 'Law and disorder', *Nursing Times*, Vol. 95, No. 8, 24 February, pp. 16–17.

O'Donnell, A. (1996) 'Legal and quasi-legal accountability', in Pyper, R. (ed.) *Aspects of Accountability in the British System of Government*, pp. 82–118, Wirral, Merseyside, Tudor Business Publishing.

Pook, S. and Copley, J. (1998) 'Inquiry after heart doctors are struck off', *Electronic Telegraph*, 'UK News', Issue 1120, 19 June.

Rodgers, S. (1995) 'Accountability in primary nursing', in Watson, R. (ed.) *Accountability in Nursing Practice*, pp. 70–91, London, Chapman and Hall.

Royal College of Nursing (RCN) (1998) *Guidance for Nurses on Clinical Governance*, London, RCN.

Skolbekken, J. (1995) 'The risk epidemic in medical journals', *Social Science and Medicine*, Vol. 40, pp. 291–305.

Smith, R. (1999) 'Editor's choice: if in doubt, start an inquiry', *British Medical Journal*, Vol. 318, 27 February.

Tingle, J. (1998a) 'Legal aspects of expanded role and clinical guidelines and protocols', in McHale, J., Tingle, J. and Peysner, J. (eds) *Law and Nursing*, pp. 49–60, Oxford, Butterworth Heinemann.

Tingle, J. (1998b) 'Nursing negligence: general issues', in McHale, J., Tingle, J. and Peysner, J. (eds) *Law and Nursing*, pp. 16–33, Oxford, Butterworth Heinemann.

United Kingdom Central Council for Nursing, Midwifery and Health Visiting (UKCC) (1996a) *Guidelines for Professional Practice*, London, UKCC.

United Kingdom Central Council for Nursing, Midwifery and Health Visiting (UKCC) (1996b) *Issues Arising from Professional Conduct Complaints*, London, UKCC.

United Kingdom Central Council for Nursing, Midwifery and Health Visiting (UKCC) (1998) *Statistical Analysis of the UKCC Professional Register 1 April 1997 to 31 March 1998, Volume 5 Professional Conduct Statistics*, July, London, UKCC.

Vinten, G. (1994) *Whistleblowing: Subversion or Corporate Citizenship?*, London, Paul Chapman Publishing.

Wagner, R. (1989) *Accountability in Education: A Philosophical Inquiry*, New York, Routledge.

Whyatt, J. (1961) *The Citizen and the Administration: The Redress of Grievances*, London, Stevens.

Winfield, M. (1994) 'Whistleblowers as corporate safety net', in Vinten, G. (ed.) *Whistleblowing: Subversion or Corporate Citizenship?*, pp. 21–32, London, Paul Chapman Publishing.

World in Action (1994) 'Whistleblowing', London. (http://www/world-in-action.co.uk/WIA_Series_Case_File/content_blowers_diary.html – accessed 13 July 1999)

Part 3
Working with
Changing Structures

Chapter 10
Understanding the policy process

Celia Davies

Stakeholders … were sometimes oblivious to
the fact that there was an indigenous
population who might well have a prior claim
to the same land.

Introduction

> Everywhere I go, the senior people tell me of progress, of better working
> methods and value for money, of objectives achieved, of changes
> delivered. Everywhere I go, I also glimpse another world, a world
> inhabited by everyone else – a world of daily crisis, and concern, of staff
> under pressure and services struggling to deliver. Both worlds are real in
> the minds of those who inhabit them. Both worlds are supported by
> objective evidence. Both views are held sincerely.
>
> (Jarrold, 1996, quoted in Hadley and Clough, 1996, p. 192)

This comment was prompted by the many visits to health care services
and facilities that Ken Jarrold made in the mid-1990s as part of his
responsibility as Director of Human Resources in the NHS Executive. It
describes a profound gulf between different kinds of staff in the delivery of
health care. The senior people (general managers and clinical directors)
were telling him that the policy changes of the early 1990s were working.
They were saying that the new health authorities and trusts in their
relationships as purchasers and competitive providers had indeed
generated entrepreneurial zeal, prompted new and better ways of working
and overall been a spur to positive change and better value for money.

Those delivering the service were telling him otherwise. These people felt on the receiving end of policy changes that left them under enormous pressure, starved of resources, barely coping, and suffering from stress and low morale.

The position is almost certainly more complex than this. Within the senior ranks, for example, it has been shown that the enthusiasts for policy reforms of the early 1990s were more likely to be the new non-executive directors. The sceptics, on the other hand, were more likely to be managers who had had long years of service in a different tradition (Ferlie *et al.*, 1996). The same set of studies also suggests divisions among professionals with some keen to take on the new hybrid roles of clinical managers and directors and others deeply suspicious of the ideas associated with this. So what are we to make of such divisions and divided ideas about the nature and impact of policy?

This chapter examines the policy process. First, it considers some of the different answers that students of public policy have given to the question 'How does policy get made?' Secondly, it explores the growing scope that new policy thinking is providing to help practitioners and others to develop and shape policies at local level. We shall see that the old model – the one that presumed policy was a rational process, taking place at the top of organisations and requiring tight control of implementation – is being replaced. A new model is starting to emerge. It recognises policy as a complex and altogether messier process with more participants, much experimentation, and multiple feedback loops. In the era of transition from the Conservative governments of the 1980s and early 1990s to the policy changes that are being created under Labour, this is an important theme for all who work in health and social care.

1   Policy as 'rational decision making'?

It is a comforting kind of common sense to assume that new policies emerge out of a process of decision making that is essentially rational. Policy-makers set out the goals to be achieved and gather relevant information. In the light of the information, they select the best course of action to enable the goals to be met. Later they review progress and make adaptations. Such a model can be applied to governments, to organisations of all kinds, as well as to daily life. In a classic work, first published over 40 years ago, American political scientist Herbert Simon questioned this. Real world decision-makers, he argued, are not 'maximisers' – selecting the best possible option from all that are available – but 'satisficers' – looking for a course of action that is good enough for the problem at hand. It was important to understand that people intended to act rationally, and they should probably be encouraged to do this – but 'bounded rationality' described their behaviour better (Simon, 1958).

The idea of the policy process as a set of rational steps remains. It is often portrayed as a cycle – looping round from an initial specification of the goal, through information gathering and so on, to an evaluation, which then sets the process in motion once again (Figure 1). The idea of an orderly and rational progression is still strong.

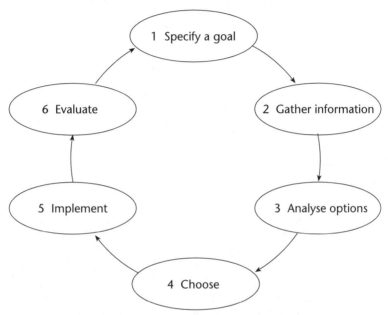

Figure 1   **The rational decision cycle** (Source: adapted from Parsons, 1995, p. 77)

Questions can be asked about each one of these stages in the real world of public policy making. Where do goals come from (step 1)? How do issues get on to the national agenda for policy making in the first place? Political parties may identify them in their manifestos and proceed to follow through their manifesto commitments when elected to office. But this only raises further questions about how decisions were taken about what was to be a manifesto issue, and how other issues emerge and are rejected or selected during a term of office. Take, for example, the case of changes in maternity policy in the NHS that were heralded by the publication *Changing Childbirth* (DoH, 1993). Where did the pressures come from that resulted in the statements this policy contains about the need for greater choice and for a 'woman-centred approach'? Who listened to whom and why?

Then there is the question (step 2) of exactly what kinds of information are seen as relevant to be gathered and what process of information gathering over what time frame is seen as appropriate. *Changing Childbirth* is again a good example. There were influential lobbying bodies not only from the medical profession and from midwifery but also from organisa-tions such as the National Childbirth Trust and the Association for

Improvement of Maternity Services. Who was on the Committee and how alert they might have been to the government agenda of the time are also relevant to the shaping of policy (see Brooks, 1999). Asking such questions politicises the policy cycle, making it altogether less neatly rational and self-contained than the model suggests.

Continuing to question the rational decision cycle, how are options analysed (step 3)? Today, formal techniques of expert option appraisal and policy analysis using statistical modelling are sometimes brought into play. However, these need to be seen as part of the information from which a choice is made rather than the mechanism for choice itself. To get at that (step 4), you might choose to listen to the debate in the House of Commons, or try to interview the civil servants. Sometimes at least, you would want to prise open the closed doors of the Cabinet. 'Implement' is less straightforward than it seems, as Box 1 demonstrates. Finally, different ways of evaluating may produce very different notions of the next step.

Box 1: A classic study of policy implementation

In the early 1970s, two American political scientists studied the implementation of an economic development programme in Oakland, California. The aim was to establish permanent jobs for a long-term unemployed minority ethnic workforce. The programme had involved the construction and fitting of an aircraft hangar, bringing together employers and shaping their recruitment policies, and establishing a government-sponsored training programme for aircraft mechanics. A new agency was created to oversee this, substantial federal funds were allocated, local officials and employers agreed to participate. Why, then, with apparently everything in favour, were the results so poor?

The authors trace in detail the different chains of decision making and where they had to mesh. They point out that a policy is not just about the first links in a complex causal chain but all the subsequent ones too. And when circumstances change, adjustments and alterations need to be made. The authors set aside the idea that we need always to find the single point of implementation failure. In so complex a process, it is not necessarily the implementation but the ambition of the initial target setting that is at fault. Policy and implementation, they argue, need to be brought more closely together. They offer the challenging observation that:

... our normal expectation should be that new programs will fail to get off the ground and that, at best, they will take considerable time to get started. The cards in this world are stacked against things happening, so much so that effort is required to make them move. The remarkable thing is that new programs work at all.

(Pressman and Wildavsky, 1973, p. 109)

In his memorably titled essay on 'the science of muddling through', Charles Lindblom (1959) argued that practical decision making involved something altogether less grandiose than a rational decision cycle. Policy developed, he suggested, through 'incrementalism': a policy 'is tried, altered, tried in its altered form, altered again and so forth' (Braybrooke and Lindblom, 1963). This at least had the advantage of testing the water and not making serious mistakes. The work of writers such as Simon, Lindblom, and Pressman and Wildavsky led others to see just how unrealistic it was to strive for control of implementation. To set out the conditions for 'perfect implementation' (see Box 2) is to show that they are never going to be met.

Box 2: The conditions for 'perfect implementation'

1 The circumstances external to the implementing agency do not impose crippling constraints.

2 Adequate time and sufficient resources are made available to the programme.

3 The required combination of resources is actually available.

4 The policy to be implemented is based on a valid theory of cause and effect.

5 The relationship between cause and effect is direct and there are few, if any, intervening links.

6 Dependency relationships are minimal.

7 There is understanding of, and agreement on, objectives.

8 Tasks are fully specified in correct sequence.

9 There is perfect communication and co-ordination.

10 Those in authority can demand and obtain perfect compliance.

(Source: adapted from Hogwood and Gunn, 1984, quoted in Hill, 1997, pp. 130–31)

Is the rational decision-making model thoroughly discredited? Colebatch (1998), an Australian political scientist who has recently reviewed the concept of policy, is among many who feel that it must be kept in play but also kept in its place. Those working within the policy process *do* strive towards a process of appraising options. They *do* call for evidence and they seek to marshal it in systematic ways. They present policies as the outcome of such a rational process of appraisal even if their rationales are sometimes *post hoc*. Actors' understandings of themselves as working in this way must have a place in the analysis. But the overall process is more complex.

Colebatch offers a useful diagram blending a vertical and a horizontal dimension of the policy process (see Figure 2 overleaf). The vertical

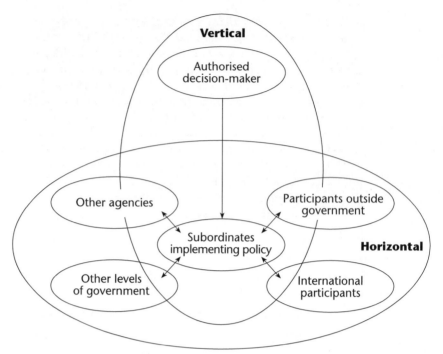

Figure 2 **The vertical and horizontal dimensions of policy** (Source: Colebatch, 1998, p. 38)

dimension draws attention to the way in which those who are in legitimate positions of authority – particularly government ministers – transmit decisions downwards for implementation. The horizontal dimension refers to those outside the line of hierarchical authority who none the less are linked together in various ways and have an important role in mobilising opinion and lobbying. Both dimensions are part of the policy process. Each is linked to the other and the answer to the question of where policy is made involves both.

The point, Colebatch argues, is not to try to 'rescue' policy from the messy politics in which it is entangled, deleting the horizontal dimension and trying to ensure greater rationality in the vertical dimension. Instead the job of policy analysis is *to understand the multiple and sometimes conflicting facets of the policy process that contribute to multiple outcomes – some intended and some unintended*. Colebatch urges those who would understand policy:

- to resist the idea of a single person or group of policy-makers – ask not 'Who makes policy?' but 'Who participates in the policy?'
- to resist the notion of policy being made in a place (at the top) – ask not 'Where are decisions taken?' but 'What networks, links and policy communities group around this issue?'
- to resist the idea of a single policy decision, which is the key determinant of practice – ask not 'What is the policy framework for this setting?' but 'What is shaping behaviour in this practice setting?'

This suggests that the policy process is complex but is also necessarily provisional and fallible. If so, then the logic may well be to call for more not less participation. While it may be right to assume that considerable work is done to explore and evaluate policy options at senior level in the civil service or in policy division in a local authority or elsewhere, this work is only one input to the policy process. Should other inputs not be encouraged to broaden and deepen the policy?

We can begin to recognise that there are *multiple stakeholders* who have an interest in this process, and they should perhaps be more explicitly involved as policy is being decided. We might also observe that certain stakeholder groups sometimes need to be fostered and developed so that their voices can be heard. This is the theme of the next section.

2   Developing stakeholder thinking

A stakeholder has been defined as 'any group or individual that can affect or is affected by the achievement of an organisation's purpose' (Freeman, 1984, quoted in Winstanley *et al.*, 1995, p. 20). Different stakeholders come into play in different areas of policy. We have already referred to some of the lobbying groups in the area of maternity policy. Stakeholders also sometimes form alliances in the policy process and exert strong influence by doing so. Stakeholder thinking can be used both to examine and contrast the way in which particular issues have been framed and discussed and to ask who is included and who is excluded in this and whether there is change over time. Stakeholders need to be seen as *all* those with an interest in an outcome and more or less power to affect it. It may be as well to remember here that the term 'stakeholder' derives from the practice of pioneers driving a stake into the ground to signify their ownership of new territory; they were sometimes oblivious to the indigenous population who might well have had a prior claim to the same land.

The stakeholder power matrix

Winstanley and her colleagues have developed what they call a 'stakeholder power matrix' and applied it to both NHS and local authority settings. They argue that there are two broad kinds of power. The first, which they call *criteria power*, is the power to define the aims and purposes of the service, to design the overall system of provision, set the performance criteria and carry out evaluations. Governments vest this power in particular departments and ministries or delegate it in varying proportions to local government or to appointed agencies. The second kind of power is *operational power* – this is the power of those who actually provide the service to decide how it should be done by allocating resources or deploying knowledge and skills in a particular way. These distinctions, the authors suggest, relate to the well-established theme of power as multidimensional, as being shaped not only by overt decisions but also by more covert methods.

Figure 3 allows the position of stakeholders to be plotted according to these kinds of power. Government as a stakeholder, for example, might be strong on defining purpose and setting systems in place but weak as far as operational controls are concerned. This makes it a stakeholder in quadrant A of the diagram, arm's length power, and represents the situation where the gap between the policy pronouncements and experience on the ground is particularly marked. However, if the government has mechanisms in place to ensure that its policy pronouncements are worked through in detail and the behaviour of service providers and users is closely controlled, then it is in quadrant B. Where a group of service-provider stakeholders has a lot of day-to-day freedom to shape the service, however, they are in quadrant D, operational power. Where stakeholders have neither the power to set the purpose of the services nor the power to influence day-to-day operation, they are in quadrant C – disempowered. Both service-providers and service-users can sometimes fit into this quadrant.

> Within the NHS, for example, there is a current issue of whether the reforms have actually created the conditions in which patients, carers and lower levels of staff are moving out of this corner, and if so whether they are moving vertically, horizontally or diagonally.
>
> (Winstanley *et al.*, 1995, p. 21)

Winstanley and her colleagues used this matrix to begin to analyse changes in local authority services and the NHS over time. They suggest that the Conservative governments of the 1980s and 1990s, for example, having created the purchaser–provider split, were committed to a central government move from quadrant B to quadrant A. Clients and patients, starting at the left-hand extreme of quadrant C, have perhaps made some small moves diagonally upwards – gaining a little more of both kinds of

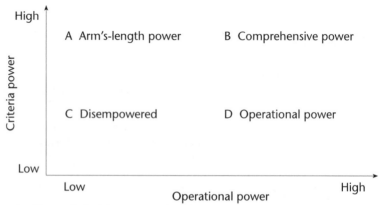

Figure 3 **The stakeholder power matrix** (Source: Winstanley *et al.*, 1995, p. 21)

power, albeit indirectly through the operation of patient's charters and the requirements that service-purchasers and commissioners respond to consumer need.

Others with practical aims of bringing stakeholders into the policy process have used the stakeholder concept in a different way (see Box 3 for one example). Alternatively, Eden (1996) has described a procedure of gathering interested parties together, getting them to identify the different stakeholders in a policy arena and to map them as closer or further away from the centres of power. He then shows how this stakeholder-mapping exercise could be sketched as a set of concentric circles with some groups in the inner circle and others in the middle or outer ones. Mapping of

---

Box 3: Using stakeholder analysis – The Netherlands

The Dutch government is committed to finding ways of involving stakeholders in decisions. It sees itself as at the centre of a network of influence rather than at the top of a hierarchy taking authoritative decisions. Two key steps in creating a more interactive process are (a) making the different stakeholders explicit by brainstorming a list and (b) facilitating group working to ensure that knowledge is shared and mutual understanding is enhanced.

The following are examples of projects stemming from this philosophy.

1 **Central government level** – the development of a national environmental policy plan by one-day meetings with 18 stakeholder groups given drafts of the preliminary chapters of the policy and asked to do a SWOT analysis (strengths, weaknesses, opportunities and threats) and then to develop their own draft of the next chapter on key issues.

2 **Regional level** – establishing a new policy for the Amsterdam–Rhine Canal by allowing four stakeholder groups, located in each corner of the room, time to develop a written plan and then asking them to rotate to review and add comments to each of the other groups' plans in turn, ending with a revision of their original plans in the light of the comments.

3 **Municipal level** – developing a shared cultural policy between two municipalities by deliberately 'pairing' individuals from each municipality and giving them tasks to work on and present jointly to the whole group, rather than letting those from each municipality keep together as a group.

4 **City ward level** – establishing priorities for a day nursery policy by bringing together aldermen, civil servants, managers of day nurseries and day nursery leaders to identify a list of issues then, with each member having four sticky-backed coloured dots to assign importance to issues, letting the ensuing dot count generate the priority listing for further work.

(Source: derived from de Jong, 1996)

this sort enables participants to articulate for themselves the potential alliances that they could form in developing a new policy direction.

De Jong (1996), working in the Netherlands, takes a different approach (as you saw in Box 3). He explains the Dutch government's commitment to get away from the familiar position where it is the civil servants who draft policies and where sending drafts out for consultation results in a series of position statements which the civil servants can then easily ignore. Instead they devised several ways to help stakeholders identify issues and actually work together on priorities. This kind of approach, which could in principle be used at different levels of the policy process, enables new solutions to emerge and creates what is beginning to be called 'collaborative advantage' (see Huxham, 1996).

All these examples offer the potential not only of a much richer understanding of the policy process but also of its practical development beyond the model that sees it only as a set of rational calculations made by one group at one particular point in a hierarchical organisation.

Beyond stakeholder thinking?

If these are some of the benefits and potentials of stakeholder thinking, does it have weaknesses? Focusing on the interactions between the stakeholders who are actually present, or who are acknowledged by those who are present to be stakeholders, has its limitations.

First, there are often potential stakeholders on any specific issue who may not always be brought into a policy process. Concentrating on the stakeholders who come forward (even those who come forward to brainstorm who the stakeholders are) may thus serve to narrow the analysis and obscure particular perspectives on the issue. *Changing Childbirth* (DoH, 1993) provides an example in its treatment of women from black and minority ethnic groups. The document contains a broad statement about respecting the wishes of women from minority ethnic groups. But, to use the words of a later study concerning the experiences of Pakistani women with maternity services in Scotland, minority voices are often 'muted voices' (Bowes and Domokos, 1996) and imaginative and sensitive ways are needed to encourage them to be heard. Bowes and Domokos suggest that, even where there have been special service initiatives, these can construct South Asian women as 'a problem' rather than finding effective ways of working alongside them to determine what the issues are (see also Parsons *et al.*, 1993). The consultation strategy of *Changing Childbirth* is relevant here. Efforts were made to gather minority group views in a survey and to hear perspectives from minority ethnic communities in a consensus conference but the expert group used the usual process of issuing a general invitation for interested parties to state views, and waiting for groups to come forward. It did not actively encourage women to get together and create dialogue in the way that some forms of stakeholder analysis are now doing.

Secondly, identification as a stakeholder does not grant stakeholders power. Even where stakeholders are present, they may face difficulties in articulating their perspectives or in getting them heard. It is all too easy for a minority arguing for something new to be constrained by the weight of the traditional thinking of the majority, to struggle against incomprehension and against those who use their experience to put apparently insuperable obstacles in the way. Stakeholders may need to take other forms of action rather than or as well as participation in a policy process if they want their viewpoint to prevail. A stakeholder process thus runs the risk of failing to uncover the underlying values and ideologies and the interests that they serve; of not recognising taken-for-granted assumptions, the prior framing of issues that, left unchallenged, supports the status quo and means that a critical consideration of the full set of alternatives remains to be made.

Is it possible to use a stakeholder analysis to get to the heart of some of the strengths and weaknesses of a particular policy? Is it possible to use it to tease out some of the aspects of power that may otherwise remain hidden? A key way of doing this, we suggest, is through developing the concept of *provenance*, which can bring stakeholder thinking into alignment with the acknowledgement of the multiple and messy character of the policy process outlined in Section 1. Dictionary definitions of 'provenance' explain that it refers to the source or origins of a phenomenon, and derives literally from the Latin meaning 'coming forth'. Using this starting-point, Box 4 (overleaf) has a checklist of questions that might be asked of a particular policy initiative. Working with questions such as these is likely to reveal not just the obvious stakeholders but the factors influencing the powerful players, the groups who are missing and the issues that do not reach the agenda at all. Chapter 13, for example, explores the provenance of policies on quality by contrasting health and social care.

3   Local level – from policy implementation to policy development

Is there always a gap between policy and practice or at the least a tension between what is on paper and what happens in the real world? This section begins with a return to the question of 'implementation' of policy discussed in Section 1. By seeing policy not as something that is given to people to implement but as something to be owned and developed by them, outcomes can be more positive. It may be that we have expected either too much or too little from policy pronouncements from the top.

Box 4: Examining the provenance of a policy – a summary checklist

1 Primary purpose

What is the nature of this new idea? What are the problems it seeks to address? What is the vision that underlies it?

2 Precedents

Where does the idea come from? (Does it borrow from another sector/ another field of activity/another country?) Who initiated it? What are the assumptions that underpin it? What sets of values, principles and ideals are on display?

3 Priorities

What pressure is there for a solution to this problem? How important is it – and for whom – to resolve this policy issue?

4 Participants

Who are the existing stakeholders with an interest in this? What is their interest and what support are they giving/withholding? Who is most strongly championing it and why? How much access has each group got to the policy process and what is the likelihood that they will be heard?

5 Processes and procedures

Who is to implement it? What training is being suggested? What financial resources are seen as required? What other support for development has been provided or assumed? What timetables are envisaged? How will resistance be responded to?

6 Practicalities

What particular approvals will have to be obtained? Who needs to co-operate with whom to make this work? What resistances is it likely to encounter? Where will they come from? What form will resistance take? What other local agendas does it dovetail/clash with?

7 Perversities

What are the unanticipated consequences (positive and negative) that this policy has had/will have? What by-products has it produced/will it produce for people not directly involved?

8 Perspectives

(If hindsight is possible) in what sense was it a feature of its time? Did it link with other measures in ways not seen until later? Did it work as part of a wider agenda? Did it help build for the future?

Paper policies and daily practice

In a classic study published in 1980 in the USA, Michael Lipsky was concerned to explain how individuals – as citizens and as workers – experience public policies and how the aggregate of their actions comes to shape that policy. He argues:

> ... that public policy is not best understood as made in legislatures or top-floor suites of high-ranking administrators, because in important ways it is actually made in the crowded offices and daily encounters of street-level workers.
>
> (Lipsky, 1980, p. xii)

Lipsky coined the term 'street-level bureaucrats' to refer to a wide array of employees, including teachers, social workers, police officers and others, who deal face-to-face with clients, making decisions to provide benefits or offer services. He recognises that they were working with a welter of policy documents, rules and guidelines, but observed that they often performed quite contrary to the rules. They favoured some clients over others and the effects of their behaviour at times actually minimised citizens' seeking of welfare benefits and services. To understand this, Lipsky argues, 'we need to know how the rules are experienced by workers in the organisation and to what other pressures they are subject' (p. xi).

Street-level bureaucrats, Lipsky explains, come into their chosen area of work because of their high ideals and have a strong commitment to the work they do. But they then face a harsh reality of high caseloads, huge classes, and so on. If they are not to drop out or burn out, they must find ways of dealing with this. Some practice a form of psychological withdrawal. Others genuinely see themselves as struggling to mitigate the worst effects of the system and work hard not to become cynical or withdrawn. They sincerely feel that they are doing their best under adverse circumstances. Yet their actions taken together serve to pervert the service ideal. Service-users are rarely in a position to challenge. They often lack the resources and understanding to question what is offered or not offered to them. If they do understand their rights and entitlements, they risk antagonising the workers by speaking out. If they organise collectively, they may get labelled as trouble-makers. Lipsky saw no point in trying to tighten the rules further: 'the fact is that we *must* have people making decisions and treating other citizens in the public services' (p. xv). The solution must be sought, he felt, in the structure of the work and in reconstituting policy. Policies should state what they want workers to do and, where objectives are in conflict, documents should indicate what is to take priority. Agencies should be able to measure workers' performance, to make meaningful comparisons between them and have relevant incentives and sanctions.

How relevant is all this to the UK today? In some instances, policy documents are not so much subverted as ignored. Staff do not consider them as resources that might be of use in their day-to-day practice. And

---

Box 5: Emma's story – policies and practices

Emma is now a senior home care assistant working for a local authority in the south of England. She has been working in home care for less than two years. She is a single parent who missed out on education and spent years at home. Now in her 30s, she is keen and enthusiastic about her job, anxious to gain qualifications, and to get on. She said 'yes' to just about any courses that were on offer. She was rapidly promoted. Emma talks eloquently about the dilemmas of home care work and the challenging situations she and her carers face and the relentless pressures of the workload. Asked what policy documents guided her, she fell silent for a moment and asked whether she could go away and check. A raft of paper emerged. There was the ring-binder she could not remember when she had last opened. There was an array of leaflets summarising policies, giving information on local services. There was the paperwork from the training courses she had attended. When we looked at this we realised that quite a number of the training events she had attended were actually based on the policy documents in the folder. There were also, she said, two box files at work. She was going to take a look at them the next day – if, that is, she got a moment to do it.

So were any of the many policy documents she held really important to her practice? 'Moving and Handling' she said immediately and the course on diabetes. She could recognise that an elderly lady lying on the floor might be in a diabetic coma and could advise the emergency services accordingly. These things were about building a knowledge base for carrying out her work. What about the local authority's policy on how to tackle difficult situations? 'Ah', she said, 'sexual harassment'.

'One of my carers came to me and said she was not prepared to visit a particular elderly man again who was regularly exposing himself to her and masturbating in her presence. I agreed with her that she should not have to put up with that and went to my manager. She said "It's all part of the job, she should be able to handle it." I disagreed. In the end my carer was moved to a different patch. Someone else was brought in. Together we then looked for the written policy. There was one, but it was missing from the file.'

---

where staff are aware of policies, they may judge them to be unrealistic or irrelevant. Emma's story (Box 5) provides one case in point.

In some areas, however, policy has been developed in great detail, both centrally and locally. Child protection is an important example, where cases in the courts and 'trial by media' have resulted in much energy being devoted to policies and policy guidelines. But with what result?

Research across England and Wales indicates uneven development and continuing areas of confusion. The findings suggest that policies have still sometimes been imposed on practitioners rather than being developed with them (see Box 6). But things can be different, as the example in the next sub-section shows.

Box 6: Policies in practice – child protection

Social workers in child protection report that policies can be of value in clarifying roles and reducing stress. However, a survey of 117 local authorities in England and Wales following the issuing of guidance on policies and procedures once a child's name has been entered in the child protection register found:

- 27 authorities had policies alone

- 37 had procedures alone

- 15 had no documentation at all.

Only two had policies, procedures and guidance and only one of these had developed standards and an evaluation checklist.

The researchers found that plans for children were unclear, action time-scales varied, and the idea of core group responsibility was blurred. They listed a range of areas where policy and procedures needed to be developed to clarify workers' roles and responsibilities. Guidance, they argued, should be embedded in the real world, acknowledging the pressures being faced so that policies and procedures can become a benchmark for quality rather than a standard against which professionals fail.

(Source: adapted from Horwath and Calder, 1998)

From paper policies to good practice – adult protection policies in Sheffield

In 1991, Sheffield City Council produced its first set of guidelines on elder abuse. The need for a co-ordinated approach was apparent. The health trust was concentrating on treating an abuse victim's injuries, the social services inspection unit was aiming to enforce Care Home Regulations, and the police were concerned with arrest and prosecution. The next eight years saw a range of developments as the complexity of defining and establishing abuse was confirmed. Following overlapping proposals to develop an interagency policy, an Adult Abuse Steering Group was set up with chief officers of the Council attending. The launch of a shared set of policy and procedures was followed a year later by the appointment of a full-time co-ordinator and in 1997 by the replacement of the Steering Group with an Adult Protection Committee (APC). A key purpose of the APC was liaison, helping to bring the organisations together at different levels and continuing to monitor, evaluate and develop policy (Quigley, 1997, 1999).

The objectives of the policy were to enhance the quality of life of vulnerable adults at risk of abuse by improving the identification of cases of abuse and setting up an appropriate process of response. Equally important was the need to agree respective roles, to establish procedures and timescales, to ensure there were ways to share information and to spell out ways of resolving disagreement. It was recognised, however, that spelling out procedures would not help with the inevitable grey areas in deciding just what was abuse and whose responsibility it was to take action. Developing trust and communicating effectively with each other were of paramount importance. Action was needed to link organisations at four distinct levels – at the front-line level of dealing with actual and suspected cases of abuse, at the management level of taking forward the investigation work, as well as at a liaison committee level and at chief officer level.

The details set out in Box 7 give an indication of how the issue was tackled. The full policy document covers the other two levels of work (the liaison committee level and the corporate level). At each of the levels, it sets out not only what the basic work is (as shown in the box) but also what the advanced work is.

Sheffield is not the only place to see developments of this kind (Brown and Stein, 1998). In 1996, the Association of Directors of Social Services passed a motion urging that generic guidelines be formulated at local levels to deal with a wide range of adult clients and with different types of abuse. A network of senior managers in social services involved in implementing policy in their areas periodically comes together to share experience and learn about the latest research and evidence. Hilary Brown, co-ordinator of the network, stresses that policies must always be revisited and rewritten and that implementation 'is a loop not a line'. Authorities, she observes, too often assign someone the task of simply writing a policy rather than of actually *nurturing* it (Brown, 1998). Interestingly, further government guidance is likely to reflect this emerging good practice rather than drive it. Policy in this case is being developed neither from the top down nor from the bottom up, but rather from the middle out.

All this is a far cry from the notion that policies are devised at the top and implemented at local level. Policies that are 'nurtured' in the way described here surely stand more chance both of being relevant to a locality and of gaining the commitment and support of staff.

Finally, the sheer complexity of the policy dilemmas being faced today in health and social care may well mean that top-down solutions in some areas are just not possible. Instead there is a need to put forward tentative approaches and accept a continual process of learning from practice. Clarke and Stewart (1997), studying local government, have gone along this route. For some issues, they argue, the problem itself is hard to define, and the causal chains are difficult, if not impossible, to unravel. Solutions are likely to be temporary ones and the issue will need to be repeatedly revisited. They refer to these as 'wicked issues' – not meaning that they are bad, but that they are tricky and resistant to solution. Where issues are like this – and they cite health and social care as one area where they often are – the policy process requires new ways of conceptualising and new ways of working. Box 8 (on p.228) summarises their key points.

Box 7: Adult protection – excerpts from a policy statement covering people working at different levels

At the front-line: working, with management support, with people from other agencies you do not know but of whom you have (it is hoped) clear expectations – people at this level need to be confident that they are part of an important and well-managed area of work.

Methods may include:

- Training, addressing areas of knowledge and skill such as basic awareness, investigating abuse, disclosure work and protection plans and recording. Training needs to be targeted at Social Services staff and others.

- Talks at team meetings in Social Services, NHS Trusts, GP surgeries, etc.

- Regular newsletters to keep staff up to date with developments.

- Achieving consistency of expectation by a wide distribution of documentation, including procedures and information leaflets.

At the management-of-investigation level: working across agencies with people you do not know but can cultivate long-term relationships with, and taking responsibility for the actions of people you directly manage. It is important to acknowledge the difficult 'balancing act' taking place at this level in organisations, trying to deliver the best process from a wide range of procedural requirements.

Methods may include:

- Designating specialist management functions, e.g. case conference chairs, and providing these managers with detailed training.

- Offering ongoing central support to these individuals, such as case advice from a central co-ordinator and/or regular meetings and updates. The purpose is to enable a core group of managers at this level to act as a consistent reference point for managers from other agencies, and to support them in resolving low-level disputes over the application of the agreed procedures to a particular case.

- Offering a source of reference material and best practice information, e.g. action on elder abuse bulletin, to a wide range of managers across all of the agencies.

- Problem-solving liaison meetings can be held at this level, leading for instance to designated contact points between different agencies, e.g. between Social Services and the police, and to clarification of roles such as those of inspection units or contracts officers.

- Paying attention to the inevitable overlap between abuse procedure requirements and requirements arising from other related areas such as 'risk', disciplinary and contract compliance procedures.

(Source: L. Quigley, 1999, personal communication)

Box 8: How to deal with 'wicked issues'

1 DO NOT search for certainty; instead accept that understanding will be partial.

2 DO NOT think in a linear way; instead think holistically and look for interrelationships.

3 DO NOT be trapped by the obvious and conventional; accept different perspectives and approaches and tolerate not knowing.

4 DO NOT consult the usual people; instead draw in as wide an array of organisations and interests as possible and be open to 'outsiders' and their new attitudes and behaviours.

5 DO NOT go for the usual answers; instead be prepared to learn and encourage experiment, diversity and reflection.

(Source: adapted from Clarke and Stewart, 1997, pp. 15–16)

As advocates of such new approaches, Clarke and Stewart perhaps underplay the adjustments needed to make a reality of this. People need not just to think differently but to develop new skills, and perhaps make changes in fundamental aspects of their identities as managers and as practitioners to work in these new ways. With a change of government in 1997, new policy documents came thick and fast – on the shape of the 'new NHS', on local government and community care, and on matters such as collaboration, quality and regulation (see Chapters 12, 13 and 14). At the same time, there were calls for bids to win demonstration site status for health action zones, primary care groups and more besides. Practitioners are thus increasingly finding themselves drawn into discussion about how to put flesh on the bones of policy and are asking how they, along with other stakeholders, can help policy development in their local areas. Will we see a real paradigm shift for the new century? Will the gulf that Ken Jarrold observed as he visited health services in the mid-1990s be bridged?

Conclusion

It is easy to regard policy as a given – a set of decisions made somewhere on high, handed down to those working in a local situation, often with little recognition of actual working conditions and scant regard for the specific nature of needs in a local area. This chapter has tried to show that there is another perspective – that of seeing policy as a process, encouraging involvement of different stakeholders in policy and facilitating the creation of feedback loops to allow learning and adjustment to occur. A critical practitioner needs to be both willing and able to take part in the policy process, acknowledging the multiple perspectives that people will bring and welcoming opportunities to engage with policy development and to make it relevant to and supportive of practice.

References

Bowes, A. and Domokos, T. M. (1996) 'Pakistani women and maternity care: raising muted voices', *Sociology of Health and Illness*, Vol. 18, No. 1, pp. 45–65.

Braybrooke, D. and Lindblom, C. (1963) *The Strategy of Decision*, New York, Free Press.

Brooks, F. (1999) 'Changes in maternity policy – who, what and why?', in Davies, C., Finlay, L. and Bullman, A. (eds) *Changing Practice in Health and Social Care*, London, Sage (K302 Reader 1).

Brown, H. (1998) *Implementing Adult Protection Policies*, ESRC Seminar Series, 2 April, Milton Keynes, The Open University, School of Health and Social Welfare.

Brown, H. and Stein, J. (1998) 'Implementing adult protection policies in Kent and East Sussex', *Journal of Social Policy*, Vol. 27, No. 3, pp. 371–96.

Clarke, M. and Stewart, J. (1997) *Handling the Wicked Issues: A Challenge for Government*, Birmingham, University of Birmingham, School of Public Policy.

Colebatch, H. K. (1998) *Policy*, Buckingham, Open University Press.

Department of Health (DoH) (1993) *Changing Childbirth Part 1: Report of the Expert Maternity Group*, London, HMSO.

Eden, C. (1996) 'The stakeholder/collaborator strategy workshop', in Huxham, C. (ed.) *Creating Collaborative Advantage*, London, Sage.

Ferlie, E., Ashburner, L., Fitzgerald, L. and Pettigrew, A. (1996) *The New Public Management in Action*, Oxford, Oxford University Press.

Freeman, E. (1984) *Strategic Management: A Stakeholder Approach*, London, Pitman.

Hadley, R. and Clough, R. (1996) *Care in Chaos: Frustration and Challenge in Community Care*, London, Cassell.

Hill, M. (1997) *The Policy Process in the Modern State* (3rd edn), Hemel Hempstead, Prentice Hall/Harvester Wheatsheaf.

Hogwood, B. W. and Gunn, L. (1984) *Policy Analysis for the Real World*, Oxford, Oxford University Press.

Horwath, J. and Calder, M. (1998) 'Working together to protect children on the child protection register: myth or reality?', *British Journal of Social Work*, Vol. 28, No. 6, pp. 879–95.

Huxham, C. (1996) *Creating Collaborative Advantage*, London, Sage.

de Jong, A. (1996) 'Inter-organizational collaboration in the policy preparation process', in Huxham, C. (ed.) *Creating Collaborative Advantage*, London, Sage.

Lindblom, C. (1959) 'The science of "muddling through"', *Public Administration Review*, Vol. 19, pp. 78–88.

Lipsky, M. (1980) *Street-Level Bureaucracy: Dilemmas of the Individual in Public Services*, New York, Russell Sage Foundation.

Parsons, L., Macfarlane, A. and Golding, J. (1993) 'Pregnancy, birth and maternity care', in Ahmad, W. (ed.) *'Race' and Health in Contemporary Britain*, pp. 51–75, Buckingham, Open University Press.

Parsons, W. (1995) *Public Policy*, Aldershot, Elgar.

Pressman, J. and Wildavsky, A. (1973) *Implementation*, Berkeley, CA, University of California Press.

Quigley, L. (1997) 'Working together to protect vulnerable adults in Sheffield', in Davies, D. and Quigley, L. (eds) *Good Policy! Good Practice? What Comes After the Policy?*, pp. 18–24, Sheffield, Sheffield Adult Protection Office.

Quigley, L. (1999) 'Why is working together so difficult? Developing policy into practice in the field of adult protection', *Journal of Adult Protection* (in press).

Simon, H. (1958) *Administrative Behaviour*, New York, Macmillan.

Winstanley, D., Sorabji, D. and Dawson, S. (1995) 'When the pieces don't fit a stakeholder power matrix to analyse public sector restructuring', *Public Money and Management*, Vol. 15, No. 2, pp. 19–26.

Chapter 11
Counting the costs

Colin Guest and Philip Scarff

The Finance Manager is seen
as the 'Abominable No-Man'
who refuses to see the merit of
new approaches.

Introduction

Too often in the public service, money, or the lack of it, is the factor that
holds back service delivery and development. The Finance Manager is seen
as the 'Abominable No-Man' who refuses to see the merit of new
approaches, cannot find the money to fund them and so stifles good
ideas at birth. In the private sector, he or she is seen as the guardian of
profit more than quality, and voluntary providers too struggle to stay in
business in the face of pressure from social services departments to reduce
costs to a minimum. In all sectors, practitioners who can see a better way
of doing things become frustrated at their seeming inability to influence
how resources are allocated.

At the core of this chapter there is a single case study aimed at bringing
to life a series of important concepts associated with the management of
budgets and to show their importance not only for specialised finance staff
but also for those who are more directly involved in delivering services.
These themes are set in the context of a transformation of the financial
regime in public services and of questions about its implications.

1   New regimes – new roles

In the years after the Conservative victory in the general election of 1979, there were moves towards more active management and new strategies for objective setting and performance management in the public sector. These moves were given a further boost after 1990 with the arrival of market competition and contracts. Local authorities became enablers of services rather than providers of them, losing many of their direct service organisations. Private providers were encouraged and voluntary organisations became service-providers on a larger scale than ever before. Newly formed NHS trusts became part of an internal market, bidding for work from the purchaser health authorities. All this gave expression to the belief that the public sector was a drain on resources and incapable of reforming itself without being forced into major change (Wilson, 1998).

The new regime brought profound alterations in roles and relationships and in people's perceptions of themselves and others. It also brought demands for new skills in relation to financial management. The case studies in Boxes 1 and 2 give accounts of the adjustments those working in health and social care had to make as they started to take more responsibility for resources.

Box 1: Mike's story – managing social services

Up to the early 1990s almost all our services for children, elderly and disabled people were provided in-house. I was a purchaser and a provider of services, although we never looked at our services in that way. I'd estimate that by 1992 only 10% of our budget was spent on private or voluntary sector services. Budgets were not of paramount importance to us, because we were primarily practitioners, who expected most of the budgeting to be done by finance specialists.

Each year we gave grants to local organisations which provided day care or home help services. Looking back, I can see that there was very little objectivity in the way we spent the grant money. We had an annual round of bidding, but didn't specify what services we needed in terms of either quality or quantity. And we had no objective means of looking back at the performance of bidders so that we could compare them or judge value for money. The result was a cosy status quo, with promising new organisations failing to break into the circle.

In 1992, when the NHS and Community Care Act began to be implemented, things began to change dramatically. Along with my practitioner colleagues in the health and voluntary sectors, I had to learn a new range of competencies. I have a budget, which I can use only for purchasing services. I can choose where I buy the services from, by referring to a list of approved in-house or external providers who meet minimum standards of cost and service quality. Some of our in-house providers have closed or been privatised. My role is very different now. I manage my budget by making choices and balancing priorities, costing the care of each client.

Box 2: Mary's story – business management in a community NHS Trust

Until 1992 I was employed by a District Health Authority and was responsible for helping to manage its district nursing service. The DHA decided how the service should be organised and it employed and managed the district nurses. The service operated very much as it had done for years – we worked closely with family doctors although we were independent of them. There was little in the way of service planning and no explicit quality standards.

In April 1993 the Community Health Trust was formed as a separate entity. I was asked to take on the role of Business Manager, negotiating and managing contracts with the DHA, ensuring that we were delivering the required service and staying within budget. I wasn't keen but I was persuaded that it needed an experienced nurse with knowledge of how the service operated, so I reluctantly took it on.

It wasn't until the second year that things really began to change: the DHA required more service, to higher standards and at less cost. We reached an acceptable compromise but I had to find savings in our expenditure and change the way some things were done. We quickly became experienced at negotiating contracts and delivering services to agreed quality standards. The DHA, which had merged with its neighbours to form a large commissioning authority, also became more experienced at identifying health needs and planning services to meet them. Another fundamental change took place when some of our GPs became fund-holders and were given budgets to purchase community nursing services for their patients. Two practices on the fringe of our area decided to purchase nursing from a neighbouring Trust: this meant that we had too many district nurses and we had to reduce their numbers. This was achieved by natural wastage but if other practices had followed suit we could have faced making staff redundant. We had to do a lot of work to make sure our service was attractive to GPs and their patients.

All this has forced us to look carefully at the quality and the cost of our service and how we do things. There has been an increase in paperwork because of contracting and the need to provide monitoring information to the health authority. The government is now talking about co-operation rather than competition in the NHS, and less bureaucracy. This will be welcome, although it would be difficult now to return to the old way of working.

If the public sector as a whole was experiencing a change in its financial regime, just what did this entail? Sheila Masters, seconded from one of the leading management consultancy firms to become Director of Finance for the NHS, describes what she found as an outsider going in at the top:

> The senior position in the NHS finance function carried the title of 'Treasurer'. That was probably what respectable accountants liked to be

called in 1948 when the NHS was founded. In 1988, however, it had no contemporary relevance.

(Masters, 1993, p. 4)

Centrally and locally, those responsible for finances were what she calls 'guardians of the cash limit'. They exercised, and to some extent still exercise, what others have explained is largely a stewardship role in relation to public funds, ensuring that these funds are spent on purposes as intended in the legislation (Tonge and Horton, 1996). Masters argues that treasurers needed to be exposed to modern concepts of financial management; not acting as the distant 'no-men' noted in the introduction to this chapter, but instead being integrated into the management team. If this were to occur, it was clear that the finance function had major adjustments to make. Revenues were already shifting from 'last year plus a bit' to a system of bidding for contracts and underpinning this with all relevant financial information. There was to be a whole new capital recording and charging system. Contracts had to be costed and settlement systems devised. A new concept of public sector financial management was being born. It involved:

> ... specifying and obtaining objectives, safeguarding and making optimum use of resources, achieving aims, and enabling something to happen according to plans and budgets.
>
> (Hill and Rockley, cited in Tonge and Horton, 1996, p. 72)

This was not a development that could be hidden away in a separate finance department. The skills in drawing up contracts and service level agreements needed to be shared effectively with those who were managing and delivering services at the front line. Local authority social workers, as care managers, found themselves among those in charge of a budget making decisions about what care services in the community to purchase for individuals and groups. Hospital clinicians were soon handling devolved budgets, embroiled in the business of calculating what a particular service or operation cost and thinking in altogether new ways about inputs, and outputs. Mike and Mary (see Boxes 1 and 2) were upbeat when they looked back. Others have been less so, focusing on broader aspects of the reforms, pointing to the insecurities and job losses that contracting has entailed, concentrating on the speed of implementation, the imposition of too rigid a notion of the market, the many things that have gone wrong and the fear sometimes of speaking out about this (Hadley and Clough, 1996).

The new financial regime certainly exposed the finance function to new ways of working on a rapid timetable when information systems and IT support were not in place. Research is now emerging to suggest how care contracting has worked, how care managers, for example – often with a training in social work values that distanced themselves from money – have had to learn to bring finances into the equation. They have struggled with the new language of economic thinking (Mackintosh, 2000); they have often had poor information and support (Lewis *et al.*, 1996). There have been new providers from the private or independent sector, whose balancing of costs, quality and profit need to be understood. There have been major adjustments of culture and style for those in the voluntary sector, who have had to balance their new provider roles with their older commitments to demonstration projects and to campaigning for change (Deakin, 1996). There is a suggestion, based on a study of London, that black voluntary organisations, dependent on local authority contracts, have done less well in gaining funding for service provision than their white counterparts (Butt and Mizra, 1997). In all, a great deal of 'juggling and dealing' has clearly needed to happen to make a reality of services in the new system (Leat and Perkins, 1998).

Has this new financial regime been worth while? Has it clarified the true costs of service provision and made more transparent to all those involved the choices that are to be made? Or has it, to use a classic phrase, produced 'people who know the cost of everything and the value of nothing'? It is worth bearing such questions in mind while working through the case study in this chapter. It follows Marjorie as she prepares and manages her budget for Middlebrook, a residential facility for people with learning difficulties. Both Marjorie and Middlebrook are fictional, built from the experience we have had with similar practitioners and agencies.

2   Managing resources – the case of Middlebrook

Middlebrook is one of five centres operated by a national charity. Until three years ago it was run by a local authority social services department, topped up by some health trust funding. Middlebrook has 12 residents, who have daily supported employment in the neighbouring town. The centre has eight staff: Marjorie (the centre manager), four carers, a job coach, a cook and a cleaner/handyperson.

Marjorie, returning to paid work in her thirties after bringing up a family, decided to plan a career for herself in the caring field, becoming a social work assistant in her local authority. Three years later, she was sponsored by her employer to train as a social worker and, three years on from that, she was offered the manager post at Middlebrook. Her duties included the day-to-day operations of the centre, ensuring cover and supervising staff. More recently she has had to learn to operate in a new environment in which Middlebrook has had to become competitive, tendering annually for local authority and health authority contracts. This has meant careful attention to how resources are used. Each month Majorie spends a few hours monitoring the budget and forecasting what the end-of-year expenditure is likely to be. She comments:

> When I first took on budgeting I wasn't happy about it, because it got in the way of other things and I couldn't see the point in it. After a while the work got easier. I can see now that there's no point looking back – places like Middlebrook have to demonstrate that the money is well

managed and we are giving value for money. On the positive side, the financial things that I have learned to do will also be very good for Middlebrook, because I expect to develop the centre and win some more business.

Marjorie's revenue budget is a key working tool. Revenue budgets are used to meet day-to-day costs of services, such as staff, materials, fuel and relatively inexpensive equipment, and they are usually allocated for just one year at a time. (The other type of budget – the *capital* budget – is used to pay for expensive purchases, which have a longer lifetime, such as building works or equipment. Capital budgets are planned with a rolling programme, over several years.) The income and expenditure figures for Middlebrook's revenue budget are shown in Table 1. They are 'cash limits': Marjorie must not spend more than the amounts shown and must also achieve the stated income figure. In practice, there is usually scope for variations between the different items in a budget as long as the net expenditure is within its cash limit. Senior managers, such as Marjorie's line manager, who may have responsibility for several centres, will have similar discretion across all the services for which they have budgetary responsibility.

Table 1   **Revenue budget for Middlebrook**

	£000	*£000*
Expenditure		
Staff	85.8	
Premises	8.0	
Transport	12.2	
Food	19.4	
Supplies and services	8.1	
Miscellaneous	3.2	
Total gross expenditure		136.7
Income		
Social services	28.0	
Health authority	10.0	
Staff meals	4.8	
Client charges	25.2	
Total income		68.0
Net expenditure		68.7

The overall cash limits in a budget ultimately reflect political decisions about the funding that will be made available to a service year on year. They also reflect decisions taken locally by senior managers about the funding of individual services and the relative priority they attach to them. In a private organisation, adherence, or not, to cash limits can make the difference between staying in business or going into liquidation. Public sector organisations do not go bankrupt (although voluntary organisations certainly can), but an overspend in one service means less money for another and, intentionally or not, can change the priorities set by senior officers or elected or appointed members. It is a brave, or foolish, service manager who ignores the cash limits set for his or her service!

Managing a revenue budget

Table 1 shows that the centre has been allocated a cash limit of £136,700 for the financial year (see total gross expenditure). Not surprisingly for a facility specialising in providing care, a large proportion of this – in practice over 60% – has been allocated to pay the staff. There are five other types of expenditure, and together these six categories of approved costs are the 'total gross expenditure'.

Income plans are set out in the lower half of Table 1, showing the sums that are planned to be collected from social services, from the health authority, from staff who eat their meals at the centre, and from clients who pay for their care. The total of £68,000 represents the annual income Marjorie must collect to set against her gross expenditure, leaving a net expenditure of £68,700, a deficit which the charity meets centrally. Reductions in Middlebrook's income have been caused by short-term vacancies. These vacancies have a double effect as, when a resident leaves, both the social services income and client charges are temporarily lost. It is not possible to catch up on lost income by increasing the number of residents beyond the approved level of 12, for which Middlebrook is registered.

How, then, can Marjorie cut costs? Her accountant will supply a monthly report of the expenditure incurred and income collected. To get the most from that report, and to make it more accurate, she needs to be prompt in paying bills and sending invoices to social services and the health authority. The report does not tell her what her future expenditure commitments are, so she keeps her own record of her spending plans. By then combining the actual expenditure shown on her reports with her local record of commitments, Marjorie has a better picture of the financial situation.

The accountant comments:

> If you have any reductions in Middlebrook's income you'll have to reduce your expenditure to cover the losses. Look for flexibility in your budget. Separate your fixed costs from your variable ones and concentrate on reducing the variable costs.

Understanding costs

To do what the accountant suggests and to ensure she is getting the best value from the limited resources available to her, Marjorie needs a clear understanding not only of the concepts of fixed and variable costs but also of several other related ideas.

Fixed and variable costs

As a general rule, fixed costs are those which do not change in the short term, even if levels of activity vary (in this context, the term 'activity' means work or services). Variable costs, though, as the term implies, do change as levels of activity vary. However, it is often difficult to make a distinction between these two types of costs and, in reality, they tend to be semi-fixed or semi-variable. Middlebrook's budget table illustrates how the distinction can become blurred. Take staffing costs: most of these costs are fixed because they relate to permanent staff, on contracted hours. Marjorie is committed to spending these fixed costs, but knows that there can be some variability in her staffing costs, as the job coach and two carers are sessional staff, who work as and when required. This means she can regard the staffing budget as having both fixed and variable elements, and she could have some flexibility within the monies allocated for sessional staff. For example, she can offset some of the income losses caused by residential vacancies by reducing the hours worked by sessional staff until those vacancies are filled, but she needs to budget for deploying sessional staff to cover sickness, training and holiday absences, too.

Looking further down Middlebrook's budget table, costs can be categorised as follows.

- **Premises** – this is a fixed cost to meet a head office contractual payment.
- **Transport** – this contains a fixed element of £8000 for the lease payment for Middlebrook's minibus. The £4200 balance is variable, as it pays for staff mileage, which fluctuates as the number of residents travelling to supported employment placements changes. Marjorie can avoid the need for additional staff mileage whenever she has two or more residential vacancies, as the minibus, which can carry 10 people, will then accommodate them all.
- **Food** – technically, these costs are variable, as Marjorie manages the food budget according to a weekly cost per resident. However, some of the economies of buying in bulk are lost when she buys for fewer residents, producing little or no savings.
- **Supplies and services** – little flexibility is found here, as the budget meets the costs of electricity, gas, water and minibus fuel, which remain predominantly fixed when activity reduces.
- **Miscellaneous** – Marjorie 'inherited' this budget allowance when she arrived at Middlebrook, and uses it to meet the costs of repairs to the building, replacing equipment and improving facilities. The costs are largely fixed, because they pay for the essential, planned repairs and replacements which keep Middlebrook up to registration standard. She has to keep something in reserve for emergencies, however.

Unit costs

A key concept that Marjorie has learned to use with good effect, as we shall see below, is *unit costs* – that is, the costs of an individual unit of service, for example, one week of care for one resident in a home or an hour of domiciliary care. By calculating unit costs she knows how much is being spent on Middlebrook's activities and services. Unit costs are increasingly used to assess whether value for money is being given by one provider compared with another. They can equally be used internally, to see whether costs are stable or changing. Sometimes, a manager like Marjorie will calculate unit costs herself, as a local management tool. However, it is also likely that target unit costs will be set by others, such as senior managers, auditors or those who commission services. Since the 1980s it has been government policy to set a range of performance indicators, including unit costs, for health and social care services.

The arithmetic for calculating unit costs is not complicated – you add up all the costs incurred in providing a service and divide them by the number of units of service provided. Thus:

$$\text{Unit cost} = \frac{\text{All the costs of providing a service}}{\text{The number of units of service provided}}$$

Problems can arise, however, in getting agreement about which costs are to be included in the calculations. For example, some resources, such as equipment, staff or accommodation, may be shared between providers and 'ownership' of such costs may be uncertain. This issue is touched on below, when we look at direct and indirect costs and overheads. Working from the revenue budget for Middlebrook and her monthly expenditure reports, Marjorie calculated unit costs for the Centre's three main categories of service.

1   The unit cost for the overall care of residents, produced by adding up all Middlebrook's costs for that month and dividing them by the number of clients resident in that same period.

2   A unit cost for Middlebrook's supported employment services, produced by separating the costs of staff time, transport, administration, etc. that were put into the service that month and dividing them by the number of days of supported employment provided in the same period.

3   A unit cost for the meals prepared in the Centre's kitchen – Marjorie calculated these to help her manage the kitchen more effectively and to see whether the information would help reduce waste. The monthly costs of staff, food, fuel and materials were separated and divided by the number of meals provided during that period.

Up to this point, the revenue budget has been taken as given, but those accountable for resources need to be aware of direct and indirect costs and of overheads that may be allocated. Understanding these, and successfully challenging them, may make a dramatic difference to budgets, unit costs and the amount available to spend on services.

Direct and indirect costs

These two terms are used to signify where a cost belongs, how it is to be allocated, or which budget it belongs to. A cost is called *direct* if it is clear who is responsible for it. For example, at Middlebrook the costs of salaries, food and transport are clearly the responsibility of the Centre and are 'direct'. *Indirect* costs, however, are harder to pin down. These are costs that are shared and apportioned between budgets – often using a formula that can be related to the level of activity. For example, the costs of putting clean linen into a hospital ward have a range of elements, including the actual laundry costs (probably contracted out), porters and administration. One arrangement for allocating these costs would be to charge them to each ward according to the number of occupied bed-days on each ward. If it is not entirely clear how indirect costs are comprised or who is responsible for them, they might be apportioned wrongly, or neglected. When they are neglected, indirect costs tend to produce winners and losers, because *somebody* ultimately picks up the cost and it may be by default, causing a budget problem.

Middlebrook is a relatively small organisation with a self-contained budget, sharing no facilities or activities with other organisations. Its revenue budget shows that Marjorie meets the direct costs of her services. Marjorie would be well advised, however, to find out from her head office whether she will be expected to pay for any hidden indirect costs. These could, for example, be a commitment on the Centre's 'miscellaneous' expenditure heading shown on the budget table. 'Indirect' costs need to be watched very carefully and minimised or eliminated wherever possible!

Overhead costs

Sometimes called 'on-costs', 'overheads' is a loose term used to describe the range of costs associated with making a service possible, but not directly connected with front-line activity. There is no strict convention or rule defining what should be included in overheads, but common examples are the administrative functions such as personnel, finance, and legal and property services which support organisations. In the 1990s new public sector overhead costs have been created in developing the internal market and purchaser and provider functions. During that time, however, some internal overhead costs have been 'externalised' through contracting out. Overhead costs are a perennial preoccupation, usually coming to the fore during the major budgeting exercises which follow financial crises or budget cuts, the aim being to reduce 'non-essential' expenditure by targeting the activities which surround and support practitioners. It can be an exceedingly problematic process to decide what (and who!) constitutes an overhead cost, where the cuts will be made, and how the remaining costs should be shared.

Understanding fixed and variable costs and being able to calculate unit costs in these ways does not mean that a budget-holder is then entirely free to allocate spending as he or she sees fit. Marjorie's spending authority is limited to £1000 on any item, and she must obtain three written quotations before going to her line manager to spend in excess of that amount. Most organisations impose constraints on their employees, limiting their authority to ensure that financial probity is maintained, as well as accountability to shareholders, elected representatives or the public at large. In the fields of health and social welfare, too, practitioners and managers are constrained by limits to their individual authority to spend money, or vary from service plans, as a means of ensuring that resources are used only for the purposes for which they were intended.

3   Budget plans and business plans

So far we have been considering Middlebrook's revenue budget simply as a table of figures, giving Marjorie a set of parameters for the activity of the Centre, only some of which she can change. A budget is not just a set of figures, however. To be useful, a budget should be part and parcel of a written plan, describing what the priorities are, what staff are going to do and the resources that are to be used, *expressed in financial terms*.

This brings us to the concept of business planning. The practice has its roots in commercial businesses, which have seen the process as an effective means for defining and meeting their objectives. In cases where the creation of the business plan remains the firm prerogative of senior managers and accountants and is not clearly understood and accepted by front-line managers and staff, there is considerable research to suggest that budgets will be resented and perhaps subverted (Williams and Carroll, 1998, pp. 65–6). An alternative is to engage the workforce in:

- determining what the organisation is in business for – its mission
- analysing the organisation's strengths, weaknesses, opportunities and threats
- setting specific business objectives
- devising a plan for implementing the objectives
- clarifying who is accountable for the implementation
- agreeing how and when the plan will be reviewed.

The motivator for business planning seen in this way is the sense of ownership which the workforce can develop by taking part in the planning process, the greater understanding of their roles and of the resources available to them in going about their work.

In the 1990s, business planning – or what some people prefer to call service planning – has become an increasingly accepted and developed discipline in non-profit-making organisations which compete for contracts. Most health and social welfare providers produce some form of annual business plan, for internal and external consumption (see for example, CPS, 1993). Effective business planning should connect with and involve key people at all levels, enabling them to influence the outcome and communicate the message across the organisation. Kevin Teasdale, a finance manager in the NHS, describing the preferred NHS approach to participative business planning in the period after the NHS and

Community Care Act 1990, points to the move to clinical directorates in many hospitals as an example of this. He adds:

> If business planning ideas have something to offer the NHS, then managers at ward or department level may wish to produce business plans for their own areas. The only constraint is that these plans must be compatible with the plan for the unit as a whole. However, ideally, the business plan for a provider unit might evolve from the detailed plans made by committed staff at department or ward level.
>
> (Teasdale, 1992, p. 35)

Some agencies take business and service planning still further, involving customers and service-users in the planning process, and seeing this as very much part of their strategy for quality (see Chapter 13).

If the budget is a plan then, like all plans, it should be open to change, if circumstances alter. The amounts of money available, or service priorities, may change during a financial year and the budget plan provides a point of reference to check progress against targets, aims and objectives, or to see whether new service choices or priorities are possible. Some organisations incorporate their budget plan inside their business plan and use them as a management tool, in a continuous process of service delivery and control, changing the plan when necessary, using their resources flexibly to respond to threats and opportunities. In the next sub-section we show how Marjorie, working in this way, turned a potential crisis into an opportunity.

Responding to budgetary problems

Last year Marjorie organised a business planning workshop for members of Middlebrook's team and the charity's board. The workshop produced a mission statement for the Middlebrook Centre:

> To provide high quality care and guidance which enables people with a learning disability to maximise their potential and lead rewarding lives in the community.

During the workshop, board members confirmed two rumours that had been circulating:

- that the social services department had changed its funding rules for people with a learning disability – this would produce a 15% drop in Middlebrook's social services income next year, amounting to £4200.
- that the charity which operates Middlebrook was in financial difficulties and would be forced to reduce the deficit funding it provides (see Table 1) by 10% – this would amount to £6870 in a full year.

The total loss for the next year was thus predicted to be £11,070.

Marjorie was able to set out a plan for Middlebrook which could potentially replace the income losses, reduce the financial risks caused by short-term vacancies and also provide surpluses which could be used to improve the Centre's residential capacity. She explained that she had been invited to put in a bid to an international trust which would provide £65,000 over three years if Middlebrook would provide additional supported employment opportunities for learning disabled clients with neighbouring organisations. The financial case that Marjorie successfully put to the charity's board was as follows.

> Twelve residents attend supported employment placements in town each weekday. Under present working practices, the direct costs of the supported employment services are mostly fixed, consisting of payments to staff who transport the residents to town and back, plus sessional payments to a job coach who arranges placements and monitors and records progress. These costs do not change in direct proportion as the numbers of placements rise and fall. The other major cost is for transport, using the minibus and staff cars. These costs are fixed, unless the number of clients travelling falls to ten or less, when only the minibus is needed.

In working out her proposal, Marjorie calculated the daily unit cost of providing supported employment from Middlebrook. Here is the formula she used:

Direct costs plus **Indirect costs** divided by **Number of**
(staff and (percentage of **days' service**
transport) management, **provided**
administration,
insurances, etc.
that go in to
supported
employment)

Here is that formula again, this time with the figures included:

$$\frac{£35,000}{2940} \frac{\text{(total direct and indirect costs for a full year, before proposed savings implemented)}}{\text{(12 clients} \times \text{245 days supported employment days each)}} = \frac{£11.90 \text{ unit cost}}{\text{per client per day}}$$

On the basis of these calculations, Marjorie explained, the trust would contribute £65,000 over three years in equal instalments, in return for the provision of 10 more supported employment placements. These 10 clients would be available from three local day centres.

Marjorie persuaded the charity's board that she could take on the extra workload and further reduce the unit costs of Middlebrook's supported employment service by making changes to the way in which clients travel to their placements in town. The aim would be to prepare as many clients as possible for travelling to work by public transport. This preparation could be achieved without additional costs, using existing staff. For a minority of clients, public transport would not be possible, as they worked away from bus routes or would be unlikely to achieve the necessary competency. For this minority, transport would be provided by contract with a local taxi company. The plan, however, would replace the current costly practice of deploying two staff to transport 12 people. Very importantly, at the same time it would address the mission – enhancing client independence. Marjorie calculated that, after taking into account a small increase in the job coach's hours, the new travel-to-work practice could produce salary and mileage cost savings of £8000 in a full year. Further savings of £5000 a year could be produced by disposing of the minibus and hiring one when necessary.

Marjorie calculated that when next year's income losses (£11,070) were offset by new income and costs savings (£21,666, £5000 and £8000), an annual surplus of £23,596 could be achieved. She proposed that a new business plan should be developed, investing the surpluses in Middlebrook to increase the Centre's residential capacity and sustain the supported employment service once the trust funding finished in three years' time. The trust offering the funding had indicated that they were impressed by the quality of Middlebrook's services and would see their services as giving good value for money to the trust, particularly as the Centre could provide services immediately, without funded development time. Marjorie calculated the unit cost to the trust of supported employment for the additional 10 clients as follows:

$$\frac{£21,666}{2450} \quad \begin{array}{l}\text{(all costs } - \text{ £65,000 divided by 3)} \\ \text{(10 clients} \times 245 \text{ days supported} \\ \text{employment days each)}\end{array} = \begin{array}{l}\text{£8.84 unit cost} \\ \text{per client per day}\end{array}$$

Marjorie also calculated the *overall* unit cost to Middlebrook of providing supported employment for the 22 clients:

$$\frac{£22,000}{5390} \quad \begin{array}{l}\text{(all costs)} \\ \text{(22 people working 245 days each)}\end{array} = \begin{array}{l}\text{£4.08 unit cost} \\ \text{per day}\end{array}$$

This represented a dramatic reduction in present costs. The new proposals would need to be explained to all Middlebrook's staff and there would have to be discussions with the staff affected by the new travel-to-work arrangements. The board, however, felt that the arguments for going ahead were overwhelmingly strong and that staff would see that there were longer-term benefits. The accountant commented that the previously fixed costs to Middlebrook would be drastically reduced. The partnership with the trust would, he said, provide excellent value for money for all parties. He would help prepare a five-year business plan.

4   Value for money and value for mission?

The previous sections have demonstrated what might be achieved in a service delivery agency such as Middlebrook through embedding the revenue budget in the overall business or service plan and through better understanding of the components of the budget and the extent to which they could be changed. Financial information, however, cannot stand alone. It needs to be set alongside information on the quality of the service to be achieved.

In following her accountant's advice to look at fixed and variable costs, for example, Marjorie noted that there was some flexibility as far as the deployment of sessional staff was concerned. In principle, she could offset some of the income losses by reducing their hours. But should she do this? On the face of it, it was more *economical*. She would certainly save money. However, she might run the risk of resignations and incur recruitment and training costs when resident numbers picked up. In the long run therefore, the cost savings might disappear, so it might not be *efficient*. Then there is the consideration of the quality of service residents are receiving from long-standing sessional staff and the extent to which their satisfaction with the service is based on the familiarity and continuity that the present system offers. Marjorie needs therefore to bear in mind that reducing hours could mean a lower quality, less *effective* service.

The three Es – economy, efficiency and effectiveness (see Box 3) – have become something of a mantra in the public sector in recent years as services have been subject to competition. The Conservative governments of the 1980s and early 1990s encouraged numerous Value for Money (VFM) studies, starting in the local government sector and then extending to the NHS. Such studies often brought in external people with private sector experience to question practices in social and health care and, indeed, in a wide range of public sector services. VFM studies also became a feature of the work of the independent Audit Commission, formed in the early 1980s to cover England and Wales, and of the parallel Accounts Commission for Scotland.

Box 3: The three Es

Economy

The utilisation of resources of appropriate quality at the lowest possible price.

Efficiency

The relationship between goods and services provided and the resources used to provide them. An efficient activity produces the maximum output for any given set of resource inputs; or it has minimum inputs for any given quality and quantity of service provided.

Effectiveness

The extent to which an activity or programme achieves its intended objectives. It will often be examined in terms of the nature and severity of unwanted side effects.

(Glynn *et al.*, 1996, pp. 246–7)

Is VFM just a synonym for cost reduction? Providing that all three Es are taken into account, the answer is no. When VFM is seen more narrowly, however, the results can be thoroughly counterproductive. Case Study A in Box 4 provides an example of this, where management action to tackle cost reduction had a series of negative consequences. It threw other equally important performance indicators off balance. As a result the quality and quantity of social work service was adversely affected. The next two case studies, however, illustrate more positive outcomes. Case Study B (Box 5) tells a story in the statutory sector of costing activities, utilising business planning, involving staff and developing targets which were achievable and shared. Case Study C (Box 6), from the voluntary sector, had a similarly positive outcome and a crucial one for an organisation that needed to continue to attract contracts.

Box 4: Case Study A – unforeseen consequences

A busy social work department in a large hospital introduced a computerised case management system, which depended on social workers completing a form for each client, for prompt input to the computer. The administration manager became concerned about the amount of time spent by expensive social workers in completing the forms, and concluded that the practice constituted poor value for money. Consequently, the staff budget was adjusted to allow clerical staff to be recruited to complete the forms, reduce social work costs and free-up time for other tasks.

However, problems arose when the clerical staff, understandably limited in their specialist knowledge, constantly needed to refer to the social workers with queries arising from the forms. New clients also objected that they were being denied access to social workers and many of them logged formal complaints, which of course needed proper administration, involving the customer service unit and the hospital social work team. Health practitioners also confirmed that a backlog of referrals had been created. The management action had achieved reductions to the payroll costs of the social work team, but simultaneously lowered the quality of the service and increased administration costs elsewhere. The administration manager was advised that service quality had been reduced unacceptably and that social workers should resume the form-filling until the training needs of the clerical staff had been addressed.

Box 5: Case Study B – bringing in business planning

A county Social Services department had a central unit to provide occupational therapy services – major and minor adaptations to disabled people's homes to enable them to continue to live there rather than in residential accommodation. The unit employed 20 occupational therapists (OTs), organised into area teams, and a number of support staff. Its revenue budget, covering staff and running costs and minor adaptations, was £1.25 million and its capital budget, for major adaptations such as lifts and bathroom extensions, was £2.5 million.

In 1993 the unit overspent its revenue budget by £200,000 and underspent its capital budget by £1 million – effectively denying service to clients who needed it. Members of the Social Services Committee were asking 'Why are we employing all these staff when they are not delivering the service?' There was a real danger that the unit's budget would be cut and its staff reduced.

An investigation revealed that:

- none of the unit's managers had any experience of budget management or business planning

- there were no systems in place to record or forecast expenditure or activity

- approval of a major adaptation took several months and often money allocated in one year was not spent – replacement funding had to be found in the following year

- there was no process of planning for the coming year's activities.

The Director of Social Services was persuaded that a part-time business manager should be appointed to deal with these problems. The unit had to give up an OT post to meet the cost of the business manager. A business plan for the coming year was prepared and all the unit's staff had an opportunity to contribute or comment. The plan set out the current year's activity and budget as a basis for the coming year, for which targets for major and minor adaptations were set. The cost of the staff and other running costs were calculated accurately and systems were introduced to monitor both revenue and capital expenditure each month. Realistic forecasts were made of the time-scales for individual major adaptations so that money could be allocated to the financial year in which it would be needed. Links were formed with the finance staff to make sure the unit had timely and accurate information about its expenditure.

At the end of the first year of this process the capital budget was 85% spent, and there was only a very small overspend on the revenue budget. The unit had reached its targets on the number of minor adaptations to be provided. Other benefits included a rational basis for allocating resources to meet competing demands and resolving conflicts about resource allocation, and a new spirit of partnership between the unit and colleagues in the Finance section. By demonstrating its ability to manage its budget and plan its activity the unit gradually gained credibility and was able to attract additional capital and revenue funding to expand its activities. Since then it has taken over responsibility for services to people with hearing and sight impairment. Its revenue and capital budgets have doubled and the services it provides are a major component in the county's community care strategy.

Box 6: Case Study C – calculating the real costs of a service

A voluntary organisation (VO), which was providing meals on wheels on behalf of the Social Services department and running a lunch club for elderly people with funding from the district council, was finding it difficult to meet increasing costs and demand within fixed budgets. The meals on wheels and the lunch club meals were cooked at the VO's kitchen using the same food and staff. The VO had a contract with Social Services for the meals on wheels which was based on unit costs for each meal. The unit cost included the cost of the fresh ingredients from which the meals were prepared, the cooks' wages and a proportion of the running costs of the kitchen as well as mileage payments to volunteers who delivered the meals using their own cars. The lunch club was partly funded by a grant from the district council which had not been increased for some years.

The unit cost for meals on wheels had been calculated some years before and stood at £1.75 per meal. When this cost was reviewed it was found that:

- the ratio of lunch club meals (which the district council funded) and the meals on wheels had changed – as a result Social Services were not meeting their full share of the food and premises costs and staff wages

- the unit cost had not been increased to reflect increased mileage payments to volunteers

- the costs of the staff who administered the meals on wheels service had never been included

- unused food worth approximately £7000 was being thrown away each year due to poor ordering practices and lack of portion control.

When these points were taken into account the true unit cost was £2.85 per meal. The councils were unable to increase their contribution so the VO decided to put the service out to tender. A private company offered to supply frozen meals for both the lunch club and the meals on wheels service at £1.25 each. The VO was able to reduce the kitchen staff at the lunch club, as the frozen meals simply required reheating.

There were, however, some additional costs to be met in the first year of the new arrangements – £10,000 to purchase special ovens to reheat the meals and adapt the kitchen to accommodate them and redundancy payments of £3000. A good deal of time had to be spent negotiating with the district council, which was eventually persuaded to pay for the ovens, while the other additional costs were met by an increase of 50p in the cost of each meal – a decision that caused some soul-searching. But the other, ongoing, savings reduced the unit cost to £1.65 per meal, which kept it within the funding provided by Social Services and allowed scope for future growth in demand.

The final case study in this section brings in the topic of external partnership funding – something that we saw Marjorie use to good effect for Middlebrook. Partnership funding is currently important and can often seem to offer a way forward: supplementing an organisation's own budget by attracting funds from other sources, such as the UK government's Single Regeneration Budget or various European Funds. Another recent innovation is the introduction of Health Action Zones to fund projects to increase the overall health of people living in deprived areas. These funds, however, often have strict eligibility criteria and may not always be relevant. Almost all require close working between organisations in different sectors; the issues of allocating overheads for somewhere like Middlebrook can pale into insignificance beside the negotiations that need to go on. Case Study D (Box 7 overleaf), however, shows how a small voluntary organisation secured funding to continue a successful pilot project.

What can be concluded from this series of case studies around the theme of achieving better value for money? First, dialogue between team members, across teams and between teams is essential if unacceptable, unforeseen consequences of value for money initiatives are to be avoided or overcome (Glynn *et al.*, 1996). Finance specialists, service managers and practitioners need to work together to ensure issues of quality and cost are considered together rather than either one dominating the other. Marjorie's travel solution demonstrated this – it was value for money because it was value for mission too. Secondly, however, there is what we might call, building on Chapter 10, the missing stakeholder problem. Notably absent in all the examples here, including the Middlebrook example, is the involvement of service-users in issues of financial planning and management. Yet service-users are stakeholders just as much as the service-providers are. If financial thinking can be extended to practitioners and service-providers in the ways this chapter has shown, can it not be and should it not be extended to the users of those services too? There is research to show that learning disability service-users can be very effectively involved in evaluating residential services in the community and that, when they are, the thinking about service priorities changes (Whittaker, 1994). In Case Study C – to take just one example – we might legitimately ask what the people eating those new meals thought and whether the changed arrangements represented value for money from their perspective, too.

Finally, we need to draw attention to some of the hurdles and the constraints the case studies tend to neglect. Financial management and budget handling are not always as straightforward as the positive examples here might seem to suggest. Financial accounting systems, designed to meet the needs of specialist finance staff, have sometimes not been able to produce the rapid, detailed and easy-to-use information that service managers need. It has not been uncommon for budgets to be notified to managers as late as three months into the financial year and then for monthly monitoring reports to be inaccurate and incomplete.

Box 7: Case Study D – partnership working for more effective use of limited resources

A voluntary organisation which provided treatment and rehabilitation services for drug misusers had run a pilot 'cell intervention' scheme. Under this scheme a trained cell intervention worker visited drug-misusing offenders immediately after their arrest or remand by the courts and offered them the opportunity to be treated for their addiction. The project involved close liaison between the cell intervention worker, the police and the probation service and its aim was to provide treatment for people who had not previously had that opportunity and so improve their lifestyle and reduce the chances of their reoffending.

The pilot project was successful but the organisation, a charity, had no money to continue it. They then had the chance to join a partnership of public and voluntary organisations that was bidding for money from the government's Single Regeneration Budget (SRB). This programme provides money to support innovative schemes that contribute to physical and social regeneration of deprived areas. SRB usually contributes around 40% of the cost of a project: the balance is 'match funding' which can be existing expenditure that contributes towards the regeneration process.

The charity needed £50,000 per year to employ and support the cell intervention worker, which had to be fully funded from the SRB money. Match funding was found by calculating the value of the time spent by police officers in dealing with arrested drug misusers and by the probation service in dealing with those remanded or convicted of an offence. This amounted to some £75,000 per annum and provided sufficient match funding to enable the SRB contribution to be obtained.

As a result, the charity can continue its successful project for the next six years, dealing with some 200 drug-misusing offenders per year. Many of them will receive treatment that would not otherwise have been offered to them, breaking their cycle of offending and reoffending, with consequent benefits to themselves and the community and reductions in cost for the criminal justice system. Lasting partnerships will be formed between the police and the probation and drug treatment agencies, which will aid the development of similar collaborative working in the future.

(Note: cell intervention schemes of the sort described here are now referred to as arrest referral schemes.)

Even when good information is available choices may not be clear-cut, and it may be difficult to make the kinds of judgements that are needed in the complex case, for example, of creating a care package for someone in need of care in the community (Leat and Perkins, 1998). Sometimes, too, there is just not enough money available to keep services going for certain client groups or to fund important new developments, especially for smaller organisations which do not have the flexibility in the use of their budgets that larger organisations have. There are limits to creative thinking and active financial management if the purse is just too small.

Conclusion

Since the 1980s there has been unprecedented change in the structure and culture of organisations in the health and social care sectors. New financial regimes with a higher profile for budgetary management and business planning are an important part of this. The treasurer no longer holds the purse-strings as of old and financial information is more widely shared and understood. Greater transparency in the financial management process, as some of the material in this chapter has demonstrated, can bring considerable benefits – aligning goals and resources more closely, clarifying policy choices, bringing more stakeholders into the policy process and sometimes, indeed, allowing more service or better services with fewer resources.

Yet the ability to count the cost is no panacea. Budget managers, as this chapter has also emphasised, have to work within constraints and may not be able to reach the happy solutions that Marjorie found for the Middlebrook Centre. Purchasers and providers still need to negotiate over contracts, debating the amount and quality of service and watching how shared costs will fall. With year-on-year demands to find cost savings, the argument that the total resource has become insufficient sometimes needs to come to the fore. Certainly it must be acknowledged that, however well they manage budgets and forecast expenditure, people at all levels in health and social care will continue to work with limited resources and hard choices need to be made. Being able to work with the basic concepts outlined here is thus a key requirement for critical practice as discussed in this book, but it is by no means the only one.

References

Butt, J. and Mizra, K. (1997) 'Exploring the income of black-led voluntary organisations', in Pharaoh, C. (ed.) *Dimensions of the Voluntary Sector: Key Facts, Figures and Trends*, West Malling, Kent, Charities Aid Foundation.

Centre for Public Services (CPS) (1993) *A Detailed Handbook for the Public Service and Business Plans*, Sheffield, CPS.

Deakin, N. (1996) 'The devil's in the detail: some reflections on contracting for social care by voluntary organisations', *Social Policy and Administration*, Vol. 30, No. 1, pp. 20–38.

Glynn, J., Perkins, D. and Stewart, S. (1996) *Achieving Value for Money*, London, W. B. Saunders Co. Ltd.

Hadley, R. and Clough, R. (1996) *Care in Chaos: Frustration and Challenge in Community Care*, London, Cassell.

Leat, D. and Perkins, D. (1998) 'Juggling and dealing: the creative work of care package purchasing', *Social Policy and Administration*, Vol. 32, No. 2, pp. 166–81.

Lewis, J. with Bernstock, P., Bovell, V. and Wookey, F. (1996) 'The purchaser/provider split in social care: is it working?', *Social Policy and Administration*, Vol. 30, No. 1, pp. 1–19.

Mackintosh, M. (2000) 'Flexible contracting? Economic cultures and implicit contracts in social care', *Journal of Social Policy* (in press).

Masters, S. (1993) 'Financial management in the NHS', *Public Money and Management*, Vol. 13, No. 1, pp. 4–5.

Teasdale, K. (1992) (ed.) *Managing the Changes in Health Care: An Explanation and Exploration of the Implications for the NHS of 'Working for Patients'*, London, Wolfe.

Tonge, R. and Horton, S. (1996) 'Financial management and quality', in Farnham, D. and Horton, S. (eds) *Managing the New Public Services*, London, Macmillan.

Whittaker, A. (1994) 'Service evaluation by people with learning difficulties', in Connor, A. and Black, S. (eds) *Performance Review and Quality in Social Care*, London, Jessica Kingsley.

Williams, J. and Carroll, A. (1998) 'Budgeting and budgetary control', in Wilson, J. (ed.) *Financial Management for the Public Services*, Buckingham, Open University Press.

Wilson, J. (1998) 'Financial management: an overview', in Wilson, J. (ed.) *Financial Management for the Public Services*, Buckingham, Open University Press.

Chapter 12
Inter-agency collaboration – a sceptical view

Bob Hudson

... whether the collaborative
imperative is in practice compatible
with the competitive imperative.

Introduction

People in need do not want to know that the service they are looking for is
the responsibility of yet another agency. They do not want to move from
one waiting list to another. They certainly do not want to find out that
they fall into the cracks between service provision. Governments have
recognised this – again and again exhorting public sector services to work
more closely together. In recent years, policy documents have begun to
recognise that the NHS and social services need to co-ordinate and to link
what they do more effectively to other areas of public provision –
education, housing and policing, for example. The relationships of these
bodies with private and voluntary sector providers have also come on to
the agenda. Yet, although terms such as inter-agency collaboration, joint
working, co-ordination, co-operation, teamwork and joint planning have
been around for a long time and the problems created by fragmentation
are now more widely recognised, the reality is that policies have tended to
be half-hearted and achievements are sometimes negligible. There is a
paradox here, with 'collaboration' seen as both problem *and* solution –
failure to work together is the problem, therefore the solution is to work
together better!

It is important at the very outset to recognise that interorganisational relationships are largely built upon *human* relationships, and that this makes the whole issue both more complex and more fascinating. As Gillett ruefully observes:

> The difficulty is that whilst it takes thirty seconds or less to say 'and there shall be co-ordination between the various forms of provision', the actual day-to-day carrying out of this co-ordination is a different kettle of fish ... behind an apparently rational statement is the whole range of human intractability, incompetence, power politics, greed and negativity, together with, of course, sweet reasonableness, great imagination, creativity, generosity and altruism.
>
> (Gillett, 1995, p. 356)

Successful interorganisational activity is no arid, managerial exercise. The challenge is to create the right climate for collaboration, to recognise the different contributions that participants can make, and to devise organisational arrangements and incentive structures that foster collaborative working. If teamworking has challenges (see Chapter 8), then inter-agency working has these challenges writ large. The literature constantly focuses on *barriers* to collaboration and failure to overcome them. Box 1 shows the breadth and depth of the barriers that can be involved.

Box 1: Five categories of barriers to interorganisational co-ordination

Structural
- Fragmentation of service responsibilities across agency boundaries, both within and between sectors
- Interorganisational complexity and non-coterminosity of boundaries

Procedural
- Differences in planning horizons and cycles
- Differences in budgetary cycles and procedures

Financial
- Differences in funding mechanisms and bases
- Differences in the stocks and flows of financial resources

Professional
- Differences of ideologies and values
- Professional self-interest and concern for threats to autonomy and domain
- Threats to job security
- Conflicting views about clients/consumers' interests and roles

Status and legitimacy
- Organisational self-interest and concern for threats to autonomy and domain
- Differences in legitimacy between elected and appointed agencies

(Source: Hardy *et al.*, 1992, p. 12)

How can such barriers be overcome? What are the factors that promote or impede joint working? What lessons can be learned from the long history of largely unsuccessful experiences? Focusing particularly on the health and social care boundary, the following key areas will be considered in this chapter.

- *The what and why of inter-agency collaboration*: what do we mean by the term and why has it become a significant goal of public policy?
- *The history of a policy concept*: in what ways have governments sought to combat fragmentation between health and social care agencies?
- *Collaboration and competition*: how did ideas about collaboration fit in with the emphasis during much of the 1990s on markets in health and social care?
- *New partnerships*: in what ways has the new Labour government attempted to shift the emphasis from competition to collaboration since 1997?

1   The what and why of inter-agency collaboration

Precision or agreement about the meaning of terms in this area is rare. Confusion is deepened where – as is typically the case – authors use the same or similar terms, but attach their own definitions to them. Terms such as 'co-ordination', 'co-operation' and 'collaboration' are so often used interchangeably that any attempt to impose our own definitions in this chapter would simply add to the confusion, rather than resolve it, although we shall use the term 'collaboration' as our general descriptive term.

Most serious conceptual explorations or policy applications take this confusion as the starting point. Aiken *et al.* (1975, p. 6) describe 'co-ordination' as a term which is 'overworked, underachieved and seldom defined', whilst Challis and others say of the same concept:

> ... if the word is once again back in favour, it remains precisely that: a word in search of ways of giving it effective meaning in practice ... a largely rhetorical invocation of a vague ideal.
>
> (Challis *et al.*, 1988, p. x)

Weiss takes this argument further and points to the link between conceptual vagueness and political action:

> The definitional ambiguity which makes co-ordination a handy political device has led to a chasm between rhetoric and operationalisation: co-ordination is discussed in the political arena as though everyone knows precisely what it means, when in fact it means many inconsistent things, and occasionally means nothing at all.
>
> (Weiss, 1981, quoted in Hallett, 1995, p. 41)

What *is* possible, however, is to use some general and inclusive definition which is sufficiently wide to encompass *all* of the variants. Warren *et al.* (1974, p. 16), for example, define co-ordination as:

... a structure or process of concerted decision-making wherein the decisions or action of two or more organisations are made simultaneously in part or in whole with some deliberate degree of adjustment to each other.

Although this sort of definition is at a very high level of generality, and therefore in danger of appearing somewhat trite, it does contain the crucial ingredient that separate but related organisations adjust their behaviour in some way that takes account of each other's interests. Exactly *why* and *how* they should do so is the meat on the collaborative bone.

While definitions are unclear, there is no lack of clarity about the need for some sort of joint approach to many problems in health and social care. Organisational autonomy has been increasingly recognised to be inadequate in the face of complex problems which require multifaceted responses. Huxham and Macdonald (1992) identify four examples of what they term 'pitfalls of individualism' (Box 2).

Box 2: Pitfalls of individualism

repetition:

where two or more organisations carry out an action or task which need only be done by one;

omission:

where activities which are important to the objectives of more than one organisation are not carried out because they have not been identified as important, because they come into no organisation's remit or because each organisation assumes the other is performing the activity;

divergence:

the actions of the various organisations may become diluted across a range of activities, rather than used towards common goals;

counter-production:

organisations working in isolation may take actions which conflict with those taken by others.

(Source: Huxham and Macdonald, 1992, p. 52)

Individualism has also been seen as less appropriate in the public – as opposed to the private – sector. Metcalfe and Richards (1990, p. 237), for example, suggest that the distinguishing feature of public management is:

... that good results depend on co-operation among many organisations with interdependent functions ... it is intensive and sustained interorganisational co-operation that is the hallmark of success in public management, rather than the single-minded pursuit of individual organisational objectives.

In fact, collaboration now tends to be seen as a virtue in both the public *and* the private sector. Whatever term is used, then, a joint approach to problem solving is now widely – if not universally – seen as essential. If the *what* remains vague and confused, the *why* is clear and paramount. The rest of this chapter considers the application to the boundary between health and social care services.

2 The history of a policy concept – collaboration or fragmentation?

The main interest in social policy co-ordination has developed since the Second World War. The creation in 1948 of one of the UK's most popular and enduring institutions – the NHS – was initially seen as an opportunity to integrate a diverse range of voluntary and statutory activity. The outcome, however, was to introduce elements of fragmentation which still affect relationships within the NHS, and relationships between the NHS and social services. Of particular significance was the compromise reached over administrative arrangements. In order to secure the support of the leaders of the medical professions, it was necessary to take account of their vehement opposition to local authority control of hospitals, and of their desire to maintain the independence of GPs. As a result of this, the NHS acquired a tripartite structure consisting of hospital authorities (to run all hospitals, including those which had previously been run by local authorities), executive councils (to administer the contracts of independent GPs) and local health authorities (responsible for community-based health care services other than those provided by family practitioners). In addition, local education authorities retained their responsibility for the administration of the school health service.

This amounted to 'a representation of what was possible rather than what might have been desirable' (Ham, 1992, p. 15). Instead of a unitary structure which could have facilitated the development of a more integrated approach to the delivery of health and social care services, this tripartite structure only served to reinforce divisions. The first major review of the funding and organisation of the NHS recognised this; it was not only critical of the inadequate liaison between the three separately administered arms of the service but also it emphasised that:

> ... a more important cleavage than the division of the NHS into three parts is that between hospital services and the social care services provided by the local authorities.
>
> (Guillebaud Report, 1956, para. 151)

Local authorities saw little incentive for local ratepayers to support the expansion of community services as alternatives to the hospitals which had been taken from them and were now directly funded by the Treasury – an early example of awareness of what these days is termed 'cost shunting'. At the same time, both acute and long-stay NHS hospitals tended to concentrate on *intra*-organisational concerns, leading to the reinforcement of an organisational and professional dichotomy between the worlds of hospital and community.

Developing a collaborative strategy: the 1960s and 1970s

The early 1960s brought the first attempt to co-ordinate health and social services through national planning systems, with the introduction of 10-year plans for hospital and community care services (Ministry of Health, 1962 and 1963 respectively). However, local authorities were merely exhorted to take account of proposed developments within hospital services, and central government had neither the means nor the inclination to ensure that the two sets of plans were brought together at local level. In any case, the initiative proved to be short-lived.

The reorganisation of the NHS in England and Wales in 1974 is particularly significant in the history of joint working. It sought – through the creation of new Area Health Authorities (AHAs) – to bring the different health services under the same organisational umbrella. The main way in which it did this was by moving most of the local health authority services out of local government and into the NHS. The list of transferred services was long, covering community health services for mothers and pre-school children, school health, vaccination and immunisation, home nursing, health visiting, domiciliary midwifery, family planning, health education, chiropody and ambulance services (Ottewill and Wall, 1990). General practitioner services, however, continued to be separately administered. Although this change was intended to secure a more integrated approach to the provision of *health care* services, it clearly also had the potential to further deepen the cleavage between health and social care services, as well as other local authority services which contributed to health and well-being. In particular, the changes reduced the potential for social workers in the new social services departments to work closely with community nurses, who now had different employers and possibly different priorities. Also the public health duties of local authorities were fragmented by the transfer of the role of Medical Officers of Health to the health authorities. The pattern outside England and Wales was broadly similar. Health Boards and the new Social Work Departments in Scotland, for example, also found problems in working together, although Northern Ireland's integrated Health and Social Services Boards, as we shall see later, offered a somewhat different picture.

To counteract divisive tendencies, two other measures were introduced. First, the boundaries of the new AHAs were, in most parts of England and Wales, made *coterminous* with those of local authorities providing personal social services – in other words, the two organisations shared the same geographical and administrative boundaries, and thereby served the same population. Second, the two types of authority were required to set up joint consultative committees (JCCs) composed of members (rather than officers) to facilitate the collaborative development of services (DHSS, 1973). Parallel forums for officers (Joint Care Planning Teams) were subsequently established in 1976. NHS monies were made available for projects in the interests of both the NHS and the local authorities, and a five-year project timetable was later extended to seven and later 13 years (DHSS, 1983). It seemed a new era was set to begin with a policy lead from the top and a financial incentive to kick-start change.

The amount of joint planning that resulted from the 1970s initiatives was generally disappointing (Nocon, 1994). It was argued that this was partly because of the over-emphasis on structural links and processes – a preoccupation with *means* rather than *ends* (Wistow, 1990). Box 3 summarises the findings from an investigation into joint finance by the National Audit Office for England and Wales in 1987. Although in themselves many of these initiatives may well have been useful, they need to be set alongside broader patterns of public expenditure. For example, in 1985–6, the total expenditure on the NHS and personal social services was over £20 billion, whereas joint finance did not even amount to £100 million. The point being made here about joint finance, then, is not that useful things did not happen, but rather that the amounts involved, and the strings attached to them, were not conducive to significant and systematic collaboration.

Box 3: The experience of joint finance

A National Audit Office investigation found:

- between 1976/7 and 1985/6 expenditure of £604 million had been incurred on joint finance schemes

- between 5000 and 7000 schemes were thought to be in operation at any one time, ranging from single grants of less than £1000 to voluntary bodies to grants of £2 million for an adult training centre over eight years

- the Department of Health collected no information about individual schemes.

Examples of schemes funded by joint finance included:

- Five *'Care in the Community'* Officers to support social workers in maintaining elderly, and physically disabled people and children in their own homes (£140,500).

- A *Mental Illness Day Centre* to provide a 'drop-in' centre for people in the community and managed by the National Schizophrenic Fellow-ship (£19,500).

- An *Elderly Persons Home* to provide half the capital costs for a 40-place residential home for elderly people (£425,000 capital).

- *Domiciliary Nursery Nurses* to provide care for children with develop-mental problems or at risk from inadequate parenting (£176,200).

(Source: compiled from National Audit Office, 1987)

Collaborative disillusionment: the 1980s

If the 1970s could be said to be the policy era when the health–social care divide was both recognised to be problematic and had – for the first time – an ostensibly coherent strategy, the 1980s was the decade when it all seemed to go wrong. At first, things looked promising. Nocon (1994) suggests that the 'Care in the Community' initiative in 1983, geared to the transfer of long-stay hospital patients into the community, actually 'gave a new lease of life to collaborative working' (p. 11). It permitted the transfer of both responsibility and resources for such hospital residents from the NHS to local authorities, partly through the extended 13-year tapering of joint finance, but mainly by allowing health authorities to 'offer lump-sum payments or continuing grants to local authorities or voluntary organisations for as long as necessary in respect of people to be cared for in the community instead of in hospital' (DHSS, 1983, para. 6).

However, the success of Care in the Community should not be exaggerated. Local authorities were concerned about the facilities available for people who, in the past, would have used the wards and hospitals that were closing down, and arguments about the amount of money to be attached to individual patients (the 'dowry') were common. It is easy to see how the welfare of individuals could get lost in inter-agency financial wrangling.

At the same time, a more significant factor affecting the climate for joint working was growing in influence – the provision of a subsidy through social security entitlements paid directly by the DHSS for people who entered residential or nursing homes provided by either the private or the voluntary sector. In 1979 this subsidy was relatively minor and amounted to only £10 million, but a widening of the regulations in 1980 resulted in a massive expansion. By early 1986 the bill had reached £459 million, with the number of residents funded by this route rising from 12,000 to 90,000 – a trend which was to go even further in the following decade. Although initially the Conservative government of 1979 had seen this trend as striking a blow for the privatisation of welfare, the fact that this private supply was almost entirely paid for by public subsidy soon led to alarm about the rising scale of public expenditure. Less obviously, the policy had also dealt a severe blow to the fragile arrangements for joint working between the NHS and local authorities. Acute hospitals seeking to discharge elderly people who were 'blocking beds' and long-stay hospitals wishing to reduce in size or close completely now had an alternative to painstaking negotiation with the local authority. It was an alternative that was cost-free to the NHS and required no assessment of need other than the individual finances of residents and patients.

The seeming inability of health authorities and local authorities to work together began to attract political interest as the 1980s progressed, with two particularly critical reports about fragmentation in community care coming from the House of Commons Social Services Select

Committee (1985) and the Audit Commission (1986). In the wake of this sustained criticism, Sir Roy Griffiths was commissioned by the Conservative government to do an independent review of the financial and organisational arrangements for community care. His report denounced the approach of central government to joint working as 'the discredited refuge of imploring collaboration and exhorting action' (Griffiths, 1988, para. 27), but he also emphasised that mandatory administrative restructuring would be unduly disruptive. Rather, he felt that the essential change needed was to specify responsibilities more clearly and to hold authorities accountable more effectively. He accordingly proposed that effective collaboration should be a condition for receipt of a new specific, ring-fenced grant, with payment dependent on the submission of community care plans which demonstrated appropriate commitment. The lead role in these arrangements which Griffiths envisaged for local government did not find favour with a Conservative government intent on reducing the powers and responsibilities of local authorities. The absence of an acceptable alternative, however, resulted in a broad affirmation of this lead role in the 1989 White Paper *Caring for People* (Department of Health, 1989) and the subsequent NHS and Community Care Act 1990. Despite a record of shortcomings and failure, inter-agency collaboration was back on the agenda. However, it also was to have a strange new bedfellow – the quasi-market.

3   Collaboration or competition? The pattern after 1990

As we saw in Chapter 1, the 1990 Act (and the Health and Social Services Order (Northern Ireland) 1991) introduced the notion of markets to health and social care, based on a separation of responsibilities for purchasing and providing. As far as collaboration between health authorities and local authorities was concerned, the implication was that purchasers could simply require providers to work jointly through contractual obligations, and that this would be most effective where purchasers themselves acted in concert – what came to be termed 'joint commissioning'. The reforms were concerned with general ideas and processes rather than specific user groups. The only exception to this was the Care Programme Approach (CPA) for people with a mental illness. Introduced initially only in England, this was seen as a means of systematically assessing people's health and social care needs and providing the necessary services to meet them (Department of Health, 1990).

The introduction of markets, however, posed a fundamental dilemma: while collaboration has long been recognised as the essence of effective service delivery in health and social care, the essence of markets is competition. Wistow and Hardy (1996a and b) ask whether the collaborative imperative is in practice compatible with the competitive imperative. There is little doubt that the Conservative government of the time did *not* see the two as mutually exclusive. For example, the then Minister of Health for England, Brian Mawhinney, was highly critical of early approaches to so-called 'macho' purchasing in the NHS based on 'stand-off' relationships between purchasers and providers. Rather, he argued for relationships built on partnership and long-term agreements (Mawhinney, 1993).

The 'fresh approach to collaboration and joint planning' of the 1989 White Paper, however, fell short of Griffiths' proposals in some important respects. In particular, the link between collaboration, planning and resource allocation was not acted upon. However, inter-agency working was given a more extensive statutory basis than previously – the Secretary of State was given enhanced powers of direction, inspection, inquiry and default, and local authorities were required to publish community care plans annually, and to consult with health and other agencies on their content. Of course, at the same time as the introduction of the quasi-market in social care, the government also introduced the 'internal market' in the NHS, which similarly separated purchasing from provision through the creation of NHS trusts which were separate from district health authorities. This not only introduced an element of competition between NHS providers but also further fragmented local arrangements for health and social care. GP fundholding, introduced on an optional basis, further complicated the mosaic of purchasers and providers across the spectrum of health and social care.

However, a significant push for collaboration arose from the transfer of responsibilities and funds for independent residential and nursing home care from the social security system to social services departments – a move which greatly reduced the opportunities for unilateral action by the NHS in discharging people from both acute and long-stay hospitals. In the past, health agencies had been able to take advantage of individuals' entitlements to social security benefits to 'clear' beds, control throughput and fund residential and nursing care for former patients. Now they would need to engage in joint assessment and care planning if they were to secure access to equivalent funds from social services departments (Henwood and Wistow, 1993). If exhortation and goodwill had proved to be inadequate collaborative incentives, access to someone else's budget might turn out to be more effective.

What, then, is the answer to the question posed by Wistow and Hardy about the compatibility of the collaborative and competitive imperatives? The authors were convinced of the need for collaboration to ensure that services could be integrated at the level of individual users. They agreed, however, that:

• collaboration was more complex in the face of multiple suppliers
• getting a balance between trust and competition was difficult to achieve.

There remained a need to counteract the continuing incentive to 'minimise market shares' – or 'cost-shunt' responsibilities (Wistow *et al.*, 1996).

In general during the 1990s, the boundary between health and social care still threatened to be a focus for competition and conflict between agencies and professions, rather than for co-operation and collaboration. It was unclear whether the introduction of assessment and care management would remove the differences in professional perspectives and status that had bedevilled multidisciplinary working in the past, particularly since social services had no power to require the involvement of any other agency or profession in the process. In the absence of a single health and social care budget, individual care managers would be no more able to commit resources for a unified package of care than their predecessors. In parallel with this, acute trusts were under pressure from the Department of Health to reduce waiting lists and increase throughput, as a result of which the prospect of 'bed blocking' – due to a shortage of social care facilities in the community – became a potential 'hot spot'. Even where agencies were prepared to work together much more closely, there remained legal ambiguities which could restrict them. All of this proved to be fertile ground for conflict and confusion. Two well-known examples are briefly described in Box 4 and Box 5 (overleaf).

Box 4: Conflict at the health–social care boundary – continuing care

In February 1994, the Health Service Commissioner reported the results of his investigation on behalf of a woman whose husband, suffering from severe brain damage, was discharged to a private nursing home when he no longer needed acute hospital care. Her complaint was that she had been placed under an obligation to pay for continuing care which should have been provided free of charge by Leeds Health Authority. The Commissioner upheld the complaint. He noted that no one disputed that the man was in a seriously incapacitated condition or that he needed full-time nursing care. He held that the health authority's policy of making no provision for the continuing care of patients with neurological conditions amounted to a failure in service and recommended that the health authority take over responsibility for funding the patient's nursing home fees. In response, the Department of Health issued guidelines on NHS responsibilities for meeting long-term health care needs which emphasised the importance of effective collaboration with local authorities in agreeing or changing their respective responsibilities.

Box 5: Confusion at the health–social care boundary – joint commissioning

In the early 1990s in Lewisham, the local authority and the health authority (HA) developed an interest in jointly commissioning services for people with a learning disability. The route chosen was for the social services department (SSD) to establish a not-for-profit company – the Lewisham Partnership. This was intended to provide, on contract to the SSD and HA, the full range of commissioning of services, the provision of housing management services and the employment of a multidisciplinary team to co-ordinate the purchasing of individual care packages. Shortly before the Partnership was due to start, the District Auditor raised serious queries with the local authority about its specific powers to establish the company, and about the proposed financial and accountability arrangements. The legal uncertainty and the Auditor's concerns about the adequacy of accountability led to this particular approach being abandoned.

---

4   New labour, new partnerships?

The Labour government came to power in May 1997 with a clear view that the quasi-market approach to health and social services had been a failure, and that the key to effective service planning and delivery lay in the development of 'partnerships'. Health ministers talked incessantly about breaking down the 'Berlin Wall' between health and social services, and managers of both services were warned that collaboration was no longer an optional extra (Hirst, 1998). The shift in values seemed to be clear; collaboration was not simply back on the agenda, it was at the very heart of new policies on health and social care in the shape of 'partnership'. This renewed emphasis is evident in reform of the NHS, reform of policies on public health and reform of the personal social services. New policy documents rapidly emerged for the different parts of the UK (see Box 6). They were similar in key respects, although there were differences in terminology and detail that reflected local circumstances.

Box 6: All change!

Elected in 1997, for the first time in 18 years, Labour lost no time in setting out new policy frameworks for health and social care, for the NHS and local government.

A   On improving the health of the population and reducing health inequalities

---

- Department of Health (1998) *Our Healthier Nation: A Contract for Health*, Cm 3852, London, The Stationery Office.

- Scottish Office, Department of Health (1998) *Working Together for a Healthier Scotland*, Cm 3854, Edinburgh, The Stationery Office.

- Welsh Office (1998) *Better Health – Better Wales,* Cm 3922, Cardiff, The Stationery Office.

- Northern Ireland, Department of Health and Social Services (1997) *Well into 2000: A Strategy Document for the HPSS in Northern Ireland*, Belfast, DHSS.

B *On reforming the structures of the NHS*

- Department of Health (1997) *The New NHS: Modern, Dependable,* Cm 3807, London, The Stationery Office.

- Scottish Office, Department of Health (1997) *Designed to Care: Renewing the NHS in Scotland*, Cm 3811, Edinburgh, The Stationery Office.

- Welsh Office (1998) *NHS Wales: Putting Patients First*, Cm 3841, Cardiff, The Stationery Office.

- Northern Ireland, Department of Health and Social Services (1999) *Fit for the Future: A New Approach*, Belfast, DHSS.[1]

C *On social services*

- Department of Health (1998) *Modernising Social Services*, Cm 4169, London, The Stationery Office.

- Scottish Office (1999) *Aiming for Excellence: Modernising Social Work Services in Scotland*, Cm 4288, Edinburgh, The Stationery Office.

- Welsh Office (1999) *Social Services. Building for the Future: A White Paper for Wales*, Cm 4051, Cardiff, The Stationery Office.

- Northern Ireland, Department of Health and Social Services (1998) *Fit for the Future: A New Approach*, Belfast, DHSS.

D *On central and local government*

- Department of the Environment, Transport and the Regions (1998) *Modern Local Government: In Touch with the People*, Cm 4014, London, DETR.

- Welsh Office (1998) *Local Voices. Modernising Local Government in Wales: A White Paper*, Cm 4028, Cardiff, The Stationery Office.

- Prime Minister, Minister for the Cabinet Office (1998) *Modernising Government*, Cm 4310, London, The Stationery Office.

> **Note**
>
> ¹ *Fit for the Future*, not formally a White Paper, was a summary of a
> consultation process. When it was issued, the plan was that it would be
> fed into the new Northern Ireland Assembly for final decision. Further
> consultations relating to certain of the changes in *Modernising Social
> Services* then followed.

Reform of the NHS and public health

The government's proposals for change in the NHS in England (Department of Health, 1997) made the link with local authorities a priority.
Perhaps most significantly, the dismantling of the NHS internal market
signalled a return to coterminosity (see Section 2), not – as has
traditionally been the case – between health authorities and local
authorities, but rather between the new Primary Care Groups (PCGs)
and social services. The White Paper made it plain that PCGs were to work
closely with social services on the planning and delivery of services, and
that arrangements should 'develop around natural communities'. For
smaller local authorities, there was to be 'whole organisation coterminosity', whereas larger local authorities may have up to 10 PCGs in or on
the borders of their area. The White Paper also stated that the local
authority Chief Executive would participate in meetings of the health
authority, and that PCG governing bodies would include social services
membership.

Section 10 of the NHS Act 1973 had placed health and local authorities
under a statutory duty to co-operate with each other, but this duty was
general rather than specific, and was not supported by formal accountability arrangements. The 1997 NHS White Paper revisited this type of
legislative partnership and proposed a new statutory 'duty of partnership'
to require NHS bodies and local authorities to 'work together for the
common good'. A prime vehicle for this duty will be the joint
development of a Health Improvement Programme (HIP) in each local
area. These will be the means to deliver national targets in each health
authority area and, although the HA will have lead responsibility for
drawing up a local HIP, the process is portrayed as an inter-agency activity.

Arrangements for the NHS in other parts of the UK are developing
within broadly similar overall frameworks. Scotland's local health care
co-operatives – working within primary care trusts – and the new local
health groups in Wales are both being discussed in a framework of
partnership working and greater collaboration and service integration (see
Box 6, B). Northern Ireland's proposals for Health and Social Care
Partnerships and primary care co-operatives are designed to foster closer
integration despite a structure which, as we shall see at the end of this
section, was already a more integrated one.

Plans for public health (see Box 6, A) also contained collaborative proposals. The English Green Paper recognised, for example, that local authorities – with their responsibilities for social services, education, transport, housing and the local environment – have the capacity to make a big impact on the health of local communities. To reflect this role, it was proposed to place upon them a new duty to promote the economic, social and environmental well-being of their areas – something which requires a close relationship with NHS agencies. The Green Paper also encouraged local authority participation in health authority planning activities, with reciprocal arrangements for Directors of Public Health to attend relevant meetings of each local authority (Department of Health, 1998a).

A second area of public health policy with a strong collaborative dimension has been the creation of Health Action Zones (HAZs). In April 1998, 11 areas were designated HAZs by the Department of Health and allocated £34 million for setting-up costs and for joint spending between participating agencies. A further wave of pilots began in April 1999. One of the key expectations of HAZs is that inter-agency partnerships will lead to improvements in people's health and involve a 'whole systems' approach to managing change. Minister Alan Milburn described them as 'the trailblazer for a new approach to more integrated care' and able to 'cut through red tape barriers between health and social care' (Department of Health Press Release, 97/312, 30 October 1997).

Reform of the personal social services

In November 1998, the government published its long-awaited White Paper on the future of the personal social services – *Modernising Social Services* (Department of Health, 1998b). The title infers the existence of an outmoded system needing a 'third way' to drag it into the new millennium – a clean break not only with the traditional 'Old Labour' approach but also with the quasi-market model. Ideas about partnership were central and the document firmly grasped the importance of making partnership working conditional upon access to resources. There was £1.3 billion of new money contained in the Social Services Modernisation Fund and, in particular, two 'Promoting Independence' grants – the Partnership Grant and the Prevention Grant – which between them totalled almost £750 million over a three-year period up to 2001/2. The largest of the two, the Partnership Grant, was intended to foster partnership between health and social services in promoting independence as an objective of adult social services, with a particular emphasis on improving rehabilitation services; whilst the Prevention Grant focused more on developing preventive strategies to target people most at risk of losing their independence. In both cases, local authorities were required to draw up plans jointly with NHS agencies, and experience with such measures as Winter Beds monies suggests that this can be an effective way to promote joint working. Policy proposals for Scotland and Wales and a consultative document for Northern Ireland then followed, adapting the major ideas to the different circumstances of these settings (see Box 6, C).

Reform at the health–social services boundary

In summer 1998, the government went one better and brought out a Discussion Document, *Partnership in Action*, which specifically addressed the interface between the NHS and social services – both the nature of the problems and the ways in which they might be overcome (Department of Health, 1998c). In the Foreword to the document, issued jointly by Alan Milburn, Minister of State for Health, and Paul Boateng, Parliamentary Under Secretary of State for Health, there was a stern warning about the sterility of boundary disputes:

> All too often when people have complex needs spanning both health and social care, good quality services are sacrificed for sterile arguments about boundaries. When this happens people ... and those who care for them, find themselves in the no-man's land between health and social care services. This is not what people want or need. It places the needs of the organisation above the needs of the people they are there to serve. It is poor organisation, poor practice, poor use of taxpayer's money – it is unacceptable.

This is certainly the strongest political warning to the two agencies that has ever been issued in an official publication. Although it conveys a feeling of 'drinking in the last chance collaborative saloon', it nevertheless rules out a further reorganisation:

> Major structural change is not the answer. We do not intend to set up new statutory health and social services authorities. This would involve new bureaucracy, and would be expensive and disruptive to introduce.
>
> (Department of Health, 1998c, para. 1.5)

For the foreseeable future, then, the answer to fragmentation is not unification, but collaboration: separate organisations must somehow be persuaded to work together. Given the disappointing past record of achievement in this respect, what new ingredients are proposed in *Partnership in Action*? Three levels where joint working is needed are identified (see Box 7 opposite).

Much of this seems similar to previous attempts at collaboration through exhortation, even if the exhortation is more systematic and the tone more strident. However, there is a recognition in *Partnership in Action* that more needs to be done and three proposals for allowing more flexibility between agencies are made. First, there is the legalisation of pooled budgets to allow health and social services to bring resources together to commission and provide services in a way that would be accessible to both partners in the joint arrangements – the sort of arrangement that was ruled illegal in Lewisham (Box 5). Of course, where

---

Box 7: Three levels for partnership working

Strategic planning: at this level, agencies will need to plan jointly for the medium term, and share information about how they intend to use their resources towards the achievement of common goals. The means for doing this are identified as Health Action Zones, Health Improvement Programmes and Joint Investment Plans. The latter (the framework for which was in place by April 1999) are based on a joint assessment of need and shared objectives, initially for older people.

Service commissioning: here it is expected that, when securing services for their local populations, agencies will have a common understanding of the needs they are jointly meeting, and the kind of provision likely to be most effective. The move to Primary Care Groups (in England) is seen as providing a unique opportunity for the key partners to test new approaches to joint commissioning, and yet more guidance on good practice from local joint commissioning initiatives will be issued.

Service provision: regardless of how services are purchased or funded, the key objective is that the user receives a coherent, integrated package of care, and this is the third identified level of joint working. Fresh opportunities at this level are to be found in the emerging Primary Care Trusts, the Primary Care Act pilot schemes, and the experiences gained from special initiatives such as the Winter Beds money. In the particular case of older people, the government further required that by 1999 a framework was in place for multidisciplinary assessment in community health and acute care settings, with local authorities required to spend part of their funding in support of rehabilitation and recuperation facilities.

(Source: derived from Department of Health, 1998c, para. 1.6)

---

there is mistrust between agencies, and a fear of 'cost shunting', then there would also be an unwillingness to commit budgets to the pool. Greater legal flexibility is no panacea for a basic lack of trust!

The second flexibility is lead commissioning, where one authority is permitted to take the lead in commissioning the range of services for a particular group on behalf of both agencies. Learning disability and mental health are cited as examples where this could be usefully applied. Again, such an arrangement could only flourish in a collaborative relationship already characterised by a high degree of mutual respect and trust. And finally, there is the suggestion of permitting more integrated provision by allowing health and social services agencies to take on at least some of each other's functions.

As described earlier in this chapter, past incentives to joint working have concentrated mainly on additional financial incentives from central government, with local agreement between NHS and local authorities serving as a requirement for access to the funds. This time the government wished 'to see joint working as a true part of core business' (para. 4.45) and proposed greater flexibility for authorities to transfer mainstream funds between each other. This involves extending the current capacity of NHS agencies to transfer money to local authorities and – for the first time – allowing local authorities to reciprocate. Joint finance, which for so long has been seen as the core of financial collaborative incentives, was to be abolished, and incorporated in mainstream budgets. The statutory requirement to have a Joint Consultative Committee will also be relaxed. The use of these new powers will, however, be at the discretion of local agencies.

As far as monitoring is concerned, and again for the first time, the government issued national priorities guidance for both the NHS and social services, part of which required a contribution to joint objectives (Department of Health, 1998d). Joint working will also be part of the performance frameworks being established, and will be jointly monitored. It is too early to assess the impact of *Partnership in Action* or the way in which its proposals, tailored to England, will be modified and developed in Scotland, Wales and Northern Ireland. It is important, however, to recognise that effective collaboration is based on a stable and trusting relationship between two or more autonomous parties. Such a relationship cannot be properly produced through either the availability of more flexibilities or the threat of external monitoring, although these may well provide an environment in which it is more *likely* to happen.

The Northern Ireland model

This chapter has concentrated on the position in England but it is also important to look at experiences from elsewhere in the UK. In particular, since 1973, Northern Ireland has had integrated health and social services authorities. In effect, this arrangement has removed the long-standing separation between acute, community health and social work budgets which has characterised England, although the funding for general practice and primary care has remained separate. After the introduction of the Health and Social Services (Northern Ireland) Order 1991, the four health and social services boards became integrated purchasing authorities, while acute and community health services were managed and provided by trusts, with social work services usually managed and provided within community trusts. Some of the strengths, as well as some of the continuing problems, associated with this approach to delivering support have been assessed in a recent case study (Rummery and Glendinning, 1998).

The Health Select Committee (House of Commons, 1998), in its investigation of the health–social care relationship, visited Northern Ireland to see what lessons could be learned from their experience of this integrated structure (see Box 8). It was sufficiently encouraged to

---

Box 8: Lessons from over the water?

In Northern Ireland, unlike in England, Scotland and Wales, health and personal social services have been provided through an integrated structure since 1973. Area health and social services boards are responsible for commissioning health care and social care from health and social services trusts. ... Some witnesses indicated that there were problems with the integrated system in Northern Ireland. ... However, we do not consider that these problems are either unique to Northern Ireland's integrated service or necessarily impossible to overcome. We strongly endorse the practice we saw in Northern Ireland. ... The integrated health and social services system seems to us to be sensible. We consider that it is a pragmatic approach to service provision and has major benefits for users and carers as it allows a seamless service between health and social care to develop.

(Source: House of Commons, 1998, paras 62–3)

---

recommend an integrated model for England also, and to argue that problems of collaboration were not going to be solved until integration of some kind occurred.

Hence, for the Health Select Committee, the answer to fragmentation was not collaboration but *unification* – an opinion out of step with that of the Labour government and which casts doubt upon the attainability of 'partnership'. Unification, of course, would raise other problems. The Committee acknowledged that it would still leave other increasingly important intersections (such as those with education and housing) untouched. Equally significantly, it would create huge political difficulties, with none of the NHS and social services agencies wanting to be 'taken over' by each other. The fact that the Committee felt unable to make specific recommendations on which organisation (if either) should have overall responsibility is an indication of the scale of political sensitivity. Interestingly, however, proposals for substantial change to foster greater integration have since emerged from within Northern Ireland (see Box 6), suggesting perhaps that there is more to be done than the Select Committee realised in promoting the elusive notions of collaboration and integration.

Conclusion

This chapter examined the conceptual confusion surrounding terms such as 'collaboration' and looked at the reasons why working across agency boundaries has become more significant in the field of health and social care. The policy history of collaboration has not been markedly successful, although it is rather early to be making any judgement on the most recent initiatives. Some specific explanations for this lack of success were alluded to throughout the chapter. In particular, there were references to the inadequacy of exhortation, to the problems of reconciling competition and co-operation, and to the ways in which organisations have discovered joint working to be unacceptable when it collides with organisational self-interest.

To secure a better understanding of the mechanics of joint working, it is vital to explore these ideas in a more systematic and theoretical way. Public policy on collaboration could be said to have been largely a-theoretical, in the sense that it has rarely been based on explicit and sustainable assumptions about individual or organisational behaviour – or even on more specific empirical findings. For example, the general thrust of policy has been to assume that organisations will collaborate purely for the good of the individuals and communities they serve, if only the virtues of this action are pointed out to them. More recently, however, the emphasis appears to have shifted to a more sceptical view, with the Labour government prepared to adopt an array of sanctions and incentives in an attempt to bring agencies together – an implicit acceptance that exhortation alone is insufficient. These respective positions deserve to be developed and explored further.

References

Aiken, M., Dewar, R., Di Tomaso, N., Hage, J. and Zeitz, G. (1975) *Co-ordinating Human Services*, San Francisco, Jossey-Bass.

Audit Commission (1986) *Making a Reality of Community Care*, London, HMSO.

Challis, L., Fuller, S., Henwood, M., Klein, R., Plowden, W., Webb, A., Whittingham, P. and Wistow, G. (1988) *Joint Approaches to Social Policy: Rationality and Practice*, Cambridge, Cambridge University Press.

Department of Health (1989) *Caring for People*, Cmd 849, London, HMSO.

Department of Health (1990) *The Care Programme Approach for People with a Mental Illness Referred to the Specialist Psychiatric Services*, Joint Health/Social Services Circular HC(90)23/LASSL(90)11, London, HMSO.

Department of Health (1997) *The New NHS: Modern, Dependable*, Cm 3807, London, The Stationery Office.

Department of Health (1998a) *Our Healthier Nation: A Contract for Health*, Cm 3852, London, The Stationery Office.

Department of Health (1998b) *Modernising Social Services: Promoting Independence, Improving Protection, Raising Standards*, CM4169, London, The Stationery Office.

Department of Health (1998c) *Partnership in Action: A Discussion Document*, London, DoH.

Department of Health (1998d) *Modernising Health and Social Services: National Priorities Guidance 1999/00–2001/02*, London, DoH.

Department of Health and Social Security (DHSS) (1973) *A Report from the Working Party on Collaboration between the NHS and Local Government on Its Activities to the End of 1972*, London, HMSO.

Department of Health and Social Security (DHSS) (1983) *Care in the Community and Joint Finance*, Circular HC(83)5, London, HMSO.

Gillett, A. M. (1995) 'Future challenges of the social services in the building of the European welfare society', *Jornades Internacionales de Surveis Sociales*, Barcelona, Generalitat de Catalunya Benstar Social, pp. 355–60.

Griffiths, R. (1988) *Community Care: Agenda for Action*, London, HMSO.

Guillebaud Report (1956) *Report of the Royal Commission on the Cost of the NHS*, London, HMSO.

Hallett, C. (1995) *Interagency Coordination in Child Protection*, London, HMSO.

Ham, C. (1992) *Health Policy in Britain* (3rd edn), London, Macmillan.

Hardy, B., Turrell, A. and Wistow, G. (1992) *Innovations in Community Care Management*, Aldershot, Avebury.

Henwood, M. and Wistow, G. (1993) *Hospital Discharge and Community Care: Early Days*, London, Social Services Inspectorate/NHS Management Executive.

Hirst, J. (1998) 'Inequalities could outlive the Wall', *Community Care*, 7–13 May, pp. 6–7.

House of Commons (1998) *Health Select Committee, Session 1998–99, First Report. The Relationship between Health and Social Services*, Volume 1, London, The Stationery Office.

House of Commons, Social Services Select Committee (1985) *Community Care*, Second Report, Session 1984–5, HC13, London, HMSO.

Huxham, C. and Macdonald, D. (1992) 'Introducing collaborative advantage', *Management Decision*, Vol. 30, No. 3, pp. 50–56.

Mawhinney, B. (1993) *Purchasing for Health: A Framework for Action*, Leeds, NHS Management Executive.

Metcalfe, L. and Richards, S. (1990) *Improving Public Management*, European Institute of Public Administration, London, Sage.

Ministry of Health (1962) *A Hospital Plan for England and Wales*, Cmnd 1604, London, HMSO.

Ministry of Health (1963) *The Development of Community Care*, Cmnd 1973, London, HMSO.

National Audit Office (1987) *Community Care Developments*, London, HMSO.

Nocon, A. (1994) *Collaboration in Community Care in the 1990s*, Sunderland, Business Education Publishers.

Ottewill, R. and Wall, A. (1990) *The Growth and Development of the Community Health Services*, Sunderland, Business Education Publishers.

Rummery, K. and Glendinning, C. (1998) *Working Together: Primary Care Involvement in Commissioning Social Care Services*, Manchester, National Primary Care Research and Development Centre, University of Manchester.

Warren, R., Rose, S. and Bergunder, A. (1974) *The Structure of Urban Reform*, Lexington, Mass., Lexington Books.

Weiss, J. (1981) 'Substance vs. symbol in administrative reform: the case of human services co-ordination', *Policy Analysis*, Vol. 7, No. 1, pp. 21–45.

Wistow, G. (1990) *Community Care Planning: A Review of Past Experience and Future Imperatives*, Caring for People Implementation Documents, CC13, London, Department of Health.

Wistow, G. and Hardy, B. (1996a) *Balancing the Collaborative and Competitive Imperatives*, Paper presented to the European Health Management Association Conference, University of Leeds, Nuffield Institute for Health.

Wistow, G. and Hardy, B. (1996b) 'Competition, collaboration and markets', *Journal of Inter-professional Care*, Vol. 10, No. 1, pp. 5–10.

Wistow, G., Knapp, M., Hardy, B., Forder, J., Kendall, J. and Manning, R. (1996) *Social Care Markets: Problems and Prospects*, Buckingham, Open University Press.

Chapter 13
Improving the quality of services

Celia Davies

Who is in the room when objectives are
set, measures are agreed and results
are reviewed can make a real difference
to the outcome for those who use services.

Introduction

Quality was barely visible as an issue on the agenda of public sector services for much of the first 30 years since 1948. The vision that inspired the NHS was to make medical and related services free at the point of use to all who needed them and to plan to provide the skilled workforce and the appropriate facilities and settings in which this could occur. The concern of local authority welfare and personal social services was to follow the central guidance about statutory services for children, older people and those with disabilities and to offer services locally – always paying attention to councillors' concern with the ways in which ratepayers' money was being spent. It was a time when the professional experts of the welfare state – the doctors, teachers, social workers and others were accorded considerable deference and respect (see Chapter 4). Lay people were not expected to ask questions.

Thirty years on, when fears about public expenditure were intensifying, questions about the quality of services started to emerge too. It was not just a matter of how much money was being spent, it was whether services were effective and were what users wanted. Quality initiatives became part and parcel of the new public services culture from the 1980s onwards. Some practitioners were enthusiastic, others distinctly lukewarm. This chapter offers a tour through the quality maze. What does quality mean when the term transfers from the product on a production line to the complexity of a human service? Who is – and who should be – involved in defining what quality is and assessing how far services come up to scratch? The detail of designing a quality assurance system is not the concern of this chapter; rather it is the significance of the many and varied arrangements for quality that service-providers have made and the involvement of practitioners and lay people that is at issue.

1   Quality evolves

Efforts at definition

There is a bewildering array of terms in use in the quality field in health and social welfare. Newcomers need to negotiate the differences between quality control, quality assurance and perhaps quality improvement. They need to be able to relate audit to these terms and distinguish between medical, clinical, uni-professional and multi-professional audit. The literature is not only voluminous but also inconsistent and confused.

One influential stream of thinking came from industry. Traditionally, quality control on the factory floor meant repetitive, assembly-line jobs for the workforce and an inspector at the end of the line accepting or rejecting the final product. From the 1950s onwards, things began to change. *Quality control* began to be replaced by *quality assurance* (Kogan and Redfern, 1995, pp. 8–9). The new approach was more proactive and preventive; work groups were given greater autonomy and responsibility for the quality of their work. Efforts were made to encompass all activities in the organisation, ensuring that they dovetailed to produce products that met the specification and satisfied customers (see Ellis and Whittington, 1993, Chapter 3). The Conservative governments of the 1980s became particularly interested in what industry had to offer and could teach public services about customer care and consumer satisfaction.

A second stream of thinking came from the use of the term *audit*. The idea of an auditor scrutinising the finances of an organisation and testifying that expenditure is in order has long been a familiar one in the private and public sectors and in voluntary organisations (see Chapter 11). Today, the term has extended far beyond this. Audit is now used to refer to any form of checking of practice against a set of standards or objectives. As a result, it can mean the work of *external* bodies inspecting an agency under statute or coming in on a voluntary and invited basis to see whether it meets independent accreditation standards. It can also refer to *internal* enquiries about performance, especially ones undertaken by uni- or multi-professional groups examining the work of a provider group or service area. This chapter focuses on internal initiatives on quality to do with both quality assurance and audit. External checks on quality are considered in Chapter 14.

Do distinctions between terms and their different pedigrees actually matter? Can such issues not be left to those whose daily work involves them directly in designing and operating quality systems? Ann James, a specialist in organisation development who has a social work background, suggests that quality is important as 'an intermediate language between managers, professional practitioners and politicians' (1994, p. 212). And she warns:

> By ignoring the language of quality ... professionals reduce their ability
> to communicate and, inadvertently, marginalise themselves and thereby
> give power away to those who are able to speak in other tongues.
>
> (James, 1994, p. 212)

Other writers have insisted that there have been and are several languages of quality and that it is important also to understand *whose* languages they are, what assumptions are built into them and which language is spoken in a particular place at a particular time. In other words, there is a *politics* of quality.

The politics of quality

Naomi Pfeffer and Anna Coote (1991) from the Institute of Public Policy Research – a body that described itself, when set up in 1988, as an alternative to the free-market think-tanks – have drawn attention to the practical significance of debates about quality and their human consequences. Their argument that five very different approaches to quality may be distinguished has been particularly important for those who want to understand the pitfalls and the potentials of quality projects (see Box 1).

Box 1: Five approaches to quality

1   The *traditional approach*: to convey prestige and positional advantage.

2   The *'scientific'* or *expert approach*: to conform to standards determined by experts.

3   The *managerial* or *'excellence' approach*: to measure customer satisfaction, in pursuit of market advantage.

4   The *consumerist approach*: to empower the customer.

5   The *democratic approach*: to achieve common goals in the interests of the community as a whole.

(Source: based on Pfeffer and Coote, 1991)

Pfeffer and Coote set aside the first approach. Going for quality in the sense of producing a superior or luxury product such as an expensive perfume, perhaps, has little direct relevance to welfare services, since when we say we want 'better services' we mean better than before not better than others receive (p. 24). But they suggest that all four of the other meanings of quality are in play in various combinations in the quality assurance systems that have been devised in the public services. And they need to be discussed. What, for example, represents quality in the case of hip replacement operations in an acute general hospital? An *expert* approach will usually mean that the surgeon's interest in the technical success of the operation is uppermost. A *managerial/customer satisfaction* approach could well be concerned with the overall environment of care, the ward and the hotel services, the supportiveness of the staff. A *consumerist* approach would perhaps shift towards giving service-users a chance to define the key quality issues for themselves. Pfeffer and Coote make a point of underlining the distinction between the customer/ consumer (in approach 4), who has interests as a user of specific services at a specific time, and the citizen (in approach 5), who might want to have a say about what constitutes a quality service. They regard the *democratic* approach as in strong need of development. In their view:

> The whole system needs to be redesigned and redirected, in order to cultivate and sustain the active support of the public it is there to serve.
> (Pfeffer and Coote, 1991, pp. 61–2)

Pfeffer and Coote insist that 'quality is not something that floats above politics' (p. 2), instead it reflects the politics of the time and place. This message that different interests drive quality initiatives at different times threads through this chapter. The following sections explore the provenance of quality policies by:

- contrasting the different pathways of development of quality initiatives in health and social care, exploring reasons for this and consequences
- considering some of the common challenges that have arisen as people try to measure quality and put it into practice
- examining two recent developments in the quality field – 'best value' and 'clinical governance'.

2   Divergent developments

In the climate of the 1980s, both the NHS and social services departments imported models of general management from industry, and quality projects were refracted through these models. But there were also some clear contrasts. In the NHS, a *managerial* approach to quality was evident, laced with very strong doses of *expert domination*. In social services, the cocktail was more varied and volatile. With less in the way of expert domination, and more social-science-based research and in some places strong user involvement, there has been greater diversity, including, perhaps, more use of *consumerist* and *democratic* approaches. Social services also, however, faced a growing external inspection regime after several highly publicised cases where quality of care had deteriorated in a major way.

The NHS

Directors of Quality Assurance, with places on trust boards, were expected to take the new 1980s NHS quality agenda forward. Experienced nurse managers often took up these posts (their old jobs having disappeared with the restructuring). Nurse managers' visions and their power or lack of it to effect organisation-wide change were thus central to the initial push for quality. Nurses were already familiar with an array of instruments for measuring the quality of services in the acute sector. With a wider brief, they were inclined to take a fairly holistic view of the patient experience and quality projects often meant working with therapists, and with ancillary and managerial staff, and consulting with patients. By the end of the 1980s, there were nearly 1500 quality initiatives under way in England and Wales. They included:

> ... patient satisfaction surveys, the writing and distribution of patient handbooks, new signposts around hospital sites, improved complaints systems, more liberal visiting hours, creation of 'patients' perceptions groups' and so on.
>
> (Harrison and Pollitt, 1994, p. 107)

In 1989, the government funded a series of pilot Total Quality Management (TQM) projects. TQM, stemming from industry, has been a management-inspired idea, stressing ownership from the top of the organisation and development of a culture of quality that permeates all levels and is committed to continuous quality improvement. These demonstration projects, it was hoped, together with the way in which purchasers would be writing quality into contracts, would start to bring more integration and coherence to work on improving quality. In the event, alongside TQM, other approaches proliferated – business process re-engineering, ISO 9000 and benchmarking, for example. These could generate uncertainty and confusion and too easily be seen as 'alien implants', thus presenting a real barrier to change (Pollitt, 1997).

The emphasis at this point was often on the quality of the organisation rather than on the quality of clinical care. Doctors, in particular, were not on board. Although they were encouraged to audit their practice – guidance on medical audit came at the time of the 1990 legislation, with funding attached – it proved to be a rather watered-down affair (Harrison and Pollitt, 1994). 'Nice little research projects' was one rather cynical description of the upshot of this policy development. Some did begin to take on performance thinking, but the culture change that was required was unlikely to occur overnight (see Black and Thompson, 1993). In all, the drive towards quality in the NHS at this point remained fragmented, single-profession-led and erratic.

By the mid-1990s, the idea that the quality of clinical practice must be based more directly and demonstrably on the most recent and robust research evidence, and that common standards could be set, had become highly attractive to several groups within the medical profession – public health doctors, for example. What was to become known as the movement for 'evidence-based medicine' (EBM) and later, more broadly, 'evidence-based practice' (EBP) was on the scene. With funding from central government for research and development, for the development of advice and guidelines and for the dissemination of findings, the result of all this was a veritable evidence-based industry in the medical field. Nursing, with far greater numbers but substantially less resourcing (Kogan and Redfern, 1995, pp. 11–12), followed suit. There were new centres and institutes, new journals, conferences, seminars and training programmes and an alphabet of new acronyms for practitioners to understand. Scotland's smaller size gave an opportunity for creating a set of organisations and relationships that was more readily understandable to busy practitioners (see Box 2). Even so, the systems set up under the heading 'clinical effectiveness and quality' were complex ones.

Box 2: '... an alphabet of new acronyms'

Scotland's size and lack of a regional tier makes for good relations between the variety of bodies set up to improve clinical effectiveness in the NHS. Even so, things can be bewildering to a newcomer. The Scottish Needs Assessment Programme (SNAP) reports on areas of specific clinical need; national projects are then set up through the Clinical Resources Advisory Group (CRAG), which also funds the development of evidence-based clinical guidelines through SIGN (Scottish Intercollegiate Guidelines Network). These guidelines then influence commissioning by being issued through the Scottish Health Purchasing Information Centre (SHPIC). Meanwhile an important database of all clinical audit projects is maintained by the Scottish Clinical Audit Research Centre (SCARC) – itself also funded by CRAG.

(Source: based on Farquhar, 1996)

Some people might say that medicine had captured the NHS quality agenda, but with this bewildering array of quality initiatives on the scene, and proliferating advice and guidelines from the centre on clinical effectiveness, performance review, continuing professional development and more, the picture locally was often one of overlapping structures and responsibilities. In such a context, it can be hard for many practitioners – let alone users – to enthuse about quality or to see direct links to practice improvement. A recent study of nurses' attitudes to quality in two general hospitals revealed a sense of isolation and alienation from action on quality and suggested a deep gulf between those at board level and those in the front-line (Clarke and Yarrow, 1997). Others have wondered whether the quality movement has lost its way (see Box 3). What those close to the ground often look for is practical, non-threatening and inclusive ways of examining services. Patients' journey projects are one such way (see Box 4 overleaf).

In short, while some people were feeling that the quality movement had lost its way in the NHS, there were also examples of important and worthwhile ways of reviewing and developing services that it had promoted.

Box 3: Doubts about clinical audit

In a review in 1997, a health authority in the (then) Oxford and Anglia Region explored whether staff felt that its substantial annual investment of over half a million pounds on clinical audit was actually improving clinical care. The comments from interviews with 30 clinicians and managers – involving representatives from primary care trusts, the Community Health Council and the health authority – supported the principles of reflective practice, peer review, development and monitoring of evidence-based standards in trusts. But there were also widely shared fears that audit and the drive for quality had failed to bring people together and had lost direction.

'You get some real enthusiasts who do excellent audit work and take it very seriously, but the majority of doctors aren't interested. What does that say about the quality of care?'

(Audit committee chair)

'There are very few GP practices who carry out regular audits – the good ones really stand out. GPs will say they have enough on their plates ... '

(Primary care facilitator)

'I'm not sure how it relates to quality – the emphasis has always been on counting things rather than looking at the quality of the process or the outcome for patients.'

(Senior manager)

'Because audit is run by the clinicians, with no senior management involvement at all, it can't link to the strategic work of the trust. All the trust board gets is a very detailed annual report listing lots of very admirable but itty-bitty projects. What are we supposed to do with it? We just "receive" it – the whole thing should be locked into trust strategy – we should be involved in setting the agenda in the first place.'

(Trust executive director)

Box 4: The patient's journey

A patient's journey through any health service department can be seen as consisting of six stages: referral, pre-contact, arrival, assessment, contact, and transfer/discharge. By examining each of these stages and how they fit together, quality improvements can be planned – especially at the interface between parts of the organisation where problems often occur. Interviews are held with every staff group and with patients and carers if they are able and willing to take part. The resulting report can be used as a basis for developing a department's agenda of audit, research and education.

After completing patients' journey projects covering A&E, day hospitals and community-based services in one local area, a co-ordinator listed the following benefits.

- A complete understanding of the workings of a department in logical sequence

- A chance for all staff to be heard

- Involvement of users

- Identification of the department's strengths and not only its short-comings

- The recommendations can be used to kick-start audits, research projects and education programmes.

- The method is compatible with care pathways.

- Staff report that the method is 'user-friendly' and relevant, it is relatively free from the usual quality assurance hassles of jargon, paperwork questionnaires and long meetings.

(Source: K. Mowbray, Milton Keynes Community NHS Trust, March 1999, personal communication)

Social services

The debate about quality has had a very different flavour in social services Concern with quality of care, and with the underlying quality of life tha services allow, can be traced back to the early 1960s, when a pioneerin sociological study uncovered unacceptable and sometimes shockin conditions experienced by older people in residential homes (Townsend 1962). This work marked the start of serious attention to residential car and a tradition of evaluation research which put matters such as space, th design of buildings and the daily regime as they affected the quality of lif for everyone in residential care on the agenda. Demands began to be mad for a system of state registration and external inspection of homes

Legislation in 1984 gave local authorities new powers and guidance made clear that an inspector needed to examine both inputs (such as staff ratios, buildings and equipment) and outcomes (in the shape of the day-to-day experience of the residents themselves) (see Chapter 14, Section 2).

A study of five social services departments (SSDs), as the NHS and Community Care Act 1990 started to take effect, showed a variety of quality initiatives in relation to the whole field of their work. Some agencies were looking to registration and inspection units to provide the whole of quality assurance. Some were seeing the matter as requiring specialist input, whereas others were encouraging staff themselves to explore the quality of the services they offered, and to devise their own standards and indicators. Still others were making deliberate efforts to bring in *all* the stakeholders – senior, middle and junior managers, together with professionals and ancillary and support workers and users – to make quality assurance systems relevant to all (James *et al.*, 1992). There are examples of working together across health and social care: for example in mental health services in Wales, where in Mid Glamorgan joint observation teams were set up to interview managers, staff and users (Leckie, 1994).

One user-led initiative is described by Whittaker (1994). An SSD, together with the regional health authority, commissioned People First, the pioneering campaigning group for people with learning difficulties, to carry out a down-to-earth evaluation of what users really needed as they made the transition into residential care in the community. With two service-users involved in designing the study, interviewing and analysing the material, the results led staff to realise just how inaccessible traditional planning approaches were and just how much unnecessary jargon there was. The Divisional Director of Social Services said the project had:

> ... given us all a very clear reminder that our services are about people with strong views about what they like and do not like, and that by ignoring the crucial information within these personal views and opinions, we ignore a way to develop services which properly meet the needs and wishes of individuals for whom they are intended.
>
> (Quoted in Whittaker, 1994, p. 105)

Questions about effectiveness and demands that interventions should be 'evidence-based' began to emerge, just as in the health field. Some writers, however, had fundamental doubts about whether the complexity of social work goals and practice could ever be unambiguously evaluated; the randomised controlled trial might be fine exploring the results of a new drug, but evaluating care management, for example, was a different matter (see Cheetham *et al.*, 1992; MacDonald *et al.*, 1992). Furthermore, social work has not had the established infrastructure of institutions, skilled enthusiasts and funding support that is available in medicine. At its many conferences, the evidence-based health care movement has not been above promoting itself by disparaging the apparent lack of evidence in social work and social care!

Alongside all this, however, events have brought even more serious and sustained challenges to SSDs' claims to be providing high quality services and to the competence and self-esteem of the social work profession. The well-publicised trial of her stepfather for causing the death of Maria Colwell in 1973 was followed by a concentration of child death cases in the mid-1980s and much negative publicity (Aldridge, 1994). Scandals about physical and sexual abuse of children in care continued to dog social services through the 1990s. In a rather more muted way, elder abuse also came on to the agenda. Neither external inspection nor in-house procedures for ensuring quality seemed to have been able to prevent this. Press and politicians have not been slow to criticise – child care is one area where a great deal of policy guidance has emerged in relation to child protection, not always with positive results (see Chapter 10, Box 6). More recently, the programme 'Quality Protects' was initiated (see Box 5).

Box 5: Quality in children's services

In September 1998 'Quality Protects', a three-year programme designed to improve the management of local authority services for children, was launched. The government set eight key objectives and required local authorities to prepare action plans. Among these objectives were:

- protecting children from emotional, physical and sexual abuse and neglect

- ensuring that they are with carers capable of providing safe and effective care for the duration of childhood

- ensuring that looked-after children gain maximum benefits from educational opportunities, health care and social care

- ensuring that young people leaving care are not isolated and participate socially and economically as citizens.

There was an emphasis on involving children in policy development and extending the limit of the duty to care to age 18. The importance of working across agency boundaries was highlighted. Local councillors were reminded of their duties to see that the authority was acting as a 'good corporate parent'. Extra funding was available but performance was to be closely monitored. The White Paper *Modernising Social Services* (DoH, 1998a) linked this with the government's commitment to action on a wide front to strengthen family life, and to reduce social exclusion and anti-social behaviour among children.

(Sources: DoH, 1998a; 1998b)

Criticism in the press had another dimension. Several of the child death cases had occurred in left-wing London boroughs which had taken a strong lead in devising policies around race awareness, cultural sensitivity and equal opportunities more broadly. The work of CCETSW, the training body for social work, was called into question. There were bitter debates about the length and content of social work training and the way it was or was not to deal with issues of equal opportunities. Social work operates in the eye of a potential political storm in a way not true of the health sector. There is a contested social control agenda around a number of social work activities – supporting people diagnosed as mentally ill, for example, or weighing the risks of enhanced independence for people with learning difficulties. Without agreement on the fundamental question of just what we want services to achieve, an assessment of quality is impossible. This can often overshadow achievements, in providing guidance about residential homes relevant to minority ethnic elders (Black Perspectives Sub-Group, 1993) or, for example, preparing a Black Community Care Charter (National Association of Race Equality Advisers, 1992), and in creating specific projects involving local community groups.

In all, then, by the final years of the 1990s, as a new government took office, what was the position as far as assuring the quality of services in health and social care was concerned? On the positive side, there had been many successful local projects, and an array of techniques and practices to audit services and settings and monitor performance had been developed. Professionals were now asking questions about the outcomes of their practice in ways that had not been at all apparent in the years before 1980. Clinical guidelines, checklists and standards had emerged. Yet quality was still a maze of fragmented initiatives and neither the government's hands-off approach in health, nor its rather more interventionist line for aspects of social services, had simplified matters. Some service-providers had found the new focus on quality liberating. Others, equally committed to improving the quality of services for users, were still reluctant to set foot in the quality maze. One reason for this is the sheer technical difficulty of translating thinking about quality in a sensitive and appropriate way into practice.

3   Putting quality into practice

Whether in education, health or social care, and whether at national level or at the level of the smallest quality assurance project, the underlying issues to be faced are the same.

- What are the objectives of the service?
- What are the best indicators of achievement of those objectives?
- How can we review results and integrate them into an ongoing action plan to create a cycle of continuous improvement in services?

Answering these questions is never straightforward. A broad objective ('to provide the best possible quality of service for the people of ... ') generates agreement but fails to provide a guide for action. Trying to specify things further – as those who have tried to write a mission statement or get involved in business planning know – can be a minefield. The following seven quality questions drawn from the field of health have often been taken as a starting point.

Is this service:

1   Accessible to all?
2   Relevant to the needs of the whole community?
3   Effective for individual patients?
4   Equitable and fair?
5   Socially acceptable?
6   Efficient and economical?

(Source: adapted from Maxwell, 1984, p. 1471)

Work is always needed to translate questions like these into a series of goals that make sense in a specific setting – be it in child care, mental health, A&E services or whatever. Taken outside of health – and sometimes inside it too – there are nagging doubts. Are questions 1 and 2 always relevant? Question 5 rules out social work with unwilling clients and ignores the fact that some objectives are strongly politically contested. Four further issues are discussed below.

Indicators are often second bests and substitutes

Performance indicators abound, but the question of what they are designed to be indicators of – and what the underlying objective is – can be neglected. Take the case of the proportion of clients with learning difficulties who have been supplied with personal assistance, or the proportion of frail older people who receive a particular service. These can be seen as substitutes for measuring an underlying objective of securing greater independence. Take the proportion of elective surgery cases treated within 12 months. This is 'a very crude proxy for the saving in pain, discomfort and lost earnings brought about by the health services' (Smith, 1995, p. 15). Focusing on the indicator without asking the question 'in order to ... ?' runs the risk of failing to see that there might be other ways of meeting the objective or indeed of measuring whether it has been met.

It has become customary in quality assurance to refer to 'standards'. No audit can be carried out unless standards are set against which performance can be measured. It is important to ask whether the standard relates clearly to the underlying objective of the service and it may have to be a proxy. There may sometimes be other indicators that singly or in combination relate better to measuring how far the underlying objective is being reached. An example, drawn deliberately from a different field, makes this point. Box 6 shows how a working knowledge of day-to-day practice in the field, together with an appreciation of and sympathy with the overall goal of quality improvement, can result in a constructive proposal for change and one with the potential to gain support from key stakeholders. It also shows how, once a goal is set and an indicator is

---

Box 6: Are we measuring the right thing? An example from education

In October 1998, the Secretary of State for Education announced new secondary education targets. Among them was the aim of raising the percentage of pupils attaining five A* to C grades to over half of 16-year-olds. Chris Bridge, headteacher of a school that already far exceeded the target, took issue. Teachers would focus on the target, become expert at guarding the borderline between C and D grades, urging pupils to make that extra effort to gain a C. A chasm would open up between successes and failures. Pupils who had made tremendous efforts and secured a D grade would see themselves as failures. It would be impossible to urge a pupil to shift from a G to an F or from an F to an E. 'We are in danger', Bridge argued, of 'further alienating the least able third of students whom the English educational system has traditionally failed' (Bridge, 1998, p. 5). His preferred target was 2+2 – aiming to add two levels to each child's performance between key stages 2 and 3, and 3 and 4. Such a target was inclusive, ambitious and reinforcing of self-esteem for all pupils. It would actually push up the A* to C results on the way. This headteacher was not rejecting performance indicators as a measure of quality out of hand. But he was deeply disturbed about the real world impact of one of the indicators chosen.

---

chosen, it can result in *perverse incentives* – encouraging people to act in ways that no one intended.

Results can be a function of factors outside the control of the organisational unit

Just as the educational attainment standards of a school are likely to reflect the composition of the local area in which it is found, so the work of agencies in health and social services will reflect the characteristics of local areas. Higher proportions of surgical complications in a hospital, for example, or higher rates of re-offending among young people might say much more about the social characteristics of the area than about the skills of surgeons or the competencies of probation officers. This is one important reason for resistance to the publication of league tables. In some cases, providers cannot actually do anything to change performance expressed in such terms.

Increasingly, too, the required outcomes are a function of joint activity across agencies and the quality of service will be a function of the combined efforts and the extent to which collaboration has been achieved. Quality measures often assume a more self-contained world. Furthermore, as Chapter 12 shows, we probably still do not know enough about how to promote collaborative working.

The single most important message from all of this is probably that indicators are likely to remain partial and incomplete. They must be used *pragmatically*, and be interpreted with care and with full understanding of the local situation to which they apply. Writing on the complexity of the public sector and its experience with performance indicators, Peter Smith, a specialist in economics and public finance, accepts this, and warns that because there are so many different users of performance indicators (PIs), with different interests:

> ... it is important to recognise that there is no single way of interpreting performance data ... PIs have a role to play. However, they need to be provided within a framework which enables the legitimate variety of stakeholders to come to their own interpretation.
>
> (Smith, 1995, p. 16)

Smith urges us to design systems that providers can support and users can be involved in – and to recognise that these will always need developing and changing. This is an important message as new rafts of performance frameworks are published for local government and the NHS.

Outcomes are of different kinds

Appraising economic efficiency often rests on a model of inputs and outputs and on success as more output for a given level of input. But 'output' seems to take us in the direction of mere activity counting. 'Deaths and discharges', regularly recorded for the first decades of the NHS, is one of the very clearest examples of an indicator of activity that ignores the notion that different groups might think of different outcomes differently!

As people have tried to find ways of using not 'outputs' but wider notions of 'outcomes' of human services, so definitions have proliferated. Cheetham *et al.* (1992), rejecting 'outputs' as economic jargon, suggest that we should examine *service-based outcomes* and *client-based outcomes*. We can also distinguish, for example, between *quality of service* and *quality of life*. Osborne (1992, p. 442) points out that it is quite possible for an adult with learning difficulties to experience a poor quality of residential service, but to have a considerably higher quality of life because of involvement in excellent day care.

Working with users to define outcomes that are relevant to them can serve to reorient services considerably. In an extensive review of user and carer outcomes in community care, for example, Nocon and Qureshi (1996) found that outcomes specified by users and carers are by no means always the same as those that providers specify. A survey of a wide range of user and carer organisations confirmed that what people want is:

- *relationships* that create credibility, respect, confidentiality, and that are courteous, honest, reliable and empowering

- *skills* that involve listening and understanding, are enabling and result in practitioners who have a knowledge of local services and a good sense of judgement about risks
- *services* that are flexible, culturally appropriate, allow choice and control and are accessible, fair and prompt.

(Source: adapted from Harding and Beresford, 1996)

Detailed comments from members of the user and carer organisations contacted by Harding and Beresford showed just how far services still need to go. Older people and young people had criticisms; so too did users of mental health services, and black groups (see Box 7). Some people objected to being described as 'users' and 'carers'. They see themselves as *recipients* of services they do not always want or as *survivors* of a system they feel works against and not for their well-being.

Box 7: Some black perspectives on service standards

'There are stories of our elders who are vegetarians being provided with meat dishes from the meals on wheels service ... There is a lack of respect, inadequate provision for dietary needs, skin and hair care, language and emotional needs ... The list is endless.'

(Standing conference of ethnic minority senior citizens)

'For black and ethnic minority users and carers, a language barrier hinders a prompt and effective service. People are sent to different sections without understanding why; procedures are not explained to them so that they understand; they do not get the interpreting help they need and have to rely on a relative or child, which is quite unacceptable and lacks confidentiality.'

(Newham Black and Ethnic Minority Community Care Forum)

'Many individuals [from Asian communities] felt isolated and alienated from mental health facilities. A number of people expressed concern about medical treatments and needed more thorough explanation. Others felt that drug therapies must be accompanied by counselling interventions and help with social problems ... There was little evidence to support the assumption that "Asian people prefer to cope without services".'

'Preventative services should be developed which provide advocacy as well as befriending, emotional support and legal advice, complementary treatments such as Al-Hickmet, Unani Desi and spiritual approaches alongside mainstream treatments to all mental health users.'

(Asian Black Community Mental Health Project)

(Source: based on Harding and Beresford, 1996)

Users at the centre of quality

Are we really integrating users into the quality process or are we still paying lip service to user involvement? The Citizen's Charter, launched in 1991, was described by Conservative Prime Minister John Major as aiming 'to give the customer more clout and the manager more responsibility' (quoted in Black, 1994, p. 215). The initiative spawned the Patient's Charter, a Mental Health Charter, the Children's Charter and many more. All these set out rights that service-users have and standards that services must reach. They are associated with published measures of performance – whether, for example, out-patients had been seen within 30 minutes and so on. A review in 1998 suggested that local charters, built up with user involvement represented a better direction for the future (Dyke, 1998).

Beresford and his colleagues (1997) cite the Wiltshire and Swindon Users' Network as one of the best examples of really concentrated effort to empower and involve service-users in relation to quality (Box 8). User involvement, they argue, is a *route to quality* in the sense that users are then fully involved in defining, developing, monitoring and evaluating quality according to their own values. It is also a *measure of quality* 'since a key objective is that service users have more say and control over their lives' (p. 79). There is an important reminder here that who is in the room when objectives are set, measures are agreed and results are reviewed can make a real difference to the outcomes for service-users.

Box 8: Wiltshire and Swindon Users' Network

This Network has a broad membership drawn from disabled people, older people and psychiatric service-users. Strong backing and financial support from the social services department give it continuity and a 'safe base' in which growing expertise can be shared and developed and from which people can go out to engage with service-providers. By 1993, the Network had been involved in 71 projects, including:

- setting up a crisis response system for psychiatric service-providers

- carrying out a user-led review of how occupational therapists organise their work, with suggestions for greater follow-through from hospital to community

- planning training for social services receptionists to help them understand why people need information and how to deal with anger and abuse.

Projects have been both independent and collaborative. Network members have chaired inspection committees and joint working groups between health and social services providers and have participated in training professionals.

(Source: based on Beresford *et al.*, 1997, pp. 73–4)

This is perhaps beginning to come close to Pfeffer and Coote's democratic approach in Section 1 – the redesign that they were calling for 'to cultivate the support of the public it is there to serve'.

4   A new quality agenda from government?

The Labour government's White Paper *The New NHS*, published at the end of its first six months in office, signalled an intention to write quality more firmly into health care. 'Every part of the NHS and everyone who works in it', it proclaimed, 'should take responsibility for working to improve quality' (DoH, 1997, para. 3.2). Quality and efficiency needed to 'go hand in hand', but the definition:

> ... must be quality in its broadest sense: doing the right things, at the right time, for the right people, and doing them right – first time. And it must be the quality of the patient's experience as well as the clinical result – quality measured in terms of prompt access, good relationships and efficient administration.
>
> (DoH, 1997, para. 3.2)

To achieve this, every trust must 'embrace the concept of clinical governance' (para. 6.2). This means setting up a framework to show it will be accountable for continuous improvement of performance and how it will create an environment in which excellence in clinical care will flourish. More practically it means: devising a clear structure to review clinical performance (through a subcommittee of the trust's board perhaps); giving clear responsibility to a named senior clinician to devise internal arrangements; and ensuring that professionals at ward and clinic level are involved.

> NHS Trust boards will expect to receive monthly reports on quality, in the same way as they now receive financial reports, and to publish an annual report on what they are doing to assure quality. Quality will quite literally be on the agenda of every NHS Trust board.
>
> (DoH, 1997, para. 6.15)

New structures at national level are also part of the clinical governance framework. A National Institute for Clinical Excellence (NICE) started work in April 1999. Its aim is progressively to spell out standards for each area of clinical service in the NHS. National Service Frameworks are being devised centrally for various care areas, starting with cancer care, coronary heart disease, care of older people and mental health. A Commission for Health Improvement (CHI), requiring legislative action to implement, will systematically review trusts' activities on quality and respond to government requests for local investigations. The new model was later described as:

> ... a marriage of clinical judgement with clear national standards. It
> involves a partnership between the Government and the clinical
> professions. In that partnership, the Government does what only
> government can do and the professions do what only they can do.
>
> (DoH, 1998c, para. 1.13)

Moves towards a new framework for quality in local government services
began at around the same time. Following a consultation paper and a call
for pilot sites, a White Paper took the concept of 'best value' forward in
summer 1998:

> A modern council – or authority – which puts people first will seek to
> provide services which bear comparison with the best. Not just with the
> best that other authorities provide but with the best that is on offer from
> both the public and the private sectors.
>
> (DETR, 1998, para. 7.1)

Compulsory competitive tendering was no longer seen as the route to
quality. The White Paper explained that obtaining best value was a matter
of accepting a duty to deliver services to clear standards and finding the
most effective and economic means of doing this, whether by providing
services directly or arranging to provide them through others. To aid this,
the government would set new national standards of performance. Social
services was identified – along with education – as among the areas where
it was particularly appropriate that government should take a lead on
standards. Local authorities would be required to start a programme of
fundamental performance reviews and set up action plans. An entirely
new Best Value Inspectorate would now work alongside the existing
specialist inspectorates and the importance of this stronger independent
external review, together with internal quality and audit measures, was
strongly underlined. Local authorities were to have a statutory duty to
obtain best value in their services.

The new approach to quality is broadly similar in both sectors. It
involves the government taking a national lead on standards of
performance in public services yet an acceptance that much can be and
should be worked out locally (see Box 9). But there are at least two major
differences.

First, the local government measures are set in a wider frame. The duty
of local councils to provide community leadership and to promote the
economic, social and environmental well-being of their areas is to be
enshrined in legislation. If they are to provide services that promote well-
being and respond to need, they should develop a corporate sense of
direction and do this by consulting widely – with taxpayers and service-
users, with business and with trade unions. The first step for a
fundamental review is to ask why and how a service is being provided
and to be prepared to search for answers from multiple stakeholders.
Arrangements for clinical governance seem more profession-led and
inward-looking when set alongside this. Secondly, the themes of external
inspection and audit are stronger in the local government context. There

	Box 9: Central/local partnerships for improving quality	
	'Clinical Governance' in the NHS	*'Best Value' in Local Government*
	Both to have a new statutory duty to provide quality services	
At the centre	National Service Frameworks spelled out by NICE	New national performance indicators (set in consultation with the Audit Commission)
Inspection	Regular reviews and spot-checks by CHI	Independent audit, extra and strong powers to intervene
At local level	Locally decided but clearly indentifiable arrangements for clinical governance	Fundamental performance reviews and local performance plans

will be new powers to require authorities to draw up and adhere to agreed action plans, or to force them to accept external help. In serious cases there will be powers to remove services from their jurisdiction altogether (para. 7.47). The words and the tone here contrast sharply with references to 'partnership' and 'marriage' in working with the professions in the NHS.

At the time this chapter was written, however, much remained to be seen about how these new arrangements would develop. A survey of people working most closely with clinical governance in the NHS was carried out on the eve of its full implementation in spring 1999. It showed that the majority were still feeling their way and many were not entirely confident that they had the systems in place for trust boards to judge matters of clinical performance (Corbett-Nolan and Malcolm, 1999). The negative publicity surrounding the case of the child deaths during surgery at Bristol Royal Infirmary, which had grabbed the headlines throughout 1998, was still reverberating. While the government stressed that the new health arrangements were about developing a learning culture and not a blame culture, inspection mechanisms in operation could prove to be as tough as those for local government.

Finally, with devolution, differences between the four parts of the UK may well grow larger (see Chapter 14, Box 6). There have already been different histories of development in the quality field. Scotland's strongly focused push for progress on audit and effectiveness through the Scottish Office Clinical Resource and Audit Group, the NHS Wales' Clinical Effectiveness Initiative, the early steps taken and built upon in Northern Ireland to devise standards for social work practice – all were suggesting that distinctive approaches could be around the corner. Policy thinking across the UK (see Chapter 12, Box 6) strongly stresses responsiveness to local circumstances. The Scottish Parliament and the Assemblies in Wales (and, it is hoped, Northern Ireland), which were taking shape as this book went to press, could prove to be new vehicles to lead change. Regionalism in England, if it develops further, could mean another source of diversity.

Conclusion

This chapter reviewed the twists and turns of efforts to improve the quality of services in health and social care throughout the 1980s and 1990s, drawing attention to different influences and different emphases in the two sectors and to the real difficulties of setting out objectives and devising measures. Where is the policy debate on quality going? The terms 'best value' and 'clinical governance' may develop or fade from view, but the issue of how to improve the quality of services and who should be involved will not go away. One thing that is certain is the quality question is shifting away from 'What is quality and how shall we as professionals seek to achieve it?' It is now closer to 'What action for welfare improvements is desirable here and how shall we – as professionals, lay people, managers and others, both locally and in central government – be rendered accountable for it?' It is no accident that the term 'accountability' is coming ever more to the fore and this is the theme of the final chapter.

References

Aldridge, M. (1994) *Making Social Work News*, London, Routledge.

Beresford, P., Croft, S., Evans, C. and Harding, T. (1997) 'Quality in personal social services: the developing role of user involvement in the UK', in Evers, A., Haverinen, R., Leichsenring, K. and Wistow, G. (eds) *Developing Quality in Personal Social Services: Concepts, Cases and Comments*, Aldershot, Ashgate.

Black, N. and Thompson, E. (1993) 'Obstacles to medical audit: British doctors speak out', *Social Science and Medicine*, Vol. 36, No. 7, pp. 849–56.

Black, S. (1994) 'What does the Citizen's Charter mean?', in Connor, A. and Black, S. (eds) *Performance Review and Quality in Social Care*, London, Jessica Kingsley.

Black Perspectives Sub-Group (1993) 'Black perspectives on residential care', in National Institute for Social Work's *Residential Care: Positive Answers*, London, HMSO.

Bridge, C. (1998) 'Sitting targets', *Guardian Education*, 27 October, pp. 4–5.

Cheetham, J., Fuller, R., McIvor, G. and Petch, A. (1992) *Evaluating Social Work Effectiveness*, Buckingham, Open University Press.

Clarke, D. and Yarrow, D. (1997) 'I find the term consumer offensive', *International Journal of Health Care Quality*, Vol. 10, No. 7, pp. 267–76.

Corbett-Nolan, A. and Malcolm, A. (1999) *Quality Improvement and Assurance in the NHS: Confidence Levels of NHS Trust Boards*, London, King's Fund, Health Quality Service.

Department of the Environment, Transport and the Regions (DETR) (1998) *Modern Local Government – In Touch with the People*, Cm 4014, London, DETR.

Department of Health (DoH) (1997) *The New NHS – Modern, Dependable*, Cm 3807, London, The Stationery Office.

Department of Health (DoH) (1998a) *Modernising Social Services*, Cm 4169, London, The Stationery Office.

Department of Health (DoH) (1998b) *Quality Protects: Framework for Action*, Local Authority Circular LA(98)28, London, DoH.

Department of Health (DoH) (1998c) *A First Class Service: Quality in the New NHS, a Consultation Paper*, London, DoH.

Dyke, G. (1998) *The New NHS Charter – A Different Approach*, London, DoH.

Ellis, R. and Whittington, D. (1993) *Quality Assurance in Health Care: A Handbook*, London, Edward Arnold.

Farquhar, W. (1996) 'Clinical effectiveness – making it happen', *Audit Trends*, Vol. 4, September, pp. 85–87.

Harding, T. and Beresford, P. (compilers) (1996) *The Standards We Expect: What Service Users and Carers Want from Social Services Workers*, London, National Institute for Social Work.

Harrison, S. and Pollitt, C. (1994) *Controlling Health Professionals: The Future of Work and Organisation in the NHS*, Buckingham, Open University Press.

James, A. (1994) 'Reflections on the politics of quality', in Connor, A. and Black, S. (eds) *Performance Review and Quality in Social Care*, London, Jessica Kingsley.

James, A., Brooks, T. and Jowell, D. (1992) *Committed to Quality: Quality Assurance in Social Services Departments*, London, HMSO.

Kogan, M. and Redfern, S. with Kober, A., Norman, I., Packwood, T. and Robinson, S. (1995) *Making Use of Clinical Audit: A Guide to Practice in the Health Professions*, Buckingham, Open University Press.

Leckie, T. (1994) 'Quality assurance in social work', in Connor, A. and Black, S. (eds) *Performance Review and Quality in Social Care*, London, Jessica Kingsley.

MacDonald, G. and Sheldon, B. with Gillespie, J. (1992) 'Contemporary studies of the effectiveness of social work', *British Journal of Social Work*, Vol. 22, No. 6, pp. 615–43.

Maxwell, R. J. (1984) 'Quality assessment in health', *British Medical Journal*, Vol. 228, 12 May, 1470–72.

National Association of Race Equality Advisers (1992) *Black Community Care Charter*, Birmingham, NAREA.

Nocon, A. and Qureshi, H. (1996) *Outcomes of Community Care for Users and Carers*, Buckingham, Open University Press.

Osborne, S. P. (1992) 'The quality dimension: evaluating quality of service and quality of life in human services', *British Journal of Social Work*, Vol. 22, pp. 437–53.

Pfeffer, N. and Coote, A. (1991) *Is Quality Good for You? A Critical Review of Quality Assurance in Welfare Services*, Social Policy Paper No. 5, London, IPPR.

Pollitt, C. (1997) 'Business and professional approaches to quality improvement: a comparison of their suitability for the personal social services', in Evers, A., Haverinen, R., Leichsenring, K. and Wistow, G. (eds) *Developing Quality in Personal Social Services: Concepts, Cases and Comments*, Aldershot, Ashgate.

Smith, P. (1995) 'Performance indicators and outcome in the public sector', *Public Money and Management*, October–December, pp. 13–16.

Townsend, P. (1962) *The Last Refuge*, London, Routledge and Kegan Paul.

Whittaker, A. (1994) 'Service evaluation by people with learning difficulties', in Connor, A. and Black, S. (eds) *Performance Review and Quality in Social Care*, London, Jessica Kingsley.

Chapter 14
Frameworks for regulation and accountability: threat or opportunity?

Celia Davies

New agencies are by no means free-
floating. They are surrounded by contract
specifications, financial targets, audit
and performance review.

Introduction

> ... one of the characteristics of Welfare State service providers ... is ... that they tend to regard themselves as accountable to their peers and are thus not linked into the institutionalized system through which political and managerial accountability flow.
>
> (Day and Klein, 1987, p. 52)

Patterns of accountability were changing even as these words were written. Those working in health and social care have found their work being increasingly scrutinised from outside the workplace as well as in it. External audits and inspections have proliferated. New techniques have been devised for measuring output, assessing effectiveness and questioning whether established procedures and patterns of work represent value for money. Governments, as described at the end of Chapter 13, have become more and more determined to set national standards and national frameworks for public service delivery.

Change, however, has brought to light a profusion and a confusion of ideas about *accountability upwards* to central departments and to the government of the day, *accountability downwards* to service-users and to citizens and *accountability horizontally* to professional peers. This chapter explores the importance of the changing regulatory environment both by teasing out some of the ideas underlying the present structures and by asking what impacts – some intended and some not – different kinds of regulation have. In Section 1, we shall consider accountability upwards in the shape of a deregulatory Conservative government leaving a legacy of more regulation. We shall consider the inspection model, its dilemmas and dynamics, as part of this upward accountability model in Section 2. Section 3 turns to the horizontal dimension, focusing on how the long-established tradition of self-regulation by many professions has been called into question. Finally, we consider new accountabilities to service-users and citizens locally and some of the ideas about facilitating dialogue and creating new kinds of accountability that are innovative and energising to all concerned. Are there, we ask, ways of turning the threat of accountability into an opportunity?

1   New forms of accountability upwards

Accountability has already been considered in several chapters of this book. Aspects of accountability for practice were considered in a discussion of ethics in Chapter 6, and the links between individual accountability and legal, professional and employer accountability were explored in Chapter 9. Demands for more accountability to consumers were the focus of Chapter 5, which began to look at new mechanisms to give a greater voice to service-users. Nowhere, as yet, however, have we considered what is referred to in the opening quotation as 'the institutionalized system through which political and managerial accountability flow'.

'Hands off the professions' – the public administration model

There was a clear consensus in the years following World War Two both about the importance of developing public services and about how such services could best be delivered. There was a strong belief that the state – through a well-organised, centrally-planned, bureaucratic machine – offered a way forward that was far superior to the previous mix involving large doses of private and voluntary initiative. As a direct provider, government could guarantee access to provisions and a broad equality of treatment across all parts of the country. For this, it was seen as vital that the contribution of professionals in health, education and social services should be facilitated. The result was a strong professional/bureaucratic alliance with 'uniform and expanding services, defined according to the professional paradigm' (Ranson and Stewart, 1994, p. 270). Political accountability would be secured by electors making a five-yearly choice between governments offering different overall directions and priorities. Butcher (1995) summed all this up in what he calls the public administration model (see Box 1).

Box 1: The public administration model

Bureaucratic structure

- clear hierarchies, accountability upwards, and reliable rule-following; detailed control of staff allows accountability and aids uniformly equal treatment.

Professional dominance

- professionals deliver services, also make some key decisions about resource allocation and policy direction; this was well-established at the outset in education and health, less so in social services and housing.

Accountability to the public

- the senior office-holders in the bureaucracy report to elected representatives at local or national level. They also account to watchdog bodies (e.g. ombudsmen and Audit Commission) for efficient administration and use of funds.

Equity of treatment

- legislation sets out what is to be available and public servants are expected to treat like cases alike.

Self-sufficiency

- the public service responsible for a function usually carries out that function itself, directly employing staff to do so, i.e. it is both funder and provider.

(Source: Butcher, 1995, pp. 2–7)

The public administration model implied a strong distinction between the public servant and the professional. The public servant was the loyal bureaucrat, committed to the proper functioning of the state machinery, working in a hierarchical way in obedience to rules. The professional, by contrast, having followed a lengthy training and intense socialisation into the profession, was deemed to have a commitment to practice, an internalised sense of the rules and values of a wider professional community that did not require to be monitored in any way. A professional could be trusted to work as an autonomous practitioner in the interests of each particular patient or client.

The rise of a regulatory state

Butcher was able to identify change to all five features of the public administration model he had outlined by the mid-1990s. Large *bureaucracies* were being replaced by decentralised operational units – local management in schools, responsibility to care managers in social services and fund-holding GPs, for example. 'Control by contract' has replaced 'control by hierarchy' (Hoggett, 1991, p. 250, cited in Butcher, 1995, p. 157). With insistent new references to efficiency and consumerism, *professional dominance* was no longer unchallenged. On *accountability*, Butcher traces, on the one hand, moves towards new forms of user participation (discussed in Chapter 5) and, on the other, the rise of new kinds of non-elected bodies with responsibility for services (the boards of NHS trusts for example). 'Equity' had in important ways been replaced by 'choice' as a leading value and the institution of provider competition was, of course, a major device to promote this. Finally, *self-sufficiency* had been turned on its head with the purchaser/provider split.

Does all this mean that the state has relinquished its powers? Certainly there are now more diverse organisations in the public, private and voluntary sectors delivering public services. Writers have suggested that what we have is no longer a *unified* system of government with a clear bureaucratic hierarchy of accountability upwards to ministers and parliament, but a *differentiated* set of loosely linking networks of providers in and across the public sector. Rod Rhodes, a political scientist who has specialised in studying central/local relations and traced the decline of local government in the 1980s, argues that we should see the shift *from government to governance*:

> 'Governance' means there is no one centre but multiple centres; there is no sovereign authority because networks have significant autonomy. The distinction between the public, private and voluntary sectors becomes meaningless. All play the game of 'grantsmanship'. These game-like interactions are caused by the need to exchange resources and negotiate shared purposes.
>
> (Rhodes, 1997, p. 109)

Interorganisational networks such as we now have are exceedingly difficult to control. Attempts at control produce unintended consequences, implementation gaps and what Rhodes calls 'policy mess'. But this is only part of the story. Long chains of bureaucratic command may have gone but new agencies are by no means free-floating. They are surrounded by contract specifications, financial targets, audits and performance reviews. These are remote controls, operated by new experts – the auditors, inspectors and management consultants whose reports now proliferate. A government committed to deregulation of business has introduced re-regulation in the public sector with an 'audit explosion' (Power, 1994) and 'centralised decentralisation' (Hoggett, 1997, p. 427).

These changes have reverberated widely in central and local government, in the voluntary sector and in health authorities. A future, after
local government reorganisation, where virtually the whole of the work of
local authorities is about getting contracts, and where it is ever more
difficult for councillors to get a sense of service provision at all, is one
scenario. In the small unitary authorities of local government reorganisation, social services has become:

> ... the last major function over which local politicians can exercise any
> real control in terms of priority setting, charging policies or methods of
> delivery.
>
> (Bransbury, 1996, p. 185)

Voluntary organisations have felt the effects of change particularly
acutely. Under the public administration model, their role was often to
comment, criticise and campaign for the take-up of statutorily permitted
services, playing a part in calling public services into account, and perhaps
sometimes using local authority grants to demonstrate alternatives. Once
they were drawn into bidding for contracts, negotiating the details,
supervising and monitoring staff (including volunteers), things changed.
There were contract negotiation and human and financial resource
management responsibilities on an altogether new scale. This can drive
away people who have a sense of active citizenship, and lead to a search
for those with financial and business skills. As a result, the diversity of
social and cultural groups that voluntary organisations had brought into
the public services arena and the dialogue and choice that such
organisations offered are in danger of attenuation (Harris, 1998).

In the NHS, consistent with the belief that the public sector needed to
learn from business, the health authorities and trusts after 1990 had new-
style boards with equal numbers of executive and non-executive directors,
mirroring a recently overhauled structure for the world of business. Board
members were to ask tough questions about efficiency and performance,
supporting the competitive culture and challenging the established
practices of the professions. The strong emphasis in the Secretary of
State's appointments was on people with business experience. Research on
how the new authorities have worked suggests confused and conflicting
ideas about accountability persist in this new arrangement (Ferlie et al.,
1996). Boards have needed considerable time to develop the levels of
familiarity and trust that allow them to take a strategic view. The
appointments process under Labour brought more new blood, focusing on
people with commitment to the NHS and to the locality. Once again there
was a learning curve for them to climb.

Hoggett urges us to think of the new modes of control over work in the
public services that these confusing and contradictory changes imply. He
offers the warning (implied perhaps in Rhodes' references to grantsman-
ship in the contract culture) that performance management systems can
shape behaviour in dysfunctional ways:

> Clearly, many individuals and groups have become highly adept at impression management whilst others have become equally skilled in the art of performing to target, even though this may run counter to the need to do the right job ...
>
> (Hoggett, 1997, p. 432)

He suggests (p. 432) that for many professionals:

> ... this leads to the invalidation of work which is non-visible and non-measurable – crucially this means that the care and attention given to service users or fellow members of staff suffers as it fails to contribute to the immediate output measures upon which the organisation's success stands or fails.

Is this dismal conclusion, with its echoes of the themes of Chapter 13, warranted? The next section examines some of the ways in which inspection has developed, extending scrutiny to the heartlands of professional practice yet seeking to acknowledge and value the commitment and motivation of staff. Can it be done?

2   Inspection in action

The extension of inspection to the fields of health and social care since the mid-1980s has brought several challenges. These have included: how to locate inspection units so that they can handle necessarily sensitive relationships with care-providers; how to identify appropriate methodologies for inspection; and how to develop the skills and competencies of inspectors. Before the 1980s, inspection by local authorities of residential services or by the NHS of nursing homes was fairly minimal. But, with the arrival of contracting, services no longer sat inside the bureaucratic chain of public accountability of the public administration model. Debate started to emerge about 'the motivations and characteristics of the new cadre of care entrepreneurs' (Peace *et al.*, 1997, p. 99) and the quality of the service they were offering. The Registered Homes Act 1984 and the Registered Establishments (Scotland) Act 1987 responded to this by allowing for the registration and regular inspection of private and voluntary residential care, nursing home care and other independent units such as private hospitals.

As the new system began to take hold, the independent providers complained about the inequity of a system whereby their facilities were inspected and could be closed down, whereas those directly provided by the local authority remained outside these arrangements. This, together with some high profile scandals about care in local authority provision, made it inevitable that the NHS and Community Care Act 1990 and associated and later legislation would further extend and develop inspection. Inspection in England, for example, was now placed at arm's length from the social services departments (SSDs) and 107 independent inspection units were established. These now covered *all* residential homes, including very small homes, children's homes, boarding schools and day care facilities for children, and provided for voluntary registration of domiciliary and other day care services. The wider remit and the 'arm's length' principle were adopted across the UK, including Northern Ireland where health and social services inspection, reflecting its integrated structure, was joint.

Departmental guidance set out tasks of evaluating quality of care and quality of life, of attending to all contracted-out services and of ensuring consistency of approach across sectors. Advisory committees with representation of the various interests were to be set up and, in 1994, provision was made for lay assessors to be integrated into the work of inspection. Alongside all of this, the Social Services Inspectorate (SSI) from the Department of Health and the National Inspectorates in Scotland, Wales and Northern Ireland had their own programmes of topic and locality-based inspections.

How, then, has this work evolved? On the positive side, frameworks for regulation in the residential care sector moved from a focus on checklists on matters such as room size towards a consideration of the quality of care and quality of life for residents. An initiative in North West England, called 'Homes Are for Living in', for example, created a matrix for evaluating residential homes based on values such as privacy, independence, dignity, choice and fulfilment. There were specific indicator questions to tap into daily practice – checking, for example, how staff addressed residents and whether they knocked on doors (see Kellaher and Peace, 1993). Also, whereas initially there was no clear specification of the qualities and experience inspectors should have and no way for them to share experience, training materials were developed, competencies were identified (see Box 2) and a National Association of Inspectors and Registration Officers was founded in 1991.

Critics, however, have pointed to variations in standards between local inspection units and to the continuing problem of subjective judgements. They have questioned long, drawn-out tribunal proceedings when home-owners contest the decisions of inspectors. They have noted the multiple and sometimes conflicting standards that are in use – when internal quality systems, contract specifications and registration standards can come into conflict with one another. Day and her colleagues (1996) stressed that some of these features are the 'growing pains of a regulatory state' (p. 43). At a more fundamental level, however, they also suggested that inspectors face three underlying dilemmas:

- *Policing versus consultancy* – is the job to enforce the rules and punish non-compliance or to seek improvement through collaboration and persuasion?

- *Rules versus discretion* – is the job to create detailed rules and inspect by ticking boxes or is it to give an outline and leave inspectors room to make judgements?

- *Stringency versus accommodation* – is the task to go by the book, insist on every detail and set a rigid timetable or to listen to difficulties and give latitude in the move towards improvement?

Box 2: CCETSW core competencies for inspectors

General	Includes contextual knowledge, knowledge of law and business finance; ability to articulate a value base, create trust, recognise and respect difference, facilitate others and make balanced judgements.
Enables user/carer involvement	Ability to identify and challenge institutional racism and discrimination and create a climate to reduce these; ability to evaluate services for their impact on specific groups; ability to facilitate users – involving them in quality control, enabling complaints; skilled in assessing risk, safety, costs.
Sets standards	Able to interpret and apply law, regulations and guidelines; able to develop frameworks for assessing standards; understand the complexity of quality assurance; can facilitate change to improve standards.
Registers provision	Able to process applications and follow correct procedures; able to judge fitness of people/ premises/management and assess financial viability.
Inspects provision	Able to plan and carry out annual inspections; to develop and apply relevant tools; to observe, record and report and to offer advice about change.
Audits quality	Able to develop audit tools and apply them; to facilitate and advise others in making changes.
Regulates provision	Able to handle complaints promptly; collect corroborating evidence; weigh evidence; and participate in prosecutions, tribunals and high courts.

(Source: adapted from Davis *et al.*, 1992, pp. 31, 47)

In reality, some balance needs to be struck between all these. Too much stringent policing of the rules results in 'regulatory unreasonableness', defined as 'a pedantic insistence on following the rules without making any allowances for ... particular circumstances' (Day *et al.*, 1996, p. 31). An overly collegial consultancy approach, however, can result in 'regulatory capture', where the system becomes dominated by provider rather than consumer interests.

A working paper produced by CCETSW summed up several of the real world obstacles to be overcome:

> ... inspectors may have to consider practice undertaken by longstanding colleagues; local authority members may impede taking action against

local small businesses for political reasons; tribunal decisions may not uphold an inspector's view. Quality assurance and improving standards can often only be achieved through encouragement when a service does not clearly infringe legal parameters. Lastly, the ultimate sanction of closing down an independent home is likely to put considerable pressure on the SSD who may themselves have to take responsibility for the care of residents.

(Davis et al., 1992, para. 3.14)

How fully any system of inspection can investigate and represent the interests of those who use the service is another debatable point. Kellaher and Peace (1993), coming from a tradition of research into the quality of life of residential homes for older people, suggest that value for money and service efficiency still dominated the inspection process in the early 1990s. Quality assurance systems that bring users into the design and monitoring of practice, they felt, may be able to do more on this front. Their later work hints at a suggestion that government might be better to stick to a role of quality control (of inputs), leaving quality assurance (covering outputs and experiences) to more local and user-centred evaluations (Peace et al., 1997, p. 105).

At national level, however, joint reviews of SSDs to be carried out by the Department of Health's SSI and the Audit Commission have emerged (Box 3). Each body has moved in the direction of the other. The SSI is looking to blend managerial with professional aspects of their reviews and the Audit Commission has expanded its original efficiency brief to consider service delivery objectives and the conduct of front-line work. Methods include coverage of a wide array of statistical indicators, use of a user/carer questionnaire and substantial fieldwork discussion in each SSD (Audit Commission/SSI, 1998).

Box 3: Do external reviews help?

The Joint Review Team for Social Services in England had done 29 reviews by early 1999. It argues that it: gives an outside perspective; checks from a sample of users, carers and service-providers what is really going on; listens to users and others saying what they think of services; and analyses the whole system, identifying organisational, cultural and practical obstacles to better performance. It highlights what councils are doing well and how they might build on it; examines costs and opportunities for saving; and supports staff with a snapshot of their performance and how it could be improved. It warns that reviews only work if councils prepare well beforehand and develop action plans afterwards.

Feedback has been positive but it has also raised questions about the methodology and language of the reviews, the impartiality and credibility of the staff, the accuracy of the reports and the extent to which the uniqueness of each setting is understood.

(Source: based on Audit Commission/SSI, n.d., pp. 28–9)

There is little in the way of independent research to reveal how the various forms of inspection work in practice and the effect they have on motivation, morale and behaviour. A study of voluntary accreditation in the health field suggests that a successful outcome depends on matters such as good prior preparation, so that staff understand the purpose of the visit, credible assessors who demonstrate their understanding of the issues and are not simply inquisitorial, appropriate feedback and a commitment and a capacity in the organisation to address deficiencies in a positive way (Scrivens, 1995).

Labour government policy has taken things further. The White Paper *Modernising Social Services* (DoH, 1998) sets considerable store by strengthening the inspection function in order to provide stronger safeguards and protection for children and vulnerable adults. It describes a 'new regulatory landscape' in England with eight regional Commissions for Care Standards, bringing health and social care inspections together and covering a wider range of services, including domiciliary services. Standards are set to be the same across the voluntary, private and statutory sectors and health and social care professionals are likely to work together and across the old boundaries in the work of inspection. There is recognition of the importance of inspectors having a credible knowledge base and, interestingly, *Modernising Social Services* suggests that 'a spell as an inspector should form part of a career path' (DoH, 1998, para. 4.17).

Just how different developments in Scotland, Wales and Northern Ireland will turn out to be is still an open question. It remains true, however, that:

> ... the challenge is to devise a system where the credibility of professional peers and those with local/regional intelligence can stimulate providers and users alike to participate actively and to positive effect with the new arrangements.
>
> (Peace *et al.*, 1997, p. 110)

3   Changing perspectives on professional self-regulation

What does all this emphasis on a regulatory state, on inspection and on externally-set standards say about professional self-regulation (PSR)? PSR claims that a profession can maintain standards from within. Medicine, nursing and the therapy professions have Councils, set up by statute to maintain a register of qualified people. These Councils decide what qualifications are necessary to enable people to describe themselves as registered and they remove those whose behaviour amounts to professional misconduct. A review of the most well known of these Councils, the General Medical Council (GMC), in the 1970s explained:

> An instructive way of looking at regulation is to see it as a contract between the public and the professions, by which the public go to the profession for medical treatment because the profession has made sure it

will provide satisfactory treatment. Such a contract has the characteristic of all freely made contracts – mutual advantage.

(Merrison Report, 1975, para. 4)

It is important to ask whether this high-trust regulation system, run largely by the professions themselves, and bypassing the time, the expense and the sensitivities of inspection can stand as alternative to it. One observer who is well placed to form a view about the workings of PSR in the medical case is Margaret Stacey. A sociologist and lay member of the GMC between 1976 and 1984, her assessment acknowledged the continuing strength of the service ethic in medicine: the genuinely felt dedication to the interests of patients. She gave credit to the GMC for establishing procedures to deal with sick doctors, developing the scope of its disciplinary machinery and gradually introducing lay members to more parts of its proceedings. Overall, however, she felt that the GMC was changing only slowly and under pressure. It tended 'to favour the profession over the public' (Stacey, 1992, p. 204). She sums up much of what goes wrong in the legacies of the GMC's nineteenth-century origins:

> In 1858 the GMC was effectively a gentleman's club. Its promise that the public could trust those it registered amounted to ensuring that there were no 'bounders' in the medical fraternity (sic) who would do dastardly things such as no gentleman would do – or permit himself to be found doing. In the mid-nineteenth century committing adultery was a prime example of such inappropriate behaviour, as was making sexual advances to a patient or getting divorced. Committing murder was also not on ... When I joined the Council in the mid-1970s it still had some of that air of a gentleman's club about it. One felt that change was accepted reluctantly and that tradition dominated. It was a place for white men for whom good food and drink was provided as a proper accompaniment to the serious work that was undertaken.

(Stacey, 1992, p. 204)

Five years later, Allsop and Mulcahy's (1996) review of criticisms of the GMC's professional disciplinary machinery underlined the slow process of change. Box 4 teases out further some of the key assumptions – none of them relates well to today's world of health care. We need to ask whether a nineteenth-century concept of a professional practitioner – with its associated ideas about exclusiveness and class and gender superiority (Davies, 1996) – has adapted or whether it needs root and branch reform.

Other health professions never fitted easily into this medical model of PSR. They have not been part of a small, high-status élite in the same way and they have not enjoyed the same status, power and prestige. They have found themselves more closely monitored by management hierarchies in the workplace and often also by the medical profession. The result is that PSR, on the surface the same, in practice operates in a different way. In their relationships with government, nursing's statutory bodies, for example, long found themselves the weaker partners in their battle to improve educational standards. This, together with proposals for higher-level educational entry and for increasing the proportions of qualified staff

---

Box 4: The classic model of professional self-regulation

Responds to the nineteenth-century professional ideal by:

- selecting people from homogeneous élite backgrounds
- instilling sufficient knowledge for a lifetime of practice
- refining their sense of appropriate professional behaviour
- respecting their right to autonomous practice.

In consequence it assumes that:

- few will fall below an acceptable standard of behaviour
- informal pressure from peers will usually be enough to maintain standards
- removal from the register will be rare and a result of gross misconduct.

---

in care settings, has been interpreted as self-interested professionalising rather than as an attempt, as its supporters would put it, to improve the protection of the public through improving the quality of care.

Since coming into operation in the early 1980s, the reformed, UK-wide registration body for nurses, midwives and health visitors – the UKCC – has been very active in promulgating educational reform, developing a code of practice and sharpening its disciplinary machinery. It has pioneered requirements that registrants should demonstrate what they have done to update their practice. There are worries, however, about whether a disciplinary machinery grown from the roots just described can deal appropriately with the reality of pressures on those in the front-line who do not have the autonomy and command over resources that the medical model assumes. Jean Orr, a UKCC member, draws attention to the inadequacy of a discussion of accountability without acknowledging power relations, illustrating this with cases before the UKCC's professional conduct committee. She urges the statutory body to speak out on matters such as inadequate resources, so that nurses can feel supported by it (Orr, 1995).

Writing in 1992, Margaret Stacey called for an independent inquiry to assess all forms of regulation. She felt that:

- PSR was not meshing well with employer and legal accountabilities
- accountability was often joint between professional groups and some mechanism of collective regulation was needed
- regulatory procedures needed to be more open and to encourage dialogue with a range of health workers as well as patients and the public.

Her vision was of a new form of regulation, guaranteeing competent and conscientious practice, ensuring that patients, colleagues and subordinates were not exploited, allowing access and compensation for patients but also affording adequate protection to practitioners against wrongful accusations (Stacey, 1992, p. 253). Stacey's call for an inquiry was not heeded, but the debate has not gone away.

Reforming regulation in the health professions

In February 1995, the Conservative government announced its intention to conduct an independent review of the professions regulated under the Professions Supplementary to Medicine Act 1960. That Act had set up an overarching Council of Professions Supplementary to Medicine (CPSM) and a series of Boards to deal with the business of each individual profession. By the time the review work began, there were seven professions under the CPSM umbrella – chiropody, occupational therapy, dietetics, physiotherapy, orthoptics, radiography, and medical and laboratory science. Others were looking to gain the same status and the government appointed a firm of management consultants to carry out the review.

The reviewers argued that statutory regulation was costly and had drawbacks (JM Consulting, 1996). It should only be used where there is 'the potential for harm arising either from invasive procedures or application of unsupervised judgement by the professional which can substantially impact on patient/client health or welfare' (p. 6). They offered four strong challenges to the operation of PSR.

1 *Professional interests and public interests are not necessarily the same*

The professions' quest for ever-higher standards, the reviewers argued, ran the risk of creating inflexibility and failing to meet employers' demands for change in service delivery.

2 *Focusing on the essentials*

Statutory bodies, the reviewers said, should set minimum standards to protect the public – leaving matters such as further professional development and specialist roles to the professional associations.

3 *An interprofessional body*

Individual professions, the reviewers felt, have a tendency to reinvent the wheel. They recommended a Council for Health Professions to take a strong strategic lead and set a common framework.

4 *A strong lay input is essential*

More lay participation was seen as essential – ultimately, the reviewers wanted to see a lay majority on the new Council.

With a government coming to the end of its term, matters were not taken forward immediately. Shortly thereafter, however, JM Consulting won the contract to review the UKCC and National Boards for Nursing, Midwifery and Health Visiting. Once again, the implication was that the work had expanded beyond what was required of a body designed to protect the public. Once again, there was the hint that the work of statutory regulation needed to be done more as a dialogue between parties rather than as the prerogative of the professions alone (JM Consulting, 1999). Meanwhile, new thinking was emerging elsewhere.

Reconceptualising regulation in social work and social care

There has been a long-running debate about whether social work should have a full-blown statutory body with registration along the lines of the health professions. Acute awareness of their position making sensitive decisions in a world of contested and changing values, however, and alertness to the charge that professionals had both privilege and power, have been among the factors rendering social workers doubtful about the wisdom of self-regulation as a model.

A new twist to the debate emerged in 1990 with the proposal for a General Social Services Council (GSSC). The vision was of an inclusive statutory body, covering not just social workers but all care staff, and allowing them to move to full registration as vocational qualifications were extended. Ultimately, the idea was of this new body:

> ... acting as the champion of the personal social services and of those who use or need them ... It should generate a continual and concerted pressure for the preservation and improvement of standards, acting as a watchdog, advocate, source of information and advice.
>
> (Parker, 1990, p. 119)

This body would replace the fragmented mechanisms of public inquiries concerning scandals. It would be truly independent, the repository of informed opinion and pressure. It would play a major part in linking education and practice, identifying levels of practice and creating open career ladders through the full range of occupations in social work and social care. The idea took further shape over the next few years as voluntary, private and public sector employers, trade unions and service-users were deliberately drawn into the debate (Brand, 1998; Statham and Brand, 1998). By the time that Labour came to power in 1997, 13 key principles had been hammered out (see Box 5 overleaf).

Things were moving fast as the Labour government began to set out its plans for modernising health and social welfare. A General Social *Care* Council was endorsed in outline form in the White Paper *Modernising Social Services* (DoH, 1998). Some, but not all, of the proposals were in line with the General Social *Services* Council idea and in some ways the plan was overshadowed by the inspection arrangements referred to in Section 2. Also, a clause was inserted in the Health Bill going through Parliament in 1999 that would enable the government to make changes in regulation for the health professions without a major review of legislation. The intention to create a new-style UKCC, smaller and with more representation from outside the professions, was announced at the same time. All in all, it seemed unlikely either that the health professions would

Box 5: Thirteen key principles for a General Social Services Council	
1 Protecting the public	the primary purpose of the Council
2 Empowerment of service-users	in the operation of the Council and recognising user and public interests are not always identical
3 Authority and independence	to carry out its work independently of other interests
4 Stakeholder participation	to ensure participation and develop ownership of standards
5 Promoting equal opportunities	modelling good practice in relation to race, gender, age, intellectual level and disability
6 Statutory powers	to define and enforce standards, investigate complaints and apply sanctions
7 Explicit standards	providing codes of conduct and practice
8 Alignment of practice and education standards	between professional groups and across inspection and quality assurance
9 Individual accountability	to the Council for conduct and for own training
10 Registration	as a condition of employment
11 Inclusiveness	standards to cover all staff managers and inspectors in the sector
12 Non-restrictive admission	but rigorous exclusion of those shown to be unsuitable
13 Conducting business openly	and educating and involving the public
	(Source: adapted from NISW, 1997, pp. 4–5)

continue to regulate themselves as they had done in the past or that arrangements for social work and social care would stay the same. All the new bodies would have a stronger lay input than before. Exactly what shape they would take, however, and how important they would be in the face of developments such as best value and clinical governance (see Chapter 13), and the new inspection regime discussed in Section 2 of this chapter, remained to be seen.

Accountability horizontally (to one's peers) was set to diminish, whereas there was to be more in the way of accountability upwards (to the centre) and perhaps accountability downwards (to the population). What more can be said of this latter kind of accountability – more direct accountability to the user and the citizen?

4   New mechanisms of local accountability

Alongside the new forms of regulation discussed in Section 1, there has been some new thinking in both the practice and the theory of democratic participation and accountability downwards to citizens, clients and service-users. In the health field, a start was made with the emergence of the 'Local Voices' initiative in 1992 (NHSME, 1992). This marked a recognition that the purchaser authorities, making decisions about priorities in commissioning services for their local areas, have a responsibility to be accountable to the population they serve for the range and types of services they purchase and that they need to develop a strategy for this. A variety of mechanisms to create more local involvement was suggested. Public meetings could be held, contributions from voluntary groups could be solicited, and focus groups, health forums, telephone hot-lines, opinion surveys, patient satisfaction surveys and complaints procedures could all be drawn in.

At the time, these ideas drew a range of responses from enthusiasm to puzzlement (Cooper *et al.*, 1995). The exercise was satirised at one point as 'the unaccountable in pursuit of the uninformed' (Pfeffer and Pollack, 1993). Nevertheless, an array of innovations has emerged. Some of them have been undertaken jointly with local government, also looking to new ways of revitalising its links with the populations it serves. Stewart (1996) describes in some detail:

- *citizens' juries* – a small group of citizens representing the public meet to explore a policy issue, hearing witnesses and calling for information, and make public their conclusions
- *deliberative opinion polls* – a group of voters interact with a candidate and discuss amongst themselves before answering the pollster's questions
- *consensus conferences* – lay people meet with experts to discuss the directions that policy on a sensitive scientific issue should take
- *standing citizens' panels* – a representative sample of perhaps 100–200 local people meet regularly and are consulted by the local council
- *mediation* – parties with different interests in an issue meet perhaps to find an agreed solution or to lessen the disagreement or at least to clarify where the divergences are.

Ideas such as these received a boost with the change of government in 1997. Local government, it was stressed, needed to be 'in touch', using new ways to 'involve local people and respond to local interests' (DETR, 1998, para. 1.1). The term 'local voices' was picked up in the very title of the White Paper on renewing local government in Wales (Welsh Office, 1998). Devolution has created new spaces for experiment across the UK (see Box 6).

Box 6: A new regionalism?

UK-wide there has been a pattern of keeping largely in step with the mechanisms for accountability discussed in this chapter. Wales has usually been included in legislation for England and different primary legislation for Northern Ireland and for Scotland has tended to follow the same broad contours. Plans have begun to diverge, however, in the climate of devolution since the accession of the Labour government in 1997. Elections to a Scottish Parliament and Welsh Assembly in May 1999, the creation of regional development agencies as a potential stepping stone to direct regional government in England, and continuing consultations among the political parties in Northern Ireland increase the scope for change. Although tax and expenditure control is retained at Westminster and only Scotland has the possibility of creating primary legislation (and the power to raise an extra amount on income tax), health and social services represent a major part of the expenditure of the new elected bodies. Local pressures and continuing regional differences in economic and health deprivation could result in different structures and different priorities.

White Papers and consultative documents have already diverged. Northern Ireland is looking towards fundamental structural change to build on its already different pattern of integrated health and social services boards. In Wales, there is a commitment in health to refocus trusts, replace commissioning with an emphasis on strategic planning, and experiment in the valleys with a salaried GP service. The corporate plan for NHS Wales is likely to reflect this. Consultations around social care changes have led to a commitment to set up a Care Council for Wales and to move towards registering the whole care workforce as soon as possible. The Scottish Social Services Council, although liaising with the English General Social Care Council over matters such as standards, may, as in Wales, have a different emphasis; so, too, might the Scottish Commission for the Regulation of Care. Scotland, like Wales, has indicated a preference for regional strategic planning over commissioning and its primary care trusts and local health co-operatives are distinct.

Most of these changes, however, remain to be ratified by the new elected bodies and the future, say commentators, is impossible to predict.

(Sources: various White Papers and consultative documents. See also Chapter 12, Box 6 and *British Medical Journal*, Vol. 318, 1 May 1999, various articles)

Low election turn-outs (including low turn-outs for the first elections to the devolved bodies in Scotland and Wales), and the very small numbers who involve themselves in public meetings of any sort, can lead to doubt about what can be achieved. Yet there is a strand of excitement about the directions in which some of the recent initiatives are pointing and the ways in which participation can be secured on issues that in the past would have been seen as too complex or too technical for a lay audience to understand. User-led services too have demonstrated both the willingness and the capacity of people to shape services and participate in running them (see Chapter 5). Mechanisms such as citizens' juries and deliberative opinion polling have shown that it is possible to create structures that systematically bring information into a decision process, allowing it to be questioned and challenged by lay people. Experience with this shows it can be a process that not only develops informed opinions but also can change minds – including the minds of the 'experts' (see Box 7).

Box 7: Buckinghamshire Health Authority – citizens' jury on back pain

Fifteen jury members were recruited by an independent market research company to reflect the characteristics of the county's population. Their task was to make recommendations on whether the health authority should fund osteopathy and chiropractic for back pain by moving some resources from physiotherapy services. They sat for four-and-a-half days and heard evidence from a range of witnesses. The jury needed to weigh up a complex array of evidence on clinical effectiveness, patient experiences, professional opinions, financial information and epidemiology. Witnesses included two local back pain sufferers, a GP, an orthopaedic surgeon, a director of public health, a researcher, two finance directors (one purchaser, one provider), a physiotherapist, an osteopath, a chiropractor and a representative from the Back Pain Association. The jury was invited to call extra witnesses of its own choosing. Jurors worked in pairs or small groups to assess what they had heard and prepare questions – this helped to enable everyone to participate. Two independent facilitators helped the jurors to work as a group and supported them through the whole process. The jurors' recommendation was for an integrated, evidence-based service for back pain sufferers incorporating osteopaths and chiropractors as part of a multidisciplinary team. Jury members were subsequently invited by the health authority to join a project group to take this plan forward.

There are ways of structuring such processes to facilitate dialogue between professionals and lay people. A meeting, for example, can be arranged so that those with opposing views can be asked to present the case of the others and have their accounts agreed before going further – a tactic which means that each group has to 'hear' the other more effectively. A facilitator can be used to comment on the process but not the content of the discussion, or a mediator can be used to put forward suggestions to overcome deadlocks, perhaps meeting the parties jointly and separately in order to do so. One small scale but particularly clearly described case of a facilitated dialogue is given in Box 8. The example is from the USA, the subject matter is environmental protection and the context is a university setting. But the underlying notion of facilitation has echoes in the citizens' jury example and is more broadly generalisable.

Box 8: Creating a forum for facilitated dialogue

Four guests – two pairs of friends – were invited to speak to a class at the University of Virginia. Each pair represented an opposing position on the subject under discussion. They were invited not to a 'debate' but to a 'dialogue'.

They were asked to:

- explain the basis for their own perspectives
- understand the perspective of those with whom they disagreed
- feel free to 'pass' on questions without explanation
- feel free to question others
- follow a rule whereby initial questions were clarifications only.

They were asked NOT to:

- speak for or as a representative of a group
- defend their views
- search for weaknesses in the position of others
- characterise the position of others unless asked to
- attack others.

The facilitator introduced the process as follows.

'We see the dialogue as an educational opportunity for participants and audience to gain an understanding of the issues and, most importantly, the people behind the issues – their real beliefs, values, goals and fears ... We hope we can demonstrate the benefits of creating a safe climate for dialogue, even in situations where parties hold (and will continue to hold after the dialogue) very different views on the divisive issues.'

Initial tension drained away as each person described what was at stake for them and as questioning progressed from clarification towards deeper understanding. Common ground across the two positions was discovered. Two participants felt able to admit to uncertainties about their positions and later class evaluations of the event showed that this generated sympathy and respect.

(Source: adapted from Dukes, 1996, pp. 70–71)

In his review of innovations in democracy in local government, Stewart (1996) argues that we need to extend the notion of a citizen's charter so that it names rights that facilitate participation. His list starts with the right to vote but goes much further to name other rights that are needed if people are to participate in making decisions about areas that concern them. These include being heard and listened to in government, being entitled to an explanation, being given an account by their representatives and having access to the information on which decisions are made.

This approach can be thought of not only as giving rights to people as citizens but also as laying corresponding duties on those who manage services and those who provide them to ensure that these rights are realisable. But we could also say that for a dialogue such as that being envisaged here, managers and professionals need to be assured of comparable rights themselves. And, as we have just seen, specific techniques for creating effective dialogue are beginning to be recognised and put to the test. Perhaps it is time to recognise that for an open and accountable process of accountability to work, not only are mechanisms of quality and performance review needed, but also skills of democratic dialogue. Professionals working in health and social care need to understand this growing armoury of skills and add them to their practice repertoire.

Conclusion

This chapter explored the changing frameworks for regulation and accountability. It traced the way in which professionals in the early post-war years were granted considerable freedom to deliver services as they saw fit and later experienced increasing amounts and types of performance review. The direct involvement of users and potential service-users in accountability structures is increasing. This can be seen in the role of lay assessors in the inspection process, the place of lay panels in the professional disciplinary procedures and in the creation of altogether new ways of debating apparently technical issues – through citizens' juries, for example.

Today's practitioners need a better understanding of who needs to be accountable to whom, when and why. They need to work both *in* and *with* changing structures. More than this, however, they need to recognise the *processes* that allow dialogue and create the momentum for constructive change. This chapter shows how some of these changes are beginning to emerge through inspection and review and through concepts such as facilitated dialogue. The watchword this book has tried to encourage for critical practitioners is not *defensive* but *defensible* practice.

References

Allsop, J. and Mulcahy, L. (1996) *Regulating Medical Work: Formal and Informal Controls*, Buckingham, Open University Press.

Audit Commission/Social Services Inspectorate (SSI), Department of Health (1998) *Reviewing Social Services – Guiding You Through*, London, Audit Commission.

Audit Commission/Social Services Inspectorate, Department of Health (n.d.) *Getting the Best from Social Services: Learning the Lessons from Joint Reviews*, London, Audit Commission.

Brand, D. (1998) 'The General Social Care Council: some implications for learning disability services', *Tizard Learning Disabilities Review*, Vol. 3, No. 4, pp. 35–41.

Bransbury, L. (1996) 'Local government reorganisation in England and Wales: the implications for social services', in May, M., Brunsden, E. and Craig, G. (eds) *Social Policy Review*, Vol. 8, London, Social Policy Association.

Butcher, T. (1995) *Delivering Welfare: The Governance of Social Services in the 1990s*, Buckingham, Open University Press.

Cooper, L., Coote, A., Davies, A. and Jackson, C. (1995) *Voices Off: Tackling the Democratic Deficit in Health*, London, IPPR.

Davies, C. (1996) 'The gender of profession and the profession of gender', *Sociology*, Vol. 30, No. 4, pp. 661–78.

Davis, A. with Mansell, C., Mansell, P. and Winner, M. (1992) *Exploring Competence in Registration, Inspection and Quality Control*, Paper 24.1, London, CCETSW.

Day, P. and Klein, R. (1987) *Accountabilities: Five Public Services*, London, Tavistock.

Day, P., Klein, R. and Redmayne, S. (1996) *Why Regulate? Regulating Residential Care for Elderly People*, Bristol, The Policy Press.

Department of Health (DoH) (1998) *Modernising Social Services*, Cm 4169, London, The Stationery Office.

Department of the Environment, Transport and the Regions (DETR) (1998) *Modern Local Government: In Touch with the People*, Cm 4014, London, DETR.

Dukes, E. F. (1996) *Resolving Public Conflict: Transforming Community and Governance*, Manchester, Manchester University Press.

Ferlie, E., Ashburner, L., Fitzgerald, L. and Pettigrew, A. (1996) *The New Public Management in Action*, Oxford, Oxford University Press.

Harris, M. (1998) 'Instruments of government? Voluntary sector boards in a changing public policy environment', *Policy and Politics*, Vol. 26, No. 2, pp. 177–88.

Hoggett, P. (1991) 'A new management for the public sector?', *Policy and Politics*, Vol. 19, pp. 243–56.

Hoggett, P. (1997) 'New modes of control in the public service', in Hill, M. (ed.) *The Policy Process: A Reader* (2nd edn), Hemel Hempstead, Prentice Hall/Harvester Wheatsheaf.

JM Consulting (1996) *The Regulation of Health Professions: Report of a Review of the Professions Supplementary to Medicine Act (1960) with Recommendations for New Legislation*, Bristol, JM Consulting Ltd.

JM Consulting (1999) *The Regulation of Nurses, Midwives and Health Visitors: Report on a Review of the Nurses, Midwives and Health Visitors Act 1997*, Bristol, JM Consulting.

Kellaher, L. and Peace, S. (1993) 'Rest assured: new moves in quality assurance for residential care', in Johnson, J. and Slater, R. (eds) *Ageing and Later Life*, London, Sage/The Open University (K256 Reader).

Merrison Report (1975) *Report of the Committee of Inquiry into the Regulation of the Medical Profession*, Cmnd 6018, London, HMSO. (Chairman: Dr A. W. Merrison)

National Institute for Social Work (NISW), General Social Services Council Implementation Group (1997) *General Social Services Council: Principles and Concepts*, London, NISW.

NHS Management Executive (1992) *Local Voices: The Views of Local People in Purchasing for Health*, London, DoH.

Orr, J. (1995) 'Nursing accountability', in Hunt, G. (ed.) *Whistleblowing in the Health Service*, London, Edward Arnold.

Parker, R. (1990) *Safeguarding Standards*, London, NISW.

Peace, S., Kellaher, L. and Willcocks, D. (1997) *Re-evaluating Residential Care*, Buckingham, Open University Press.

Pfeffer, N. and Pollack, A. (1993) 'Public opinion in the NHS: the unaccountable in pursuit of the uninformed', *British Medical Journal*, Vol. 307, 25 September, pp. 750–51.

Power, M. (1994) *The Audit Explosion*, London, Demos.

Ranson, S. and Stewart, J. (1994) *Management for the Public Domain*, London, Macmillan.

Rhodes, R. (1997) *Understanding Governance*, Buckingham, Open University Press.

Scrivens, E. (1995) *Accreditation: Protecting the Professional or the Consumer?*, Buckingham, Open University Press.

Stacey, M. (1992) *Regulating British Medicine: The General Medical Council*, Chichester, Wiley.

Statham, D. and Brand, D. (1998) 'Protecting the public: the contribution of regulation', in Hunt, G. (ed.) *Whistleblowing in the Social Services*, London, Arnold.

Stewart, J. (1996) 'Innovation in democratic practice in local government', *Policy and Politics*, Vol. 24, No. 1, pp. 29–41.

Welsh Office (1998) *Local Voices. Modernising Local Government in Wales: A White Paper*, Cm 4028, Cardiff, The Stationery Office.

Index